Here's what people are saying about He Doesn't Look Like a Murderer But Margie Is Dead

The Bostrom's sad story is one of deep tragedy and great personal courage. Their daughter was murdered, as are many young women, by her intimate male partner. Shirley and Larry's eloquent and heart rending account of their loss, as well as their constructive commitment to prevent this from happening to others, is an object-lesson in the art of community and caring for others.

Neil Websdale, Author of
Understanding Domestic Homicide

Shirley Bostrom has written a powerful book that strips away any unsatisfying academic explanations for the tragedy of domestic violence. Her knowledge of this devastating and often deadly abuse, found too often in relationships, comes from the pain of a mother's heart. She tells of the permanent grief that defines her life from having her daughter Margie murdered by a violent husband in her own home. Her book is special because it shows how this mother found the courage to tell Margie's story in hope of exposing the truth of domestic violence so that more help can be given to other women who are in danger behind the closed doors of their home. This is a must read book.

Antoinette Bosco, mother of a murdered
son and daughter-in-law and author of
Finding Peace Through Pain

No one who has ever loved—child, parent, partner, friend—can fail to be deeply moved by the poems in Shirley Bostrom's book. In mourning her daughter Margie's tragic murder, Shirley brings us with her through the joy of loving, the agony of loss, the frustration of a sometimes erratic justice system, and the tidal waves of pain that murder sends to our every shore. Sometimes raw, always honest, these poems expose deep nerves within us. They also inspire and remind us to never stop loving, and to never take our loved ones for granted. You may cry as you read, but the experience will be worth every tissue. Don't miss it.

Amy Dawson,
Fight Crime: Invest in Kids

I refer to Shirley's chapter, We Are Not Contagious, when I offer support and guidance to family members of murder victims. It is helpful for them to know that other survivors have similar feelings and reactions. It can also help friends and care givers to understand how to be truly supportive. This is a chapter that is worth reading twice.

Charles A. Lexius, Victim Services
Supervisor, Office of Victim Services,
Judicial Branch, State of Connecticut

Funny—He Doesn't Look Like A Murderer But Margie Is Dead is written with a mother's heart, a writer's eye, and a society's conscience. It matters not whether you have knowledge about abusive relationships or our culture's legal system because Shirley Bostrom's account of this horrific crime will teach you about a problem none of us can afford to ignore. Margaret is our friend, our sister, our mother, our colleague, and we need to heed her call for help.

> Mary T. Mackley, Director, Connecticut Writing Project, Department of English, University of Connecticut

Shirley is such a close observer of her own feelings and experiences that her book develops as a faithful chronicle of emotional trauma, grief and healing processes.

> David Kaczynski

...In this remarkable book Shirley recounts, in personal and reveling detail, what it has been like for her family to come to grips with Margaret's murder .... In this important text, Shirley provides much more than an inspiring story of surviving the unthinkable. By melding together the detailed, sometimes moment-by-moment, account of surviving the murder of a child with current social science literature in the area of violence and prevention. She has provided a book which is a must read....

> Mario T. Gaboury, J.D., PhD.
> Associate Professor of Criminal Justice, University of New Haven

...Shirley and Larry Bostrom have taken a bold and proactive approach to combat victimization. They have turned their grief...into a life-altering lesson for offenders. Through the VOICES program, Victim Offender Institutional Correctional Education Services, the Bostroms vividly detail to inmate audiences the impact of homicide on the victim's family. Their message to offenders is simple yet powerful, when you're released stop before you act, think of the options and choose one that is non-violent. They have my respect, appreciation and admiration....

> John Armstrong, Commissioner, Connecticut Department of Correction

When a young woman's life ends in domestic violence, her parents die too. Yet the inspiring story the reader is left with is of the remarkable union that urges and accompanies the author in her resolute quest to educate others about domestic violence: the union between a daughter's guiding spirit and her mother's voice....The Connecticut Coalition Against Domestic Violence, Inc. is extremely proud of Shirley's book....

> Lisa Holden, Executive Director, Connecticut Coalition Against Domestic Violence, Inc.

FUNNY—
HE DOESN'T
LOOK LIKE A
MURDERER

But Margie Is Dead

FUNNY— HE DOESN'T LOOK LIKE A MURDERER

But Margie Is Dead

SHIRLEY PIERCE BOSTROM

CALIE BOOKS
Marlborough, Connecticut

Although the author and publisher have made every effort to ensure the accuracy and completeness of information contained in this book, we assume no responsibility for errors, inaccuracies, omissions, or any inconsistency herein. Any slights of people, places, or organizations are unintentional.

Author's Disclaimer: This book is my version of our story. Others who are involved may remember the events very differently. I am not presenting this book as the absolute truth but as my truth.

All legal quotes used in the book are from written documents submitted by the judge, attorneys, and experts or the court transcripts of the Williamsport Division of the Middle District of Pennsylvania.

Original cover photo by Robert Charles Photography, East Long Meadow, MA.
Author's photo (back cover) by Cromwell Photo, Cromwell, CT.
All photos not credited in the book are from the author's own family photo collection.

First printing 2002

ISBN 0-9720218-3-3

LCCN 2002105199

ATTENTION CORPORATIONS, UNIVERSITIES, COLLEGES, AND PROFESSIONAL ORGANIZATIONS: Quantity discounts are available on bulk purchases of this book for educational, gift purposes, or as premiums for increasing magazine subscriptions or renewals. Special books or book excerpts can also be created to fit specific needs. For information, please contact Calie Books, 24 Pond View Lane, Marlborough, CT 06447; ph. 860-295-1217.

DEDICATION

For Margie, my family, friends, the
caregivers, and other co-victims who
experience a similar grief. You have
helped me find purpose in my life.

*Timothy's
Fight violence
everywhere. You
count!
Shirley Pierce Bostrom 10/03*

TABLE OF CONTENTS

PREFACE

Margaret's life was as unique as her fingerprints, so she was the only one who could accurately record her experiences, but she is no longer here. So I, her mother, have written our story as I know it, including my truths while trying to carefully preserve my memory of her. Margie's personality, relationships, and values were complex so some details of her life will always remain a mystery to me and others. Writing this book has been painful, but the process helped me understand and accept our tragedy. Our lives are not the same—nor will they ever be, but they are richer because of our fond memories of her.

My daughter Ruth, Margie's sister, told me, "Ma, you have to write a book so domestic violence will be exposed. Please let people know it can happen anywhere. If one woman's life is saved by sharing Margie's death, it will be worth it." Her plea broke my heart—again.

This book is part of my ongoing effort to adjust to her brutal murder and live a productive life. Since her death, years have come and gone and life for our family has changed drastically—in ways we could never have predicted. While our path is not one we would have chosen we've made many new friends through our dedication to violence prevention—especially against intimate partners. Margie's brief life does have meaning and we have many reasons to go on living. No one could have predicted how far and wide our message against violence would, or may yet, extend.

FOREWORD

by David Kaczynski

What a serious reader hopes for in a book, regardless of whether it's a life account or a work of fiction, is the ring of truth. We want to be told things we don't already know, but we also look for points of reference in our own experience. We begin to absorb our belief and sympathy in a book's characters and situations only once we've settled in our own minds that the storyteller is herself honest and perceptive, aware of an underlying connectedness with her readers, able to invoke our shared human world—yet in a way that uniquely influences and deepens our understanding of it. We also want to care about the book's subject matter. The story must somehow align itself with our predetermined interests, or else it must create an interest we didn't have (or know we had) beforehand. Only books with "big," universal themes can draw in a wide audience, because only such books deal with issues that are meaningful to all readers: themes like love, death, spirituality, family, crime and punishment, trauma and loss, betrayal, healing, and justice. Something I find fascinating about Shirley Bostrom's utterly honest and unpretentious book is the way in which it wrestles with all of the above. It does so quietly, with mature dignity and acute anguish, never offering hasty answers to difficult questions, neither demonizing nor canonizing its human subjects, but relentlessly, courageously posing questions that fly to the heart of what it means to be human.

No one can be prepared for a murder in the family. That much is clear to me from reading Shirley's book and from speaking with dozens of family members of murder victims. Thus, no one could know, in advance, how he or she would react to such an event. Undoubtedly, some readers of this book have lost a loved one to murder. An even greater number, I'm sure, will have some personal experience with domestic violence, either directly or through its impact on someone close to them. The circle of pain from a violent act spreads out in all directions, even across time. To a greater or lesser degree it affects us all and belongs, in some half-acknowledged sense, to our understanding of the human condition. On one hand, we "know" that human beings hurt and kill one another. On the other hand, we tend to imagine some special immunity for ourselves and for our loved ones. We want to believe that it can't happen to us. We think that if such a tragedy did strike close to home, it would come from afar, like lightning. So we lock our doors and feel safe, refusing to imagine that the killer could be someone we know, perhaps intimately. For imagining the latter would be to acknowledge that sometimes we don't really know the people who are close to us. It would call into question our trust and faith in others. It would challenge us to examine more directly and intimately the seeds of violence in human beings.

Readers who have survived violence will know why they are reading this book and will find much comfort and inspiration in it. They will admire the author's honesty and courage, and they will appreciate her determination to confront the unbearable, because they understand that denial, avoidance or distortion brings no lasting solace, and that most people who experience traumatic losses are left with no choice about confronting their pain, one way or another, sooner or later. Shirley has chosen a path that is direct and welcoming to others. General readers will learn much about domestic violence, its patterns, disguises, and warning signs—information that may prove useful (in some cases life-saving) to themselves, their loved ones, and acquaintances. As we read this book, we join a family as it copes with an unexpected and devastating act of violence; we walk beside a grieving mother as she is confronted with a multiplicity of new life tasks—including dealing with an unfeeling criminal justice system; we revisit a dangerous relationship as it unravels toward its shattering end; we ponder the human pieces that must be put back together somehow, albeit with a different understanding than before. The story has tragic resonance. The task for the reader as well as for the author is to derive sense and meaning from a senseless act, to pose questions that deepen our understanding, even if some of them must remain unanswered, to rescue faith, kindness, and life's very meaning from violence and cruelty. The ultimate task Shirley has set for herself is to create an apt memorial for Margaret, to convey a sense of the person she was, to bind her own story to Margaret's foreshortened legacy as a prison psychologist—the legacy of someone who'd committed herself to helping others. In this, I believe, she succeeds poignantly. The author becomes a mother in a second sense. By the end of the book, Margaret is very familiar to us: She could be anyone's daughter, sister, or aunt. We almost experience Shirley and Larry's loss in its heartbreaking finality. We feel the urge to treasure and protect each and every Margaret in our world.

Verisimilitude, emotional complexity, and large themes frame this harrowing account of one family's tragedy. But I think another measure of the story's importance lies in its ability to accommodate a variety of personal references. Shirley and Larry could easily have been my parents, or indeed any caring and committed parents who must wrestle with doubts about a grown child's choices, who must balance their protective instincts with an offspring's genuine need for autonomy. This walk of faith transforms itself, during times of stress and worry, into an emotional high-wire act where balance and perspective are singularly hard to maintain. When we raise our children to be competent and independent, we free them to answer life's challenges. We do our best to view their mistakes as learning opportunities and hope for the best, knowing that every person must ultimately stand or fall on his own. But every parent likewise carries the memory of their child as an utterly dependent, vulnerable being. Nagging worries may represent merely a projection of that memory, an unhelpful regression; or they may represent a parent's privileged intuition, a voice that gives warning when their child is in danger.

Unfortunately, parents can never know the truth until something good or bad happens. Whereas some parents struggle for control long after their children are grown, others like Shirley and Larry understand that their role has changed. They can be as loving and supportive as ever, but they know that interference comes at a high price. The parent of an adult child becomes, in essence, a good friend—but a unique kind of friend who expects nothing in return other than the joy of watching another, separate being blossom. The parent who was once almost a god in the child's eyes, now becomes more like an angel: inconspicuous, nearly invisible at times, watching fondly from a distance as the child creates her own life. Surely, there is no crueler fate for the parent than to see a child's life destroyed. I don't know which is crueler—to see the child's life slowly eaten away from within by addiction or mental illness, or to see it snatched away in bloom, a victim of someone else's demons. Certainly, the parent of a murdered child must live with added burdens of injustice and anger. In either case, there are sorrows, questions, and regrets; emptiness where fullness ought to be; an unreasonable but potentially toxic sense of guilt born from the failure to foresee and protect. As I read this marvelous book, I saw my own parents mirrored in Shirley and Larry, sometimes in detail, always in the larger outline. It helped me to understand my parents better and to appreciate them more. At times, my eyes welled up with tears as I superimposed their sorrows and losses onto Shirley's and Larry's.

I first met Shirley and Larry during a difficult period in my life. Not the most difficult period, of course—that had ended a year before with a plea agreement that effectively spared my brother's life.* However, I was experiencing some symptoms of depression. A burden of fear was lifted, but also gone was the urgency to act and to speak out, leaving many complicated and troubled feelings in its wake. How would I ever come to terms with what Ted had done? Or with what I had done—turning my brother in to the FBI, exposing him to possible execution, breaking my mother's heart? I imagined that most people I met had questions about me that they felt unable to ask, questions as unsettled as my own heart. I confided in my wife Linda and a few close friends, yet my sadness seemed incoherent, unable to make itself understood. A great many people, friends and strangers alike, expressed sympathy, in most cases obviously heartfelt. However, as much as I treasured this kindness in people, I felt an emotional blockage, a mass of unresolved feelings that dimmed my responses to life, distanced me from other people, shrouded my heart. Paradoxi-

---

*Author's Note: David Kaczynski is the brother of Theodore Kaczynski, the Unabomber who eluded the F.B.I. for 17 years, during which time he orchestrated 16 explosions that killed three people and injured 23 others. Convicted in 1998, Ted Kaczynski is now serving four life sentences plus 30 years in prison.

cally, depression feels like an utterly unique experience, yet it is common. When its origins are situational, as opposed to primarily chemical, it may signal our incompleteness, the need for resolution and integration at a deeper level. However, it generally doesn't tell us where to look or how to go about restoring wholeness. When, in addition, we must deal with some irrevocable loss—a betrayal, a terrible sin, a lasting injury, a death—the challenge may seem overwhelming.

Dr. Samuel Rieger, president of Survivors of Homicide, the most influential victims' advocacy group in Connecticut, had invited me to address an annual anti-violence conference sponsored by his group in the spring of 1999. It was there that I first met Shirley and Larry Bostrom. The invitation from Dr. Rieger had sparked in me a small feeling of hope. After listening to the very moving victim impact statements at my brother's trial, I had some sense of the violation and emotional devastation that family members of murder victims experience. Although I had expected to hear testaments of pain, still I couldn't help feeling shaken by them. Now several months later, it intrigued me that a group of such family members—not my brother's victims, but someone's—would have an interest in hearing my thoughts and feelings. Clearly, they were reaching out to me, offering me kindness, the opportunity to tell my story, to reconcile on some level. Of all the speaking opportunities I've had, it's still the one I value most; the one I credit with helping me to find words for some of my elusive feelings—feelings about my brother, my family, the many who were hurt, the difficulty of keeping hope alive at times, the need to recognize our deep human connectedness. Even before I delivered my speech, however, I felt recognized by the Survivors' members—and I don't mean recognized as a quasi public figure, but rather as another survivor. Amazingly, unlike any other people I'd met outside my immediate family, they seemed to have an intuitive understanding of what I'd been through. Not that my pain is comparable to theirs. Rather, it seemed to me that each had been deeply hurt, deeply tested; each had developed strategies to survive, the foremost being their compassion and support for one another; each had acquired a survivor's wisdom, the understanding that life and happiness are not less meaningful because they are fragile; that healing is both a process and a path; that helping others is the best way to help oneself.

Among the important themes encompassed in this book, I found myself paying special attention to the issues of grief, survival, and healing. While I have personal reasons for doing so, one doesn't have to be a survivor of homicide, either in Shirley's sense or mine, to take an interest in these processes. Loss is an inevitable feature of human experience. We hope to grow wiser as we age. With age comes loss and pain; with loss and pain, we hope, some kind of wisdom: self-acceptance; the will to benefit others, and the ability to do so. Shirley is such a close observer of her own feelings and experiences that her book develops as a faithful chronicle of emotional trauma, grief, and healing processes. Instead of telling us what she may want us to think and feel, she tells us exactly what she thought and felt. There is no distortion here, no bending of the truth to accommodate a personal or philosophical agenda; no false sentimentality. In my view, only this sort of unvarnished account can afford us a glimpse into the human situation as it was and is. Shirley's life journey is not finished, and her book leaves us with a sense of that fact. The story itself endlessly widens. It is complex, with interconnecting parts. The feelings branch out, reaching unexpected places. By the end, we have a pretty good sense of Shirley's secret—how she has been able to survive.

I'm proud to call Shirley my friend. I feel honored that she has asked me to write this foreword. We are both, in our own ways, committed to bringing some light from the darkness of our family tragedies. This book will instruct many and comfort others. It humanizes what we all need to learn about domestic violence, and about the shattering effects of interpersonal violence in all forms. Through remembering her daughter in this way, Shirley Bostrom has given shape to Margaret's legacy, and has probably saved some lives as well.

Lewisburg, PA—Friday, August 16, 1996

A Lewisburg Federal Penitentiary clinical psychologist, Dr. Margaret E. Bostrom, 31, was pronounced dead at 11:30 A.M. today —the victim of an apparent homicide. She had been stabbed sixteen times in the chest with a butcher knife. One blow was so violent that it went through her slender body. Any one of nine wounds would have been fatal. Eleven additional slicing cuts on her arms, hands, and chin were sustained when the victim attempted to defend herself. The FBI would give no further details.

CHAPTER 1

Every Parent's Worst Nightmare

On Friday, August 16, 1996, I'm thinking about a weekend of relaxation and camaraderie as I drive south on I-91 to Hartford and east on Route 2 to Marlborough. The car is packed with clean bedding, food, beverages, and photographs of my friends and me with sand castles built in years past. Later, I will wonder how I could be so blissfully unaware of the life-changing tragedy that was taking place.

Delilah, sitting in the passenger seat, is watching me with her big brown Sheltie eyes. She's just been groomed and her sable-colored fur is smooth and soft. "You're sure a pretty girl," I tell her. Her ears perk up and come forward as she moves her head toward my lap. I bite off a piece of the apple I'm eating and hold it to her. She takes it gently and chews on it—savoring all the flavor before swallowing.

Delilah is my daughter Kathy's dog but is with us because Kathy knew she wasn't taking care of her. Kathy's problems with drugs and alcohol have recently escalated—again. She feels she has caused us enough pain and grief and doesn't want to put us through any more so she has cut herself off from the family. I told her, "This hurts us too. You need to stay in touch." But we haven't heard from her in over six weeks.

I look at the brilliant blue sky decorated with white puffy clouds and think what a beautiful summer day it is. I can't wait to bask in the sun. The last three months have been hectic. My brother Jack died of a heart attack and I retired in June after thirty-two years of teaching.

My retirement party was a tribute to me both as a teacher and as a mother. My three beautiful daughters—Ruth, Kathy, and Margie—were there, looking lovely and charming all my friends. Abby, my seven-year-old granddaughter, was so excited to have her dad together with Mom, Aunt Margie and Uncle Mitch, Aunt Kathy, Grandpa Larry and Grandma, and younger brother Jacob at home with Nana—excluded from the festivities because of his age. I feel warm and content when I remember Abby's speech, "I'm glad Grandma is retiring. Now she'll have more time to play with me." Ruth read it after her own touching tribute to me as her mom and as a teacher.

I had agreed, "Yes, I will, Abby!" I'm ready to begin this new phase of my life. It will be a wonderful adventure.

My youngest daughter, Margie, and her husband, Mitch, seemed so happy. They had been together in Lewisburg for three weeks. The tension caused by previously being apart for six months, when she began working at the Federal Penitentiary in Lewisburg and he remained in California, appeared to be gone.

Margie's eyes sparkled with pride when she watched Mitch go to each table with the video camera and solicit candid remarks. I haven't watched the tape yet, but from the raucous laughter he elicited at the table with my male cohorts, I know I'll enjoy it. My friends and fellow teachers were all impressed with my family and it was nice for my family to hear me praised as an educator.

When the school year was over my husband, Larry, and I went to a fiftieth wedding anniversary party for his brother and sister-in-law in Jamestown, New York. The next week I started a writing course at the University of Hartford that met two nights each week for four weeks, and there was a lot of writing to do. The last session was just last night.

"Yes, I'm going to rest, but you, poor Delilah, won't get any peace with Abby and Jacob after you all the time. But look at it this way: It's better than being cooped up with that crazy puppy, Calie."

Larry is home at our condominium in Windsor fixing the air conditioner before Margie arrives. She is driving up from Lewisburg to leave her year-old golden retriever while she attends a week-long conference on Cape Cod. I'm leaving Delilah with Ruth. "The two of you dogs in one house is too much for Grandpa to handle." I look at Delilah's slightly cocked head and wonder if she understands what I'm saying.

I'm planning only a brief stop. I'll drop off Delilah, hug the kids, and make sure Ruth plans to go to the Native American PowWow on Sunday afternoon. I hope I'll see Margie at the powwow, but if I don't I'll see her the next weekend when she comes back from Cape Cod.

Then I'll be on my way. I'll have plenty of time this afternoon to get the camper ready. I have to make the beds, dust, sweep off the deck, and wash off the outdoor furniture. I know my friends have to work this morning. They won't be ready to start until around 1 P.M.

As I turn onto Emily Road I reflect on how good my life is and tell myself, "I don't want to die, but if I did right now I couldn't complain—I have a wonderful family, close friends, and I just retired from a challenging, rewarding career as an educator. Now, I have time to complete my book about growing up on an Indian reservation."

Late in August, Mitch will be at Cornell University pursuing a master's in business administration, which will give Larry and me more time to spend alone with Margie. This fall we will explore Lewisburg with her. We have fallen in love with the small city with its Victorian storefronts, homes, and small taverns that have good food and plenty of atmosphere. The small boutiques hold promises of many pleasant hours to be spent browsing with Margie. If Margie and I are lucky we'll convince her father not to join us for this activity. She and I will have many chances to talk about what she wants to do about pursuing the divorce.

At 12:25 P.M. I pull down into Ruth's driveway, stop, open the door, and lift Delilah down. She is only two years old but has hip dysplasia. We go through the garage and the screen door into the mudroom. I see Ruth in the kitchen, her face contorted, arms flapping as she hangs up the phone. In the seconds before she speaks I anticipate that Kathy, my second daughter, has been hurt or killed.

I'm not prepared for, "Margie's dead. They found her—murdered!" Ruth gasps for air as I try to comprehend what I heard. The prison chaplain had called our home and Larry just called Ruth. "Daddy doesn't know any more. He said we can call the assistant warden, Frank Adair, for more information."

I know we'll have to go to Lewisburg, but there are things we must do. First, I call my friend Shirley King. I want to reach her before she and the rest of the "play therapy group" leaves to make sand castles. "Shirley, don't start for Rhode Island. Margie is dead. I'm sure Mitch killed her. Will you call Barbara, Carol, and Marj for me?" She offers to help any way she can. I know she will.

Ruth repeats over and over, "What am I going to tell Abby?" Seven-year-old Abby and her Aunt Margie adore each other. I have no answer for Ruth. She continues, "I need more information. I'm going to call the assistant warden."

"Ruth, wait. He is going to ask about our plans. What do you need to do before we can leave?"

"Abby is at the Connecticut shore with the Brownies. Can you pick her up at the church at four? I have the au pair coming on a bus to Farmington at three—if it's on time. I'll call Abby and Jake's dad. I'm sure he'll come watch them while we are gone."

"Ruth, what should I tell Abby?"

"Try not to tell her anything. I'll do it when I get back. You might want to tell Colleen, though—if you get a chance to see her alone." Colleen is a Brownie leader, but also Abby's and Jake's baby-sitter.

"Ruth, I need to call Daddy back now. Poor guy, he was all alone. I hope he's okay. Telling you couldn't have been easy."

Larry answers on the first ring. I tell him it is me and he begins, "I was in the basement when the phone rang. I thought it was probably someone trying to sell aluminum siding or pushing a different long distance company, but it could have been Margie so I ran up the stairs. I still had the screwdriver in my hand and was puffing as I answered. I heard a heavily accented Spanish voice asking if I was Mr. Bostrom. He told me, 'This is Sergio, a chaplain at the prison in Lewisburg.' I wondered if Mitch had caused more problems for Margie at the prison. Then I heard him say, 'Your daughter Margaret—she's been attacked.' There was a long pause, 'She's dead.'

"I couldn't reply. I just stared at the stove. I wanted to cry but I couldn't. Sergio asked, 'Are you still there?' I did manage to get the phone numbers and names of who to call for more information. He told me how sorry he was. He was floundering for words—I could tell he was upset too. When we hung up I just stood there—immobilized. Finally, I dialed Ruth's number. I hoped you hadn't been there and left already. I didn't know what to say or how you and Ruth would react.

"I told Ruth, 'I got some bad news.' Then I blurted out, 'Margie's dead.' Ruth cried, 'Oh no! Oh no! Poor Margie.' Then the screen door slammed in the background and I heard you ask, 'What's wrong?' Ruth said, 'We'll call you back.' I hung up and waited for you to call."

We agree that we have to go to Lewisburg, but I hate asking him to pack some good clothes for me. Under different circumstances our conversation would be situation comedy material.

I feel numb and disoriented and have no understanding of what we face in the days to come. "Bring my plain beige top and green skirt."

"There are three beige tops." Larry's voice is flat as he responds.

Do I really have three beige tops? "It's the one with the thin piping around the neck and it's sort of ribbed." Does it really matter which one or am I just trying to keep my mind occupied with mundane matters?

"Huh?" Long pause. "Oh, I think I found it. Does it have short sleeves? I don't see a green skirt."

"Yes. The skirt has a pink and beige seashell print. It isn't really a skirt but culottes. On my dresser there's a jade-colored necklace and earrings to go with the outfit. The ones I bought with Margie—when we were last in California." I quickly shut out the memory of that warm, sunny day when we visited the winery in Poway and were unexpectedly treated to several, small unique shops. I feel a small tinge of guilt because Margie wanted the green necklace too, but there was only one—so she let me have it and took a black one instead.

"I need pantyhose, underpants, and bras."

"I thought you packed that stuff for the camper."

"Most of it's ratty and old or for the beach." I wonder, do I really care what my underwear looks like?

Larry promises to try to bring what I need. I can hear his confusion and the fatigue in his voice. He needs to call his brothers. I tell him that Shirley King will feed and care for our twenty-one-year-old cat, Felicia. Barbara, who lives near us on Strawberry Circle, will give her our key. Both of them are part of my Rhode Island "play therapy group," whose session has just been canceled.

I hang up and turn to Ruth, "I'm worried about him driving here."

Ruth says, "Let me have Steve get him when he comes to stay with the kids." The anger and frustrations that led to Ruth asking for a divorce, which became final last week, are now forgotten. Steve readily agrees to help in any way he can.

Our need to know everything is unquenchable. It consumes us, but details come only in bits and pieces. We call Assistant Warden Frank Adair, who tells us they have Mitch, her husband, in custody. "Oh, my God. No. I knew it!" I ask, "Where is Margie now?"

"Her body is still in the house. Mrs. Bostrom, we have rooms reserved for you at the Days Inn."

"Thank you, but can you try to get one room with two double beds? I think we want to be together. It'll be a late arrival."

"Certainly. They're going to hold the reservations until ten P.M. When you get in call me at the prison. I'll be working late. Everyone will."

Ruth goes upstairs to get her two-and-a-half-year-old son, Jacob, and herself ready to go to Farmington. If Jacob likes the new au pair she will be a great help to Ruth. A live-in baby-sitter can get the kids up in the morning, put them to bed at night if necessary, and be with them when they are sick. With her demanding job Ruth needs this support.

I take the cordless phone and go into the family room to sit on the sofa. The bright primary colors all appear the same shade of dull, bleak gray. I begin dialing. My friend Judy isn't at home. How do you leave such a message? I must tell her something—so she doesn't hear it from someone else. I blurt out, "Margie's dead. She was murdered. Mitch did it. I'm sorry to have to let you know this way."

I hang up and dial the Windsor Locks Funeral Home. "Hello, John? This is Shirley Bostrom."

"Hi, Shirley. How can I help you?"

"I always told you that I planned to use your services, but I didn't think it would be this way. My youngest daughter was murdered in Lewisburg, Pennsylvania. I don't have any details. We don't know when her body will be released. I'm just calling to alert you."

"Shirley, don't worry about the details. We'll take care of everything. The medical examiner will probably have to perform an autopsy. Call us when you know the name of the funeral parlor that will be in charge of her body in Lewisburg. Take care and our thoughts are with you."

I hang up, thankful that we won't have to deal with complete strangers. I taught John's oldest daughter, Sherry, in fourth grade. Later, when I was a learning disabilities teacher and coordinator, I worked with Gina, one of his twins, from first grade through to her graduation. She's a true success story and holds a special spot in my heart. John is also second selectman in Windsor Locks. I saw him last fall and told him, "If I lived in Windsor Locks I'd vote for you." He laughed and offered to have a room built on the back of his house for me. I wonder how he felt getting this call.

I call Larry back and tell him Steve will pick him up. Then I ask him to call the doctor and hospital to cancel my breast surgery scheduled for Tuesday, August 20th. He hesitates and I explain, "All the information is there on my dresser." He agrees to do it.

Next, I leave a message on Arlene's answering machine. "I won't be able to do the writing workshop for the teachers in East Windsor on Wednesday, August 27th. My daughter was murdered." I feel a moment of sympathy for her when she does listen to my terse message. Then I giggle at the absurdity of it all: *Bet no one has used that excuse before.*

Judy calls back and after we talk I let the horror sink in—briefly and as deeply as a mother can—so soon. I do my primal scream! Repeating over and over between howls and sobs. "Mitch, why? You bastard! My baby's dead. You killed her. Why? How am I going to live without her?" Without this release I couldn't have continued to function.

Thinking about what must be done is easier than facing the horrendous truth. Keeping busy helped me when my dad died and later my mother. I'm not noted for my housekeeping, but now I find vacuuming, taking sheets from the dryer, making Abby's bed, and folding clothes welcome tasks which help distract me from my loss and the terror I'm trying to keep under control.

I must go out to the driveway to unpack the fun-filled contents of my car because we'll take it, a new Caprice Classic, to Lewisburg because it is bigger than Ruth's. This task reminds me that our lives, not just someone else's who you read about in the papers, can change in an instant—never to be the same again. Sheets, blankets, a DustBuster, extra lights, swimsuits, sand toys, insect repellent, novels, and women's magazines will now clutter Ruth's living room and garage.

I see the Southern Comfort lying on top of the clothes basket. Shirley King and I have made it part of our yearly ritual. While the others are enjoying wine or beer, she and I savor the memories of all our years together in Special Education as the sweet flavor slips down our throats. I reach in the trunk to take it out but change my mind. *I might need this where I'm going. No, I'll definitely need it!*

At 3:55 P.M. I leave for the Congregational Church, dreading my mission. The Brownies are late. I don't mind. It's a brief respite for me. I'm relieved when I see Steve and Larry drive by. Soon a caravan of minivans, four-wheel drives, and station wagons arrive. Abby sees me, "Grandma, why are you here?" Without waiting for an answer she hands me a shell. "Here, this is for you. It's a lady slipper." Then she runs to her friends, extending the excitement of the day a few moments longer.

Silently, I encourage her. Enjoy it while you can, honey. Colleen is alone now. Time to tell her. She says she'll call Steve later to see what she can do to help. Gradually the girls are gathered into waiting vehicles and Abby and I are in the car—alone. I tell her that her daddy and grandpa will be at the house when we get there. She asks where Mommy is. I remind her that Tina, the au pair, is coming today and Mommy and Jakie are getting her now.

Satisfied that everything is right in her world, Abby begins a monologue about the shore and its creatures that lasts the few brief moments it takes to get home. I'm behind Abby as we walk in the door. I shake my head back and forth sideways to tell Steve that Abby doesn't know. He understands. We make small talk until Ruth returns with Tina.

A car door slams and a tall blonde German teenager follows Ruth, who is carrying Jacob, into the kitchen. Ruth tells us, "The bus was an hour-and-a-half late. Traffic was heavy. Typical Hartford on a Friday afternoon. Everybody, this is Tina."

When everyone has settled around the kitchen table, Ruth who is still standing turns to Abby and says, "I have some very bad news for you." Abby runs to her mother and tries to pull her into the front hall to be alone, but Ruth stops her and says, "Your Aunt Margie is dead."

"Which Aunt Margie?" Abby is hoping her mother means her great, great, aunt Margaret. I marvel at her brain's attempt to protect her, even at such a young age.

"The only Aunt Margie you have. My sister!"

"How?"

"She was murdered." Abby's face contorts with pain. Tears flow unchecked down her cheeks. She pulls her mother toward the hall. This time she succeeds.

Later, Ruth tells us. "Abby asked how Mitch could stab Margie if he loved her. I hadn't told her Mitch killed Margie and at that time I didn't know she was stabbed, so I couldn't have told her that. I think Margie stopped on her way to wherever she was going, to tell Abby what happened. She had to let Abby know the truth, but she wanted to comfort her, too." Sounds like Margie.

Abby wants to come to Lewisburg with us. Ruth explains, "Abby, I need you to stay and help Tina get used to living in Marlborough. Your daddy and Jakie will get lonesome if we all go. Besides it won't be fun for any of us." Abby accepts that she can't come more easily than we expect.

I'm struck by Tina's plight—a young girl in a foreign country plunged into our tragedy. In Germany they have certainly heard about the violence in America. She doesn't know anything about our family, really. Does she understand that she is in no danger? If I were her parent I'd tell her, "I'm sending you money. Get the first plane back home." And if I were her, I'd go.

I write this poem to show how quickly our priorities change when tragedy strikes.

Loss and Guilt

On the day you died
you were coming home.
I grumbled as I cleaned your bed.
I was going to Rhode Island

to build sand castles with my friends.
I knew you'd understand.
I'd see you Sunday, or next Saturday.

If you were coming home today
I'd change all my plans.
I'd clean your room from top to bottom.
There'd be chili and pecan pie.
I'd wait with roses and Mouton Cadet,
in eager anticipation, for your arrival.
What a difference a day makes!

CHAPTER 2

God Must Be
Really Angry at Us

It is 5:35 P.M. when we start for Lewisburg. Almost five-and-a-half hours have passed since Larry got the call. How can that be? I sit alone in the backseat with a pillow. I can't decide whether I want my feet on the seat or the floor. Ruth and Larry are in the front seat. They will share the driving. Larry tells Ruth to drive first. He knows it will make us feel safer. As Ruth backs out of the driveway he decides we should go through Middletown and avoid the Hartford traffic. We take Route 66 and cross the Connecticut River. In Middletown the traffic lights slow us down. Larry says, "This was a mistake. We should have gone through Hartford." He'll worry all the way to Lewisburg about whether they will hold the room. He is our official family worrier.

Thirty minutes later we're finally out of Middletown and flying along I-691, trying to make up time. Our relief at finally reaching I-84 just north of Waterbury is short-lived. There is a solid line of vehicles going up the long hill before the Cheshire exit.

The car is an imperfect cocoon. It neither fully protects me against the outside world nor insulates me from the painful metamorphosis taking place in my life. I'm amazed, angry, and incredulous that other people are going on with their lives as if nothing has happened—I'm not ready to admit that for them nothing has changed.

Rude drivers toot their horns, pass on the right, cut us off with looks that tell us they resent our confusion but don't fathom our loss or pain. How can the world be so blissfully unaware? The sun should stop shining, the clock stop ticking, and the radio fall silent.

Near the highway, in Danbury, is the Ethan Allen Restaurant where we first met Mitch's parents and sister four years ago during Christmas break. His family drove up from New Jersey with Mitch and we brought Margie with us from Windsor. Margie kept telling us, "You'll like Mitch's family. His dad is outgoing and friendly—a good salesman. His mom studied to be a special education teacher and his sister loves animals just like we do."

We were introduced and Mitch's father laughingly told us, "Don't blame us for the way Mitch is. We aren't that way and we don't know how he got that way either." We all chuckled and relaxed ready to enjoy the evening.

Our shared interests in best-selling novels led to lively discussions of certain authors' strengths and weaknesses and added to our lists of books we must now read. Clive Cussler and his superhero, Dirk Pitt, stimulated a lively discussion as did Jonathan Kellerman and his psychologist, Alex Delaware.

There were many similarities between our families. Larry and Jordan reminisced about being in the navy at about the same time. We discovered Jordan shared an interest in photography with us. Michelle, Mitch's younger sister, worked with animals at Pace University. When dinner was over, we were sad to leave. We would miss Margie who was going home with Mitch to spend a few days with his family. Alone in the car on the way home Larry and I agreed that we liked Mitch's family—maybe even more than we liked him.

Now, fleetingly, I think of his parents. Do they know? How awful for them. Their son a murderer! They loved Margie, too. Now, my memory of the evening we met is forever tainted. Mitch has made adversaries of friends. I'm sure they're stunned and grief-stricken by his actions, but they are his parents. They'll stick by him.

Larry interrupts these thoughts with, "I need to stop and get something to eat. I haven't had anything since breakfast." Ruth and I aren't hungry but she takes the exit when Larry tells her, "It says there's a McDonald's here."

Soon he's apologizing for his "blunder" as we waste time winding along little back roads before reaching the restaurant. After we eat Larry drives for a while.

I reflect on the last time we saw Margie alive in Rhode Island at our trailer. Mitch and she had been in New Jersey along with Ruth and her children for the July 4th fireworks Abby and Jacob call, "Jordan's."

Abby loved all the attention Mitch's parents gave her. Our whole family went last year, but this year Larry and I were in Jamestown, New York. Later Margie and Mitch drove to Ruth's home in Connecticut where they spent time before driving to our camper. On Friday, July 5th, Larry and I drove the five hundred miles from western New York back to our home in Windsor, Connecticut, washed some clothes, and left to meet everyone in Rhode Island.

At the campground I was greeted by both Margie and Ruth. "Boy, are we glad to see you. Abby says no one is any fun at the beach but Grandma."

I laughed and told them, "She's right."

Soon Margie and Mitch were arguing about when he should jog— before we went to dinner or after. Ruth shook her head and whispered to me, "They've been going at it like this since they got to New Jersey. Last night in Marlborough he got on her case because she was having another glass of wine. She got mad and went to bed. Then he poured himself a glass of Scotch. Make sense to you? It hasn't been much fun for me. I got a divorce because I couldn't stand the tension. Now I have to listen to them."

I got Margie alone, "Margie, it doesn't make that much difference. We're only talking twenty minutes."

"Ma, you don't get it. He's got this new guru whose book tells him how to make his life perfect. He wants me to jog with him after I've worked all day and he's sat around the house. Some days I just can't do it. You should see the lists. He has them posted all over. Little reminders to keep him on track. He tells me, 'When I get my MBA you won't be good enough to be my wife.'"

"Oh, Margie, you don't believe that, do you?"

"Of course not, but it hurts anyway. Right now I just want to relax. I've got a cold and haven't had much sleep. He's insisting we visit his uncle on Long Island and go out in the boat Sunday. I've told him it's too much. We should do it another weekend. I have to go to work Monday. We won't get home until late. He doesn't care. He can sleep all day."

Things eventually calmed down and Mitch told us he was treating Larry and me to dinner because our anniversary was July 2nd. We interpreted this as a positive sign that Mitch was maturing. But Margie told us, "He spent a lot on dinner for his parents' anniversary last week so order what you really want. He has to do it."

Mitch told her, "Margie, that's not called for. I want to do it for your parents."

Margie answered, "Oh I know. I'm just teasing."

I knew she wasn't. She has told me several times about how tight Mitch is with his money—and hers. He hasn't let her buy anything for the house with the wedding money and he expects her to turn over her paycheck for him to manage. I remember going to visit them in Poway, California, in April 1993. Mitch sat in a rose-colored lounge chair reading the want ads. From time to time he would circle a job with a highlighter and tell Margie, "Here's a job you should call about."

She ignored him for a while. Then she told him, "I'm getting ready for my oral exams. I don't get the doctorate if I'm not prepared. I'm not ready to give that up for a few bucks. Are you?" Money has always been an issue between them.

Riding to our anniversary dinner in the backseat of our car, with Abby on his lap, he told us the house in Poway had just been sold. He cleared eighteen thousand dollars on the sale. I wondered silently when we would get the money they owed Larry and me. We're retired. We could use that money as well as they could. We loaned them money for mortgage payments when he was out of work and for a down payment on the Volvo they had leased nine months ear-

14

lier when Margie took the job in Lewisburg. I made a mental note to talk to her about when they would start paying off these loans.

Dinner at the Larchwood Inn in Wakefield was pleasant. We were seated in a small, almost private, colonial-style dining room with historical prints on the walls. Jacob entertained us with his two-and-a-half-year-old antics after eating several maraschino cherries a doting waitress put in his Shirley Temple. Abby sat at the head of the table between her aunt and uncle.

Mitch told us, "My parents would like you to go on a cruise with them this November. I have the brochures in my car. I'll give them to you when we get back to the trailer. You have to make a deposit by July 10th if you decide to go." It sounded like something we would enjoy.

After leaving the Larchwood, we returned to our trailer, which sleeps four people comfortably. There were five adults and two kids, so sleeping arrangements had to be carefully negotiated. Mitch told us he didn't mind sleeping on the queen-sized air mattress, but Margie said, "I'm sleeping on one of the twin beds."

Our last good picture of Margie was taken in May 1996.

Abby asked, "Can I sleep with Uncle Mitch?"

Mitch agreed and that's what happened. Now, after what has occurred, I think to myself, *Abby slept in the same bed with the man who killed her aunt.* I can't comprehend how we let that happen.

Margie and Mitch were gone when I woke up Sunday morning. He wanted to catch the early ferry to Long Island and they didn't want to disturb me. Now, little more than five weeks later, tears flood down my cheeks as realize I didn't even get to say goodbye and there will be no more chances to do so!

We were surprised when we called Mitch's parents late Sunday evening to tell them we wanted to go on the cruise. Margie and Mitch were still there. We knew she was upset. She would get home to Lewisburg very late. I didn't know I'd never see her alive again.

"Oh my God, Larry, we can't go on the cruise with Jordan and Aileen. What are we going to do?" Our anticipated enjoyment of Acapulco, going through the Panama Canal, and stopping at several Caribbean islands now feels like a cruel joke. We'd never been on a cruise. Jordan and Aileen, cruise veterans, were going to show us beginners how to get the most out of the experience.

Larry assures me. "When we get back home, I'll have someone call the travel agent and cancel the trip. We may not get our deposit back."

I look out the window seeking distraction from my melancholy thoughts. I see we are near Scranton and it's getting dark. I notice that Ruth is again behind the wheel, driving through stretches of stop-and-go traffic. Now, I begin to wonder if the motel will hold our reservations if we're late. I tell myself, *Yes, of course.* Soon there's one lane of traffic because of construction. Flashing lights, sirens, ambulances, and tow trucks are clues that accidents are also contributing to the nightmare. Hours go by. We are helplessly stuck. "Why, God? Haven't we gone through enough? You must be really angry at us."

Later, a state policeman tells us that part of the problem was that a trucker had fallen asleep with his vehicle stopped in the right-hand lane of traffic. The trip to Lewisburg usually takes about five-and-a-half hours. We've been trying to get to Margie for eight hours. It is 1:30 in the morning. The motel has held our reservation. Does the clerk know why we are here? Who cares. In the room I call Frank at the prison as he had asked me to do. He is at home, but he immediately calls back offering to come to our room with a chaplain right away. I doubt we will sleep, but I know we are too exhausted to see anyone or understand what they're telling us. I ask, "Can this wait until morning?" We agree to meet at 9 A.M. Larry, Ruth, and I prepare for bed. Morning, in the daylight, will be soon enough to face the details of our hell.

CHAPTER 3

Mister Rodgers'
Neighborhood

At a little past eight we are at the Perkins Restaurant next door to our motel. We're surprised we slept as well as we did. Exhaustion, we decide. I tell Ruth and Larry, "I didn't think I was going to be able to sleep even with the Southern Comfort, but I did. You'll probably think I'm crazy but I pulled a chair next to the bed and told Margie, 'Come sit here. Let me know you're okay. If you do that I'll get through this.' She came. I couldn't see her but a soft gray shape leaned over me. You know how we always teased Margie about her patting our backs when she hugged us? Well, she patted mine. For just a second or two I felt the most incredible peace and love."

They listen politely as tears stream down my cheeks in the crowded eatery. I don't even worry about people seeing me cry. Who has more of a right?

Ruth and I are seated opposite Larry in a booth. I like to face the door—this need goes back to watching too many John Wayne movies, I guess. So we see people coming and going and wonder aloud if any of them is from the penitentiary. We go back to our room at 8:55 A.M. Soon there is a knock on the door. When Larry opens it, Frank Adair holds out his hand and introduces himself and Joe Pryor, one of the chaplains. They sit on chairs we had taken from beside the small table in the corner of the room and placed in the open space near the door.

Frank begins, "We cannot imagine your pain and suffering, but Margaret was a part of our family here at Lewisburg Federal Penitentiary, so we are feeling a loss too."

Joe asks to say a prayer. We agree, but I'm thinking, isn't it just a bit late for this? He asks for strength and guidance through the days ahead. We'll certainly need both. When he's finished, he looks at Ruth and says, "We saw you in Perkins. I knew you must be her sister. You look so much alike." Ruth smiles.

News is filtered to us gradually. We're surprised when we hear that she was murdered on Friday around eleven A.M. instead of Thursday night. Frank tells us, "She was seen alive at 10:30 Friday morning. Lauren, one of the other psychologists, was picking up Margaret's beeper because she would be on call that weekend and nights until Margaret returned from the conference on Cape Cod. Lauren reported that both Mitch and Margaret answered the door and everything seemed okay."

Ruth asks where Margie was killed.

Frank tells her, "In the bathroom, but the FBI is in charge of the investigation, and they have ordered us not to give out information."

"But we're her family—surely they don't mean us?" Ruth asks. When Frank just nods his head up and down she continues, "So when are they going to talk to us?"

"I'm not sure they plan to." Frank explains. "Both the Bureau of Prisons and the FBI are divisions of the Justice Department. The decision about jurisdiction came from Attorney General Reno's office. Since the murder took place on federal property, the reservation housing at Lewisburg, but outside the prison, the FBI has jurisdiction. We have to live with that. If it had happened inside the penitentiary walls, it would have been our case." Left unsaid was "as it should be."

Larry, Ruth, and I look at one another. We feel caught in bureaucratic crossfire. Ruth asks Frank to call the FBI. He agrees reluctantly.

I ask, "When will we be able to get into the house? I almost had Ruth drive over there last night."

Frank looks at me. "If you had gone over, we had a guard posted at the gate to escort you back to your motel. The FBI has not released the house to us yet. We aren't sure when that will be."

Ruth and I are stunned. I tell him, "None of this will seem real until we get into the house."

"Maybe Monday or Tuesday."

We shake our heads. Not soon enough. We'll do whatever it takes to get in that house—soon. "Where is her dog, Calie? Can we at least see her?"

"She is next door at the captain's house. We'll try to arrange that."

This discussion is interrupted when an FBI agent calls back. They want to talk to us. When Frank asks where we would like to meet, both Ruth and I tell him, "Not here." The maid hasn't been in to clean the room yet and the walls are closing in on us—cabin fever.

The Pennsylvania State Police Barracks at Montandon have room for us. Frank knows how to get there, so we follow his car in Joe Pryor's big old Cadillac. Joe explains, "This car was my dad's. He died this spring. Having it makes me feel closer to him."

"I know what you mean. I got an old Chevy Impala when my mother died. It didn't have power steering and I got bursitis from driving it, but I loved it because it was hers." I continue, "Joe, we want to thank you for everything, especially your time. I'm sure there are places you'd rather be on a Saturday."

"Actually, you got me released from camping duty with my son. I was called back yesterday afternoon so I'd be available to you." I appreciate Joe's warm, open manner.

At the barracks we are introduced to FBI Agent Dick Rodgers. Then we are shown into a small office where he takes a seat behind the metal desk. Joe and Frank sit beside it. Larry, Ruth, and I sit in three chairs facing them.

Agent Rodgers is dressed in a light gray-blue suit, has silver hair, and wears wire-rimmed glasses. He is a mild mannered, soft-spoken man, probably in his late fifties. I'm sure I'm not the first person to be reminded of the children's TV program host for *Mister Rogers' Neighborhood*. When I shake his hand I think, *this is the person who will answer all our questions.*

But Agent Rodgers tells us, "You have no need to know all the facts now—later you will have them all. This way you can honestly say you don't know, and we don't risk information leaking to the press that could damage our case. News releases will be made by the FBI. And we don't give any details. I can only advise you not to talk to any reporters. But be warned that if you do they will misquote you, and then you will be more upset than you must be right now. If they persist, have them call us. We know how to deal with them."

Frank looks at us and adds, "They can call us too." Even though Dick Rodgers is silent, he is looking straight at Frank. We feel it is a definite warning to remember who is in charge.

Ruth asks, "Can't you at least tell us who found her?"

"Mitchell Paster called 911." Dick Rodgers stands and says, "Now I would like to talk to each of you alone. Frank, will you see if they have found another room for me? I'd like to start with you first, Ruth."

After Ruth has been gone for almost an hour Frank asks if anyone is hungry. I tell him, "I'm a diabetic and need to eat something soon or we'll have more problems." He and Joe take orders for sandwiches and go to pick them up.

Ruth comes back. "Ma, he's going to talk to you next. It isn't too bad. He just asked what I knew about their relationship. He did tell me that Margie was getting in or out of the shower. But when I asked if her hair was wet or not, he wouldn't answer."

I go into an even smaller office where Mr. Rodgers is seated on one side of the desk. He motions me to take a seat on the other side. "Mrs. Bostrom, what can you tell us about Margaret's and Mitchell's relationship?"

"It started during the fall of 1985, her junior year in college, when she transferred to the University of Connecticut. It hasn't been smooth. I used to tell them they would get married just so they could get a divorce."

"So they were together around eleven years. Was she planning to get a divorce?"

"Yes, she contacted a lawyer in mid-July."

"What brought it about—at this time?"

"They were having some troubles, but we all hoped they could work them out. Then he started making wild accusations about her having an affair with her boss. He even made a complaint to the penitentiary about it. The psychologist he talked to made a written memo, which she submitted to a supervisor. Margie was upset about this, but the last straw was when he took her dog, Calie, and her cat, Sebastian, to New Jersey. We gave Calie to Margie. He didn't want a dog."

"Was she having an affair?"

"No, they were trying to work out their problems but he repeatedly accused her of having an affair, which I didn't believe was true. She told me Mitch had been back from New Jersey for about a week and was trying hard to be nice. So she was pleased when he suggested he would cook dinner and she should invite her boss since his wife was out of town visiting relatives. She thought this was a sign Mitch was sorry and wanted their marriage to work out. He cooked a wonderful dinner and they were having a good time when Mitch got up and said he had to go referee a basketball game. Margie told me she and Bill went into the living room and sat talking about their jobs. She explained, 'Ma, it was just like your friends and you talk for hours about the students you work with.' Mitch came home later and was furious when he found Bill was still with her. He accused them of having an affair. She was afraid because his outburst was particularly violent. I don't know what he did but she was afraid to be left alone with Mitch and wanted Bill to get her away from him. She felt like she was on an emotional roller coaster. Mitch could be so loving one moment and so hateful the next.

"Bill took her to his house where she spent the rest of the night. She told me they had sex then—for the first time. Mitch arranged the dinner, left, and returned early because he thought he would catch them doing something and now they had."

"When did this happen?"

"The dinner was on a Thursday. I believe July 11th. She went back home to get dressed for work Friday morning. She locked the bedroom door, but Mitch broke in, took Calie and Sebastian, put them in the car and drove off. She didn't know what he was going to do with them. It ended up he took them to New Jersey to his parents' home. He told her he did it because she loved them more than him."

"What was your reaction to this?"

Margie's golden retriever, Calie, and her cat, Sebastian, lounge on Margie's bed.

"We didn't hear about it until Monday. I was really upset. I asked her why she waited until Monday to call us. She said, 'Because I hoped Mitch would bring them back on his own.' We were quite sure his parents didn't want the dog and didn't approve of Mitch's behavior. We told her that one of us would go to New Jersey to pick up Calie.

"Mitch knew how much she loved her pets. It was a cruel thing to do to someone you say you love. Margie made several calls to Ruth and me that week. But I don't think she told me he broke the lock on the door until later. She was determined to see a lawyer to get a court order to have Calie returned. She couldn't prove the cat was a gift to her from Mitch, but she had a bill of sale for Calie and we had our canceled check. She planned to have the lawyer draw up divorce papers too. She got the name of Graham Showalter, a civil attorney, from one of the attorneys at the prison. She met with him after work on Wednesday."

Dick Rodgers nods his head, "Yes, I know Graham. A good man." Then he asks, "She saw him on July 17th?"

"I believe so. I know she thought he was taking too long to draw up the papers to get Calie back. Mitch kept calling and wanting to reconcile. She told him that unless he gave Calie and Sebastian back there was no hope of getting back together. He indicated she had to come to New Jersey to get them. Something about his car being fixed. She ignored our advice and went by herself to get them. We weren't very happy about that, especially when we found out that his parents weren't there."

Dick Rodgers moves on, "Was Mitch ever abusive?"

I explain, "He was a very controlling person and mentally abusive. I have a letter he wrote to us ten years ago telling how sorry he was for an incident that occurred at our home. They had one of their frequent arguments and he called the police to get his credit cards back from her.

"When the police came, Margie asked them, 'Did he tell you about the nude pictures of me he plans to put on the college bulletin boards?' Margie gave the policeman the credit cards and he took Mitch out to the police car and had a talk. Apparently there were no nude pictures.

"Mitch's letter to us was a long list of reasons for his behavior. He had a cold, was tired, traffic was awful, his grandfather was ill, and he knew he was going to be late. Margie would be upset and he didn't want her to be—not his fault."

Dick Rodgers leans forward and asks, "Why did he write you the letter?"

"I think he knew how much Margie loved us and that our opinions were important to her. He wanted us on his side. What I got from his letter, even then, was a sense of his trying to manipulate us and refusing to be responsible for what he did."

"As the relationship progressed, how did he treat her?"

"He put her down a lot," I repeat Mitch's remark about her not being good enough to be his wife when he got his MBA.

Dick Rodgers shakes his head. "Sounds like role reversal to me. She was a Ph.D."

"That's what we thought."

The FBI agent persists. "Was there evidence of physical abuse?"

"One time, a while ago, I noticed bruises on her arm, like someone had grabbed her too hard. I asked her about it and she told me not to worry. She had handled it, and it wouldn't happen again."

Dick Rodgers raises an eyebrow and looks steadily at me.

I clarify, "I don't know if he physically abused her again but we were becoming concerned about his unrelenting verbal attacks. Quite frankly we were anxious for him to leave for Cornell. Margie decided to pursue the divorce quietly until he left. She told me, 'He'll get involved in his life there and I can get the divorce then. I'll avoid a lot of trouble that way. He doesn't care about me. If he did, he wouldn't have stayed in California all that time.' I told her to cool it with Bill. She halfheartedly agreed. I knew she wouldn't."

"Why did he stay in California?"

I'm impressed and relieved that Mr. Rodgers is gathering information about the time and events leading to the murder. "I don't know. They had only been married for a year and a half. Wouldn't you think he'd want to be with her? He said he wanted to get a bonus that he was sure was large, maybe even ten thousand dollars. He had to stay until March 1st to get it. He even went up to Orange County to work at that office for a few weeks because his position was cut in San Diego County. He got a two-thousand-dollar bonus, then he quit the job. Yet he stayed at his house in Poway two and a half more months—unemployed. He played golf and spent a week replacing the roof on his house. Margie felt lonely and kept writing notes asking him to come. In May she finally gave him an ultimatum. 'Be here by May 15th for the secretary's wedding or don't come at all.' He came. She was sure people at work were talking about her phantom husband. Her house on the reservation was large and spacious—the kind usually saved for assistant wardens, and she was in it all alone."

There is a long pause, then I express my fear, "I'm worried about Mitch getting away with killing Margie. He can be very charming when he wants to be. Especially when he is getting his own way or when it will help his cause."

"Don't worry, Mrs. Bostrom, judges see charming defendants all the time. They aren't impressed. In fact, it might count against him."

"Were all the legal procedures that protect his rights followed? Was Mitch read his rights before you questioned him?"

"No comment." His face is unreadable. I'm confused by his refusal to give me this assurance. I wonder, did they forget or ignore important guidelines and if they did will that make it hard to convict Mitch—just because of a technicality?

"I guess what you're telling me is that you are a professional and you followed all the guidelines carefully. I just have to believe that."

"No comment."

I wonder how he would feel if it were his daughter and he was being kept in the dark. But I don't ask.

There is a knock on the door and Frank sticks his head in. He has our sandwiches. He looks at me, "I thought you might need this."

Dick Rodgers tells him, "It's okay. We are about finished anyway." Then he asks me, "When did you last talk to Margaret or Mitchell?"

"I talked to Margie Monday night after we had a message on our answering machine from Mitch. I talked to Mitch about 10:15 Thursday night."

"August 15th?"

"Yes." Then I quickly relate my conversation with Mitch—just hours before he will kill my daughter.

Dick Rodgers thanks me for my cooperation and assures me, "Everything possible is being done to make the case against Mitchell airtight."

As I leave the interview room I comment, "I'm reading John Grisham's novel *The Runaway Jury*, which doesn't inspire much faith in our judicial system." Fiction and reality blend for the moment.

"Unfortunately, the book contains certain truths. Especially about jury selection. The fact that she was having an affair could inspire sympathy for Mitchell in someone who has suffered from an unfaithful spouse. They might even see him as a hero. He did what they only fantasized about doing."

Just what I needed to hear. Dick Rodgers stands, we shake hands, and I leave to eat my sandwich. He goes to find Larry.

Ruth waves me into an informal lounge or lunch room. The gray linoleum floors, Formica-topped tables, metal chairs, file cabinets, and 1970s-model refrigerator are typical government decor. I'm introduced to four state troopers and one of their wives. The atmosphere is friendly and relaxed. They banter good-naturedly about marriage, divorce, alimony, favorite junk foods, and plans for the remainder of the weekend. Eventually the conversation settles on Margie's murder.

A corporal tells Ruth. "I knew you were her sister. You look so much like her."

Ruth asks, "When did you see Margie?"

"When the 911 call came in we went to the house. I saw your picture in her bedroom too."

Another trooper also saw Ruth's picture in the bedroom. I wonder how many people stood in the bathroom door looking at my murdered daughter. Was she naked? Margie would be mortified if she knew strangers were looking at her nude body. I can't ask these men.

Ruth asks, "Where was Mitch?"

"He sat in the dining room. He's a little weasel. I sure hope he gets what he deserves," the corporal tells her and then immediately adds, "I shouldn't have told you that. We aren't involved with the case anymore."

Larry and Dick Rodgers come out of the office. Frank tells us the human resources people from the penitentiary are waiting for a call from him. They will meet us back in our room at the motel to discuss Margie's death benefits and do the paperwork. The corporal gives Ruth his business card, "Here, call me if you have any questions or need help."

We ride back to the motel with Frank. Larry comments, "Dick Rodgers isn't exactly what I expected an FBI agent to be—with all the bad publicity they've been getting lately."

Frank says, "Yeah, amongst all the agents I've met there are two good ones. You just met one. His partner is the other."

We go to our room and Frank waits outside for the human resources people. He brings them to the room and introduces Vicki and Marsha. They express their sympathy and outrage at Margaret's death. Marsha looks directly at me with her brilliant, penetrating blue eyes. The empathy I see there reflects the pain she reads in mine. "You know don't you, Mrs. Bostrom, that Margaret named you as her beneficiary? It is a sizable sum based on her pay grade and untimely death."

I'm stunned. "No, when?"

"Two weeks ago. I was on vacation but Vicki took care of it."

Vicki adds, "She was very insistent and definite about wanting to make the change immediately." She continues, "You know her smile lit up the whole office whenever she dropped by. We loved her visits."

My surprise quickly turns to relief. "Oh, thank God. Mitch won't get his hands on it." There I go. I've been cursing God and now I found a reason to praise Him.

Marsha gathers the necessary personal information about me before she hands me the policy to sign so I can receive the money. I know this is real, tangible proof of Margie's love for me. It was her way to be sure we'd be repaid for all the things we had done for her—even if she were dead. Did she have a premonition? Did she know she was going to die? That Mitch would be the murderer? All I want is her back. Money doesn't mean anything in the face of our loss.

"There will be other small amounts of money coming. Her last paycheck, payment for vacation time that she had coming and she just qualified for our savings plan. I'm not sure if you'll get these or if they will be added to her estate. If you have any questions, please call." Marsha holds out her business card. Vicki gives us hers and they are ready to leave when there's a knock on the door.

Joe is back with a note about a phone call to the prison. Margaret left several outfits at a dry cleaner in a nearby town. Who was going to pick them up and pay the large cleaning bill? Certainly a silly detail, considering everything.

Finally, we are alone. Ruth calls Steve. No one has been able to locate Kathy yet. Her landlord went into her apartment, which he described as a disaster, but Kathy was not there. Steve talked to the Hartford Police but they can't do anything. They will call him if she turns up. Ruth's friend Mary Ellen offers to look for her. We tell her thanks but not to do it. We don't need anything more to worry about. We don't know how Kathy will react if she is on drugs or drunk when she hears the news.

Silently I wonder if we would get a discount for having two funerals instead of one. Would mourning two daughters be any harder? How could it be?

We need to decide what we are going to do about funeral arrangements. I begin drafting the obituary then stop and ask, "Are we having her cremated or buried?" Ruth hesitates.

I explain, "Daddy and I aren't planning to stay in Windsor. We could have her buried with her grandmother Bostrom in Jamestown, but that seems so far away. We'd never get to her grave." I ask, "Do you know of a cemetery near you, Ruth?"

She doesn't and reluctantly suggests, "Let's have her cremated. I can keep the ashes."

Ruth and I want to see Calie and talk to Margie's neighbors, Matt and Sandy. We think it will help us to see her house from the outside—sort of a step-by-step process.

I tell Ruth, "Call Frank Adair, but be kind."

Ruth wants to know what Larry thinks she should say. He doesn't tell her, so she says, "Okay, one of you call him if you don't trust me." I refuse, so finally Larry calls. Frank offers to bring Calie to the motel.

Ruth and I look at each other. What is going on? "Ma, can't you just see that big golden retriever pup on the stairs and in this room?"

"Daddy, tell him no. We want to go to Matt and Sandy's house."

Larry is uncharacteristically persistent and we finally receive permission to go see Calie at 6:30 that evening. We arrive. There, next door, is Margie's house all cordoned off with yellow police crime scene tape. Her Volvo is parked in the driveway about two feet from the garage. It is so quiet and surreal. We see the new siding she told us about. How could such a terrible act have taken place here? Just yesterday!

Matt, Sandy, and Calie meet us at the car. Calie knows us and loves up to us equally. The captain introduces us to Manny Cordero, the Justice Department's district chaplain from Philadelphia.

"Why is he here?" I whisper to Ruth. "Must be they don't want to leave us alone with Matt and Sandy. What are they afraid of?"

Ruth shrugs and rolls her eyes.

Inside Calie and I play our favorite game, tug-of-war. She has been well taken care of and even has toys of her own. Matt and Sandy's two beagles have shared their territory, either willingly or unwillingly. We feel fortunate she has been treated so lovingly.

Matt apologizes because Margie's cat got away. "When we opened the door it took off like a bat out of hell. Don't worry though, I've set a trap. I propped the door open so he can get to his food, but the door will shut behind him."

I try to imagine what those poor animals saw and heard. They loved to lie on her bed together. I'm sure they were there that morning as she packed for her trip and undressed for the shower.

I thank Matt, "I'm sure you'll get him. I don't know what we are going to do with him, though. Ruth is allergic to cats and we have a twenty-one-year-old cat who won't be happy with a competitor for our affections. Besides we live in a condominium and plan to travel since I retired in June. He'd be left at the vet's a lot."

Matt looks at Sandy and tells us, "I think I know someone who would feel honored if you'd let him take the cat. Margaret was helping him deal with the loss of three family members. It would comfort him to know he was doing this for her."

"Wonderful! Please ask him. It would be such a relief if we knew Sebastian was with someone who cared about Margie."

Sandy gives us the names and phone numbers of people we will need to contact such as the cable company, telephone company, and Calie's veterinarian.

Ruth asks, "Do you have a leash? I want to take Calie for a walk."

"Sandy, why don't you go with her?" Sandy either doesn't hear her husband's orders or ignores them.

The telephone rings and it is Dick Rodgers telling us that the lawyer, Graham Showalter, is back in the country and will see us. We are to call him to set a time.

I ask, "When are we going to be let in the house?"

Manny Cordero answers, "Mrs. Bostrom, the FBI hasn't released the house to us yet. They will go in and get what you need."

"Even what Margie will wear for her funeral? I'm beginning to wonder what the secret is or what you have to hide."

Manny reaches out to me, "I assure you we have nothing to hide."

But I'm tired of being put off, "We're beginning to wonder—I said it because I want to get your attention."

"You got my attention. I'll talk to Frank. We'll let you know as soon as the FBI gives the okay for you to go into the house."

"If it's that you don't think we are strong enough to handle it, believe me we are. We need to see the murder scene to make any of this real, to understand that she truly is dead. Besides there are personal items we want to take, like her photo albums."

As we get ready to leave, Matt hands me Margie's engagement ring. The coroner had taken it off during his examination and asked that it be returned to us.

I look at the diamond with rubies on each side and know I never want to see it again. It is too tangible a reminder of what I have lost and why. I hand it to Ruth.

She takes it and tells me, "Ma, Margie designed that ring herself. She was very proud of it. You could have a necklace made out of it."

"Give it to Abby when she is older. By then maybe the pain will be more tolerable."

Sandy hugs me and says, "I'm sorry I wasn't at home when it happened. Maybe I could have prevented it." But all our maybes, should haves, and what ifs can't change a thing.

Back at the motel there are several messages. The lawyer wants us to call. He will see us tomorrow—Sunday at 3 P.M. The Windsor Locks Funeral Home needs information from the death certificate. Larry's brother and mine have called.

We return the calls before we walk down the street to the Panda Garden for dinner. We order mechanically and eat without tasting. They don't serve wine or beer, which might have helped us to relax. When we finish eating we decide we want to read the morning paper's account of the murder. But all the newspaper boxes in the area are empty, so we go in the motel lobby and ask if they have a copy. They do. The clerk lets us look at it.

I'm furious when I see the newspaper. "They didn't even have her name right. They called her Mary. The least they could do is get a person's name right when she dies."

When we ask if we can take the paper with us she explains, "The manager hasn't read it so I can't give it to you."

Tired and drained, Ruth gets angry. "One of the headlines is about our family. My sister was murdered, and you can't give me the paper!"

As I follow Ruth out the door, I turn to see the clerk's bewildered expression. I feel sorry for her. But Ruth needed to vent her pent-up feelings.

Back in the room, Ruth continues her search for Kathy. She calls the corporal at the Pennsylvania State Police and asks for his advice. He says there isn't much we can do while we are in Lewisburg.

We will have to be back in Connecticut to sign a missing persons form and give the police a picture and description.

I watch, amazed at Ruth's need to contact her middle sister. No, her only sister—now. She looks at me and I tell her gently, "Maybe it is best if we can't find her. If we do we'll have to deal with her problems along with everything else. She'll feel she should have done something to stop the murder. You know Kathy can't give you the support you need and I'm not strong enough to help her now."

We hug and turn out the lights. I whisper in the dark, "Oh, Ruth, I'm so glad we have you."

The first full day AMM (after Margie's murder) is over.

CHAPTER 4

Two Pairs of Slippers and a Clean White Bathroom

Sunday morning we wake early—surprised and relieved we were able to sleep at all. Larry goes next door to Perkins to get muffins and coffee. Today we want to avoid putting ourselves on display in the crowded restaurant. The call we've been waiting for finally comes. We can go into the house at eleven. Anticipation and apprehension vie for control of our feelings. We have to go but dread facing the reality of what happened there only forty-eight hours ago.

We drive north on Route 15, make a left turn, and drive past homes untouched by our tragedy. Soon we approach the wire fence that surrounds the reservation. The yellow crime scene tape is gone from the light blue-gray colonial house with white trim. Instead there are three cars in the driveway and one on the street. "So much for being alone," I mumble as I watch at least six men approach the car.

Manny Cordero reaches out and opens my door, "Good morning, Mrs. Bostrom. I'd like you to meet David Lamer,

The house on the penitentiary grounds where Margie was murdered has new siding.

the warden at Lewisburg." I turn and see a trim, light-haired gentleman in his fifties.

Behind his glasses, his eyes are filled with compassion, "I'm so terribly sorry about Margaret. I can't imagine your pain. She was part of our family here at Lewisburg, and we're saddened by our loss. If there is anything we can do for you please let us know." He extends his arms and I go gratefully into his embrace as tears blur my vision.

Larry and Ruth receive similar welcomes. I hear a slender Hispanic man tell my husband, "Hello, I'm Sergio, the chaplain who called you with the terrible news." Larry extends his hand. Introductions and condolences are quickly completed.

We're ready to go in. Walking isn't automatic. Each step is the result of repeated commands. Lift right foot. Put the leg forward. Place right foot on ground. Now do the left. Right, again. The door is open, *Margie must be here waiting to greet us*—but she isn't! I hesitate, take a deep breath, and I enter. I'm numb. This is happening to someone else and I'm just acting out their part. Inside I stand to the right of the door as everyone enters. I look at the black wrought-iron and glass table with white chairs that we bought for her when she moved to Mira Mesa. The happy memories distract me for only a moment, then I turn to Ruth and point under the window, "Is that the tablecloth you gave her?" We gaze at the deep red and green Victorian print. She nods her head.

I'm not ready to go upstairs yet, so I walk ahead into the kitchen. It looks lived-in and inviting. Two wine glasses with dried residue stand on the counter. Whose? Hers and Mitch's? Hers and Bill's? For a moment I think we have arrived unexpectedly and soon Margie will return from her brief errand. She'll be delighted to see us. Reality hits and I wonder where the butcher knife was when Mitch decided murder was the solution to their problems. I escape back through the dining room and the entry hall ignoring the stairs and small half bath to my right. I go into the living room where there are familiar, framed Dali and Van Gogh prints. "Now I won't have to get mine framed, Ruth."

"Jeez, Ma, you're worse than I am. Even I got mine framed."

I walk past the fireplace and blue, flowered sofa and love seat. She and Mitch had a real big argument when she wanted to buy these for the family room in the house he bought in Poway. She had prevailed then but lost when he insisted on buying whitewashed pine log and glass coffee and end tables. We knew Mitch felt he should have the authority to decide how money was spent but we didn't recognize it as a signal warning of future dangers. We thought when she finished her degree and had a job she would have command of her money. However, control of the money remained an issue even after she had a job where she earned forty-nine thousand dollars a year. Each month she was expected to send him at least half her paycheck. Bitter, long-distance disagreements seriously eroded the marriage.

There—sitting on white, built-in shelves—is my favorite picture. It was taken on their wedding day. Margie and Mitch are holding Abby between them and smiling at her. She is beaming with joy. Margie and Abby look so much alike. I felt so lucky that day. Now I place the picture that mocks me face down on the shelf and walk into the sunroom.

This was my favorite picture. Mitch, Abby and Margie depict what family is all about.
(Photo by Robert Charles Photography, East Long Meadow, MA)

35

Here are the pastel sofa with the abstract print and the rose-colored recliner we helped her pick out seven years ago. Both are faded now. I cross the room, sit on the sofa, and try to connect with Margie. At my feet, between the sofa and the light oak coffee table are two pairs of slippers—sitting neatly side by side. Happily? I'm reminded of a movie set and expect actors to come out and read their lines. The director will yell, "Cut!" and life will get back to normal.

Uncomfortable with the irony of what the slippers imply and the reality that surrounds me, I get up and go to the light pine entertainment center. I open a cabinet door and there are all her photograph albums neatly and carefully filled. Six of them are covered with fabric. I had taken a class to learn how to make them. Margie loved the idea and begged me to show her how. It was hard for me because she was left-handed. She looked so awkward making her first one, I had to laugh, but it turned out great. It was red satin with a big heart on the front. For Mitch. After that she made albums as gifts for her friends and family. We loved her thoughtfulness.

I look at Manny Cordero, who has been my constant shadow. "I want her pictures." I hand the albums to him one-by-one. He carries them to a box in the dining room where Dick Rodgers, the FBI agent, is sitting making out an inventory. I have an idea he is also giving his permission for us to take each item. I begin to feel like a scavenger picking over my daughter's things, but having what belongs to her helps me feel close to Margie—reinforcing precious memories.

It's time. Slowly, I start up the stairs. Manny and Matt, the captain of the guards and Margie's neighbor, both start after me. I go into her bedroom, see the family pictures, and rumpled bed. I remember the comforter.

Margie bought new bedding just before one of our visits to Poway. When she put the comforter on the bed the seams across the surface were crooked from top to bottom. She decided to return it and asked me to go along. We couldn't find another one at that store so we picked out a different, more expensive pattern. Margie loved it—so I paid the difference in the cost. We got home and I told Mitch, "We couldn't find another one of the same kind, but we found one you'll like even better."

When he saw it, he told us, "I hate it. The pattern is too small. I refuse to sleep in a bed with that on it. I liked the other one."

Margie explained, "They didn't have any more like it."

"Did you have them call their other stores to see if they had any?"

"No."

By then I was feeling like I overstepped my motherly boundaries so I told her, "Do whatever you want, Margie."

The comforter was put away and not discussed again during our visit. Later Margie returned the second comforter and searched until she found the first pattern with straight stitching. On the surface and by itself that incident wouldn't be a cause for alarm. In fact, many wives would welcome a show of husbandly interest in bed linens. What has become obvious is that he resented my influence on Margie and had to reestablish his position of authority.

I informed Larry, "If you told me you wouldn't sleep on a bed with a comforter, I'd put it on the bed and tell you you could sleep wherever you liked."

He responded, "I'd never tell you that. I'm too smart."

We laughed and agreed. Mitch just being Mitch—again.

There, off to the right, is the bathroom door slightly ajar. I take several deep breaths to steel myself against the pain and panic assaulting my body. I remind myself, *You have to see it to accept that such an unspeakable horror happened.* I push the door fully open and gaze at the antiseptic white tile floor, tub, toilet, and counters. The only color comes from the deep burgundy towels decorating the shower door and the long, narrow, brightly colored fish print framed in black that hangs over the oak toilet seat. I sit down and picture her damp, bloody, nude body lying lifeless on the floor, a pool of red blood spreading across the white tiles. Are her eyes open? Where are her arms? Over her head? Across her chest? Flung out to the sides? What kind of damage would so many stab wounds to her chest cause?

Ruth's words interrupt my gruesome reverie. "Ma, they didn't clean out the sink very carefully. There's still some blood in it."

I look up, surprised she is here, and watch as she runs water down the drain to complete the task. A large walk-in closet opens off the bath. Everything is in place; a full, white, plastic shoe bag hangs from the rod and blue, labeled sweater boxes sit on the top shelf. At the far end are shelves with neatly rolled socks and folded sweatshirts. Ruth picks up a new one with Cornell written across the front in bright red letters. She asks, "Why couldn't he have just waited two days and gone to Cornell like he planned?" I can't answer her.

Manny peeks in the door. I tell him, "We have to pick out what Margie will wear for the funeral." He withdraws. We select a gold silk pantsuit, a red dress, and a black suit. We take both red and black silk shells. Do they put shoes and stockings on the bodies before placing them in the casket? We don't know so we take a new pair of pantyhose and a pair of dark shoes.

"Ma, there are lots more clothes in the spare bedroom. Let's look there." We walk back through the bathroom into Margie's bedroom where we give Manny the clothes we have already selected. Down the hall past the second bathroom is the small airy bedroom with the furniture we bought for her. Sitting on the dresser is a framed school picture of me. Tears roll down my cheeks. The first drawer I open is full of neatly stacked tops. Sleeveless in one pile, short sleeves in another, and long-sleeved ones in the next. I grin at Manny. "How's that for being organized?"

Manny admires her meticulousness and laments, "I've never seen anyone so systematic. I wish I was more orderly."

So do I, but I know Margie had to be. She was learning disabled and received special help when she was in first and second grade. It taught her the skills she needed to compensate for her learning problems so she could use her above-average intelligence. She knew order was essential for her to function successfully.

In this closet are most of her expensive, feminine dresses. I look at each one. Some I recognize and remember how well she wore her clothes. "Look, Ruth, will these fit you?"

"Ma, I don't know if I'd be comfortable wearing her clothes." She feels the fine quality of a long, rich floral print.

"I know Margie would want you to have them. Maybe it would make you feel close to her." Ruth agrees to think about it. We add a black shift with a jacket and a blue linen dress to Manny's pile. I grab a small plastic basket full of fabric paints and a glue gun from the ironing board and walk across the hall.

Margie's dad is in the third bedroom, which Margie and Mitch were using as an office. The cute elephant wallpaper and border look out of place in a room filled with computers, desks, filing cabinets, and work space. Larry is sitting at the desk going through the papers. Joe Pryor, the chaplain, is carefully removing her degrees and awards from the walls and putting them in a file folder.

I find recent photographs in the top right-hand desk drawer. "She didn't even have time to put these in albums." I flip through them—leaving any that include Mitch. In the closet is a picture of her wearing a lovely flowered beige dress. She looks so young and innocent. The picture is surrounded with adjectives—terrific, wonderful, awesome, sweet, and so forth. When did he make it for her? It took a lot of loving time to make it. I wonder aloud, "How does a relationship get from this to the tragic, devastating situation we now face?" Mitch was so charming in June at my retirement party. He and Margie were smiling all night. How can this be? Two months later she's dead. He's murdered her.

Margie, why didn't you tell us what was happening? We would have helped you. You didn't have to handle it on your own.

Her answer, I'm sure, would be, "With my training I should be able to handle it and I didn't want to bother you with my problems."

Sure, Margie. Why didn't I pay closer attention when you told me the sex wasn't even that good anymore?

Alone for a moment, I walk back to the bathroom. Why wasn't I here to protect my baby? Did she try to defend herself? Beg or plead? Scream with terror as she realized his intent? Did she call for me? Answers elude me so I walk slowly down to the kitchen. Counting steps as I go. Thirty-nine steps one way. Seventy-eight steps if he had to go down to get the knife. Certainly time to reconsider his purpose. *Why, Mitch, did you take her life and throw yours away?*

In the dining room Dick Rodgers gives me Margie's unopened purse, briefcase, and personal identification as an employee of the federal penitentiary. His distress, watching our grief, is apparent in his subdued voice and hasty actions. Later, I will have to return her most recent bank statement for evidence.

When I pick up her briefcase I see she has a plastic card attached to the strap. It has the names and telephone numbers of people at work, including Bill Corey's. When we first arrived in Lewisburg I asked to speak to him, but I was told that was not possible. Supposedly, he was on annual leave. Now, I can talk to him anytime I want. I don't need their permission! I'm ready to leave.

I tell Larry and Ruth, "Margie's wallet has thirty dollars in it. The least she can do is buy our lunch and maybe a bottle of wine." They agree and we find a small corner deli just off the main street. Nothing appeals to me and I have to force myself to eat. It is two-thirty and time to leave for the attorney's office. At least Showalter knew Margie. She had seen him a month earlier about a divorce and to get her dog, Calie, back from Mitch. We drive up the tree-lined street to a rosy-beige stucco-finished building with brown shutters. We're early but he's already there.

The interior is pleasant with its dark wooden panels, bookcases, cabinets, and huge desk covered with papers. Graham Showalter is a tall, distinguished-looking man with prominent features and sandy hair touched with gray. He appears capable. His firm handshake confirms this. "Mr. and Mrs. Bostrom, Ruth, I am outraged this could happen to someone so sweet and naive."

I'll be forever haunted by his next words: "She felt so alone." I know Mitch wanted her to feel isolated. *Why didn't I do more?*

We discuss the murder and share background information. "If you give me her credit cards, Donna, my assistant, will notify each company of her death and check for any unpaid balances due." I give him the ones Margie had in her purse.

Larry asked about the procedure for returning a Volvo that was leased in California. "We'll contact a local dealer in Williamsport about that for you. Do you have a copy of the lease agreement?"

"Yes, I saw it on her desk."

"Did you happen to notice who leased the car? Margaret, Mitchell, or both of them? That might make a difference in what we can do."

"I'm not sure, but we loaned her two thousand dollars for the down payment." I elaborate: "He wouldn't let her use any of their money to get the car she wanted. He drove a fancy sports car but she could manage with an economy car. I'm so glad she insisted. At least she had it for ten months."

"Were you paid back? If not you can file a claim against the estate."

"No, not a dime, even when he got the money for the house."

"You'll need to file with the county clerk to become administrators of her estate. I know there is a memorial service at 10 A.M. tomorrow. Let's make an appointment for early afternoon to get some of the paperwork done."

We agree, feeling we are in competent hands, and go back to the motel. We begin working on the obituary again but we're interrupted by a knock on the door. It is Chaplain Manny Cordero delivering a huge purple tray full of vegetables, fruits, cold cuts, cheeses, deviled eggs, olives, and pickles. "The ladies of the reservation wanted to do something to let you know they are thinking of you."

"Please thank them for their thoughtfulness." I smile at him, but I see Ruth scowl. I give her a warning glance. He leaves after brief pleasantries.

"But, Ma, that was so chauvinistic. 'Ladies'!"

"They were just being nice."

"Yes, they were but couldn't he have said 'her friends and neighbors'? Even 'residents' would have been better. *Ladies!*" I grin at her and let it drop.

Ruth and I only pick at the food, but Larry finds comfort in devouring everything he can. After phone calls home we drive over to Old Towne Tavern—a place we had never been with Margie, but one she told us the people at the penitentiary come to often for happy hour. We pick a table in the corner of the wood-paneled room and observe the other patrons, diverting ourselves by trying to identify who might know Margaret. Being in the comfortable, homey setting makes us feel close to her.

Back in the motel room I call the funeral home and read the obituary over the phone to Charlie, one of the managers. He makes a few suggestions and asks us to fax him my handwritten copy tonight. He will have it typed and submitted to the newspapers.

Ruth and Larry both ask, "What did he say?"

"He wants us to fax it tonight. Margie's body will be arriving at Bradley [the Hartford-Springfield airport] tomorrow morning. She'll be home before we are. Thursday is the best day for the funeral because the *Journal Inquirer* will run the obituary in Monday's evening edition and the *Hartford Courant* will put it in Tuesday morning. This will give people more time."

Larry goes to the lobby to send the fax:

OBITUARY

(as it appeared in the *Manchester Journal Inquirer*)

BOSTROM Dr. Margaret E. Bostrom, 31, was unexpectedly found dead at her home in Lewisburg Pa., on Friday, Aug. 16, 1996. Dr. Bostrom had been employed at the Lewisburg Federal Penitentiary as a psychologist for the past 10 months.

Margaret was born in Jamestown, NY, on Nov. 6, 1964. She grew up in Suffield and graduated from Suffield High School in 1983. She received a bachelor's degree, magna cum laude, and a master's degree from the University of Connecticut.

She lived in the San Diego area for six years and earned a Ph.D. in Clinical Psychology from the California School of Professional Psychology. Margaret was a member of the American Psychological Association, Phi Beta Kappa, and a licensed psychologist in the State of Pennsylvania.

She will be sadly missed by her parents, Lawrence and Shirley Pierce Bostrom of Windsor; two sisters, Ruth Grover of Marlborough, and Kathy Bostrom of Hartford; a beloved niece, Abigail Margaret, and a nephew, Jacob Pierce Grover; and a special aunt, Margaret Bodine of Conesus, N.Y. She also leaves two much loved pets, Calie, a dog, and Sebastian, a cat.

She is survived by her estranged husband, Mitchell F. Paster.

Family, friends, and staff attended a memorial service on Monday, Aug. 19, 1996, in the chapel at Lewisburg Federal Penitentiary.

Visiting hours will be on Thursday, from 2 to 4 and 6 to 7:30 P.M., at the Windsor Locks Funeral Home, 441 Spring St., Windsor Locks. The Rev. Joseph Pryor, a chaplain at Lewisburg Federal Penitentiary will conduct a funeral service immediately following evening visiting hours.

Instead of flowers, the family is requesting that donations be made to a college fund for Abigail, 7, and Jacob, 2. Contributions may be sent to the Abigail and Jacob Grover College Fund, in care of New England Bank, 176 Broad St., Windsor, Conn. 06095, att. of Sheila Bryson.

One terrible task has just been completed so Ruth turns on the television. The local news is about a domestic dispute where an area woman was thrown to the floor and held there by her husband's foot while he shot her in the head. At this hour she is still alive. We just look at each other, but with a new understanding of what her family and friends are experiencing. Not sympathy—but empathy.

Tomorrow we'll begin to say our public goodbyes to Margaret.

Fragmented Thoughts on My Daughter's Death

Lover, Murderer,
Wife killer,
Out of control.

Butcher Knife
Clenched hands.
Instruments of death.

Recognition, Disbelief,
Comprehension, Terror,
Don't do this!

Cries, Screams,
Barking, Begging,
Death is coming.

Water, Blood,
Thirteen wounds,
Naked and lifeless.
Kitchen, Bathroom,
Thirty-nine Steps.
Time to think.

Choices, Consequences,
Walk away or pay,
An eye for an eye.

Sorrow, Pain,
Anger, Frustration,
Why's he alive?

Sister, Aunt,
No More
Love to give.

My daughter
Dead, Gone.
He killed Her.

CHAPTER 5

Was It Really Only
Two Years Ago?

I wake, remain inert, delaying, for a while, the inevitable public acknowledgment that Margie is dead. The clear, deep blue sky with fluffy white clouds scattered over the green rolling fields on this perfect August day leads my thoughts back to another summer day—July 30, 1994. Their wedding day.

Love and pride washed over me as I watched my youngest daughter pose for the photographer. Standing with one hand raised to the window she gazed into the distance with serious dark brown eyes. Her fine features, caught in profile, were framed in brown ringlets and a wedding veil. But a chill swept over me on that warm July afternoon as I wondered if she glimpsed the future.

A pensive Margie at her parents' home before the wedding. Could she see the future? (Photo by Robert Charles Photography, East Long Meadow, MA)

Yesterday, the day before her wedding, she had told me as we rode along in the car, "I'm not sure marrying Mitch is what I really want to do. Sometimes he can be such a jerk!"

"It isn't too late to change your mind. You don't have to be married before you turn thirty." But soon the subject shifted and the moment was lost. I didn't tell her that I, too, had concerns.

Margie completed her work for her doctorate in clinical psychology in June and flew home from California to take care of last-minute wedding arrangements. Her father and I willingly gave back this responsibility that had been entrusted to us while she was in San Diego. It was the first time she had been home for an extended period in over six years. We made the most of that month we had her in Connecticut without Mitch. Her sisters Ruth and Kathy, her niece Abby, and nephew Jacob joined us on many trips to the beach, shopping, and out to dinner. Gradually she began to relax and I had my baby back—if only for a month.

Mitch remained in California because he had started a new job after being out of work for over a year. He only arrived the day before the wedding—in time to play a round of golf, go to the rehearsal, and then to dinner. He hugged us. "Hi, Mom and Dad." A habit he started over a year ago when they became engaged. "Tomorrow I can call you Mom and Dad for real!"

The rehearsal at Chez Josef was disorganized and confusing. There was no clear center aisle so we had to weave our way between tables set up for a party that night. Abby told us in the car on the way from the rehearsal to dinner she was scared. Ruth tried to reassure her, "It's okay. Everyone is a little nervous."

Five-year-old Abby told her, "I didn't say I was nervous. I said I was scared to death!"

The dinner at Albert's, a local restaurant we had recommended to Mitch's parents, was festive. Our families and friends from out of town, who were staying at the same motel just down the street, were all invited. Everyone was ready to celebrate. Mitch's cousin asked, "Mitch, what took you so long? We've been waiting nine years to see you tie the knot." Everyone laughed and drank a toast to their wedding day.

"Ma, here comes Steve with Jakie." Margie's voice brought me back to the photography session. The picture of her at the door had been taken and Mr. Charles was waiting to do the family portrait.

I wondered if Steve was still angry with me about leaving him with eight-month-old Jacob so I could come home to shower and dress for the wedding. Kathy and Abby came with me because it was getting late and Margie and Ruth were still at the hairdresser.

He had promised Ruth he would mow the lawn while she was gone because we had invited people to their home in Marlborough for Sunday brunch. He told me, "I'm sick of everyone having to jump for Margaret—even Ruth. Nobody made this big a fuss over our wedding."

I told him, "Ruth had the wedding she wanted and we did what she asked."

Steve and I don't usually snap at each other, but I was hot and tired and didn't really like what was done to my naturally curly hair. Driving thirty miles in one direction to have our hair done, returning to the condo in Windsor to meet the photographer, then heading twenty miles in the opposite direction for the wedding didn't make much sense to me, but the sisters had made up their minds. At least the condo and the car were air-conditioned.

Steve and Jacob entered the house as Abby, in a white flower-girl dress and a wreath of white flowers circling her almost-blonde hair that was fixed on top of her head, came dancing down the stairs. Ruth was stunning in a sleeveless, black lace-over-fabric dress, which was straight and floor-length with a square neckline and slit up the side. Her blonde hair formed a crown above a strikingly beautiful face so similar to her younger sister's. I wondered again how I got three such attractive daughters. When the picture taking was completed, Steve took Jacob to his sister who was baby-sitting during the wedding and we left for Agawam.

We arrived at Chez Josef at 5:30 P.M., an hour before the ceremony was to begin. When we arrived, we toured the large rooms where the Jewish wedding ceremony and reception were to be held. Larry and I had accepted Margie's planned conversion to Judaism. She seemed happy about it and we thought it would make life easier for her and any children she and Mitch might have. Deep red carpet and large chandeliers with strings of lights, hanging from the ceiling

The two ladies in white are Margie and flower girl, Abby. (Photo by Robert Charles Photography, East Long Meadow, MA)

Margie, Abby, Larry and Shirley pose together proudly. (Photo by Robert Charles Photography, East Long Meadow, MA)

and reflected in the mirrored walls, made the scene appear magical. Rows of chairs faced the white tulle Chupah with ferns across the top and clusters of red roses at the corners. It sat on a raised platform and was where the ceremony would take place. We walked down the center aisle toward the foot of an open staircase decorated with large gold ribbons, white tulle, and fresh green plants.

At the top of these stairs was a private waiting area for close family and friends.

There were hors d'oeuvres, wine, and champagne for our enjoyment, but we waited for Mitch's parents to arrive. As his mother approached in a beaded and sequined dress, I realized it was the same as mine except hers was royal blue instead of burgundy. We laughed. "We sure have good taste!" We decided to tell people we planned it that way. "Bridesmaids dress alike—why not mothers of the bride and groom?"

At the rehearsal we learned that in a Jewish wedding the groom's family sits on the left and the bride's on the right. Just the opposite of what Protestants do. But I liked the idea that both parents walked the bride halfway down the aisle to where they were met by the groom.

The flower bouquets, corsages, and boutonnieres were distributed. Then the music started and Michael, our Chez Josef wedding coordinator, told Michelle, Mitch's sister, who was a bridesmaid, to start down the stairs. Abby was getting nervous so I tried to reassure her. "Don't worry, honey. Grandma will be at the bottom of the stairs if you need her."

I went down the back stairs and waited as Kathy and Ruth followed Michelle. Then there at the top was Abby. All by herself. She looked down at the crowd of guests, straightened her shoulders, and with a determination driven by love put her right foot forward. At the bottom of the stairs she looked at me. I patted her arm and guided her forward. "Abby, you're doing great. Just keep it up." She held her head up, reached into the small basket with her right hand, pulled out rose petals, and dropped them carefully on the white carpet that had been rolled down the center aisle.

When she reached the front she turned around and saw that only one side of the carpet was covered. She started back to finish her job just as Aunt Kathy reached out and said, "Abby, it is okay. Look at Aunt Margie coming down the stairs."

Margie was breathtaking. A live fairy-tale princess. I pushed lingering doubts aside and reminded myself that fairy tales always have happy endings.

Larry and I joined Margie when she reached the bottom of the stairs. We walked beside her halfway down the aisle, stopped, and kissed her. She walked ahead of us with Mitch to the Chupah. During the ceremony we stood facing Margie and Mitch while they took

49

their vows. I particularly liked the rabbi's explanation that the Protestant religion expects a newly married couple to forsake all others and to think of each other. In the Catholic religion they must fulfill their responsibilities to the church, but in the Jewish faith emphasis on being responsible members of two families continues. This expansion of our small family was welcome.

The service was long—done in both English and Hebrew. The traditional glass was wrapped in cloth and Mitch stepped on it for good luck. Ruth and the best man signed the book as witnesses. As Margie and Mitch signed their vows I looked into the crowd and saw happy tears in my aunt Margaret's eyes. After all it was her great-niece, her namesake's wedding.

Hot hors d'oeuvres, which we had upgraded to include kosher, were served by circulating staff and at a buffet table in the lounge. Meanwhile, tables were being set up behind a closed curtain where only moments before guests were gathered to watch Margie and Mitch become husband and wife. Soft piano music provided a pleasant atmosphere in which guests mingled as Margie and Mitch were whisked upstairs to have their pictures taken in the photographer's private studio. Later they joined us in a receiving line in the entry room where we relaxed and enjoyed ourselves as we received everyone's good wishes.

At eight o'clock the curtains opened and we went to our tables. Mirrors held crystal globes with floating red roses and candles in the center of the crisp white tablecloths. The napkins duplicated the color of the roses. Each guest had a souvenir bottle of champagne labeled "In Celebration of the Wedding of Margaret and Mitchell, July 30, 1994."

When the guests were seated, the members of the wedding party were introduced and took their places at a raised curved head table. Mitch and Margie were in the center. Next to Margie were Ruth, Steve, Abby, and Kathy. Abby told us, "I'm Kathy's date because she doesn't have anyone else." They enjoyed being together. From our table directly in front of them I savored watching my daughters and granddaughter celebrating exuberantly. This was what being a family was all about.

When dinner was over the traditional dancing began with the bride and groom. Soon Larry and I and Mitch's parents joined them.

Then Mitch danced with his mother and Margie with her father. I danced with Mitch's father. The song was "Unforgettable" by Natalie Cole and Nat King Cole. Then the bridal party and the other guests joined us. Abby danced with Mitch, Margie, Kathy, Mommy, Daddy, Grandpa, Grandma, and anyone else who would. At one point she was dancing with Mitch and Margie holding her between them. I told the photographer and videographer to take a picture of them then. It would be my favorite remembrance of the happiness we shared that day.

Between songs, the bandleader asked for attention and then announced, "The bride, Margaret, earned her Ph.D. in clinical psychology this June—so now she is Dr. Margaret E. Bostrom. Congratulations, Margaret. Let's have a round of applause." I was so proud. My youngest daughter had persevered and was now ready to begin her life as a wife and a professional. I was delighted all her hard work had paid off.

The marble cake's three tiers were separated by white plastic pillars. White frosting with pink accents reflected its name: "Fanciful." Margie and Mitch decided to remain dignified while cutting it. They lovingly placed pieces in the other's waiting mouth. My friend Judy hugged me as she said, "Mitch hasn't stopped smiling all night long."

I added, "Neither has Margie."

She agreed and added, "Maybe all your worries were uncalled for. They look so happy."

For a moment my joy was overshadowed by my nagging doubts, but I quickly pushed them aside and turned to see my husband raised high on a chair by several strong young men. The Jewish dance was lively and the cheering encouraged the revelry.

All too soon the evening was over and we left for home. The next morning we planned to meet at Homewood Suites for breakfast. Margie and Mitch wouldn't be at Ruth's because they couldn't be late for the cruise ship they were going on to Bermuda for their honeymoon. It was leaving New York City Sunday afternoon and Mitch's parents were driving them there. I tried not to be too disappointed, but wished they had told us before now. Most of our friends and family enjoyed a relaxing Sunday afternoon on Ruth and Steve's deck being entertained by Jacob. I know Margie would have loved being with us.

When Margie and Mitch returned from their honeymoon they went to New Jersey first. Then they visited us for a few days in Connecticut before flying back to Poway. When Mitch saw the thank-you notes with their wedding picture on the front, he liked them and told me we should get some. The photographer was offering them at a reasonable price, so I suggested, "Okay, Mitch, here is the price list. You can buy as many as you want." That was the last he mentioned about getting them. I assume he expected us to offer to pay for them.

Larry and I paid for the whole wedding, even the rabbi. Mitch's parents paid for the rehearsal dinner and the honeymoon. The guests gave them many lovely gifts and ten thousand dollars in cash. It should have been a great start to their marriage. However, the money caused heated disagreements. He took control of it. Margie was furious. "It was a gift to both of us," she protested, but he wouldn't let her spend any of the money on the household items she wanted.

When they returned to California, Margaret began her post-doctoral clinical work at a facility that treated battered women. After the murder, I learned the workers there knew she was being abused by Mitch and the police had been called to their home on at least one occasion. But at the time I thought they were settling into the routine of married life without much difficulty. They both talked about wanting to come back East to be nearer their families. We were ecstatic about this.

It is time to get dressed for the memorial service but my mind keeps trying to make sense of what has happened. I felt Mitch was cheap and self-centered. There was plenty of evidence of that. But why didn't I recognize how dangerous he was? His taking her pets should have set off warning bells. I was uneasy when I learned he had broken the lock on the bedroom door to get them, but I never thought it would come to this.

Larry calls to me, breaking my reverie: "Come on, Shirley. They're here." He doesn't want to keep the prison personnel waiting.

CHAPTER 6

Memorial at
the Big House

It's 9:30 A.M. on Monday, August 19th, when Joe Pryor's car takes us past the guardhouse into the circular drive of the large red brick penitentiary. After only a few steps we are on a portico where we are directed to wait. It's obvious that the people walking by us into the building know who we are. All but a few are silent. Soon we are escorted into the prison lobby and into a hall. Ahead of us is a locked door with metal bars. A guard stamps the back of our hands and allows us into a small chamber. Behind us the door clangs shut with a loud hollow sound. Another guard uses an ultraviolet light to see our stamped hands. He then unlocks the second door. Clang again.

We are now engulfed in a huge chamber capable of holding hundreds of people. The iron barred windows are framed at the tops with bricks placed in decorative semicircles. Our footsteps echo as we walk across the shiny floor that looks and feels like marble. "Larry, can you picture Margaret here each day—shoes tapping as she hurriedly begins her workday?"

"Not really." He doesn't want to play my little game but I try again.

"I wonder how she felt with the doors locking behind her? Did it make her feel uncomfortable or safe?"

"I'm sure she was used to it by now."

At the end of the long hall we are taken into the warden's private office. The decor is rich in leather and dark wood, probably cherry or mahogany. High-backed, winged chairs upholstered in a muted floral print are complemented by the open drapes hanging beside the tall windows that let the sunlight sparkle on the clean surfaces.

"Larry, Shirley, Ruth, I'd like you to meet my wife, Karen." Warden Lamer looks across his desk at a lovely blonde woman who is extending her hand to me.

"I'm so sorry to have to meet you under such horrible circumstances. Dave and I were in Indiana with our daughter who is starting college when we got the news. She is studying to be a psychologist—like Margaret." The soft Southern voice is friendly and comforting.

Warden Lamer motions for us to be seated. I watch as Mrs. Lamer sits and crosses her ankles. I'm reminded of our dean of women at college who always told us, "Ladies never cross their legs above the ankles—certainly never at or above the knees." This is a Southern lady.

"We've never been in a penitentiary before. Margaret was planning to get permission to bring us up when we didn't have the grandchildren along. It's quite impressive, sitting on top of the hill. You can see it from an amazing distance." This feels to me like a safe topic to discuss.

"Yes, we are very proud of our facility. It was built in 1932. Can't find workmanship like this these days and even if you could the cost would be prohibitive." The warden's pride is obvious as he continues. "We also have a great staff. We are very close. Like family. This isn't true at all federal penitentiaries. Lewisburg is pretty unique. I've worked at several locations and this is one of the best."

"Larry was born in 1932." I try for a light tone as I ask, "Well, dear, how do you feel knowing you are the same age as a federal penitentiary?"

"Old, but some good things did come out of the depression after all."

The Warden smiles as he explains, "I wanted to have you come by my office first so we could chat. I'll fill you in on what we have planned and try to answer any questions you might have. We'll be going to the chapel as soon as they let me know everything is ready."

"Thanks. It would help if we could visit Margaret's office. Being able to accurately visualize where she worked will make her job here more real for us."

"Certainly, Mrs. Bostrom. I'll arrange for it. Right after the memorial service should be fine. You may want to take some of her personal items with you."

The intercom on his desk buzzes. It is the signal we have been waiting for and now we are escorted to the chapel. It is a large room—about the size of a high school gym. Each long row of seats is full. Extra chairs have been added along the aisles, but there are still many people standing. Individual faces are all a blur as we walk down the long center aisle to the front row where there are three empty seats waiting for us. I feel like I'm in a dream or sleepwalking. Nothing seems real. My short, heavy body clad in the green culottes and beige top progresses toward the front. I know Larry and Ruth are with me but I'm not conscious of their presence—I feel all alone. I wonder what all these people are thinking. What would I be thinking if I were sitting there watching us? Something like: *Oh, those poor people. They look like they're in shock. How do they keep going? What does it feel like to have your daughter or sister murdered? I couldn't take it! Thank God it isn't me, but why them?*

We've made it to the front—finally. I sit and look at the dais. There's Joe Pryor, and Manny Cordero with Sergio and Warden Lamer. I reach for a tissue and realize my supply is insufficient. Then a gentle voice asks, "Is there anything you need?"

"Tissues, please." We've been given programs for the service. On the front below the inscription—In Loving Memory of Margaret Bostrom—is the outline of a stained-glass window with the image of a dove that seen through my tears is blurred. Solemn music fits our mood and purpose. We stand automatically for the invocation as a box of tissues is handed to me. We watch four men in uniform, the prison drill team, enter with the American flag and that of the U.S. Department of Justice. For Margie? No, for Dr. Margaret E. Bostrom, federal employee. Is Margie watching? What is she thinking? Is she impressed? We had no sons to send into battle, so this honor is totally unexpected.

Sergio, the chaplain who called us with news of Margie's murder, does the scripture reading. Psalm 23 is printed on the back of our program. I listen with a sense of irony to, "I will fear no evil." Maybe I should have. The words "Surely goodness and mercy shall follow me all the days of my life" mock my loss.

A lovely black woman, Marion Johnson, sings a touching song. I never learn the title, but I do find out she is the wife of the chaplain, Glen, who is playing the piano. It was she who arranged for the food tray from the "ladies."

District Chaplain Manuel Cordero leads the responsive reading. I'm quite angry, as I silently reject, "...he hath delivered me out of all trouble." "And the peace of God which passeth all understanding, shall keep your heart and minds...." He ends with a "prayer of comfort."

Warden Lamer gives words of condolence that are sensitive and personal. In his role as leader he is setting the tone and establishing the official policy for Lewisburg and the Bureau of Prisons employees. But I know this father has asked himself what he would feel and do if it were his daughter who lay dead instead of a young female employee. He doesn't want to know the unimaginable answer to this question. Neither did we.

Chaplain Joe Pryor reads from 1 Thessalonians 4:13–18. Then he laments for society's loss. Margaret was a caregiver. She didn't turn her back on those in need of help. He reminds us that this priority is unusual in our self-absorbed culture. Most days Margaret and he arrived at work at the same time. "I often had the opportunity to walk in with her. Seeing her smile was a great way to begin the day."

I visualize them exchanging pleasantries as he holds the door for Margie. Joe has agreed to officiate at the funeral too. Larry suggested it, but Ruth and I are pleased and relieved that someone who knew Margie will conduct the services.

When Joe completes the benediction the color guard proceeds with the retiring of the colors. The American flag is folded—ceremoniously—and presented to Margie's father. Oh, my God! She was Daddy's little girl. As a former naval officer he is fully aware of the honor. His pride and pain are clearly visible.

As the planned memorial service ends, Ruth stands and asks to thank everyone. She tells them, "Your support will help us through this and justice will be done. I believe that."

I silently muse, *I wish I did.*

Marion Johnson begins to sing "Amazing Grace." I'm reminded of my days as a devout Baptist and I'm glad it isn't "The Old Rugged

Cross." Both these songs still touch me deeply. Then we are asked to stand in front of our seats to receive condolences from two hundred teary-eyed employees. They walk by, hugging us, shaking hands, and telling short personal stories about Margie. One man worked with her in the lock-down unit and told how upset the prisoners were they couldn't be at the service. She was firm with them but well liked. Over and over we are told this is a big close family and they are hurting along with us.

When we leave the chapel we are escorted through the twists and turns that lead us to Margaret's office. There is a sign over her door. Dr. Margaret E. Bostrom. Staff Psychologist. We take it. Inside the room is sparse with no decorations or pictures on the wall. We are told all the psychology offices are this way because so much time is spent away from them counseling prisoners. We take a small radio, a figurine of a retriever, and a tin of hard candy. I see her brass name-plate mounted on wood sitting on her desk. I want it, but Mitch gave it to her when she earned her Ph.D. He seemed so proud of her then. I take it anyway. Another memory forever tainted.

We go back to the warden's outer office to say our goodbyes. He gives us mugs and pens with the Lewisburg logo. Larry receives a cap with the Department of Justice seal and Bureau of Prisons on the front, and Lewisburg Federal Penitentiary on the back. The employee's club gives us the Big House—Lewisburg Federal Penitentiary T-shirts, beach towels, and golf towels. I mention Margie had promised me a Lewisburg sweatshirt for Mother's Day, but they didn't have the right size then. They still don't, but promise to send me one. Later they send one for each of us.

As we prepare to leave, Warden Lamer tells us, "Please accept my sincere condolences again. Let us know your plans for the funeral. As many of us as possible will be coming to Connecticut with Chaplain Pryor for the services." It is almost noon.

Ruth goes back to Margaret's house with Mrs. Lamer to separate Mitch's personal items so his lawyer can claim them. We leave instructions that they are not to remove anything else. At two o'clock, an attorney from the prison will drive Ruth to Mitch's preliminary hearing in Williamsport. We are told we don't have to be there—it will be brief, probably only ten minutes, in a small room. Ruth insists on going anyway.

Larry and I aren't ready to see Mitch, his sister, or parents yet, and we have to keep our appointment with Attorney Showalter. When we arrive at his office, his assistant, Donna, meets with us. We fill out the forms to become administrators of Margaret's estate and walk the few blocks to the county courthouse to sign them in front of the county clerk. While we wait, we watch and listen to two grieving adult children deal with the paperwork caused by a father's death. When Donna gives the clerk the forms and introduces us, I wonder if she knows why we are there. Of course she does.

Back at the office we talk about the mail, telephone, having the estate assessed, and the lease contract on the Volvo. We trust Donna to take care of the details. We're not in an emotional state to think about such things. We certainly aren't capable of making important decisions. When we're ready to leave Graham comes to assure us they are here to handle the details. We aren't to worry about them. Then he adds, "I would like you to think about whether you want to bring a wrongful death lawsuit against Mitchell."

"Yes, probably, but what good would it do? He won't have any money."

"Mrs. Bostrom, we can talk about that some other time. Do you want to sue the prison?"

"No, not unless we find out they are covering up some neglect on their part." After all, they're family.

"Let me know. I don't do civil litigation, but I can refer you to a highly successful attorney in Harrisburg. The suit has to be filed within two years of the crime."

"Two years!" I tell Larry on the way to pick up Calie at Matt and Sandy's. "I can't even concentrate on two hours from now. I wonder what Graham's referral fee will be." Our stop is brief. We are afraid Ruth will be waiting for us at the park in Williamsport where we arranged to meet her. Seeing Margie's house again and saying goodbye to Sebastian, who has found a good home with Margie's friend Ed, is painful. I feel close to Sandy because I met her the weekend Margie moved to Lewisburg. She brought a fruit basket and some treats for Calie. We promise to keep in touch. I do write but never hear from them again.

Ruth is not waiting when we reach the park. Larry wonders, "Are we too late? Have they come and gone? Should we go back to

Lewisburg? Wait, maybe this is her now." It isn't and I suggest he take Calie, who is watching every car, for a walk.

As they leave, I pat her. "I know you hope Margie will be in one of them. Sorry, girl, but Margie isn't coming—ever." While they are on their walk, I finish reading *Runaway Jury* and ponder whether the criminal justice system can really be manipulated so blatantly. I've got a lot to learn.

Ruth arrives at four o'clock. The ten-minute brief charge and bail pleas stretched to one-and-a-half hours.

CHAPTER 7

"He Wouldn't Even Look at Me"

"I'm glad you and Daddy didn't go. It would have been too hard on you. They played the whole 911 tape. I could hear Calie barking in the background." Ruth pats Calie and hugs us.

"How are you doing?" I think she looks exhausted.

"I'm tired but it was important one of us be there. I found the answers to some of our questions. An FBI agent, Harold Schmidle, testified and made the criminal complaint. I have a copy of his written affidavit."

"I think we just learned an important lesson. We need to be at every court proceeding—no matter how brief or unimportant they tell us it is." Larry and Ruth agree.

Michael Sullivan, the Bureau of Prisons attorney who drove Ruth to meet us, explains they have a very strong case against Mitch and the assistant U.S. attorney handling the case is the best. We have the full support of the Bureau of Prisons and their attorneys will be available to the prosecution. They will remain in close contact with us. As Margie's family, it is comforting to know we have their support.

When we are in the car and ready to start home, Ruth turns to Calie and me in the backseat and says, "The two Mikes [both prison attorneys] sat on each side of me. I'm not sure who they thought they were protecting—Mitch or me. He wouldn't even look at me. I did catch him looking out of the corner of his eye once." Her complaint would be the same during the long months ahead: He doesn't look at us during any of the court proceedings.

"Were his parents there?"

"Yes, they sat in the back. I didn't talk to them. They brought letters from friends and community leaders attesting to Mitch's good character. At one point his sister got up and left the room."

"How come it took so long? I was ready to go back to Lewisburg. I thought we had missed you because we were fifteen minutes late."

"Oh, Daddy, you know how they said it would be in a small room that would hold no more than ten people? There were so many people they had to find a bigger room. That wasted a lot of time. The 911 tape and the testimony of the FBI agent took time, the judge looked at the crime scene photographs, and then they got into a big discussion concerning bail."

Ruth continues, "On the tape you can hear the operator tell Mitch to keep the dog away from the bathroom. Mitch tells them he shut her in a bedroom. He is moaning and asking, 'Why me?' Then he says Margie drank too much and was on Prozac."

"Oh, he killed her because she was such a rotten person?"

"Yes, he tells them he stabbed his wife because he just found out that morning she was having an affair. Here, Ma, is the FBI agent's affidavit. You can read it when you are ready."

I'm anxious to know the contents and ignore the distress that reading in a car usually causes me. There are thirteen numbered items. The first six give information about the Union County Emergency Services switchboard receiving the call from a male requesting an ambulance because he had just stabbed his wife, dispatching an ambulance, and making a call to the U.S. Penitentiary at Lewisburg's switchboard. The caller was kept on the line and reported that he put the butcher knife in the kitchen sink. When he told the operator the emergency services personnel had arrived, the operator stayed on the phone until correctional officers from USP-Lewisburg arrived and spoke on the phone.

Numbers seven and eight state that four Bureau of Prisons officers entered the house followed by emergency services personnel, learned that the victim was in the upstairs bathroom, entered the bathroom, and found Dr. Margaret Bostrom dead from apparent multiple stab wounds. The FBI was contacted.

Numbers nine through thirteen read as follows:

9. Mitchell Frederick Paster was identified as the caller and husband of Dr. Margaret Bostrom who was an employee of the Bureau of Prisons, United States Penitentiary, Lewisburg in the Psychology Department. Paster remained downstairs in the dining room under escort. When observed by a Bureau of Prison's officer, he was found to have, what appeared to be blood on his clothing.

10. An interview of Paster by this agent and SSRA Richard L. Rodgers was conducted.
    a. Paster advised that Bostrom had informed him earlier that morning that she had been having an affair with another man.
    b. Paster stated that he became extremely distraught and went into the kitchen while Bostrom went upstairs to take a shower after they had argued.
    c. While in the kitchen, Paster retrieved a butcher knife, silver with a black handle from the knife block, and started to walk upstairs.
    d. Paster further claimed he remembered nothing further until coming down the stairs with a portable phone and dialing "911."

11. A butcher knife matching the above description was found in the kitchen sink, exactly where Paster had advised the "911" emergency operator he had placed it.

12. The butcher knife was covered with what appeared to be blood.

13. Paster was subsequently arrested on suspicion of the murder of his wife, Dr. Margaret Bostrom, and detained, awaiting his initial appearance.

At the end of the written statement, FBI Agent Schmidle had declared his statement to be true and accurate.

Seeing the official report forces me to recognize the awful reality. "Oh, Ruth, I can see it all."

"I know, Ma, but try not to. It doesn't do any good."

"One of Mitch's lawyers even asked the judge what he thought the bail should be set at. The judge refused to comment and the lawyer went on to explain that Mitch is a responsible citizen who should be allowed to pursue his MBA at Cornell. He said Mitch is enrolled for the fall semester, has secured lodging there, and would be available for any court proceedings."

"I'm sure Cornell wants a murderer on its campus," I respond sarcastically. "Doesn't he know how serious what he has done is?" I answer my own question, "Obviously not!"

Ruth continues. "Finally Judge Askey got tired of the haggling and told the attorney not to worry about how much the bail should be—because bail was being denied."

I reach across the seat and pat Calie. "At least that is something to be thankful for. Right, girl?" Our mutual loss is already making our bond stronger.

It is a long ride home. When we reach Connecticut it is almost 11 P.M. Ruth encourages us to stay with her for the night rather than going on to Windsor. We agree and at a rest stop I call Shirley King and ask her to go to our house and remove the answering machine tape. The FBI has asked that we send it to them so they can try to retrieve the August 12th phone message Mitch left us. It proves that four days before he killed her he accused Margie of having the affair for a month. In his statement to the FBI he reported that he only found out on the morning of August 16th. It is key evidence because previous knowledge of the relationship refutes his claim that killing her was an immediate reaction to this devastating news. Later, we do send the FBI the tape, however, it is never presented as evidence because Mitch's story changes.

We go to sleep dreading the days and nights ahead of us. On Tuesday, August 20th, Larry and I go home to Windsor. We have an appointment at the Windsor Locks Funeral Parlor to discuss arrangements. We pick out prayer cards and thank-you notes. All the expenses for the Pennsylvania funeral parlor, flying her body to Bradley International Airport, and the cost of the death certificates are included in their bill. John Lee explains the options for displaying the body along with floral remembrances, mementos, and photographs. He wants a recent picture of Margie to help the hairdresser make her look as natural as possible. I give him one with both her and Mitch smiling at the camera. "This is just for the hair dresser. It isn't to be displayed. I'll bring those tomorrow." John writes this in large letters on a sheet of paper and attaches it to the photograph. Plans for calling hours and the funeral service are reviewed.

Then we go downstairs to select an urn. I like a green marble rectangular one with a rose etched in gold on the side, but we decide to wait to see what Ruth thinks. John tells us there is no hurry.

Later, we cannot decide which of two dresses would be best for Margie. One is blue linen with short sleeves and a square neckline. Ruth has given us a multicolored scarf in case it is needed to cover wounds to the upper chest or neck. We think we've come prepared, but John's partner Charlie looks uncomfortable as he tells us, "Yes, this is a lovely dress, but it will need to be altered if we use it. We can cut off the skirt and use the material to make sleeves."

I can't speak but Charlie sees my expression and explains that she received several slicing cuts on her arms, hands, and face. "We can cosmetically cover the wounds on her hands and face, but there has been too much damage to her arms. We decide to use the red dress which has a high neck and long sleeves. Abby will like that.

That afternoon Ruth, Tina, Abby, and Jacob come over to our house. Still no Kathy. My friends arrive. Brenda has fixed a chicken casserole that I can actually taste. Shirley King has baked a chocolate cake. The refrigerator is full with rolls, sandwich makings, and salads. Shirley and Marj fix us plates of food. Judy and Barbara explain they cleaned the condo as best they could while we were gone. Judy put the extra papers and mail in our bedroom. Barbara, who hates cats, cleaned up after Felicia's accidents. She tells me, "You know how important you are to me if I'll do that." I'm embarrassed they had to see how dirty my house was.

When everyone is gone Larry and I sit down to watch the news. There, on the screen, is Mitch being led out of the Federal Court House in handcuffs—head lowered. Ruth thought he was wearing a prison jumpsuit for the hearing. But here he is dressed in a brown and beige striped long-sleeved shirt and tan pants I recognize. Margie is dead because he killed her and he is alive. His family can still see him, hug him, talk to him, and write to him. We can't be with Margie. It isn't fair!

CHAPTER 8

Margie Arrives Early But Leaves Too Soon

Margie's death and plans for the funeral revive memories of her birth. In March 1964 Larry was teaching school in the technical department at Jamestown High School and I was a busy mom with two young daughters. Ruth would be three in June and Kathy two in May. Twins the hard way. Ruth didn't appear jealous of Kathy. But why should she? When Kathy was born she still had her bath in the morning, a bottle, and a crib. Ruth, the first grandchild, was the darling of my family with her blonde hair and large brown eyes. Kathy got frustrated because she couldn't keep up with her older sister but kept stubbornly trying. When faced with failure she became more determined. She would shake her curly light brown hair and her bright blue eyes would sparkle when she tenaciously refused to accept defeat.

Larry's mom watched the girls, as I called them, three mornings a week while I taught Spanish to accelerated sixth graders. This arrangement gave me time to be home with my daughters, but allowed me to keep teaching part-time even if I didn't have my own classroom. We were busy and content.

One evening Larry complained of pain and feeling nauseous after eating chicken. We cut down on the greasy food but the attacks continued. Finally, he came home from school because of his discomfort. I knew then it was serious. We called a childhood friend who was now a doctor. Larry told him, "I'm pretty sure it is my gallbladder." John had him admitted to the hospital.

They decided the dye tests weren't confirming the diagnosis because the passage to the gallbladder was blocked, so an operation was scheduled. I remained strong during that crisis because I had my family and Larry's nearby for emotional support and help with the two small children. However, as anyone who has found themselves traveling back and forth to a hospital worrying about and supporting a loved one knows, it was exhausting.

I grew up while facing that first real crisis in my married life. I was thirty years old. I wondered what my life would have been like if Larry had died. I didn't want to lose him. What I did want was another child—a girl. Since I was a child I had promised my favorite aunt my first daughter would be named Margaret after her. But Ruth Ann was named after her two grandmothers. Kathy was going to be named after her father until a neighbor used Laurie for her daughter. Two Lauries, a week apart, seemed too confusing. Larry and I agreed she looked like a Kathy—not a Catherine or Kathleen. Besides, several of my best students were named Kathy. We gave her my middle name—Louise.

I wasn't sure why I hadn't kept my word; maybe Margaret had seemed too big a name for a small baby, but I wanted the chance to keep my promise. Margaret is my mother's youngest sister and only twelve-and-a-half years older than I am. For twenty years she called me her favorite niece. I was the only niece. When another niece arrived she didn't call me that anymore but continued to spoil me. I knew I was still number one.

During Larry's long period of recuperation, which was required after major surgery in 1964, I began my campaign for a third daughter. Larry reasoned, "Honey, you can't be sure it will be a girl."

"But I am and her name is going to be Margaret."

It wasn't easy being pregnant during the hot humid summer, especially with two small children, but I was ecstatic. Margie—that was my nickname for my aunt and it would be hers—was eagerly awaited. Larry was taking a course in abnormal psychology at the State University of New York at Fredonia and came home with morbid tales of everything that could go wrong and cause birth defects during a pregnancy. I knew his concerns were real, but they were driving me crazy. Finally I told him, "She is going to be all right. I know that. Even if she isn't, worrying about it isn't going to help." From then on he tried to keep his worries to himself.

My due date was December 8, 1964. My best friend Agnes was expecting her second child at the same time. We planned to share a room at the hospital and have a pajama party for new moms. By early November I'd gained twenty-four pounds. The doctor insisted that the limit was twenty-five pounds. I shuttered as I thought of Thanksgiving.

Thursday night, November 5th, I went to a baby shower at my next-door neighbor's home. It was dark but I cut across the lawn and I was greeted with a deep growl. The German Shepherd who was so friendly during the day was warning me he now saw me as an unwelcome intruder. Fortunately, before I had a chance to panic the guard dog was called off. Since my next doctor's appointment was a week away, I decided it was all right to sample each delicious dish. I'd be careful—beginning tomorrow.

Around six on Friday morning, November 6th, Larry jumped up and yelled, "You just wet the bed."

I could feel the liquid oozing out of me and spreading over the sheet. "No, I think my water broke." His anger quickly became concern.

I called the doctor. He wanted me in the hospital because there was a danger of infection. This time he wanted me to go to the WCA Hospital because they had a unit for premature births. I wasn't happy with this. Both Ruth and Kathy were born at Jamestown General Hospital. Reluctantly, I agreed because it would give the baby a better chance if it was born prematurely.

Larry decided to go to work until we knew what was going to happen so I called my mom to take me to the hospital. Larry's mom would stay with the girls.

At the hospital, I was disappointed that Dr. Bugbee, my favorite, wasn't on duty. My mom had cleaned offices for him and his partners for more than twelve years. Dr. Crandall delivered Ruth. He was in his fifties and had a gruff bedside manner. Dr. Bugbee, who was very supportive, caring, and handsome, delivered Kathy. Dr. Messinger was my age and we hadn't formed a bond. But the nurses assured me that Dr. Messinger was young and familiar with all the new techniques required in premature births. He examined me and reported they were going to try to keep the baby from being born. He wanted me to relax and rest. Fat chance.

As the day progressed my labor pains continued to be sporadic and varied in strength. Gradually I became aware of the nurses scurrying around and my mother's distraction. No one wanted to tell me anything. Finally, when I became too agitated, thinking something was wrong with my baby, my mother told me there was another woman giving premature birth and it was going badly. Later I learned she lost her baby.

A little before 5 P.M. the doctor admitted defeat and I was taken to the delivery room. Still not apprehensive I joked, "Guess I don't have to worry about what I eat for Thanksgiving dinner."

In the delivery room I was told I would receive no anesthesia. I needed to be fully awake to help the baby as much as possible. This was a radical change from my two previous deliveries when I was overly sedated. If the pain got really bad they would put the ether mask on my face for a short time to give me some relief. I hated the smell of ether so when they first offered it to me I didn't breathe deeply. However, it didn't take long for me to decide the ether was the lesser evil so I took long deep breaths. From a great distance I heard the doctor, "Get that mask off her. She is going under." From then on they were careful to keep me awake.

Just when I didn't think I could bear any more pain, Dr. Messinger informed me, "We are going to help the baby along with forceps. Push hard when I tell you to." After a few moments of excruciating pain he continued. "Shirley, open your eyes. The baby is here." It was 5:34 P.M. when I heard a robust cry.

"How is she?"

"That's just what she is. A *she*. A healthy baby girl. Look." I watched as he placed her across my stomach. I'd never seen anything more beautiful than that ruddy bundle covered in shreds of white membrane with dark hair poking through it. Then, he handed Margie to a nurse to clean up while he did some stitching on me. When he finished he put her beside me on a stretcher and I rolled with her to the nursery where she was placed in an incubator crib for one night.

I was proud of myself. She was a healthy little girl and I saw her before anyone else in the family. With both Ruth and Kathy I was the last to see them. When I got to my room Larry, my mom, and my dad were all there. I was touched by how worried they all looked, especially my dad. For a moment I felt all his love and I was deeply touched. When he handed me a pair of little brown and tan moccasins for the baby, I saw the tears in his eyes. Mom later told me, "He was so worried about you. He bought the moccasins all by himself." Twenty months later he would be dead from a heart attack.

Margie weighed five pounds seven ounces, which appeared perfect for her seventeen-and-a-half-inch body. Ruth had been nineteen inches and weighed eight pounds four ounces, but Kathy weighed seven pounds eleven ounces and appeared skinny for her twenty-one-and-a-half inches. Dr. Furlong, the pediatrician for each girl, visited me and assured me the baby was healthy. There was nothing to worry about. I asked him about nursing her.

He responded, "Sometimes premature babies don't have the instinct to suck or the strength to get the milk, but we can give it a try." Margie proved her determination by vigorously guzzling down the milk. I grinned. He continued, "Many times premature babies catch up with and pass their full-term counterparts. She may be taller and have bigger feet than her sisters." We laughed, unaware of how accurate his prediction was.

I was pleasantly surprised when I saw the head nurse in the nursery was Georgia Wirtner, a neighbor when my family lived in Jamestown on Hedges Avenue. She still had a wonderful laugh and enjoyed life. She and my mother had a great reunion. Mom was reassured because "Georgia says everything is all right with the baby."

I missed Ruth and Kathy. Hospital regulations still didn't permit small children to visit. Larry brought them to the sidewalk outside my room. We waved and tried to talk but it was too far. They sent in a monkey squeeze toy and a rattle to their little sister, and some drawings for me. I was pleased to learn that Margie would be allowed to spend most of her time in my room with me. That was a positive change in hospital procedures. I held her and teased, "You're an impatient young lady. Couldn't wait to see your family and take on the world, could you? Believe me, no baby has ever been more welcome than you."

We officially named the new baby Margaret Eleanor on the tenth. Her middle name was for another great aunt. Thursday, on his daily rounds, Dr. Furlong marked her weight at five pounds and told me he wouldn't be in the next day before we were released.

Being home felt so good. Ruth and Kathy, who seemed large next to Margie, were interested in her but wanted attention from me. Fortunately I had lots of help. Larry and my mother insisted I save my strength for the night feedings. Margie quickly set a three-and-a-half-hour schedule for herself. Within a week her color had lost its ruddiness. The purple instrument marks on her forehead only reappeared when she cried hard. Everyone agreed—she was beautiful. My aunt Margaret and her husband Carl brought her namesake a pale yellow dress and matching sweater. Margaret never had said a word about my choice of names for my first two daughters, but I could tell she was extremely proud. So was I.

We sent out birth announcements. "It's a girl! Introducing our new little highness. Her majesty's name is Margaret Eleanor (Margie). She began her reign November 6, 1964. Happy subjects are Larry and Shirley Bostrom."

I got great pleasure from giving Margie a bath. I looked at each perfect little part and delighted in caressing her body as I rubbed in the baby oil. Ruth, Kathy, and my mom all watched as I lifted her off the towel, which was on the dining room table, to the baby scale. At first I didn't believe my eyes. She only weighed four pounds eight ounces. "I must be starving her. She's lost six ounces!"

Mom told me the baby was nursing well and seemed content, but suggested I call the doctor. Maybe

Margie arrives early but leaves too soon.

my milk lacked the nutrients she needed. When I told Dr. Furlong about the weight loss, he laughed. I was annoyed until he explained, "It is nothing to worry about. She isn't doing so badly. Remember I signed her release the day before she went home—when she weighed five pounds. I was afraid if I weighed her Friday her weight would drop more. Regulations require that a baby weigh five pounds when it goes home. I knew she was healthy and would receive better care with you than in the hospital. Besides I knew you'd be at the hospital all the time anyway. I'm sorry for the unnecessary concern it caused you."

I assured him I appreciated what he had done. Coming home without her was unthinkable. "It pays to have a pediatrician who knows you." I told my mother as I explained the situation to her.

In late December Agnes had healthy twin boys. Together they weighed over seventeen pounds. No wonder she could hardly walk during the month before they were born. We joked that Margie would have two men to choose from. Of course she would be an older woman. Agnes and I would be mothers-in-law to each other's children—a pleasant fantasy.

Margie thrived. At one month she weighed six pounds two ounces and was eighteen-and-a-half inches long. At six months she was fifteen pounds and twenty-four-and-three-fourths inches long. At a year she weighed twenty-two pounds. She took her first steps just before her birthday.

The blue eyes of birth changed to hazel and then to a deep brown. Margie was eight-and-a-half months old when she said her first word: "Mama." The next day she said, "Dada." I was so proud. Ruth and Kathy said "Dada" first. Margie lost most of her hair so that on her birthday she had only a curly tuft on the top of a fuzz-covered head.

In July, when Margie was nine months old, we moved to Connecticut. Larry had a job with Hamilton Standard Division of United Technologies in Windsor Locks. He was excited about working as an electrical engineer, which he was trained for at the University of Michigan. Moving away from our families removed the support I had but it also reduced my direct involvement with family problems. Our parents would miss the grandchildren but Larry and I looked forward to being a more independent family unit.

Rusty, our collie who had become so protective of Ruth and Kathy, now took on Margie as his responsibility. He sat next to her in her high chair reaping rewards of affection and food. He stood watch for hours as she played with paper cups or stacking plastic donuts. When she was awake he was never far from her.

Margie usually went to sleep easily at night to the sounds of a musical clock. However, she lost the desire or need for a nap long before I did. When I found her playing with all the toys in her crib, I removed them. Later I tiptoed into her room to find her wide awake contentedly playing with her hands. She was twisting and turning her fingers into different shapes. One day I was resting on my bed when she came toddling in—all smiles. I was afraid she had climbed over the sides. Ruth had tried that, fell and broke her collarbone. But when I looked I saw she had systematically removed the rungs from the side of the crib and climbed out, I gave up.

Every time Margie got a new tooth she had pain and the symptoms of a cold, so she didn't sleep well. I often spent those nights on the floor next to her crib with my hand on her back. If I removed it she cried. I was happy I could comfort her.

This last thought brings me back to the present. I wasn't there to comfort her when she was dying and there is little to console me as I prepare for her funeral. My thoughts are of my unbearable grief. A parent shouldn't have to go through this. Then a question forms—unbidden. Would you give up having Margie for the thirty-one years ten months and ten days you had her—even to escape this pain?

My answer is a resounding, "No!"

CHAPTER 9

Alone in
a Crowd

I don't have Margie. I can't see her, talk to her, or touch her, but I do have hundreds of photographs and mementos of her and her life. I cling to them searching for comfort, for a sign that this is all a bad dream. Gradually, I put together the story of her life that I will display at the funeral parlor. I start with pictures of the baby, the toddler, and the preschooler. My memories are so vivid. I laugh as I look at her school pictures. The early ones show her with short curly light brown hair, sparkling eyes, and a silly smile. Later, when she is wearing braces, her lips are always tightly closed over the silver-coated teeth. The pictures of her with our animals—her cat, the dogs, and horses—remind me how happy she was with them. Prom and graduation pictures portray a slender, long-haired smiling beauty full of promise.

It is hard to look at the pictures of her as a professional adult, as a proud aunt, sister, and daughter, because it reminds me of what we have lost. We will never see how she would have matured or have her at any more family gatherings. It is like driving a knife into my heart when I look at the hundreds of pictures with Margie and Mitch smiling into each other's eyes, Mitch and me, Mitch and Abby, Mitch and newborn Jacob at Christmas, Mitch and Calie, Mitch's mother and me, or Larry and me walking Margie down the aisle—giving her to Mitch, her murderer.

Pictures from eleven years are proof of our acceptance of this man who betrayed us all. It will be a while before I can begin to accept that we shared many happy times with the man who has now caused such incredible pain, but ignoring or denying those times would cheat me of most of my memories of Margie for the last eleven years.

Wednesday, we take the pictures, the U.S. flag Larry received at the memorial service, her Phi Beta Kappa pin, Ph.D. nameplate, degrees, and certificates to the funeral home to be put on display. I want everyone to know how special she was and how much we have lost.

Later that day, a hasty search of my closet reveals nothing suitable for wearing to a daughter's funeral. Shopping without her, when she enjoyed it so much, seems inappropriate. Besides I don't have the energy. Then I remember, right in Windsor is a small women's shop that I am familiar with—Martha Mcquiston Clothing. Larry goes with me.

I glance at the garments and panic. Like my closet, everything is casual, appropriate for a picnic or lunch with the girls. "May I help you find what you need?"

I turn to see a smiling clerk, probably about forty. "Thanks. I need something dressy. I don't want black." She holds up a beautiful yellow dress with bright summer flowers around the skirt and neck.

"No, not anything that fancy or bright."

"Do you mind if I ask what it is for?"

No, I don't mind. It makes sense for you to ask. But how are you going to react when I tell you? "It is for my daughter's funeral."

"Oh, no, I'm so sorry. How did it happen?" I share the details briefly. She quickly regains her composure and successfully directs me to a two-piece multicolored green rayon dress. It is loose-fitting and long-skirted. It will be comfortable and it hides my stomach. Task completed.

Larry and I go to the Windsor Branch of the New England Bank to officially open the college fund for Abigail and Jacob. We are escorted to the private office of bank officer Sheila Bryson, who is friendly and helpful. She asks what happened and expresses both outrage and sympathy. Our task is simple and easily completed. She gives us the papers to take for Ruth to sign, since she will be primarily responsible for the account. When we are ready to leave, Sheila gives us the letters and notes she has already received with deposits.

We go home, appreciating the thoughtfulness of our friends. I need to keep busy so we begin writing thank-you notes. We receive telephone messages from friends of Margie, our friends and relatives expressing sympathy. We also get a call from Channel 3 Eyewitness News. I follow the FBI's advice: "I have nothing to say. If you want information you may call the FBI."

The reporter responds, "Oh, I have all the information I need on the crime. I just wondered if you had anything you wanted to say about your daughter to help us know her better."

I tell him no and hang up. Even if I wanted to, how can I explain Margie in fifty words or less?

A reporter from the *Manchester Journal Inquirer* calls and asks for an interview. I decline but thank him for the very sensitive article they ran in their paper. It was fair and nonjudgmental. Another newspaper ran a short article on one of its back pages. In it, Mitch was quoted identifying Margaret as an adulterer. Mitch is only an alleged murderer but Margaret is dead. Obviously, Margaret's life and death were not important enough for the front page or an accurate account of the details. We were never contacted by that paper.

Late Wednesday afternoon, Larry's brother Bud and his wife Shirley are the first family members to arrive. They are the only ones coming from Jamestown. It's comforting to have them near. They love Margie too.

Soon Mary Ellen, a friend of Ruth's since high school, comes. I call her my fourth daughter because she spent so much time at our farm in Suffield. Margie was her baby sister too. She takes over, organizes the refrigerator, prepares sandwiches, delivers me a plate, and tells me to eat. I let her take on the responsibilities of a hostess while I sit in my favorite spot on the corner of our sofa near an end table with my glass of water and the telephone. I talk. No, I ramble. Midsentence I forget what I am going to say but keep on anyway. This way I don't have to think. I'm not aware of anyone's reactions.

I don't know if Thursday, August 22nd, is sunny or not. My pain-filled haze is too thick to penetrate. The family gathers at the funeral parlor at 1:30. Ruth and Steve are waiting for us in the parking lot when we arrive. We walk slowly to the door and John Lee meets us. He escorts us into a large parlor. At the other end is Margie lying in a bronzed casket. She appears to be sleeping peacefully. She is all I'm aware of as I approach her. I touch her hair. It looks and feels natural. She thought her hair was too thin and hard to manage. *No more bad hair days to worry about, Margie!* I examine her face for the cuts and bruises we have been warned about. I find a large bruise on the left side of her nose. It is covered with thick makeup. There is a cut from her lower lip to her jaw that is covered with a compound similar to Silly Putty. I might not have noticed it if I hadn't been looking for it.

My mother had insisted that I touch my father's forehead and then kiss him when he died. She told me, "You'll see there is nothing to be afraid of." What I did learn was that my dad was not in that stiff, hard-as-marble body. I kiss my daughter's forehead. Margie isn't there either. I touch the long slender sleeve of the red dress. Unexpectedly, I hear and feel paper crumple and I jerk my hand away. I tentatively put my fingers on her chest. The sound is the same. *Why?*

I look at Ruth who is standing beside me gazing in horror at Margie's hands. "Ma, they cut off all her beautiful nails."

"Oh, Ruth, they were probably broken in her struggle and I imagine they needed some for evidence." I look at the long diagonal cut across the back of her right hand. I point to it and explain, "See the cut. They have covered it with putty, too—just like her chin. They told Daddy and me the ring finger on the left hand was almost cut off, so they placed the right one on top of it." Our examination of her wounds is almost clinical. It is a safe and detached approach.

We are supposed to have a half hour for private viewing, but friends begin forming a line that is rapidly growing longer and we are anxious for the comfort they can give us. People who know Larry, Ruth, and me from our jobs come to talk and stay a while. Ruth reminds me, "Ma, you are supposed to stay in line. My friends want to meet you but you keep disappearing." I try, but the lure of familiar faces draws me to teachers, school administrators, social workers, psychologists, parents, and students who have listened to me talk about my family with love and pride. Tim, Kaitlin, Kerry, Jennifer, and Evan come with their mothers. Sean, whose mother is dead, comes. We understand each other's pain. I want to teach each of them how to cope with such a tragedy but how can I help them? I can't help myself. I had last seen many of them in June at work. This isn't how we foresaw my retirement.

There are very few dry eyes. Everyone's horror as they look at the beautiful, talented, young woman dressed in red, lying lifeless in the casket, is reflected in their eyes as they offer support and sympathy.

We still have not heard from Kathy, but three of her friends from work come to pay their respects. They don't know where she is and haven't heard from her in weeks. She just stopped coming to work. They know she will be devastated by Margie's murder. They promise to renew their efforts to find her.

A psychologist friend and mentor of Margaret's when she was doing clinical work for her master's in marriage and family therapy tells me, "I'm Bill Boylen. I was Margaret's supervisor at Altabello." It is a state facility for troubled youth. I recognize the name, but it is clear he thinks I don't. Later, I send him a letter thanking him for coming. I tell him Margie enjoyed her time with him, respected him, and appreciated his support. The letter was returned because he was no longer at that address.

The time passes rapidly, but I'm exhausted and disoriented. We go home for two hours. Mary Ellen is there and has everything under control. Larry's oldest brother Riley and his friend Esther, and my youngest brother David and his Margaret arrive. Their support soothes our aching hearts.

Soon it is almost six and we must go back for evening calling hours and the service that will follow at seven-thirty. A large white van with Pennsylvania license plates is parked along the side of the building when we arrive. The Bureau of Prisons personnel must be here. This time seven-year-old Abby is with us. She insists that she wants to see Margie. We were apprehensive, but asked the chaplain, Joe Pryor, what he thought and he suggested we bring her so he could talk to her. I watch her take his hand and go into a private room. She is so small and dainty in a favorite dress given to her by her aunt Margie. I can't fathom the depths of our pain—hers or mine. Later, Joe tells us that she had three questions. "She had the same questions we all ask and I didn't have very good answers for her."

Abby asked, "How could Mitch kill Margie when he said he loved her? Does Mitch still love us? Will I ever be able to ask Mitch to his face why he did it?" Apparently she has accepted Joe's ideas. She walks to the casket with her mom and dad. Later she takes one of the seats lined up for the family. Weeping quietly, she responds shyly to comments from friends.

The twelve Bureau of Prisons staff members solemnly pass by the photos and reminders of who Margie was and approach us with words of comfort and tears in their eyes. Annette, a secretary to the psychologists whose wedding Margie attended in May, comments that she appreciates the display. Ed Soboleski, who Margie helped deal with his loss of three family members in one year, can't say much except, "I'm so sorry." It is enough.

My friend Liz hugs me and says, "I shouldn't even be saying this, but you look fantastic. That dress is perfect." I feel a little guilty that this is important to me, but pleased, knowing Margie would approve.

I see Flo Packard. I now know some of what she suffered when her son, the father of three young children, was killed in a freak highway accident. The driver of a "cherry picker" forgot to lower the basket and when he drove under an overpass, the rig toppled onto Glenn's car. Flo hugs me and expresses her sorrow. She has a strong religious faith that has helped sustain her through her ordeal. She tells me, "Warren is sorry he couldn't be here...." I don't remember why. She promises to call, she does once—four months later.

At first I'm not sure if the young woman approaching me is Margie's closest friend from fourth grade through high school. She is and we hug. "Colleen, it is so good to see you. I thought you were still in Florida."

"Nope, I moved back to Connecticut and got my act together. My sister saw your daughter Kathy and told her to have Margie get in touch with me." Kathy later confirms this. "Would it be okay if I dropped by sometime soon? I'd love to talk."

"Of course, I'd love that." Five years later she still hasn't done so.

Jan Foster, a teacher who helped Judy Smith arrange my lovely retirement party, reaches out to me. "Jan, I wanted to take you and Judy to lunch, just to show my appreciation for all your effort."

Later Judy asks me, "Do you remember what Jan said at the wake when you mentioned taking us to lunch?" I didn't. "She told you, 'And I was going to order lobster.'" That's Jan. I get a belated chuckle.

More than two hundred people come to pay their respects and offer prayers and sympathy. At 7:30 the parlor is packed with friends and relatives when John Lee goes to the front of the room to begin the service. The music of "Amazing Grace" floats over the room. I'm glad I asked that it not be sung. I have all the pain I can bear without those words intended to comfort. Joe Pryor tells us, "Margaret's life ended much too soon. She chose to be a caregiver, which is a rare commodity in today's world." He shares a Margie with our friends and family who we will never see doing her chosen work. He laments the waste of such a productive, hardworking, intelligent person who had spent her whole life preparing to help those who needed it, even criminals in lock-down units. "She didn't walk away from the problems of our society. She worked to be part of the solution. Now she is gone and we have all lost. There is no doubt how much she will be missed." We pray.

Warden Lamer speaks but is so overcome with emotion that only the family, in the front row, can hear him say, "She was a friend and coworker that taught us all kindness. She was very proud of her job, and we were very proud of her. I have asked many times why she had to be taken at such a young age, but I have few answers. It is a waste of life." Again he is thinking of his loss and wondering how he could live through a similar tragedy.

Then Ruth begins to speak. She is dressed in a plain black shift and I can see her body shaking. Her voice quivers but she delivers the perfect tribute to her sister. Thank God for her.

Eulogy given by Margaret's sister Ruth Bostrom Grover:

> On behalf of my parents and family I would like to thank you for coming. Your support and love are certainly a comfort to us as we deal with our tragic loss.
>
> The last time I saw a few of you, I was speaking to you about my mother at her retirement party in June, voted in as the "family speaker." I definitely didn't think I'd be up here today once again perfecting those skills. My sister was known to you all in many different ways, as a friend, colleague, or as the daughter of my

parents. We were all very proud of her professionally. As you look around here this evening you see many mementos of her academic life. So as a tribute to her dedication to higher education, we've set up a college fund for my children, Abby and Jacob, in her name.

What you may not know about Margie is what type of sister, daughter, and aunt she was and how she touched the lives of those who knew her well. So I would like to share a few memories with you that I hope you will carry with you as you leave here—instead of the memory of how she died.

Margie had very long, beautiful fingernails. When we were young we would tease her, out of jealousy, on how they got that way. But if you knew her, her hands were one of her most expressive features. Please remember her beautiful hands.

Margie was extremely organized. She prided herself on her neatness. She loved to buy little containers to put everything in, from hair fasteners to closet shoe racks and boxes for sweaters. You name it—she had it, labeled it, and knew exactly where it was. Please remember her for her gift of organization.

Margie loved animals, from the horses we had growing up to her dog, Calie, a golden retriever, and a cat, Sebastian. We teased her for spoiling her dog. On her way home she let Calie ride on her lap in the car. Lewisburg is five hours away. Please remember her for the love she had for animals.

Margie loved to shop. I loved to shop with her! She could always find a bargain and had impeccable taste. I joked that we should spread some of her ashes at an outlet mall. I know she would have liked that. Please think of her the next time you're shopping.

Margie loved my children. When I had Abby she watched her for me during her summer break. Abby was only three months old. Margie loved to hold her, dress her, and was very protective of her. Even as a seven-year-old, Abigail Margaret could do little wrong in her eyes. My kids love her—her smile and laughter. Please remember her as an aunt when you hug a child.

Margie loved her family, her parents, sisters, and brother-in-law. She loved holidays and our Swedish traditions, although at Christmas she had a tendency to knock over the tree. She was so happy when she moved back from San Diego because she could visit more often. In fact, she was on her way home the weekend of her death.

She always bought the greatest birthday gifts and never forgot to send a card. She loved eating out, having veal Marsala, even with my kids. She loved reading, especially the latest diet and exercise crazes. We'd trade the latest information. She loved her work, helping others, adding value to a world gone mad. Please remember her this Christmas.

We can't explain why this happened, why to someone so young, beautiful, and caring. Our hope is that justice will be served. It won't bring her back, but it gives us the hope and courage to go on. Thank you again for coming.

The music begins and I walk to the casket to say my final goodbye. Margie's cuts and bruises are now more visible. Tomorrow her body will be taken to the Springfield Crematorium. Her ashes will be returned to us in the jade green marble urn with the engraved golden rose and this epitaph:

Dr. Margaret E. Bostrom, Ph.D.
Clinical Psychologist
Much loved daughter, sister, aunt and niece
Died too soon

I know that it should be either Dr. or Ph.D., but so what? I want both. I wait to be alone with her, but Ruth and Abby stay too. I'm not sure if it is to comfort me or for them to share this moment together with Margie. After a moment I turn, walk past the mementos of her life, and leave.

Margie's Journey Taken Too Soon

No, I don't want to go. I'm not ready.
But it's happening. I can't stop it.
My body is riddled with wounds and weakening.
I can no longer fight off the vicious thrusts of the knife.
I never thought he would attack me this way
Waiting at the bathroom door for me to finish my shower.
I can feel my heart pumping futilely.

I want to live. I have goals and plans.
My life flashes in front of me.
I hear my sisters and me bickering, teasing, giggling and sharing.
I regret the times I caused Ma and Dad to worry.
I always knew I was loved and, yes, spoiled.
Calie's barking grows fainter and
The white bathroom takes on a bright blue gleam.
My loved ones here on earth appear briefly—vaguely.
I wonder if they can hear my goodbyes
Before I'm swept away by the rushing gust of air
That propels me upward out of my body.
I feel no more pain or terror—only dismay.
I watch as Mitch walks away from my body
Naked and lifeless on the white tile floor,
Goes downstairs, puts the knife in the sink,
Calls his mother and then 911.
I feel his terror as he realizes what he has done.
Knows his dreams, as well as mine, have been destroyed.
I'm amazed that in his anger he risked so much.
Then I feel a gentle touch and turn to see
Several welcoming smiles on faces both known and unfamiliar.
My grandmothers take my hands and lead me away.
Come, we'll help you get settled.
You will like it here—once you accept what happened.
I lament unfinished work in life.
I had just begun my career helping others.
They gently explain, *You finished all you were meant to do.*
You will become reconciled to that—later.
But now you need to embark on a new journey.
Everything you puzzled over without understanding
Will be perfectly clear to you.
Let us assure you nothing you learned on earth is lost.
It will be increased and put to good use here.
I wonder about what will happen to my family and Mitch.
Soon you will know—but not yet.
Then their welcoming happiness engulfs me.
I put aside my objections and join their joyful celebration.
I look in Grandpa's eyes and we share the memory of

The little moccasins he gave me when I was born.
As we move away I become aware of a heavenly light.
But first I must stop to tell Abby that I'm okay.
I'll slip back later to comfort my mother, Calie and the others.
My transition to this phase of my existence begins.
When I accept my fate I realize it feels familiar
Like I'm home from a long and difficult voyage.
Here there are no fences, leash laws, or zoos.
Co-Co, Mac, Shawnee, Jessie, Sabrina and Felicia
Along with Shoo-Shoo and Little Brother are free to find me.
Magnificent exotic flowers grow in profusion while
Delicate shapes in all colors and sizes float where I want.
Anything is possible—limited only by my creativity.
I can move from place to place with just a thought,
Arrange to meet anyone that's here with just a mental request
Or revisit my perfect earthly body whenever I wish.
I can create sunny days and beautiful beaches, visit mountains,
Go to fancy restaurants, listen to glorious music
Or join Ma as she watches the Yankees play ball.
Depression, alcoholism and violence are no longer mysteries.
I want no more destruction, disease or malnutrition on earth
But I understand that our souls learn from such tribulations.
I wait for my loved ones on earth to join me.
Time is irrelevant because nothing really ends.
Everything is as it was and shall be. Eternity.

I know I must go on with my life even though it doesn't seem possible right now. Tomorrow is another day—without her.

CHAPTER 10

Don't Cry for Me, Argentina—Life Goes On

I have no memory of the day after the funeral. That Friday is a complete blur. But on Saturday, August 24th, Larry and I decide to go to Rhode Island. We don't feel like going but feel we should. We have tickets for Theatre-By-The-Sea's *Evita* and our friends Harry and Terry, who have the trailer next to us, are expecting us to go with them. We will have to tell them about Margie's murder. How? Do we say, "Oh, by the way, Mitch murdered Margie"? How many details do we have to give? "He stabbed her several times when she got out of the shower. He wasn't going to let anyone else have her. He wouldn't give her a divorce and accused her of having an affair with her boss. She was having the affair." Once you start telling the story it is hard to know when to stop.

Harry and Terry read the obituary in the *Hartford Courant* and they weren't sure we would even come today. They hadn't called us because they didn't want to intrude. I don't have the heart to tell them their call would have helped ease the pain. They are caring people and their compassion is obvious.

We follow our usual routine of going to dinner before the play and arrive at the theater early, so we walk through the lovely gardens. The building is a rustic old barn, painted red and made into a theater. After the performance cast members sing and do comedy routines in a restaurant that is at the back—the Seahorse Grill. Larry and I enjoy the Cabaret but don't usually go because as Harry says, "It's way past my bedtime, boys and girls."

A cowbell tolls—the signal that we may now enter the theater. Larry and I have aisle seats in row G. Harry and Terry are two rows in front of us and across the aisle. The lights dim and the play begins with Evita's funeral. The haunting melody of "Don't Cry for Me, Argentina" fills the hall. I begin sobbing out of control. The play ends with her death and the same familiar refrain. Again I'm overcome with tears. I'm enough aware of the world around me to imagine what others in the audience must be thinking—*What kind of nut gets this upset about Eva Peron's death? It happened so long ago and in a foreign country.* If they only knew!

That Sunday morning we receive a message from Ruth. Kathy called. Her landlord traced her to a motel on the Berlin Turnpike south of Hartford. Apparently she was distraught and inconsolable when the police told her that her baby sister was dead—murdered by Mitch. Kathy genuinely liked him but she feels that two people in her life have loved her unconditionally, her sister Margie and Grandma Bo. She trusted Margie with details of her addiction but not the rest of us. Margie didn't reveal Kathy's secrets to us. She would say, "Ma, Kathy's in trouble. Watch her." But never the specifics. She kept her promise. Kathy was proud of her for that.

Several months later Kathy will feel betrayed when she hears that Margie's friend Bill believed Margie's outlandish stories of affairs and drug use were fabricated from her sister Kathy's experiences and those of Margie's close female friend. She tells me, "Margie had no right to tell him." I explain that most people tell someone and she probably needed to talk about her concerns with another professional. Kathy still feels betrayed.

I'm probably more able to deal with Kathy's needs now than I was nine days ago—but not much. She reacts as we expected. "It should have been me. I want to die. It's my fault. I should have gone to live with her in Lewisburg when she asked me. He couldn't have killed her then." I listen to her, knowing that each of us has our own irrational guilt to face, but she is only concerned with her loss.

Under the influence of drugs or alcohol, Kathy denies that Margie is dead. Sober, she refuses to deal with the pain she feels. She needs more help than I can give her. I worry about what she will do.

~~~

My breast surgery that was canceled in August is rescheduled for the Tuesday after Labor Day. On September 2nd I go as an outpatient to Hartford Hospital to have the precancerous calcium deposits removed from my right breast. I have great confidence in Dr. Bloom because he operated on my left breast several years ago and removed a cyst that was not cancerous. He left virtually no scar on this body that has a tendency to form ugly keloids.

When the papers are signed, I'm prepared with hospital gown and booties and wheeled into a waiting room for pre-op patients. There I'm met by the anesthesiologist, given something to relax me, and left to contemplate my destiny. The medication is beginning to relax me when a nurse all dressed in green scrubs—even a green "shower cap"—enters the room. As she comes closer I recognize Colleen Mahoney, Margie's friend through high school. I saw her for the first time in years at Margie's funeral. "Hello, Mrs. Bostrom, I didn't know you were coming in. When I saw your name on the list for operating room one, I asked if I could be assigned there so I could care for you. Dr. Bloom is the best."

I nod and tell her, "Margie sent you. It is her way to let me know she is watching over me and everything is going to be okay." She agrees.

I didn't even know Colleen was a nurse and I certainly didn't know she worked here. Just a coincidence? Not likely. Everything is okay. They get all the suspicious tissue and five years later my mammograms remain trouble-free.

Larry and I had signed up in June for our first Elderhostel experience and an author's conference scheduled for mid-September in Presque Isle, Maine. We decide it will be good for us to go—be some place we have never been with Margie. We will be back in plenty of time to go to Williamsport, Pennsylvania, for Mitch's arraignment on September 25th. I have never been this far north in Maine and find the scenery both soothing and exciting. At times I feel Margie's presence in the backseat. She taps me on the shoulder to point out a crystal blue lake, a rugged mountain top, or a rundown deserted house.

She knows they inspire my imagination. She can go everywhere with us now—even if in spirit only.

At the author's conference, which takes place just before the Elderhostel, we meet an author from the South, Dori Sanders, who is delightful, friendly, talented, and very supportive of my writing. She has written a cookbook on southern home cooking. Larry takes a workshop with her. They actually cook and he buys her cookbook. I don't tell her about Margie's murder then, but later I write to tell her how much she helped us and she didn't even know she was doing it.

The subject of the Elderhostel group is personal writing. I think Larry is going because I want to write. He often does nice things like that, but he says he is going to write. Maybe we'll both write about Margie. Fleetingly, I wonder how the other members, who have not experienced such a tragedy, will feel about being in a group with us, but decide they are adults. They may be uncomfortable but they can handle it.

We are pleased when Glena, the instructor, sets a very compassionate tone everyone else accepts and seems comfortable with. What a blessing these people are. They listen, they hug, they watch our tears and shed a few of their own—because the loss of a loved one is a natural part of life that everyone faces. Dr. Bill Orrsinger and his wife Viola's daughter had died after a long illness. They keep in touch with us long after the Elderhostel and even write a letter for the pre-sentencing impact report before Mitch is sentenced.

Our tragedy releases thoughts and emotions long held in by many of the participants. They write of their losses and pain. Maybe our being here is a good thing for them too. Larry successfully writes about the phone call parents never think they'll get and his reactions to receiving the news. It is therapeutic for him as is reading it to the group on our last night here.

The pain of our grief is never very far from the surface. Anything can bring it forward with surprising rapidity and intensity. At the Elderhostel a woman unknowingly remarks, "If I'd known thirty-one years ago, when my daughter was born, what Ann would accomplish in these years and what she would be doing now, I wouldn't have believed it."

Her sister is attending with her and I've told her about Margie's death at thirty-one. She tells her, "You don't want to know." Then asks me, "Does she, Shirley?"

Everything in my world conspires to remind me of our loss.

I love babies and young children, but smiling friendly little ones remind me I will never hold Margie's babies. Two-and-a-half years after the murder, at Abby's clarinet concert, a small girl sitting with her dad in the row in front of us smiles at me. She has short curly hair, big brown eyes, and freckles scattered across a tiny nose that stir memories of how lovable Margie was. I choke back my tears.

Seeing the trees begin to change from green to gold to crimson brings tears and sadness. I write this poem because she never got to see the beautiful fall display of color that she looked forward to viewing when she returned to the East Coast.

Eastern Autumn

The sky is so blue, Margaret.
The clouds puffy and white.
The air crisp and invigorating.
The maples are bright crimson, yellow, and scarlet.

Contrasting deep green pine trees,
Orange and golden leaves are
Also part of nature's palette.
How can I be sad on a day like this?

How can I ever be happy again?
You came east looking forward to autumn's magic.
But in August, you left this life forever.
So many dreams unfulfilled.

I feel your touch, hear your gentle whisper,
Ma, don't cry. I can see all the magic from here.
My view is vast and quite beautiful.
But I can't see you, Margaret.

Letters from childhood friends of Margie remembering something special about her are treasured but painful. Many incidents I had forgotten or never knew about. Kim Costello, the daughter of a teacher friend, writes to tell me that when we went to Hammonassett Beach to visit her family at their trailer, Kim, Ruth, Kathy, and Margie bought ice cream cones with colored sprinkles on top. Margie would always pick off the pink candy shots because she didn't like the taste of them. No one ever told her they all tasted the same. That was Margie. How many of these stories do I still not know? Will never know?

My aunt Margaret has a note that a young Margie sent her for her birthday. With it is a quarter and an apology because it isn't more. She carries it in her wallet—she shows it to me after Margie's death.

Dear Aunt Margaret,

I'm sorry I didn't send you a birthday gift. How old will you be? I know I really shouldn't ask, but I was just too curious to hold it in. We are taking tennis lessons now. I'm giving you a quarter because it is all I have. I wish I could give you more. I'm really sorry. Did you get a lot of presents? I hope so. I'm really awful at tennis but that was the first time I ever played tennis, though I could serve good.

Love,

Margie

My aunt wants it buried with her when she dies.

Reading should be an escape and it is unless I come upon paragraphs like these from Joseph Wambaugh's *Floaters*. He quotes two policemen:

"Wonder why O. J. used a blade? Why not a gun with a silencer? A guy like him could get any weapon he wanted. Why a blade?"

"Don't you know anything?" Letch, a vice cop said. "A knife is the most phallic of killing tools. When you wanna fuck your babe to death you use a knife. You stick it in all the way!"

I ask Larry who read this book before I did, "Why didn't you tell me this was here?"

His response, "I guess I forgot," seems a poor excuse.

Reading authors like Jonathan Kellerman or Mary Higgins Clark, who Margie enjoyed along with us, is sad but it is a way of staying in touch with her too. I'm drawn to TV shows and books about murder, especially if it is also about violence against women. Ruth and Larry find this interest appalling. I find shedding tears of empathy is therapeutic and releases some of my pain.

Walking into a room and unexpectedly seeing Ruth in Margie's sweatshirt with her hair pulled back in a ponytail startles, then saddens me. They look so much alike, for just a moment I think it is Margie. Then reality strikes.

Larry and I hear "Unforgettable" sung by Natalie Cole and Nat King Cole, for the first time after the murder, on the car radio. I turn off Margie's favorite song, which was sung at her wedding. Yes, Mitch is unforgettable but I don't want to think of him when I hear her song. Over time I learn to listen to it, remember her, and feel my sadness.

For the first time I have real fear of losing a family member. Margie's murder convinced me that it can happen to someone I love. Ruth and I feel a strong need to be together. Our fears and loss are easier to face together and we get comfort from being with each other.

After a few weeks we begin to talk about bringing Margie's furniture to store in Ruth's basement—but it is full and also has a water problem. We clean it out and decide it would be nice for Larry and me to have a bedroom down there. Over the next few weeks we decide to make an apartment with a living room, bedroom, and dining area. A builder is hired and plans are drawn up that now include a bathroom and a small kitchen. Later the kitchen is enlarged to include a stove, dishwasher, and refrigerator. The bathroom has a Jacuzzi and we put a washer/dryer in the storage area. Windows are added to give us more light.

Without really being aware of what is happening, over the next few months we expand a very small project into a major undertaking. It is healing because picking out the cabinets, fixtures, carpet, tiles for the kitchen and bathroom floors, countertops, and paint uses energy that otherwise would be focused on our loss. In November we have enough finished so we can put our daybed from the trailer in Rhode Island in our new bedroom at Ruth's. We start sleeping there sometimes, especially on holidays. The task of cleaning out and getting our condominium ready to sell begins, but we'll do most of it when we return from Florida in March.

After Margie's murder Barbara Carman, a social worker at the school where I taught, calls and asks, "What can I do for you?"

I tell her, "Please, find me a support group for people who have had a loved one murdered. I've gotten letters from several people telling me about support groups for those grieving the death of a loved one, but none that focus on homicide. I think we have additional issues. Especially anger at the killer and frustration with the justice system."

Barbara agrees and promises to begin her search at once. She finds Gary Merton, who founded Survivors of Homicide in 1983, after his daughter was murdered. Gary is no longer active but does serve on the board of directors and attends fundraising functions. He gives her the name of the new president of the organization, Sam Rieger. She reaches him and tells our story. Sam says he will contact us.

Sam calls, listens to our story, expresses his deep sympathy, and tells of his eighteen-year-old daughter, Melanie, who was murdered in their home by her boyfriend. She was trying to break up with him. After brutally attacking her he put her body in her brother's hockey bag and took it to a storage locker. Later, after getting a lawyer, he led the police to her body. Sam and his wife, Wanda, were in Aruba when they received the news. I know from talking to him that our tragedies are similar.

Sam invites us to a Survivors of Homicide meeting. Larry agrees to go with me, but court proceedings delay our attending until the Christmas meetings. We are hesitant because we're not in a festive mood but decide to go anyway. The Waterbury meeting is being held at a truck stop. The owner is donating the room and the meals to Survivors of Homicide. We follow Sam's directions to the back of the restaurant where several people are gathered around long narrow tables near the wall. Sam and Wanda recognize us and introduce themselves. They are about ten years younger than us and make us feel part of the group. Soon we are meeting everyone else. When I sit down, I immediately realize there is no easy way out. I will have to ask other people to move if I want to leave. That is probably what keeps me from running, but as we hear their stories and share ours, I realize that everyone is friendly. The atmosphere is caring and supportive—no one appears uncomfortable when my tears begin to flow. I'm amazed at the strength of everyone in this room. We meet another couple whose only daughter, Kate, was killed in July by the drunk driver with whom she was riding. I know I'm lucky to have my family.

The following week we meet more survivors at the Hartford area meeting, which is held at the home of Doug Isleib, whose wife was shot several times as she pulled into her driveway. Gail Isleib's daughters are here. Their mother was killed by a jealous rejected coworker. We are touched by the stories of the other survivors too.

The Uhlman brothers' mother, Ruth, was murdered in January. She was my age and dreamed of writing children's books. Her sons are frustrated because no arrest has been made in the year following the murder. They can't even get anyone in the criminal justice system to talk to them. She was beat up and tied to a chair and her apartment set on fire because the killer was mad at her youngest son. I look at my daughter, Ruth, who is with us, and wonder what would it be like for her, Kathy, and my grandchildren if I were taken away from them in such a brutal manner? Later, Gail's killer is convicted and sentenced to 65 years.

Cindy's fiancé, a postal worker, was killed while delivering mail in Hartford. The crime is a federal crime, just as ours is, because he was a federal employee doing his job. I know how cheated I would have felt if Larry had been murdered before we had a chance to fulfill our dreams. This murderer was also convicted and sentenced to life in prison without parole.

Stuart Brush, a minister and father of a murdered son who was delivering pizza in Bridgeport, leads a touching Christmas memorial service. He and his wife Laura lost their other child when he chose to commit suicide rather than face life without his brother. I reassure myself that my girls are strong. Aren't they? Yet I worry about Kathy.

I remember reading the news and hearing the television reports about all these cases. From now on our cases and our lives will be permanently intertwined. Larry and I become very active in all the activities of the group. We go to the Connecticut Legislature to lobby for victim-friendly laws, to court proceedings when a member's case is on the docket, give emotional support when needed, and do anti-violence educational programs. Larry and I quickly learn that the surest way to begin healing is to be active helping other victims.

Survivors of Homicide—a Club

Membership is open yet no one wants to join our group.
Before we were survivors we were whole, living safe busy lives
only slightly concerned with the effects of crime and punishment.

We accept mothers, fathers, sisters, brothers
and other family members who mourn a loved one
tragically taken from us by the violent act of another.

Our members are social workers, engineers, policemen, teachers,
doctors, factory workers, writers, lawyers, and lottery workers.
No one is excluded because of race, religion or economic status.

We have much in common: pain, grief, depression, anger, denial.
Each new member is welcomed with compassion and understanding.
Seasoned members explain, *What you are feeling is normal.*

Our rules of order support each member's right to grieve
in his own unique way without ridicule or censure.
While sharing what has helped us begin to heal.

Some members wallow in self-pity and stay anchored to their loss.
Others seek ways to make new members' paths easier to travel.
Helping others avoid our fate are the dues we pay.

Activities include court appearances, lobbying for victim-friendly laws,
speaking at schools and prisons to prevent future violence.
We are the club that wants no new members.

Unfortunately, five years later, philosophical differences with some of the members will cause Larry and me to withdraw from the board of directors and resign as co-vice presidents. We continue to support other survivors in court and through our advocacy. We also continue our work educating people about and against violence.

A new sense of the extent of our incredible loss arrives with Mitch's birthday, which stirs up memories of the pleasant times we shared with him. In many ways he was the son I never had. Mitch is an avid sports fan. I don't share his passion for Giants football, but we both enthusiastically support the New York Yankees and the University of Connecticut men's and women's basketball teams. While they lived in Mira Mesa and Poway, Mitch and I often called each other with encouragements at halftime during close basketball games. And again at the end, when a great shot won the game. Now I hope he doesn't even have the privilege of watching them.

I had an old Password game at the camper. When Mitch came he would talk me into playing it. He didn't have to try too hard because it reminded me of playing Touring with my mother—she cheated, or so we all claimed, and we would get so silly. Mitch and I would soon have everyone laughing because of our challenging camaraderie.

Margie and Mitch knew I loved anything with fish on it. I still marvel that the sixteen-inch powder-blue ceramic fish they brought me from Mexico to Connecticut on an airplane made it in one piece. The most touching thing Mitch ever did for me on his own was pick out a pair of fish earrings. They are handmade, wooden, a pretty turquoise color. I loved them and wore them often. I haven't put them on since he killed my daughter, but I haven't thrown them away either. How would he feel if I gave them back?

Mitch and I shared a sense of adventure. On one of our trips to Poway Mitch drove us to Mexico. We went southeast toward the border looking for Tecate. We arrived in town at siesta time and the brewery, which was supposed to have tours, was deserted. Without Mitch we probably would have turned around and gone back home, but he talked us into going west. There were wineries along the route, but they were closed too. When we neared the Pacific Ocean we saw a sign for "La Buscadero." It was now dusk and Larry was getting nervous, but Mitch took us down a narrow dirt road to discover what "La Buscadero" was. We were all delighted when we saw a water spout shoot, from between the huge rocks, into the air. We watched and waited as the pressure from the waves built and another stream of water blew toward the sky. It was late and all the little souvenir stands were closed as we walked back to the car.

We drove on to Escondido and discovered a French restaurant in the old Santo Winery. Huge ancient wooden wine casks permeated with the bouquet of fine wines, classical music, elegant table settings, impeccable service, and gourmet food made it an immediate favorite for all of us. Later we went there as part of Margie's graduation present and Mitch took his father there when he visited. Mitch's betrayal has damaged many memories for both families.

October 22, 1966

A murderer was born this day.
A fact that would be proven so
in less than thirty years.
Did anyone know or even suspect?

Amidst the revelry and good wishes
for health and prosperity,
life was full of promise.
Could the evil spirit be imagined?

95

FUNNY—HE DOESN'T LOOK LIKE A MURDERER

Carefully disguised with dark curls,
and equipped with instant charm
he allured and delighted.
Was any father or mother ever more proud?

When sister Michelle was born
she learned quickly that Mitch,
the son, was the family's shining star.
Did she sense a dangerous presence?

When boyhood friends played football
before the cheering hometown fans
or gathered in their secret hiding place
did they see the cruel side of Mitch?

College friends warned Margaret,
Stay away. Don't date him. He gave the
last girl who broke up with him a hard time.
Why didn't she listen and live?

On July 30, 1994, their wedding day,
they smiled brightly, hugged, and kissed.
Who could know or even suspect
this *love* would lead to her death?

She told me, *He broke the bedroom door.*
He took Calie and Sebastian,
and he didn't even like Calie.
Why did he have to hurt me so?

She'd have a lawyer get Calie back.
She'd file for divorce—start life anew.
She liked herself—was strong enough to break away.
Why didn't we realize she was in mortal danger?

He called me twice the week he killed her.
Said he loved her, but guessed it wasn't enough.
The call comes—She's dead—stabbed thirteen times.

How do I know he did it, not some prisoner?

We travel to Pennsylvania, see the FBI, Calie
and the already cleaned white bathroom.
It can't be real. She's not dead.
How can life go on without our Margie?

He pleads not guilty as we sit and wonder.
How can he deny he did this awful deed?
October 22, 1996, he's sitting in a jail cell.
I hope he's thinking of what he did to Margie.

Sorry I didn't feel like sending a card.
Is it a happy thirtieth birthday, Mitch?

Life goes on but every thought still turns and races toward Margie: each place we visit, event we attend, movie we see, new friend we meet, each shopping trip we take. New fashion and the changes in Abby and Jacob invoke regret she isn't here. Tears flow but I have precious memories of Margie to comfort me.

CHAPTER 11

My Little Margie

Margie was my youngest child, my baby—even when she was a thirty-one-year-old adult. I enjoyed all her stages: the early years with her silly grin and bubbly way of always being happy to see me; the years as a teenager, shy and unsure of herself but occasionally finding trouble; and the adult, sensitive and caring—a clinical psychologist working with federal prisoners. Margie always had a way of making me feel special. I'm fortunate to have been her mother and blessed with detailed remembrances of her.

In the weeks and months after the murder, I have a multitude of memories of Margie that scramble for my attention. Auspicious, frightening, mischievous, funny, or touching—they are all full of love. As soon as one recollection fades a new one appears. There is no apparent order and each image gives me a precious glimpse of Margie to treasure.

Shortly after she was born, I started having terrifying thoughts about doing harm to this child I wanted so much. I thought I was a terrible person. I delayed telling anyone because I was afraid they would think I was crazy. After a time I mentioned to my mother that I felt depressed and was worried about the strange thoughts I was having, without going into detail. She wisely advised me to talk to Dr. Bugbee, my obstetrician, who told me to come in immediately.

When I explained how I felt, he said, "I bet you think you are the only woman who has ever felt this way." I did. He explained that I was experiencing postpartum blues, which are more common after a third pregnancy than earlier ones. He gave me a small white pill—to this day I don't know what it was—and within days I was enjoying my baby. Since then I have read about mothers who don't get medical help and hurt their babies or themselves. My mother had given sound advice.

Larry and I moved our family to Connecticut when Margie was eight months old. Trips back to western New York State in the mid-sixties took twelve to thirteen hours. Since then existing roads have been improved and new roads have been built. In the 1990s, after the girls were grown, it took only eight-and-a-half hours to make the same trip.

In the days before air-conditioned cars, Ruth and Kathy would fall asleep in the backseat, their young bodies soaked in sweat. It was also before child safety car seats or the accompanying laws. Margie would ride in the front seat—on my lap. The happy, contented child I loved so much quickly disappeared. She didn't sleep once in thirteen hours. I tried everything to calm her screams but was unsuccessful. I knew she couldn't be hungry but offered her bottle after bottle. She'd drink a few drops, then the screaming would begin again—her tiny body stretched taut with her feet pressing painfully into my abdomen. Thirteen hours of this and I was ready to toss her from the car. Many years later I found out she had been carsick. I wish I had known. I would have spared each of us that repeated experience and enjoyed visiting Jamestown more.

Margie was a year and nine months old when my father died. My mother used some of the insurance money to buy me a puppy, which she sent to us on an airplane. The airport was very close to where we lived in Windsor Locks. We called our new puppy Co-Co. Not very original—for a brown miniature French poodle! He was a replacement for Rusty, our collie who hadn't been able to adjust to the confines of being leashed. As a result, bladder and kidney problems developed and he had to be put to sleep. The puppy and the toddler became friends instantly and spent many happy moments together before Co-Co, at age five, decided to chase a squirrel across Windsor Locks' busy Elm Street and was killed. He was showing off for Grandma Bo, who had just come to visit. I have a favorite picture of Margie and Co-Co standing on the steps outside our kitchen door—she with very little hair at a year and nine months, dressed in a dainty feminine dress, and Co-Co a curly brown bundle of fur.

Margie and Co-Co enjoy each other's company.

The year we moved to Windsor Locks from Bloomfield, Connecticut, Ruth started kindergarten and Kathy went to the Congregational Church Nursery School. One cold snowy winter day Larry stayed home from work because he had a high fever. After taking Kathy to school I gave Margie a bath. Larry woke up long enough to tell me, "Don't bother to get her dressed to go with you. She can stay with me." This sounded good to me. I hated the idea of taking her out in the below-freezing weather after she just had a bath. I drove off, unaware that Larry had fallen back into a sound sleep, and Margie had decided she was supposed to go with me. She went downstairs, turned the door handle on the inside, which unlocked the door, and started down the driveway—barefoot and dressed for indoors. She made it to the end of the driveway before our neighbor Amy Christensen rescued her. We lived on a bend on Elm Street, which is the busy State Route 140. When Kathy and I returned there was enough guilt for both Larry and me. If it had not been for our curious neighbor, we might have lost Margie then.

We soon joined the Congregational Church in Windsor Locks. One Sunday when we came home from church, two-year-old Margie, in her little patent leather shoes, slipped on the wooden floor in the living room. She had been running to me where I sat in a wooden rocking chair and hit her head on one of the rockers. When I picked her up she was screaming and bleeding profusely. I knew this was not the time for ice and Band-Aids, which worked to heal most of her boo-boos. I remembered that my mother put flour on my little finger when I fell on an axe and almost severed it. I did the same thing, and the bleeding stopped and we rushed her to the hospital. In the emergency room Margie decided it was my fault she got hurt and wanted her daddy. The doctor thought I was crazy for using the flour and suspected I was a child abuser. Larry assured him I was neither.

Another time Margie and I went to the store where I bought a large container of laundry detergent. When we arrived home I placed it at the top of the cellar stairs because the minister was ringing the doorbell. As I welcomed him in we heard a loud thump-thump. I knew what it was. When I reached the top of the stairs I saw Margie lying unconscious on the cement basement floor. I held my breath as I raced to her. Thankfully she was breathing and further inspection revealed no serious damage. I told Reverend Samsvick we had a hook for the door but hadn't gotten it put up yet. He decided to do it for me—then. Larry was embarrassed when he came home and found that the minister had done his job, but thankful his procrastination didn't have more serious consequences.

We celebrated Margie's third birthday with our good friends Bunny and Neil Daniel and their children. Leslie was the same age as Kathy and Christopher was Margie's age. Bunny volunteered to make Margie a fancy birthday cake that had a small doll head and upper body on top and the cake formed a billowy full skirt. It was beautiful. Margie, unconcerned about the hours of work Bunny put into it, took one taste—"Uck, this frosting is yucky." She pushed the cake away and refused to try any more. I was mortified even though Bunny kept assuring me it was okay.

Impish eyes are a tip-off that she is considering some devilment.

Margie's Grandma Bostrom gave her a big stuffed rabbit for her third birthday. It was over two feet tall and made from red polka-dotted cotton. Margie fell in love with it immediately, and it replaced the tattered blanket that she carried everywhere. After a year the fabric covering the bunny started to wear out. In places the stuffing was peeking through, so I suggested to Margie that I get some material and recover her friend. She agreed so I bought some pink furry material—more appropriate for a bunny, I thought. As I was working on the project I kept reminding myself that it might be for naught. Margie probably would take one look at it and cry, "That's not Bunny. I want Bunny back." And it would be too late. I was pleasantly surprised when I showed the new bunny to her. She smiled and hugged it. She knew Bunny was still the same inside and that was what counted.

The following summer we took the girls to New York City. At the Bronx Zoo, Ruth and Kathy stayed near us and were easy to manage in the crowd, but three-and-a-half-year-old Margie refused to hold my hand. In spite of my warnings, she would give me her impish grin and wander off. I was able to keep her in sight, but eventually she turned around and couldn't see us. I can still see the look of pure terror on her face. I had taught her a valuable lesson but the price was too high. She used her usual explanation: "The devil god made me do it." This statement always made me uneasy because we never understood where it came from.

Even in the late 1960s, New Yorkers had the reputation of being unfriendly. We found the opposite was true. Once a waiter in a fancy English restaurant volunteered to split a piece of roast beef three ways and give each child her own baked potato—for the price of one meal. One time we were walking down Fifth Avenue with the girls, in pink and white lace dresses, when a woman stopped us, leaned over, and smiled at them, "What beautiful young ladies. I hope you are enjoying your visit to our city."

They were. So were Larry and I.

On another visit to New York City we went to a Yankees game. We had second row seats behind the plate on the third base side. Craig Nettles was playing his last game as a Cleveland Indian because he became a Yankee the next day. Margie always took lots of teasing about being left-handed but in the late innings she saw that Sparky Lyle, who came into the game as a relief pitcher, was a lefty. From then on she reminded us that left-handers can do great things—just look at Sparky Lyle.

Bunny and I led a Brownie troop that Leslie, Ruth, and Kathy belonged to, and Margie and Chris enjoyed playing together during the meetings. Our families always got together to celebrate Memorial Day and the Fourth of July—usually with picnics. Eventually, the older girls moved on to Girl Scouts and a new leader. One November day they went on a hike up a mountain. I allowed Margie to go because the leader was Margie's kindergarten teacher and said she knew the trail well.

When it was time for them to return, Neil Daniel went to wait for them to come down the trail from the mountain. He waited and waited. No scouts. Finally Bunny called me with the news. We waited in terror, wondering if they had matches, a flashlight, or blankets. The day had been warm and they wore only light jackets but it gets cold and dark early in November in Connecticut. Finally, at about ten that night Bunny got a call that they were safe. They had come from the woods at a different point than they had expected and called from a nearby home. We might have lost all three of our daughters and their friend. They got lots of hugs that night.

My three girls are only three-and-a-half years apart in age and I had no built-in baby-sitters, so when Ruth began dancing lessons so did Kathy and Margie. Margie was only three when she started and the teacher demonstrated great patience. For one dance at the recital the class was dressed as little yellow ducks. On stage Ruth, Kathy, and the other girls carefully performed the dance, but Margie, on the left end facing the audience, stood, fascinated by the crowd. When she glanced at the other dancers she copied their moves, but she was late so when they were twirling she was facing the back of the stage and wiggling her

Margie is doing some last minute practice before the big recital.

tail feathers at the audience. The gales of laughter confused the other dancers but Margie, unaware she was responsible for the hilarity, kept opening and closing her little fingers and singing, "Quack, quack, I'm a little duck." She was adorable and I loved her so much—still I couldn't stop laughing.

My mother used to tell me, "I'm glad I lived long enough to see you get the child you deserve." Margie was a climber—apparently so was I. Margie was like me in many ways. When I was a young child I gorged on butter, got terribly sick, then wouldn't eat butter for years. One evening Margie ate too many strawberries and broke out with a terrible rash while we were at a drive-in movie. Another time, she ate too much lobster when we stopped at Booth Bay to buy cooked lobsters to eat at a roadside picnic area in Maine. It was years before she would try either one again. Many of my friends still tell me how much Margie looked like me and even though she was much better-looking, I enjoy hearing it.

I had a miscarriage when Margie was five. When I came home from the hospital, she and Co-Co climbed up on the sofa bed that Larry had prepared for me in the living room. Margie told me, "I'm your baby. The only baby you'll ever need." Her voice was full of reassurance but also indignation—that I apparently didn't know this.

Margie loved books and playing library. She taped letters and numbers onto the book spines, and stuck date due forms and check-out cards inside the back covers. Each night before bed I would read one of the books to the girls. They took turns choosing which one it would be, but it didn't matter—all three would choose *Larry the Canary*. It wasn't great literature but it used their dad's name in a silly way. Finally, in desperation, I limited its reading to one night a week. It was falling apart and its pages were crumbling before they finally stopped requesting it.

Winning was important to Margie—she hated to lose. It didn't matter if it was at Candy Land or cards. Soon we limited the number of games we played in our family because none of us wanted to deal with her distress at losing, which happened often—just because she was the youngest. However, even as an adult she still wanted to win. One Christmas she and Mitch gave Larry and me a VCR horse racing game, *Let's Go to the Races*. Players bid on horses, rolled the die, and watched the taped race. Both Mitch and Margie needed to win. When he won, Margie announced disgustedly that she wasn't going to play anymore. I was reminded of the saying—your greatest strength is also your greatest weakness.

When we lived in Windsor Locks, Larry was getting his master's degree from Rensselaer and he needed quiet time, especially on the weekends. I began taking the girls to the Wadsworth Atheneum, an art museum in Hartford. They developed a love for Salvador Dali paintings, especially the soft clocks in *The Persistence of Memory* and *Apparition of Face and Fruit Dish on a Beach*, which also looks like a large dog. Van Gogh, Monet, Cezanne, and other impressionists became favorites too. On weeks we didn't go to the Wadsworth we visited Mark Twain's home on Farmington Avenue in Hartford or other historic sites.

These jaunts became special memories for us.

Margie had two older girl cousins who tormented her when she was small. Ruth and Kathy did what they could to protect her and when that failed they would find me. One cousin shut her in a dark closet and waited outside the door. When Margie got out the girl sprayed perfume at her eyes. Another cousin who was only a few months older than Margie but much bigger took her presents at Christmastime. I would quietly retrieve them, but one time the cousin used force to get something she wanted and Margie clobbered her with a new winter boot. I was startled by the cheers from my mother, brothers, and sisters-in-law. My brother said, "About time, Margie." He wouldn't listen to his daughter's complaint. He told her, "You've been asking for it."

When the girls were small we enjoyed hiking, camping, and picnicking. Our walks had a definite pattern. Margie would tire easily because of her little legs and we would end up carrying her. When we tired we would take a short rest, give her a LifeSaver, and her energy would be magically restored for a short while. Then the cycle was repeated. Campfires, usually with Margie on my lap, meant I had to tell ghost stories just as my dad had done for us. It is a family tradition that my grandchildren now enjoy. However, when I started teaching again and the girls went to the baby-sitter's home, they complained the Duponts made them watch *Dark Shadows*, which was the hit afternoon soap opera at that time, and it gave them nightmares.

The next year the girls were allowed to attend Union School, where I taught. It made it easier because they could ride to school with me in the morning and come to my room after school. Each afternoon when the four of us arrived home from school, I asked for twenty minutes alone to go from being a teacher to a mom. Ruth and Kathy were very good about giving me this time, but Margie would come running into my bedroom and jump on top of me. Her "I love you, Mommy," usually earned her hugs and kisses instead of reprimands.

When Margie was in first grade we had her tested for learning disabilities because she was experiencing some problems with academic tasks, even though we knew she was bright because of her oral vocabulary and comprehension. When she began to write she did perfect mirror writing, which was a signal that she might be processing things differently. Her disabilities were diagnosed as disgraphia, directionality (couldn't correctly identify right and left), and spatial relations. As part of the testing she had to have a psychological exam. Dr. Glass, a clinical psychologist the school contracted with, met with Margie. She commented when it was over, "I didn't like that man. He thought he was funny but he wasn't."

When I met with him I was devastated by his perceptions and remarks. He told me I put too much pressure on her to succeed. He conceded that it might not be intentional, but he saw me as very goal-oriented and assumed my husband was too. He saw Margie as a very sad and unhappy child whom he couldn't get to smile. I wanted to tell him he wasn't funny but resisted.

Then he told me about a drawing Margie had done. He said it was about death, the colors were all purples and blacks and it was of a cemetery. That was the last straw. Margie had drawn that picture at the request of the then-Governor Ella Grasso's daughter, who was an art student. Margie had a very good idea of what death was. Just weeks before, her aunt and young cousin died in a fiery car accident. A secretary, trying to be helpful, had shown it to him. He was surprised when I told him about our losses, but he continued to blame me for her imagined problems. When I left his office I made it to my friend Judy's classroom before the tears began to flow. She consoled me by assuring me I was a great mother and Margie was a happy child. Since then I've asked myself, *How dare he?*

I talked with Margie about her grades and how hard school was. I explained that if she agreed we could have her spend another year in first grade with the same teacher. That way next year she would be in the top reading group instead of the lowest and school would be more fun. She accepted this idea, especially when I told her she could have a new bike because she helped make such a mature decision. She had a fantastic learning disabilities teacher who worked with her each day during that repeat of first grade. She taught Margie ways to compensate for her learning problems. This intervention, along with the fact that she was more mature, resulted in Margie's grades shooting straight up. Thus she began her long, successful academic career. She even won first prize in the school science fair that year.

My aunt Margaret and uncle Carl made regular visits to Windsor Locks. Carl always gave each girl a silver dollar and it became a ritual for him to take the kids to Riverside Park, which was a local amusement park in Agawam. The girls always looked forward to these visits.

Aunt Margaret created three complete wardrobes: wedding gowns, coats, skirts, sweaters, fancy dresses, pants, and shirts for their Barbie dolls, which Margie and her sisters played with by the hour. When the girls tired of playing with the dolls alone, they added their plastic horses. Carl died about a year-and-a-half after my dad but Aunt Margaret continued to visit. Sometimes she would get my mother to come with her.

Margie could entertain herself for hours with her Playskool toys. She had all of them—the house, the barn, the schoolhouse, the school bus, and the boat. When, as an adult, she came home from California and saw her niece, Abby, playing with them she reminded me that they were hers. It was okay for Abby to play with them, but she wanted them kept for her children. I promised they would be. They are now neatly boxed and labeled as hers and sit in the storage area above Ruth's garage. Someday I may give them to a women's shelter—but not yet.

Margie was an impish, adorable five-year-old. Her short, light brown hair curled tightly around her head. Freckles spread across her cheeks and dotted her delicate nose. Dark brown eyes fringed with long lashes sparkled with excitement. One hot and humid afternoon filled with the threat of thundershowers, I was in the kitchen at the ironing board when she came in the door and held out her hand. On it was perched a blue jay. Its blue-gray coat was trimmed in black with a white vest and on its head sat a crest or tuft of feathers. Margie giggled as it jumped onto the ironing board. "She's my pet. Can I keep her?"

I was speechless, but Ruth and Kathy chimed in, "Please, Mommy."

"We'll see." I gave my standard noncommittal answer as I moved toward the ironing board. Close up, I saw that it had red markings on its tail and around one leg. Margie saw it about the same time I did. "Ma, is it hurt? Is that blood?" A large tear rolled down her cheek.

Fortunately I could reassure her. "Looks like fingernail polish, not blood. She is already someone's pet and I bet they are looking for her. We'll have to let her go when she's ready." All three girls groaned.

We watched the blue jay walk around, calmly devouring the bits of cookie crumbs placed on the white ironing board cover. Ruth brought a saucer of water for it to wash down the bits of food. The bird sipped, extended its neck into the air, and swallowed. I could almost feel the cool water sliding down my own throat.

I remembered the little Brownie camera. "Stay still. I'm going to get the camera to take a picture. Don't scare the bird." It was light enough in the kitchen so that I didn't have to use a flash and take the chance of startling it. "There, Margie, now you will always be able to prove that a blue jay visited you."

Then the blue jay flew off the ironing board and around the room. Margie held out her hand. It landed on her index finger, returned her gaze with its bright black eyes. I snapped another picture before it soared out the door.

Stunned. We didn't say anything for a while. Soon, nine-year-old Ruth put her arms around Margie's shoulders. "It'll come back to visit. I'm sure." Then they ran outside, slamming the screen door behind themselves. For a few days they watched faithfully for their winged visitor to return. It never did but I still have those pictures.

I felt honored when my cousin Tim, Rance and Peggy's son, and Sue, his bride-to-be, asked for one of my girls to be their flower girl.

I picked Margie because I felt there would be less jealousy than if one of the older girls had the honor. Aunt Margaret made a long, bright green dress of organdy with a colorful sash around the waist. Margie looked adorable. I was a little apprehensive because she was young and I would be the only one at the wedding she knew well. She charmed everyone at the rehearsal dinner but fell asleep. At the ceremony she performed perfectly and I was so proud of her.

When I started working full-time we began saving for our Christmas trip to the newly opened Disney World. Margie was six when we went and unfortunately she didn't remember much about the trip except that was the year Santa didn't come. On Christmas morning the girls woke up expecting their stockings to be there and filled. They weren't. They reminded me that sometimes when we were in Jamestown for Christmas, Santa visited our house in Windsor Locks, so they returned home to full stockings. They quickly decided that was where he went instead of our motel. I knew he hadn't. At first I was angry because I thought they were being ungrateful for the expensive trip, but gradually I realized they were truly disillusioned. It wasn't the best way to teach them about Santa Claus.

We took the girls to Cinderella's Castle for lunch to help ease the pain. Cinderella walked around and greeted everyone. They enjoyed all the characters who shook their hands and told them how cute or good they were. Margie had a little purse that she left every time we went from one place to another. Usually I reminded her to get it, but one time I didn't notice until much later. I had no hope that it would still be on the bench where she last remembered having it. Fortunately, when we returned to look, there it was.

From Disney World we went to Everglades National Park to see the alligators and the famous sunsets. Then we went to Key West, where we spent a half day deep sea fishing from a boat. Kathy caught a good-sized grouper, which everyone told us was an excellent tasting fish. They suggested we take it to a restaurant and ask them to prepare it for us. We did and they agreed. Kathy was so excited and proud of herself. We waited and waited—the restaurant was very busy. Before the food arrived Margie was sound asleep with her face on the table. We assured Kathy that meant there was more for each of us.

In second grade Margie had a teacher who encouraged individuality, creativity, and independence. Margie made close friends with a girl whose parents were wealthy—at least by Windsor Locks standards. Alicia would spend time in our home and Margie in hers. One day during a class discussion Alicia told the teacher she had sixteen telephones in her home. Margie raised her hand, "I only counted nine." Later the teacher told me it was good for Alicia to have Margie for a friend because she provided a reality check for Alicia.

Unfortunately, not all the teachers were as child-focused as Margie's teacher. Apparently on a trip to the bathroom, Margie decided to do a cartwheel in the hall. That day two teachers visited me after school. Linda, a first-grade teacher came to tell me that when she looked out the window in her classroom door, to her surprise, she had seen a pair of feet go by in a perfect arc. I knew she was telling me because it was Margie. She recounted how she stopped Margie and told her how dangerous it was. She might have bumped into another student or fallen and hurt herself. Furthermore, it wasn't lady-like and distracted other classes. I listened politely but wished I could give Margie a hug. When Margie's teacher showed up she looked at me and knew Linda had already made her visit. We both wondered why she had made such a big deal of it.

Margie went into fourth grade the year we moved to Suffield. I went in during the summer to register her and was told she was lucky because she would be in a class of seventeen students. I looked at the class lists and saw that all the other fourth grade classes had over twenty students. I thanked the secretary but asked that Margie be placed in one of the other classes. As a schoolteacher I recognized a class that is so much smaller may mean that parents have requested their children not have that teacher. I was right and as it turned out Margie was placed with teachers who team taught and she loved them. She also met her friend Colleen in that class. It was an eventful year. They wrote an editorial for the fourth grade newspaper about the conditions of the school restrooms. They described them as dirty and stinky. Margie would not use the bathrooms at school. She waited until she got home.

Margie decided to play the French horn. We were puzzled about the appeal of this instrument that was larger than she was but agreed. Later, when she decided it was too much for her, she told us, "I chose it because it was rent-free. You had to pay for the other instruments." We appreciated her thoughtfulness but reassured her that we could pay for an instrument if she really wanted to play one. We bought a piano and the music teacher at Union School began giving the girls lessons after school. His attitude and their abilities doomed that venture.

Margie wrote a paragraph describing her mother when she was in fourth grade. I've kept it because it is a precious tribute to me:

My Mother

My mother is not selfish at all. She is a very consiterert (considerate) person. She is nice to us to (too). She is nice to everbody (everybody). She never is uncensitarit (insensitive) to anybody. I enjoy being with My Mother to (too). She tris (tries) hard to make us happy. She (is) not perdjadic (prejudice). She never critasires (criticizes) us to (too).

Words in parenthesis are corrections made to the rough draft done in fourth grade.

When Margie was little and had her picture taken, she always wore a silly grin. She scrunched up her eyes and nose and stretched

her tightly closed lips into a huge upturned arc. She thought that was what we wanted. Ruth and Kathy loved it—something more to tease their baby sister about. When she was a teenager she continued to keep her lips firmly together because she didn't want anyone to see the braces.

The summer Margie was six-and-a-half we took a vacation in New Hampshire at the Robinwood Inn, a bed-and-breakfast near North Conway. There the girls had met Ziggy, a shaggy pony the owner led around with them sitting on its back. They were quickly hooked on horses, just as I had been since childhood.

That fall we all began taking riding lessons at Fox Run Farm in Suffield and their dancing careers were forgotten. We didn't realize at the time that six-year-old Margie's learning disabilities contributed to her inability during her riding lessons to determine from which side she should mount the horse. The following June we bought our first horse, Shoo-Shoo, and on this 15.2-hand horse she was small but had excellent balance. We bought Shoo-Shoo's brother the next year, at the same time we purchased the eleven-acre farm in West Suffield. Eventually, we got Sara Lee, our third horse. All three girls became excellent riders and competed in shows—often winning in their classes.

When we moved to West Suffield, the bedrooms were not yet ready for the girls to sleep in, so they chose to sleep on cots in the barn near their horses Shoo-Shoo and Little Brother. They

The beginning of six-year-old Margie's love affair with horses.

thought they were living every girl's dream. I had no objection to them sleeping in the barn for a few nights, but I was concerned when I came home from school one afternoon and they had invited Little Brother into the house. He had his two front hooves inside the mudroom and was lifting a back foot—trying to decide if he really wanted to do it.

When we first brought him home he was skittish because a jockey used an electric prod on him in the starting gate of a quarter horse race. We had worked long and hard to build his trust but he was still easily spooked. If he panicked the damage to the house would be extensive and Little Brother or maybe even the girls could be seriously hurt. My fear was that his nine hundred pounds would be too much for the old floorboards and he would break through them. I circled through the kitchen door and into the mudroom where I gently pushed his head back through the door. The girls were upset. They didn't understand that my arrival may have saved him from the same fate as Rumpelstiltskin. I had to admit that bringing him into the house was an intriguing thought—if the consequences had been less frightening.

When Ruth got older, she went from hunt seat competition to three-day eventing. Margie followed Ruth's lead and did extremely well before Shoo-Shoo went permanently lame. In fact, she rode in her only three-day event while I was in Jamestown because my mother, who suffered from emphysema for ten years, was near death. When Margie and her dad arrived for the funeral, he told me she had done extremely well. I still wish I could have seen her ride then.

Even when our horses and the farm were gone, we still enjoyed riding. Margie went trail riding with Larry and me in the Blue Ridge Mountains on one of our trips to Lynchburg College. Best of all, Margie was there when I fulfilled my dream of galloping a horse in the ocean's surf in Ensenada, Mexico. An added pleasure was that Margie's horse was a new mother and her foal went with us. We had tried riding on the beach once before with Ruth at Rosalito, Mexico, but the horses were lazy and the owners mistreated them when we complained they wouldn't even trot. Their quick sharp slaps to the horses' rumps with a whip caused them to buck—not to move forward. The men stood and laughed—no doubt hoping we would fall off. We were proud we didn't but Margie and Ruth had saddle sores from clinging to the cheap saddles. When we go riding now, I know Margie is with us.

When we moved to Suffield Margie wanted a cat so we took Sam, the black cat from Fox Run that the owner, Jack Coonan, was happy to get rid of because of his bad habits. Sam didn't want to stay with us and found his way back to Fox Run. We brought him back and he disappeared again. This time he didn't return to the stables.

I saw an ad in the paper for kittens and Kathy helped me pick out an orange, long-haired, female kitten with double paws—extra toes—to give Margie for her tenth birthday. She loved the kitten and named her Sabrina. About a month later, while Sabrina was cleaning herself, we realized the kitten was male. Margie refused to change his name. He remained Sabrina for the sixteen years we had him. We teased her about the sexual identity problem she caused the poor confused cat. Everyone else called him Sab.

She gave Sabrina regular baths and after one she proudly showed her father and me that she had trimmed his whiskers—for neatness. We told her gently that cats need their whiskers to warn them when they're putting their heads in spaces that are too small to be safe. She felt guilty and fretted until the whiskers grew back.

Margie was in seventh grade when she went to a middle school dance. We dropped her off and then went to the grocery store. When we reached home the phone was ringing. It was the school nurse. Margaret had been outside the school drinking from a cola bottle. Apparently it was laced with Wild Turkey. Margie—young, thin, and inexperienced with alcohol—was being taken to the hospital. We rushed to Hartford. Margie was having her stomach pumped. When I saw her I was still worried but relieved the doctors thought she would be okay. As I waited by her bed she woke up and told me, "I'm so sorry. I'll never drink again. I promise." She didn't keep that promise but she did understand how serious a problem drinking could be.

In middle school Margie smiled so no one could see her braces.

I promised Margie she could have her ears pierced when she turned thirteen. When the time came I mentioned that I had been thinking about having mine done too. Of course the girls were thrilled and insisted I should go with Margie. I was worried it would hurt too much, so Margie told me, "I'll get mine done first and I'll tell you if it's painful. Then you won't have to get yours done." She sat quietly through the procedure and at the end assured me, "It didn't hurt a bit."

The relief her assurance gave me quickly disappeared as I felt the quick sharp puncture in my right earlobe. Margie was looking out the window—avoiding eye contact. The pain was enhanced by my knowledge that the left ear must be done too. I certainly wasn't going around with a hole in one ear. Afterward, I asked Margie if it really hadn't hurt her. She grinned and told me, "Of course it did, but if I had told you, you wouldn't have had yours done. Ruth and Kathy warned me not to let you know."

We took teenage Margie and Colleen on a trip to Niagara Falls in our pickup camper, stopping at a campground in the Berkshires that had a swimming pool, which kept them entertained for hours. At Niagara Falls we went under the falls. They looked so cute in their yellow raincoats and boots.

Colleen often went with us on Ruth and Little Brother's three-day events. Margie and Colleen found many innocent ways to cause my hair to turn gray—like sneaking away to attend a local dance held at the racetrack where we camped for an event in New Hampshire. Ruth found them and brought two very sheepish girls back to the camper. Mostly, we just enjoyed having the two of them with us.

Thankfully, the majority of my memories of Margie's middle and high school years are of a bright hardworking student. Margie asked me to help her with a research report when she was in ninth grade. I spent hours showing her what to do. It was a very good paper so I was disturbed and amazed when she got a C for a grade. We decided the teacher thought Margie didn't do it. She wasn't too upset because she knew what she had learned would help her later.

Margie never needed to be reminded to do her homework. Once I asked her if she had finished it and she replied, "I always do it. You never had to ask before. Why now?" Why indeed? I never made that mistake again. She had already set goals for her life. When she was afraid she might lose track of them she asked to see a counselor before a serious problem developed. She established a relationship with a woman psychiatrist, Dr. Schaefer, that she maintained into her college years.

Margie had a mole over her left eye. It became the focus of Kathy's jokes and many times I'd hear her teasing Margie by calling her "mole face." Finally, when Margie was in high school, she'd had enough and asked to have it removed. I agreed because I knew a surgeon, Dr. Bloom, who had removed a cyst from my breast and left only a small scar. He removed her mole in his office. Margie wanted me with her. I agreed but panicked when I saw all the blood.

Margie had no serious health problems growing up. She did inherit her father's and my tendency to get cysts. She also had trouble with nosebleeds. One time I got a call from Suffield Middle School that she needed medical attention. I took her to a doctor and he cauterized it, but before we got home she was bleeding more than before. We had to go back so he could do it again.

When Margie turned sixteen, Larry and I took her to New York City for her birthday. A bizarre thing happened when we went to our room. We found a man sleeping or in a drunken stupor still in bed. We were given another room, but Margie used her imagination to create an intriguing mystery.

We went to Sardi's for lunch, saw *A Chorus Line,* and learned that Linda Ronstadt was at Radio City Music Hall. The only way we could get in was to buy tickets from the scalper outside the theater. We got two seats together toward the front and one further back. Larry gallantly volunteered to sit alone and Margie and I found our seats. A man in his late twenties was sitting in the seat next to me. He appeared to be sleeping with his head forward onto the back of the seat in front of him. After we had been seated for a while he sat up and asked me if I wanted to share his marijuana joint. I thanked him politely but refused the offer. Margie never forgot that. It was one of her favorite stories. She'd laugh as she told her friends, "My mother didn't get upset. She acted like it was a perfectly normal and acceptable suggestion. She was so cool."

Margie was shy and didn't date much in high school so she was amazed when she was asked to two proms. She looked so beautiful all dressed in the long feminine gowns that were popular at the time. I was happy for her. I was getting a glimpse of just how beautiful a woman she would be.

A shy Cinderella poses with her prom date.

Ruth and Kathy worked in tobacco as young teenagers. In Connecticut the tobacco is shade grown and it is hot and humid under the white gauze-like cloth that covers the plants. Many of the adults were migrant workers that were brought in each year. The girls were exposed to language and sexual remarks that I had only read in books. Physically, it was dirty, smelly work so they'd strip off their clothes and take long showers when they came home. Still the tobacco smell remained. They worked hard and faithfully and were rewarded with money that they got to spend on anything they wanted because I didn't have the heart to take it away from them. They were very well-dressed teenagers. Later their constant refrain became, "Why doesn't Margie have to work tobacco?"

Later Ruth went to work in a local drugstore. When she was older Margie worked for the same druggist for a while. Later she and Kathy worked at a nursing home. I'll never forget the night they came home and talked about putting a man in a body bag after he died. I knew my girls had grown up.

She's ready to begin her college career—high school graduation.

Evaluating Pain

A childless friend used to tell me
How painful baby showers were
    for her.
She mourned what she never had.
I didn't understand—still don't.
I felt your tiny fingers grip mine.
I nursed, bathed, and held you.
Watched you grow, looked at
    your beauty,
Marveled at giving birth to someone
    so lovely.

I laughed and giggled with you—
    and at you.

120

Scolded your thoughtless and careless deeds.
Took pride in all you accomplished.
Our futures appeared long and bright.

Which is worse? Her pain or mine?
Neither—they are just different.
I'm fortunate for I had you for a while.
No one can take that away from me.

But there will be no more happy memories.
No more long talks, or hugs, or kisses.
No more honors gained or goals reached.
No more tiny fingers—I'm just beginning to understand.

You won't be here when I'm old and feeble.
But you'll be waiting when I'm ready to join you.
We'll dance and hold each other.
What a celebration that will be!

But for now we continue to celebrate life both as it was before Margie's murder—BMM—and now, after Margie's murder—AMM.

CHAPTER 12

Celebrations, the Lonely Year, and Beyond

When November 1996 arrives there is no scurrying around to pick out the perfect birthday card for Margie and get a gift mailed on time. There will be no money sent for her to do something special—go out to dinner, buy flowers, or enjoy a special bottle of wine. No phone call. Last year on November 6th when Margie turned thirty-one, we were excited because she would soon be moving back East from California and we would be able to spend her thirty-second birthday together. Now she is with us—in a green marble urn in Ruth's family room.

I wake on Tuesday, November 5, 1996, Election Day, with an overwhelming sense of despair. Margie is constantly on my mind. I can't make myself get out of bed. Why should I? Who cares if Bill Clinton gets elected or not? Larry brings me my morning coffee in bed but is unable to find words to console or inspire me to crawl out of my cocoon. Here in my stupor I find not peace or solace, but a dulled sense of my pain.

A woman whose husband died unexpectedly when his dosage of medication was not monitored for toxic side effects calls. She tells me, "The day before the death anniversary or birthday is always the worst because of the anticipation and the question—how am I going to get through this?"

I go to the computer but can't concentrate on my book about growing up on the reservation. A poem begins to take shape as I wonder what Mitch said to her as he killed her. I call it:

Murderer's Incantation
or
What to say to your wife while stabbing her thirteen times

One—Here
Two—Take this,
Three—You bitch!
Four—You can't leave me.
Five—Whore!
Six—He doesn't love you.
Seven—Fool.
Eight—You're mine.
Nine—Forever!
Ten—Fuck You.
Eleven—You should have known
Twelve—I'd never let you go!
Thirteen—Got to stop—I'm tired.
Why Me?

We later learned that he stabbed her sixteen times. Guess I could now add Fourteen—I hate you, Fifteen—No one else will have you, Sixteen—Die, slut.

I show it to Larry and his comment is, "You certainly got in touch with your anger in that poem." Since I rarely feel my rage I interpret this as progress. I read somewhere that anger and depression are the same emotion, but depression directs the anger at yourself. Maybe. Right now I am thankful I can share my bounty with Mitch.

Ruth calls. "Ma, what are you planning to do tomorrow?"

"Stay in bed and cry all day."

"No, really. Abby thinks we should celebrate Margie's birthday in some way. Maybe Daddy can make veal Marsala and you can come over to our house."

Reluctantly I agree. All the books on loss and grief suggest that establishing rituals in memory of the loved one is an important part of the grieving and healing process. These ceremonies acknowledge the love we still share and help us survive painful reminders, including holidays.

I decide I will take her photo albums and some of mine. Abby loves to look at pictures. I spend hours, in bed, looking through moments caught on film and remember everything I can about what was happening surrounding the picture. I shed many tears.

Later I do vote but I'm definitely not up to celebrating anything, most certainly not a political victory.

I awake the next morning to find the woman is right: I can face today. I'm glad Bill Clinton will be our next president. I wonder how Margie would have voted. I'm sure Mitch would have wanted her to vote Republican.

Warden Lamer calls but he doesn't know it is Margie's birthday. It is good to talk to him. I explain that Mitch is giving us a hard time about settling the estate and I apologize about not having Margie's things removed from the house. I suggest, "If he gives us much more grief, we'll ask you to start charging him rent." Warden Lamer is willing to comply if it will help speed up the process.

We go to Ruth's for dinner. I have two albums and a small folder with pictures of our last trip together to visit Mitch's parents. It was a happy time. The photos show Abby hitting the ball Mitch was pitching to her and Jacob charming everyone with his eighteen-month-old antics. Jordan and Aileen, Mitch's parents, were plying the children with love and attention. We were all anticipating what it would be like when Margie and Mitch blessed us with a grandchild—our third and the Pasters' first.

Memories of the fun we've had with the Pasters are bittersweet now. They invited us to their home for Thanksgiving in 1995 when Margie took the job at Lewisburg. They made us feel so welcome. Abby wore a little Pilgrim outfit her mother made for her. She loved all the attention. Now, Abby and Jake want to know if we can still go to the Pasters' next summer for the Fourth of July fireworks. How do you explain the no? Losing Jordan, Aileen, and Michelle's friendship brings tears of sadness for everything both families have lost. Then anger at Jordan and Aileen creeps in. They didn't even send flowers to the funeral. I understand they probably felt unsure of our reaction and didn't want to add to our pain, but I think they should have risked it.

As we look at the albums, Abby enjoys the stories I tell her about Margie as a toddler, teenager, and college student, and the kind of daughter, sister, and aunt she was. Kathy does not want to look at pictures—too painful a reminder to her of why Margie isn't here. I'm different, I want to keep looking at pictures—maybe to soften the last time I saw her, which was dead in the casket.

Margie's Thirty-Second Birthday

I plan to stay in bed all day—cry a little,
recall the day Margie was born, the day she died,
feel my terrible loss and cry some more.

The pain of her premature birth without anesthetic,
so as not to harm the baby, was bad
but a precious soul came into the world.

The vicious killing, her premature death
leave me devastated and inconsolable.
Now I know a parent's greatest agony.

Tears and depression seem fitting
on this day of bittersweet remembrance,
contemplating the years ahead without her.

The veal Marsala, Margie's favorite meal, is tender and tasty, and we talk about the times Margie was with us at a restaurant or asked her dad to make it for her. What we all forgot is that the meal isn't complete without pecan pie—Margie's special dessert. Unfortunately, we could not find one in the local stores or bakeries and it was too late to make one. With deepest apologies to Margie, we promise there will be one next year, even if Daddy has to make it.

That fall at the flea market in Charlestown, Rhode Island, walking by Christmas stockings brings tears. I remember making each of my girls big red flannel ones with white trim and their names embroidered diagonally from top to bottom. What will I do with Margie's? At Christmas, we decide to put it on top of the urn with her ashes along with an angel figurine. I find the stocking we kept for Mitch; he is Jewish but always celebrated Christmas with us. I quickly put it away in an empty ornament box.

I know that Christmas Eve, when we open our presents, and Christmas morning, when we get our stockings, will be the most difficult holidays for us. We can't ignore them with two small children in the house, and Margie wouldn't want us to—she loved these times with her family and was always with us to celebrate. So was Mitch—for the last eleven years. Last year he wasn't going to come but Abby threw a fit: "I want my uncle Mitch to be here too." I'm sure Margie was happy he reconsidered and came.

Abby remembers that Mitch taught her how to spin the dreidel. She says, "Now I have no one to teach me about being Jewish."

This season of joy is very solemn for us. We try to show enthusiasm as Abby and Jake delight in their gifts, but Margie's absence is foremost in our thoughts. We recall the year Jacob was born when the tree tipped over—twice, when Margie was near it. We teased her unmercifully about knocking it over. I still hear her giggling denial.

After our usual quiet prime rib dinner on Christmas Day, I start vomiting and have diarrhea. Larry has felt bad for a few days and no doubt there is a bug going around as Ruth and Kathy also get sick, but I'm sure emotional stress is contributing to the severity of our symptoms. New Year's Eve is spent at home with our grandchildren, which is a family tradition that is as old as Abby. This year, I'm glad I don't have to party.

Each time we have an occasion to celebrate we also mourn our loss. My January birthday passes without Margie's call or card. On Valentine's Day I no longer send her money to do something special for herself. On March 1st, Abby gets no birthday visit from her aunt who made a particular effort to be with her on that special day.

Mother's Day always reminds me of her birth. One Friday before such a Mother's Day, I'm at court with two mothers who had sons murdered during the year. We joke about having a happy day. For Pam Cloud it is especially difficult because her son was born one May 6th and murdered on another May 6th. She did receive a belated Mother's Day gift—this May his killer was found guilty.

Memorial Day, Father's Day, Fourth of July, and Labor Day all hold special memories of her. So do family birthdays and Abby's dance recitals. Larry and I were happy Margie and Mitch went to her recital in June 1996 and took pictures. We weren't there because I was at my brother's funeral.

As the first anniversary of Margie's murder approaches, Larry and I make plans to go on a cruise to the Caribbean from August 9th to August 16th, 1997, with members of Survivors of Homicide. Dr. Henry Lee, the famous forensic pathologist from Connecticut, is traveling with us and will present a seminar. I look forward to this support in the time leading up to her death day.

It is our first cruise and we enjoy the shore excursion to Jamaica for river rafting. However, we finally realize we are being held hostage—until we agree to buy a gourd that our guide carved while taking us down the river. We pay too much and are quickly put ashore.

In Mexico we visit the spectacular Mayan ruins at Tulum, the only settlement they built near salt water. On Grand Cayman we take the Atlantis submarine trip one hundred feet below sea level. Large sea turtles and all kinds of fish appear in the waters. At Key West we ride the train that tourists take past Hemingway's home. All are interesting and divert our attention.

On the ship, we spend time with the other survivors and look forward to hearing Dr. Lee speak. We arrive at the designated room, where several people who are not members of our group have been watching a movie. When they learn Dr. Lee is going to speak, they refuse to give us their seats. He is a well-known, skilled speaker who uses humor to make distasteful topics palatable. We are dismayed by their behavior and the lack of support we get from the ship's staff—we have to adjust to the invasion by standing or taking seats in the back of the room.

Later, Survivors do have a private cocktail party with Dr. Lee. Larry and I have our pictures taken with him. We tell him our story and he offers to assist in developing the case. It helps to know he is willing to support us.

When the cruise is over, we fly home from Fort Lauderdale on August 16th with thoughts of this day a year ago when our world was changed so drastically. Soon we will be with Ruth, Kathy, Abby, and Jacob for our dinner ritual with Margie's favorite foods. As we eat the veal Marsala, and Abby and I look at the pictures of Margie, I begin to understand why one of the authors who writes about grief calls the second year the lonely year. Our loss occurred a year ago so some friends and family expect us to be "over it," or at least to suffer in silence.

Unfortunately, it doesn't work like that. Judy Smith and Bill Corey are the only friends, outside of our Survivor friends, who contact us to let us know they understand today is difficult for us.

Inevitably, events occur that cause us to relive the initial pain of our loss. One evening in August 1997, while I'm watching TV, the programming is interrupted by a special bulletin. Princess Diana has been rushed to a Paris hospital after being injured in a car crash. She, like Margie, had been struggling to get her life back together. I pray she will have that chance but the next day I learn that she too has died.

Abby and I curl up on my sofa watching the news unfold and she tells me, "Margie has probably met Princess Di by now. I wish I could have met her." I hug Abby as I ponder who Margie has met. But the agony Prince William and Prince Henry must feel is intertwined with my personal pain. The world's public mourning for this young woman whose life has been so open to scrutiny opens anew my private wounds.

Larry and I attend group counseling sessions provided by the state during the summer and then we begin private therapy sessions with Lillian Serrano, who was one of the group counselors. She is a skilled social worker and I do some very difficult work with her. Some survivors feel that anyone who has not survived a murder cannot possibly understand our loss and therefore is not able to help us. Larry and I do not find this to be true. Counselors only guide us along the path to healing—we provide the labor.

In my fifth session I express great respect for the person I used to be—or thought I was. I want to be her again. Suddenly, I burst into facetious laughter, "My God, I was a wonderful person." I know that is ridiculous. I was no saint. Then, I thought I had control of my life. Now, I know I don't and that makes me weak—which I can't stand.

I admit I have difficulty feeling my anger at Mitch for what he did. Lillian helps me understand I'm most likely reluctant to deal with my anger at Mitch until after the trial, which we believe will begin soon. She assures me this is okay and probably a wise decision.

"Did you ever get angry or annoyed at Margie?"

I smile as I remember. "Yes, I got tired of listening to her complaining."

Lillian helps me to stop glorifying who I was and who Margie was. We were both fallible human beings. Every once in a while, I need to replay that session in my mind when I start to fantasize about how perfect everything used to be.

The lonely year finally ends. August 16th is on a Sunday this year—1998. We begin observing the anniversary on Friday, the actual day of the week she was murdered. I had been working for weeks on an article about domestic violence that I planned to submit to a magazine on Sunday but finished early. When I went to the post office to get the right amount of postage, I learned large envelopes must be sealed, weighed, and sent out at the same time. I guess they think we might sneak in additional material. So the manuscript goes out on the twelfth—the same as the last day I talked to her two years ago. (After eight months the editors decide not to publish the article.)

Earlier in the week, when we were in Rhode Island, Calie came and lay on the bed, between Larry and me, with her head on our pillows. It felt like Margie was there with us. She loved to crawl into our bed as a child, and as an adult she would sit there talking to me. On Friday, Kathy, Abby, and Jake join us. As the trailer was the last place we saw Margie alive, it felt appropriate being there.

We return to Marlborough on Saturday and I keep busy with things I like to do. We go to dinner and rent two movies—*Midnight in the Garden of Good and Evil* and *As Good As It Gets*. We make plans to go to a powwow on Sunday because that was what we planned to do with Margie if she had lived to come home in August of 1996.

On her death day anniversary, after watching *Sunday Morning* on CBS, I work on my flowers, a task Margie and I both enjoyed. I do some weeding on the patio and because it is so very hot decide not to go to the powwow. I watch a Yankees ball game on TV in our air-conditioned living room. The game is tied for much of the time. The Yankees miss several opportunities to win, but in the ninth inning Bernie Williams hits a game-winning home run. I like to think Margie might have had something to do with it because I began asking for her help in the seventh inning. I learn some interesting trivia—this is the day, fifty years ago, that Babe Ruth died and twenty-one years ago so did Elvis Presley. Two years ago it was Margie who died.

Abby and Jake come downstairs and draw pictures of Margie for me. Then we look at photographs of her and have the veal Marsala and pecan pie Larry made. Shirley King calls but she doesn't remember that this is the day Margie was murdered. When I tell her she apologizes, "Maybe I shouldn't have called." If people only understood that we don't want to forget Margie. We can't forget the day she was murdered and a kind word helps so much.

Later, Larry and I watch a movie and read in bed. When I look at the clock it is one A.M. We have survived another anniversary but I think about that long drive to Pennsylvania and how exhausted we were at this time in the morning of the seventeenth—two years ago.

The year that follows is very busy. We have court dates, vacations, and many speaking engagements. We find it a little easier to get through the special days since we have been through all of them twice without Margie.

Meanwhile, the numerous court appearances, briefs, and appeals that began in 1996 seem to be never-ending. They are more about Mitch and his case than about Margie or our healing. But our memories of Margie keep us going and for each new event to have meaning I must be able to relate it to Margie in some way.

CHAPTER 13

The *Criminal* Justice System—1996 Style

After the bail hearing on August 19th, which Ruth attended, Magistrate Judge Askey schedules a preliminary hearing for Thursday, August 29th. However, the prosecutor presents the government's case to a federal grand jury on August 28th. Because grand jury proceedings are conducted in private, this keeps him from having to disclose evidence to the defense at the hearing. Only the grand jurors, witnesses, a court stenographer, and the U.S. attorney, in this case Wayne Samuelson, are present. Just the grand jurors remain during deliberations.

We are pleased to hear from Wayne that "the grand jury voted a true bill of indictment on the charges presented, which means Paster now stands charged with first-degree murder of your daughter." Everything is going according to schedule.

The next step in the process is Mitch's arraignment on the charge before a federal judge. Wayne tells us, "This will be a very short and simple proceeding. Paster will appear before the court with his defense counsel; I will represent the government." The judge will explain the charge and ask how Mitch pleads. Wayne has no doubt he will plead not guilty. It is the only way he can get a trial.

Wayne thinks the arraignment will be within two weeks and the trial scheduled for December, but explains, "Although the trial will be 'scheduled' for December, it will most certainly be conducted months after that. This is because the defense will undoubtedly file numerous pretrial motions, some of which will require hearings—

including testimony—and submission of written briefs on various legal issues." Truer expectations were never written.

The arraignment is scheduled for September 25, 1996, in Williamsport, Pennsylvania. On September 24th, Larry and I drive to Harrisburg airport where we pick up Ruth at 7 P.M. She has been in Chicago on business. We drive to the Days Inn in Lewisburg, where we have reservations. It may be painful staying at the same motel we were at the night of her murder, but the Country Cupboard, where we stayed last November when Margie moved here, is full. We plan to go to her house in the morning and to Graham Showalter's office at 2 P.M., before going to the arraignment at 4 P.M. We will leave for home when it is over.

The FBI released the house on September 23rd. When we arrive her car is still in the driveway but it has been moved. Donna Joy, the appraiser, and Michael Tafelski, an attorney for the Bureau of Prisons, meet us there. Michael tells us that the investigator for Mitch's attorney has been there and picked up Mitch's personal things. He also photographed and made a video of the house.

When we were there in August the house still felt lived in. Now, just over a month later, the empty house feels abandoned. No warmth or part of Margie remains even though her possessions are still here. It is deserted, lonely—lacking its original personality. I'm happy to leave when we have the trunk of the car filled with more of Margie's personal belongings—mostly clothes Ruth now feels she wants to have. Michael Tafelski is keeping a record of what we take that will protect us and the BOP (Bureau of Prisons) against claims Mitch may make.

Our meeting with Graham and Donna is brief. We get information about the Volvo and learn that Margie's student loans will indeed be paid off. The appraisal should be ready in two weeks but we learn that Mitch is claiming many of the items in the home were purchased by him before they were married—therefore his. We cannot get into the house to remove everything until these property issues are resolved.

We arrive at the Federal Court House in Williamsport early to meet for the first time with Mr. Samuelson, in his office, along with the two FBI agents assigned to the case. During this meeting he tells us he represents the government—not us. It is the federal government that is prosecuting Mitch. We as survivors have no role in the court proceedings until sentencing, when we will be allowed to make an impact statement before the judge.

I ask if we should hire our own attorney. I'm told we do have that right but we'll lose all rights to personally communicate with the prosecution team if we have our own attorney. All contact would be through our lawyer, isolating us more than now. Besides, that attorney would have no role in the court proceedings. Why bother? For the first time I realize we are truly alone, even though we are kept informed.

We are fortunate to have a sympathetic, skilled U.S. attorney. Now he tells us what will happen in the courtroom and assures us there is nothing to worry about. We go up one level to the courtroom.

The Pasters enter shortly after us. Ruth goes across the aisle and extends her hand. I'm proud of her. I wish I had done so. Jordan and I look at each other, he comes forward, gives me a hug, and says how sorry he is. Aileen hugs me and says the same thing. I think she looks awful. I hug her and tell her, "I know you are going through your own hell." She shrugs off my concern. Mitch's Aunt Fran hugs me, says she's sorry, but doesn't want to talk. Michelle, his sister, is distraught. Her face is swollen from crying. We hug and I tell her, "I love you." She says she loves me too. Ruth tells me Mitch came in and saw us hugging. Good. I hope he feels some remorse for what he has done. Margie was a strong bond between our families.

Mitch and his two attorneys look like triplets. All are short with dark hair and wear dark business suits. I wonder how anyone can defend a murderer when they know he did it.

Today in court we learn for the first time she was *getting out* of the shower when he killed her. Also, she spent the night before the murder at a local motel. She was at a social gathering with prison personnel and drove by the house. When she saw Mitch's car she wouldn't go home.

Jordan takes the stand and tells about the kind of son Mitch is and that he was a very concerned husband. He worried about his wife's drinking and her alleged affair. He only wanted to help her. Jordan reports he has seen Margaret drunk. He also knows Mitch is not a criminal.

Wayne shows Jordan an autopsy photo and asks him what he thinks when he sees it. Jordan is stunned speechless, then he murmurs something about how awful it is.

Mitch pleads not guilty to the charge and files a "motion for release from pretrial detention" along with proposed findings of fact and conclusions of law. Judge Muir tells the defense that Judge Askey has already ruled he be detained. Therefore, the request is a "motion for review of a detention order."

Court is adjourned. When the arraignment is over, Wayne Samuelson asks, "Why didn't he just walk away? Look at how many lives he's hurt."

I, too, have asked that question innumerable times.

We return upstairs, but this time to a small conference room to discuss the case further with Wayne and the FBI agents: Dick Rodgers and Harold Schmidle. Wayne sits at the end of the rectangular table. His back is to the window. I am at the other end near the door. Harold and Dick are on the side facing the door and Ruth and Larry have their backs to it. Wayne is an ex-marine whose hair is still short with a few flecks of gray in it. He is tall and trim, and wears glasses on a clean-shaven face that has strong regular features. He could have been on a recruiting poster representing the perfect marine. He is an attractive man in a light-colored suit who exudes strength and determination. He begins, "That went well and as expected. The bail hearing will be more involved. How are you folks doing? Any questions?"

We tell him we are okay and then I ask if the FBI was able to get anything from our phone's answering machine tape. Harold tells me they weren't but could do further tests if the need arose.

Months later I hear the police told Sam and Wanda Rieger, members of Survivors of Homicide, the same thing when their daughter was murdered. Then just before the trial, the police admitted they had gotten her murderer's threats from the tape. Their story will make me wonder if the FBI really could retrieve Mitch's message and will tell us this later.

I tell the three men, "Mitch called his mother before he called 911. We got their bill from the Buffalo Valley Telephone Company. There was a call to Caldwell, New Jersey, at 11:08 that morning."

134

They stare at me in stunned disbelief. The 911 call was placed at 11:13 A.M.

Ruth adds, "We know because I called the New Jersey number and his mother answered the phone. It was the law office where she works. I just hung up."

Wayne remarks, "So he got to talk to his mom and an attorney all with one call—convenient." Everyone nods.

Larry adds, "We're sure they're the ones who convinced him to call 911."

Harold asks if we have a copy of the bill with us. I do.

The trip home to Connecticut is a quiet one. We are all drained.

Later, we are given copies of the motions and briefs and reply briefs regarding release from detention (bail) to read. We will be making another trip to Williamsport—soon!

Defense reasons for release from detention include: Mitch does not pose a danger to the community nor a risk of flight. They argue that the court can impose conditions that will reasonably assure his appearance, including parental supervision, travel restrictions, regular reports to an appropriate agency, psychological or psychiatrist treatment, and the forfeit of bail. They argue that the chief of police of Montville, New Jersey, Carl DeBacco, has offered his services to monitor Mitch's movements. A report by Dr. Kool, a forensic psychiatrist, is given as proof that Mitch will not flee and is not a danger to himself or others.

In their written opposition to Mitch's release on bail, the government argues: Mitch admitted he stabbed his wife and she died from multiple stab wounds. The magistrate judge heard the same defense arguments and denied bail. Judge Askey did so because Mitch can get the maximum penalty of death or life imprisonment. The grand jury has indicted him for first-degree murder.

The government concludes that Judge Muir may review the case without holding a new hearing. All he has to do is consider the transcript of the hearing. The detention order should not be revoked unless it is clear that errors were made. Wayne's brief cautions that there are no conditions to reasonably ensure safety of persons in the community and the risk of flight is great. The crime was violent and the evidence is overwhelming.

The judge decides there will be a hearing to review the detention order. It will be in Williamsport Federal Court on October 7, 1996. Mitch's family had presented the court with letters from several family members and friends at the arraignment in September. We ask Wayne if we can write a letter opposing the granting of bail. He tells us to send him one but cannot assure us that the judge will choose to see it. On September 30, 1996, we send this letter:

Dear Mr. Samuelson,

The family of Dr. Margaret Bostrom opposes the granting of bail, in any amount, to Mitchell F. Paster. Due to the strong evidence against him and the likelihood of life-long incarceration, flight to another country is an attractive alternative. It is also a real possibility considering the support the family is receiving from friends and relatives.

Mr. and Mrs. Paster are honorable respectable people and would want to do the right thing. However, Mitchell is their only son. As parents, we understand their position. Keeping a son free, even if you couldn't be with him, has to appeal to their parental instincts. We would sacrifice everything we own to have Margaret back. Are we so different from the Pasters?

In the past, Mitchell has done things without parental approval. Certainly, they did not want him to kill Margaret. After a recent argument, he stole her dog and cat and took them to New Jersey. We do not believe his parents approved of this behavior, but the only way Margaret was able to get them back was to agree to talk about a reconciliation. She had to go pick them up. We do not believe the Pasters have the necessary influence on Mitchell's behavior to guarantee he will be available for trial if granted bail.

Ruth Grover, Margaret's sister and mother of Abigail and Jacob, now has the dog. She is concerned that Mitch may try to contact her or her children, or take the dog again.

The letters of support from all of Mr. and Mrs. Paster's friends are a touching tribute to the family. Would these letters be the same if Margaret were a local Montville woman or the daughter of a friend or neighbor? We think not. Many expressed surprise that anything like this could have happened. They would not have predicted his violent act of stabbing Margaret thirteen times. Mitchell can be charming in non-stressful situations. This is exactly our point. When Mitchell feels out of control we cannot predict his behavior. Bail will only serve to give him more options.

We think Mitchell murdered Margaret because he was losing control of her. Now, he must feel that he has totally lost control. What does he have to lose by fleeing?

Sincerely,
Margaret Bostrom's family

We are told Judge Muir chose not to see the letter, but Wayne makes several of these points in his oral opposition to Mitch's release on bail.

The bail hearing goes well for us. Mitch is ordered to remain in detention until his trial takes place. We sigh with relief. At least we will know he is in jail—not exactly where, because we have been told he is being moved from one county jail to another, for his protection, as space is available. *Oh yes, let's be sure we protect him.*

We have a quiet month. In early November I go to a Connecticut Writing Project retreat for writers at Wisdom House in the Litchfield Hills of Connecticut. My writer friends—Pat K, Mary, Penny, Jenny, Jo, Sheila, Anne, and Kathy—are all very helpful. We stay up until 2 A.M. on Saturday night talking about death after Pat reads my poems about Margie aloud to the group. Anne gives me a bookmark with "'Love never changes" written on it. Each of us has suffered from the death of a loved one and experienced grief, so healing takes place for all of us. It is a productive weekend even though my memoir, *Allegheny Native*, doesn't receive the attention I planned to give it.

Sunday, as I'm driving up the small incline near home, Larry is out walking Delilah. I stop and he tells me my aunt Margaret called. My uncle, her brother, is in the hospital suffering from a serious heart attack and pneumonia. He is unconscious, heavily medicated, and on a respirator. Rance is a very special uncle—my mother's oldest brother. Fortunately he does survive and lives for a year-and-a-half longer. We visit him during the summer of 1997 and he looks great.

Next Larry says, "Wayne Samuelson called. Mitch's lawyers are presenting a motion to suppress the FBI confession so it cannot be submitted as evidence."

This news brings back my fears, which resulted from my conversation with Dick Rodgers, on August 17th, when he would not confirm or deny that Mitch was read his rights. I was upset for two weeks until Wayne Samuelson assured me Mitch was informed. Now, three months later, it may be a problem after all.

The hearing is scheduled for Friday, November 22nd. Right before Thanksgiving. We know we have to go. It means we will miss our first meeting of Survivors of Homicide so I call Wanda. I learn more about her daughter's murder. Melanie was killed by a jealous boyfriend with whom she was trying to break up. Control issues were involved but he also threatened her and her family. He was found guilty and sentenced to sixty years in prison. Melanie was murdered on May 24, 1994. Two-and-a-half years later their pain is still raw. I gain the knowledge that my grieving will never be over.

Ruth isn't going this time because Larry and I want to leave during the day on Thursday. It gets dark so early in November, why take unnecessary risks driving after dark? I take my computer in the car and spend the time writing, mostly to meet a deadline on my memoir. It makes the trip pass more quickly.

We stay at the Country Cupboard this time and eat at Rusty's Café, where we went once before with Margie, Ruth, and Abby. We also went there with Ruth on a previous visit.

Friday morning we are at Showalter's office for an 8:30 meeting. As administrators of Margaret's estate, we have not received a completely acceptable accounting of their assets, including wedding gift money of ten thousand dollars, eighteen thousand dollars cleared on the sale of the house, and where the eleven thousand plus dollars paid to Cornell University came from. There is a bill for forty-five hundred dollars on Margie's credit card and we don't know what was charged. We believe Mitch paid for his new computer with it. Mitch bragged about stocks he had, but we cannot confirm this. We never will get a truly satisfactory accounting of all the funds. He claims the money isn't there. Maybe not, but where did it go?

There are new developments: Margaret's name has been taken off the lease for the Volvo and Mitch's family have agreed to take care of that matter. Mitch will allow us to sell the marital property but still insists most of the bedroom and living room furniture are his because he purchased them before they married. Maybe, but Margie helped pick them out and they were probably paid for by credit cards, in both their names, which weren't paid off when they got married. The attorney and his assistant expect us to make decisions. We can't. We thought we only had to sign a few checks before we went to Williamsport. These things seem unimportant compared to what we face at 10 A.M.

When we enter the courtroom we are surprised to see Michael Tafelski, an attorney for the BOP. We sit next to him. Mitch is the first to testify. It is our first chance to see his face or hear him testify. He does not look good. He has gained weight and he appears depressed. I wonder what it must be like to know your whole life could be spent in a prison cell. However, my sympathy is short-lived. When he begins to talk he is very self-centered.

His family must have gone through hell knowing he killed Margaret, not knowing what was happening to him. The defense elicits the information that Mitch called his mother and that the attorney she works for told him to call 911. They must have found out we knew about that call. The defense states in its findings of fact statement that Mitch's parents had tried to contact him several times that day. Mitch alleges the FBI refused his many requests to talk to his mom. They would only let him talk to her if he finished answering their questions. When the judge asks if he was allowed to talk to her when the interrogation was over, Harold Schmidle replies, "He never asked to, your honor." I believe he cares for no one but himself—not Margie; not his mom, dad, or sister; and certainly not us.

He complains of rough, threatening treatment. He gives the example of a jumpsuit being pulled up on him so hard it hurt his groin. He claims he overheard a guard say, "He'll not last long in prison when one of those big boys get hold of him."

Mitch, at some point during the day of murder, was handcuffed by a BOP officer—for his own protection and that of others. The defense suggests the concern was that he might hurt himself. Later, the officer explains he was trying to ensure that Mitch did not hurt anyone or get another weapon that may have been in the house at the time.

The defense claims Mitch was subjected to repetitive forceful orders by the agents of U.S. Penitentiary (USP) and the FBI. These claims are later denied by personnel from both agencies. In fact, his

139

handcuffs were removed at the training center where the FBI took him for interrogation late that afternoon. He was offered cigarettes, sodas, water, and food while there.

Mitch describes himself as having been distraught, wanting to call his parents and unable to focus at the time of the interview. On the stand, it appears to me that when he thinks an answer will get him in trouble, he says, "I don't recall." He says he can't remember if they read him his rights or not. He hadn't been able to read the form because he couldn't focus on it. He is shown a signed form and confirms, "Yes—that's a shaky version of my handwriting." The defense claims he signed it because of "surrounding pressures and in response to false promises" and "Paster was led to believe he would be incarcerated at Lewisburg if he did not cooperate with the agents."

That would have been all right with me. Margie's friends are there.

Mitch also claims that people were leering in the windows at him. He complains about having to remove all his clothes, except boxer shorts, and stand exposed, while handcuffed, with the blinds up for forty-five minutes before pictures were taken. The photographer refutes these claims. He says it was more like ten minutes and the blinds were lowered when Mitch asked that they be.

I want to shout, "What about Margaret having to lie naked and dead for men to see and touch?"

On cross-examination, Wayne shows photographs that prove the blinds were drawn when the pictures of Mitch were taken. He also elicits the information that there were red stains on Mitch's clothes and the phone. Mitch admits they look like blood. The photographs also show a red mark on his face.

The BOP plumbing foreman, Timothy Kline, who was told to guard Mitch, reports he sat with Mitch in the dining room while other people were up in the bathroom with Margie's body and Mitch kept saying, "Oh, my God! Why me?" repeatedly. He never once asked about his wife.

I want to stand up and shout, "Oh, my God! Why my daughter?" Why me? I'm glad he didn't think to fake concern.

Kline also testifies that Bill Corey was the first to touch Margie's body. He tried for a carotid pulse—there was none. She was dead.

The judge adjourns for lunch and we go across the street to a small restaurant with Michael Tafelski. He tells us we are still part of the USP family and they are very interested in seeing Mitch get a just penalty.

After lunch Wayne cross-examines Mitch. "How old are you?"

"I'm now thirty."

"August 16 of 1996 you were twenty-nine; is that correct?"

"That's correct."

"You're a college graduate?"

"That's correct."

"And when did you graduate college?"

"Nineteen-eighty-eight."

"And what college?"

"The University of Connecticut."

"And what was your degree?"

"I had a bachelor of science in business."

"And you were born in the United States."

"That's correct."

"You read and understand English; is that correct?"

"That's correct."

I think Wayne has shown Mitch's claim he didn't know what he was signing for the agents is questionable and self-serving.

Wayne continues. "All right. Now, on August 16th, at about 11:15 A.M., you called Emergency Services; is that right? You testified to that; is that correct?"

"That's correct."

"Why did you call them?"

Mr. Kyle Rude, one of his attorneys, objects to this question as beyond the scope of direct examination. After a brief discussion, the judge decides Mr. Rude opened it up and overrules the objection.

Wayne asks again, "Why did you call emergency personnel?"

Mitch responds, "I was told to."

"You were told to. By whom?"

"By an attorney."

"By an attorney. Okay. And where was the attorney? Was he at your house?"

"No, sir."

"Where was this attorney?"

"In New Jersey."

"And how did you happen to talk to that attorney?"

"I had called my mother at her place of work."

"And this was before you made the 911 call; is that correct?"

"That is correct."

Later, Wayne asks, "Now, you didn't tell anyone throughout that day you had talked to an attorney, did you?"

"I was never asked that question."

"Okay, but you never told anyone that, did you?"

"I didn't know I had to."

Wayne continues with questions about the blood on Mitch's clothes and body. Then he moves on to Mitch's complaints about the blinds being open in the dining room where he waited during the day. Mitch admits that some of the blinds were closed when he asked for them to be. Then Mitch is shown photographs taken of him in that room that reveal the blood and blinds that are closed.

Later, Wayne asks, "And you said no one explained the condition of your wife at that time; is that right?"

"That's correct."

"You never asked about her condition, did you?"

Mitch doesn't respond, and Wayne asks, "You never once asked about her condition while you were in the house, did you?"

"No, I did not."

"Did you at any time while you were at the Training Center [with the agents] ask about the condition of your wife?"

"No, I did not."

"Because you said all you wanted to do was stay alive and talk to your parents; is that correct?" Mitch agrees that is what was primarily occupying his thoughts at that time.

When Mitch is excused, I think that I'm glad I'm not him. I don't think he helped his case much. The prosecution has effectively responded to each defense claim, I believe.

When court is dismissed we go to Wayne's office. He is feeling very good about how it went. "If they are smart they won't put Mitch on the stand again. He isn't a strong witness." Wayne theorizes that maybe they asked for the suppression hearing just to see what kind of witness Mitch would make.

Wayne's teenage daughter is in court today. She had a day off from school and wanted to see Dad at work. I tell Wayne, "I'm sure glad you are on our side. I wouldn't want to be cross-examined by you." His daughter readily agrees and says she is never going to get on his wrong side again. We all laugh. She has no desire to become a lawyer, however.

Today, three months after the murder, we learn Mitch was not the first or only suspect. The FBI hadn't heard the content of the 911 tape until Sunday afternoon and were unaware he told that operator he had stabbed his wife. The camp inmates on work detail were questioned and accounted for. Bill Corey was taken to the prison and questioned. Ironically, he was in marriage counseling with his wife.

The defense states in its closing, "In short, the government, through whatever organization was supervising him at the time, created a puppet, and that puppet was doing whatever they wanted him to do during the interrogation...When he was asked questions, they [the supervising organizations] were answering...his will was overborne."

The government argues, "In the statement it says he remembered getting the knife and he remembered coming back down the stairs afterwards, and that, oh, the knife was in the sink because that is where he thought he heard someone say it was. But he doesn't even admit to that.

"He, in essence, wants to divorce himself from the entire situation but only lay out any possible justifications that he may have for his actions on that day; and we submit there are none." (Mitch talked at length about the events leading up to the murder and what Margaret had done to provoke him.)

We drive to Connecticut and wait for a decision. Thanksgiving comes. We still don't know what the judge has decided. Harry and Terry Fitzgerald and Margie's friend Hope are the only friends or family who call to offer love and support on Thanksgiving. Their thoughtfulness means so much. Larry and I laugh about Margie calling us from San Diego for directions on how to prepare a turkey. We missed having her home for Thanksgiving all those years. We were looking forward to being with her this year. If the USP at Lewisburg was in lock-down we would have gone there. Or maybe we would have returned to the Pasters', where we had such a wonderful time last year. But that was not to be. We try to be thankful in spite of our loss.

On December 8, 1996, Wayne calls. We are relieved to hear Judge Muir has denied Mitch's request for suppression of the FBI interrogation. There will be no more trips to Williamsport in 1996. We now face our first Christmas without Margie and with the knowledge that the task of emptying out the house on the reservation at Lewisburg still lies ahead.

CHAPTER 14

Our Last Trip to Her Home
on the USP Reservation

The arrival of 1997 brings little solace. We have a new potential court date for jury selection—February 13th, 1997. Larry and I have rented a modular home in Englewood, Florida, from January 15th to March 15th. What should we do? By now we are skeptical about the likelihood of it happening, even though we acknowledge the possibility we may need to travel to Williamsport during that time, so we don't change our plans.

We begin to feel we are imposing on Warden Lamer and his staff, who have been extremely understanding and patient regarding our inability to remove Margaret's belongings. The prison has been in lock-down but that hasn't caused the delay. It is because we cannot get Mitch's release for us to buy or sell the belongings. Finally we receive word he has agreed.

Relieved, we leave Ruth's home about 7:15 A.M. on Monday, January 6, 1997. I am vaguely aware of the pain and distress that going through Margie's things will cause. We arrive in Lewisburg at noon and go to the restaurant at the Country Cupboard to eat lunch and call Donna. She has Mitch's signature so we go to Graham's office, sign the agreement, and make out a check for Mitch's half of the appraised value of the estate, which will be deposited through his attorney in a bank account for Mitch.

Donna tells us she was at a social gathering for Dick Rodgers, who is retiring from the FBI. A former psychologist at the prison who trained Margaret before he retired, told her we should be suing the government. "Bill's attention to Margaret was sexual harassment and the government should have stopped it." Mitch's complaint to the prison would help our case. We know Margie wanted the affair with Bill and she was worried he would lose his job. She would hate it if we helped cause that to happen. They were both adults and did what they wanted to do. We can't morally hold the government responsible and we don't want to go against Margie's wishes. Her involvement with Bill helped her gain enough strength to pursue the divorce from Mitch, which she had determined she wanted. She felt it was too soon to be concerned with how that new relationship would eventually develop, but she did not want Bill to be blamed for it. Larry, Ruth, and I are not ready to consider suing, at least not now. As Larry says, "If we sue now the very people who are currently representing us will become our adversaries." Our purpose presently is to see that Mitch gets justice. We don't need distractions.

We check into the motel and wait for word from Michael Tafelski that we can go to the house. At about 2:30 P.M. Michael lets us in the house and leaves us to our grim task. We work from 3 to 6:30 P.M., sorting, saving, and discarding. We find Margaret's and Mitch's goals written down. I'm reminded of how upset she was the last time we saw her—because of these goals, but she had reached some of hers. She had lost the weight she previously gained, passed the licensing exam for psychologists, and been promoted to level thirteen at work.

Mitch's goals were:

1. to play on the Cornell football team
2. to network at Cornell
3. to get high grades
4. to be financially stable
5. to invest in the stock market
6. to eat right and take care of his body

I tell Ruth, "Unfortunately his behavior is keeping him from reaching most of these goals. I notice there is no goal about working on his marriage. I guess saving their relationship wasn't important enough to warrant a goal."

Little things are precious reminders of Margie. There is the perky little bright green alligator candle sitting on the sink in the spare bathroom and a memo pad holder that looks like a black and white cow's head whose mouth you open to get the paper. A lizard, bought in the Southwest on her cross-country trip to begin the career she had trained eleven years to do, crawls up a wall in the sunroom.

I carefully pack the little snowman that moves in a jerky little walk when it is wound up. Jake will enjoy this. I wonder where she got it and if she had kept it for him.

In the kitchen I imagine the fun she had buying the teakettle that looks like a black cat. I marvel at how perfect the basket she used to hold her dish towels looks and wonder where she got the idea. I'll never know. I'll take her cookbooks to Kathy, who loves to cook.

I remember being with Margie at the Wadsworth Atheneum in Hartford when she bought the print by the Hudson River artist Albert Bierstadt, which now hangs over the mantle in her living room. Her dad and I bought the Salvatore Dali prints at the museum of his work in St. Petersburg, Florida. They'll hang in my home now. I have always been pleased I was able to pass my interest in art on to all my daughters.

Sitting on the cold, paint-flaked, concrete floor of the basement, I go through box after box of files, keeping any reports or notes she had written. I have this nagging feeling I'm missing something important—something that would help me understand why she stayed with Mitch so long or more about who she was.

I'm not prepared for the gut-wrenching sense of finality I feel when I'm forced to sort through the backup materials for her dissertation. I wonder how much Margie's personal contact with alcoholism and problem drinking has influenced her choice of a subject for her dissertation. All three of my brothers suffered from the disease. Margie witnessed her sister's battle to overcome addiction and felt the devastating effects it had on our family.

During Margie's teenage years Larry had a very demanding job as an electrical engineer and I was a special education coordinator. Having three teenage daughters, the farm, an old house in need of remodeling, and three horses added more stress. Larry and I used alcohol to relax and drank too much during those years. Fortunately, we easily reduced our drinking as the number of stressors diminished. Since Margie's death we recognize that alcohol does not provide escape. We have chosen to face our pain with the help of each other, our family, our friends, and Survivors of Homicide.

I find her dissertation, *The Relationship Between Parental Alcoholism, Family Environment, Alcohol Expectancies and Drinking Styles in Adult Males*, which she never had bound. The acknowledgments confirm her love for all of us, including Mitch. The following is a quote:

> I am indebted to my parents who inspired me to pursue my goals with their love, understanding, and support both financially and emotionally and for their reassurance and belief in me. I also want to thank Mitch for standing by me through all my years of school, for moving across the country, and for his love, tolerance, and support.

Why? Such a tragic loss. All the time and energy she used to get her Ph.D.—would she have spent her time differently if she had known how little time she had? Quickly I direct myself away from such useless thoughts. I carefully put her dissertation aside. I'll have two copies made and bound to give to Abby and Jacob when they are older.

As the discard pile grows so does my sense of loss. I know that some of what she wrote she never intended for us to see. I feel like I'm invading her privacy—similar to what a mother feels when she reads a teenager's diary, I suppose. Then I tell her, "If you didn't want me to see this you shouldn't have gotten yourself killed." I sound flip, but that notion helps me to continue my gruesome task. I read this weekly journal entry she had done for a class:

> After class I found myself feeling very lucky to have both my parents living. I often take for granted that they will always be there for me forgetting that some day they will die. I know that I will never be prepared to deal with their death but now, at least, I will not take them for granted. My first experience dealing with the death of a close relative was four years ago when my grandmother died. She was the only living grandparent I had....My grandmother lived in upstate New York which was over five hundred miles from where I was in Connecticut. I decided not to go

to her funeral. In retrospect, I wish I had gone because I think attending her funeral would have made her death a reality. Although I mourned her death that week, I think, in many ways I denied it.

My sister (Kathy) was very close to my grandmother and was devastated by her death. She has tried to bring up my grandmother's death on many occasions. However, our family usually changes the subject....In the future, when my sister brings up my grandmother; I am going to listen and respond instead of moving on to another topic of conversation.

It is ironic that Margie worried about dealing with our deaths and never had to deal with them. She was going to listen to Kathy talk about the death of her grandmother, but her sisters don't feel comfortable when I talk about Margie's death. A parent isn't supposed to have to do this. Margie should be here to help Ruth, when I die, sort through my disorganized papers and materials gathered throughout a long life.

In a later entry she writes about volunteering to share in class:

Initially, I was afraid I would not be able to control the degree of exposure that volunteering implies, however; I never felt uncomfortable or that things were getting out of hand.

Since participating in class, I have found it easier to balance school and practicum with my outside interests. Once I realized I was not alone in my lack of motivation, I was able to accept that part of myself. Furthermore, once I gave myself permission to spend time doing things I enjoy; I was able to concentrate more on my school work.

...I never realized that I am usually harder on myself than other people are on me. It felt good to hear others' approval and validation of my feelings.

I have often wondered how hard it was for Margie to stay focused on getting her Ph.D. Now I know she struggled at times with the long process. I'm glad someone gave her permission to pursue other activities—have some fun. In the last entry for that class she wrote about a visualization exercise:

I was surprised at how easily I slipped into my imaginary world. All of a sudden, I was able to utilize all of my senses. I could feel the sun warming me through the trees. I could hear the birds singing and the wind blowing through the trees. I could smell the pine scent. I saw the forest, the animals, and the winding pathway all around me.

At first I had trouble with the wise figure. Eventually I pictured an old man with a long white beard, dressed in a white robe. He had a kind, gentle face. I trusted him immediately. He told me that the answer to my question (What is the secret to happiness and self-confidence?) was inside of me. The wisdom would come to me when I was ready to take the steps necessary to achieve my dream of contentment and inner peace.

Then he gave me three gifts: a mirror, a pair of eyeglasses, and a key. The mirror would allow me to see both my inner and outer self more clearly. The glasses would let me view others without distortion. The key would give me the ability to return to the forest whenever I wanted to and to seek the answers to other questions.

I think my dad would be proud of this third-generation storyteller. I feel happy for her as I read the teacher's comments:

Margaret, you are so beautiful—inside and out—those gifts were wonderful. You might consider mentioning them in class—others may want similar gifts for themselves.

You are showing yourself that there is so much inside of you. So much that is wise. Also so much that you have kept hidden from yourself.

I find a folder that has several letters of recommendation. I read them and get a better sense of how capable she was and the respect her supervisors felt for her. Dr. Frederick G. Humphrey, a professor of Family Studies at the University of Connecticut wrote:

In appearance Margaret is always attractive, neat and well groomed. She demonstrates an emotional maturity beyond her years and always uses excellent judgment....I have been on or chaired our Graduate Admissions Committees many times over the 25 years of my University teaching and I believe Margaret to be one of the most able and fine candidates for doctoral studies that I have had the pleasure of admitting and teaching. Were she to apply to our own doctoral program in Family Studies I have no doubt that she would be readily accepted.

I feel so much pride before the pain and the enormity of our loss take over. If only Margie had shown the same good judgment in her personal life. Margaret's supervisor at Altobello, an adolescent psychiatric hospital, found her to be an integral part of their multi-disciplinary treatment team. He wrote:

> Her insights into the patients and their families were immensely valued by our evaluation team as she was able to integrate a scientific attitude with an empathetic understanding of family dynamics.

Margie had a friend, Jenny, at California School of Professional Psychology—San Diego (CSPP) whose father was a professor. He employed Margaret as a research assistant and worked on her doctoral dissertation committee. His letter contained the following statements:

> Ms. Bostrom has performed her job functions superbly. She has displayed an impressive degree of motivation and independence, as well as intelligence, insight, maturity, sensitivity, interpersonal skills, good writing ability, and the ability to respond well to feedback. I have seen her demonstrate these same exceptional attributes in her work on her nearly completed doctoral dissertation, a fine study on alcoholism. She has evidenced extreme interest in the subject matter of clinical psychology, along with sincere dedication to the profession. I recommend her highly and without reservation for any position she seeks.

Wow! I don't think, as her mother, I could have said it better. Dr. Paul Goldstein, the clinical coordinator at Harmonium Counseling and Community Services, writes this about Margaret:

The main impression I have of Ms. Bostrom is that I was frequently surprised and impressed by the quality of her clinical work. The surprise has come from the fact that she was so unassuming and modest about her own accomplishments and abilities, which contrast markedly with her actual level of clinical competence....I was quite impressed with Ms. Bostrom's willingness to take risks in order to expand her experience and improve her skills.

None of my girls ever "brag" about themselves. They let people find out for themselves how capable they are. I think Dr. Goldstein was fortunate to have that chance. I particularly enjoy Shawn Miyake's personal touch:

Ms. Bostrom has displayed a willingness to perform tasks outside her job description and on occasion, has come in on days off to fill in for co-workers in other departments. Furthermore, she has dealt with difficult situations admirably. One such situation involved a patient who presented a challenging placement problem. Ms. Bostrom worked diligently on finding a placement that would benefit this patient. She looked for creative solutions to obstacles, while working together with co-workers and outside agencies. When she found an ideal placement for this patient, the physician was so appreciative, he brought in a cake to her unit.

That must have delighted Margie. This incident gives me a clear picture of her contributions—as a professional member of a team. Dr. Lorraine Watson, director of clinical services at Bayview Hospital and Mental Health System, supervised Margaret's post-doctoral training. She wrote:

Dr. Bostrom has functioned as the "senior" psychology intern, responsible for providing informal supervision for pre-doctoral interns working in the various hospital programs. During her tenure at Bayview, I have found Dr. Bostrom to be a highly competent, responsible and enthusiastic professional. She is viewed by peers and colleagues as a very strong member of our multidisciplinary team. She has demonstrated superior psychological assessment and report writing skills and has been helpful to other interns, provid-

ing peer supervision. Her clinical judgment and ability to inter-
face with a large multidisciplinary staff is outstanding....

Dr. Bostrom has demonstrated excellent skills in working with
very difficult psychiatric populations. She has been able to effectively manage patients with overt psychotic symptoms without
interfering with the therapeutic tone of her groups....I recommend her without reservation.

I am struck by the progression I see in her skills and confidence
from the first letter to the last. She demonstrated real growth. I'm
pleased with what I see but also feel a strong sense of loss. What
would she have been able to accomplish if she had been allowed to
live out her life? We'll never know—I can only fantasize.

I skim through papers filled with her personal and professional
observations. All of them are now precious—because there will be
no more. Her life and her career are over. I see checklists where she
describes me as a caring mother who listened to her and praised her.
She recognized I was interested in her and felt that I encouraged her.
She understood I was proud of her and liked being with her. She did
feel that sometimes I was too busy to pay attention to her and I
forgot to do things I was supposed to do for her. *I wouldn't be too busy
or forgetful now. I promise you that, Margie.*

The results of the psychological testing she did on all of us are
neatly filed along with her interpretations. I'll keep them to study at
a future time. On a questionnaire about male sex partners, she admits to being jealous of Mitch's old flames and reports that he did
physically abuse her once. Another checklist is about her perceptions of herself and there is one on family alcohol use I'll look at
later. I add these papers to my stack of mementos I collected upstairs. Before we go back to the motel, I take pictures of the bathroom
and the outside of the house. I want to remember the details.

We go to dinner at the Temperance House in Lewisburg. It is a
nice restaurant we found accidentally the last time we were in
Lewisburg. During the meal I feel uncomfortable and can't finish my
food. Later that evening I have severe diarrhea and projectile vomiting similar to what I experienced at Christmas. We have all been
battling a particularly nasty strain of the flu, even though we received shots. I'm sure the emotional strain of our loss and the holiday

season have also weakened our systems. I face the emotional stress of moving day, drained and with less than four hours of sleep.

When we arrive at the house at 9 A.M. on Tuesday, there are at least six packers ready to begin work. They each take time during the day to express their sympathy and some remind us that they were the ones who moved Margie into the house in November 1995. Repacking her things, because Mitch killed her, is difficult for them.

Tom Bruno, from the office of Mitch's attorney, is here to pick up more of Mitch's personal things. Yesterday I placed Mitch's Christmas stocking that Margie made for him with a box of his family photos. I also jokingly suggested that a small bottle of champagne from their wedding, found in the large cherry hutch, be given to him since everyone at their wedding received one. Later, Ruth tells me she did put it in Mitch's pile. We feel a bit guilty because we know his parents will go through his things—not Mitch.

We have agreed to allow Mitch's family to purchase, at the very low appraised price, Margie's china and a Lladro bride and groom they gave her as a wedding present. The movers agree to pack them first so Mr. Bruno can take them.

Mr. Bruno thanks us for being civil to him. I ask, "What good would it do to be vengeful with you? You didn't do anything to us."

He answers, "You'd be surprised. Lots of people take out their anger on anyone who is aiding their murderer."

I respond, "This is a very hard situation. Everyone is suffering—even Mitch in his own sick way."

Mr. Bruno looks out the window and responds in a quiet resigned tone, "You would hope so." As a former policeman who is now a paralegal, he explains, "I went to college so I wouldn't have to do things like this," while he points at Mitch's possessions and laughs at himself.

We learn from Mr. Bruno that Mitch will never get to spend the money from the sale of the property. Under the Pennsylvania Slayers' Act it will be kept in trust to be returned to Margaret's estate upon his death, but he can use the interest. When we signed the agreement we didn't think it was fair but had accepted that Mitch would spend this money on his defense. We wonder if he thought he could too. Certainly we have no objection to this restriction. However, this information clarifies the purpose of the slayers' act, which previously seemed to protect his interests.

At 10 A.M. the auctioneer, who was also the appraiser, comes with his daughter to take the things we don't want or can't use. We decide the blue-and-white flowered love seat, which Margie insisted on buying when they moved to Poway, is in poor condition and not worth keeping. Sebastian, the cat, has clawed it badly and Calie has chewed the cushions. This decision is right but feels bad. Somehow the scratches and chewed cushions are part of Margie. We decide to take the matching sofa, which is in better shape. The large office desk, printers, now-empty file cabinets, and the baker's rack she bought when we were here in 1995 are all to be sold along with coffee mugs and Tupperware containers. We will receive three hundred dollars for the items sold at auction.

Ruth wants the hutch that is in the dining room. Margie and Mitch both were so proud when they bought it at an auction for their home in Poway. It is a lovely piece of furniture and was out of place with their lighter California-style furniture—but they were planning for the future.

We have planned our apartment with the bedroom furniture, entertainment center, and glass-topped kitchen set in mind. I find that her things make me feel closer to her. The fish print that hung over her toilet, along with other fish pictures, will provide splashes of color in my all-black-and-white bathroom. We purchased them on a visit to the Stephen Birch Aquarium-Museum, which is on a hill above Scripps Institution of Oceanography in La Jolla, California.

The food is separated into three piles. One pile is for the local food kitchens, one is damaged or opened containers to be discarded, and the last pile is what we will take with us to Connecticut. These include the more unique items—guava jelly and black bean dip. I even take the microwave popcorn to try out in my new microwave at our apartment in Ruth's house.

Warden Lamer, his wife, and daughter Tamara stop to visit. We hug and I'm again impressed with the genuine compassion they show. Their daughter is bright, open, and friendly. Her parents beam, proud of the daughter they have raised. We are happy she has Margie's psychology books and magazines. She tells us, "When I become famous and successful I am going to establish a center and name it after Margaret." She touches my heart and I wish her success.

Mrs. Lamer tells us she wants us to visit their home on top of the hill—outside the walls of Lewisburg Federal Penitentiary—when we return for the trial. The warden is retiring in June. Because of court delays we never get to make that visit. Already the people who knew Margie are leaving Lewisburg. It starts me to thinking about an appropriate memorial in her honor at the penitentiary.

Margie loved gadgets. She had every imaginable one. We take the Brita water purifier, a tiny snack-sized Crock-Pot, the bread machine, salad spinner and shooter, an electrical extension cord neatly wrapped on a plastic holder, a glue gun, and all her little containers.

Steve wants the headboard and frame from the waterbed, but first the mattress must be drained. Larry finally finds the tools, hoses, and directions to complete the job. The auctioneer doesn't want the mattress or its supports. The movers, who are kind and helpful, move them to the discard pile in the garage.

Margie enjoyed flowers and plants. Each time she went to Mexico or Old Town San Diego she returned with new pots. I take them— some have never been used. I wonder what she planned to put in them. I'm reminded of the jade plant we were able to put in her front yard in Poway. I wonder if it is still growing. We bought Margie a green plastic lounge and six white chairs in California and took them to her home in her small Hyundai. Mitch didn't think she needed them. I decide that we or Ruth can use them. They are the last things to be loaded on the truck.

At lunchtime, we go to sign a petition to the court for the right to buy most of the estate rather than selling all of it. Then we eat at the Old Towne Tavern. When we return to the house we have a note from Ed Soboleski, Margie's friend and Sebastian's adopted dad. He had stopped to see us. I am sorry we missed him but don't have the energy to call him.

I keep returning to the bathroom, drawn by the hope of feeling Margie's presence. I can't. When the movers are gone I sit on the stairs of this empty house that was Margie's home for ten months and think a nice house like this should not get a reputation as a murder site, as if it were somehow responsible. Ruth walks into the foyer and expresses similar thoughts aloud, "This is a really nice house but I feel sorry for the next people who live here. How will they feel living where a murder happened?" She continues, "They'll be okay. Margie wouldn't stick around here haunting them." We know where she will be. Picturing her spirit with Mitch in the confines of a jail cell momentarily satisfies our need for him to suffer as we are.

Larry goes up to the penitentiary at about 2:15 P.M. to tell Mike we are nearly done. He comes down, and we say our goodbyes and leave the house for the final time. We all agree it is almost worse than the funeral. It is a major milestone along our path of grief.

At the motel Larry calls Wayne Samuelson and learns that Michael T. was right. The defense has asked for another evaluation. Mitch will be hypnotized in Philadelphia. The defense feels Mitch is withholding evidence. I can't see how this will help him unless he plans to use it as a basis for an appeal. It could be self-incriminating. I should know Mitch well enough to know there will be nothing revealed that doesn't help his case—but I don't. Wayne hopes he and Harold Schmidle will be allowed to attend but that sounds optimistic to me. Certainly this means a delay in jury selection, which is still scheduled for February. Wayne is certain a defense request for a continuance into March will be granted. We know it probably won't happen until April, so our trip to Florida will not be interrupted.

Ruth calls home and checks her voicemail, trying to take care of normal business details in the midst of all this. We have a glass of wine and decide to go back to the Italian Terrace. It is the restaurant and sports bar that we went to with Margie, Mitch, and Abby on the Friday after Thanksgiving in 1995. We had spent the holiday together in New Jersey with Mitch's parents, two of their friends, Michelle, and Margie and Mitch, who had just driven across the country. Jake had stayed in Connecticut with his dad and Abby enjoyed all the adult attention.

This memory evokes thoughts of the Pasters' suffering. All my "what ifs" and "if onlys" can't be as difficult to face as theirs. Has Aileen ever regretted telling Mitch to call 911? Margie told me Mitch's father kept telling him, "Go back to Lewisburg and work it out. That is what you do when you have problems in your marriage." Sound advice, right? Margie had been pleased when Jordan told her, "No matter how this works out we want you to know that you will always be welcome in this house." What does Jordan think now?

Both families are suffering and grieving. We would benefit from each other's love and support, but I know the circumstances won't allow us that. We'd have to be better people than we are. I understand they are horrified by the murder, but they love their son and must help him through this ordeal. They don't condone his act but he is their son—blood is thicker than water. Our daughter was brutally murdered by someone we all trusted. She is gone forever. Mitch is accusing her of being a whore and a drunk. The gulf is too great for any of us to span—no matter that we wish we could.

Being at the sports bar reminds us of the dreams and excitement of a new beginning we shared with Margie and Mitch then. We cannot help but compare those feelings with the anguish and torment we feel now because of his unforeseen act.

Ruth asks not to be seated in the same area we were in before. The waitress puts us at a table next to two women and two teenagers. One of the women talks constantly. Ruth asks, "Why is it the loud and obnoxious ones are always stupid too?" We laugh and realize this woman has provided a needed distraction. We can't ignore her so we can't continue to concentrate on our loss even though we look at the very table we were at fourteen months ago. I can see Margie with Abby's head on her lap. We were exhausted then. We are exhausted now, but the emotions are so very different—anticipation versus heartache. That night the only frustration was that the University of Connecticut men's basketball team lost a close game as we watched on the bar's TV.

We return to the motel and learn the movers will be in Marlborough Wednesday afternoon. The weather report on TV shows a northeaster coming up the Atlantic coast, due to arrive in New England on Friday, January 10th. Maybe our trip to Florida will be delayed. I hope not for too long. Larry and I need the peace and diversion that new strange surroundings can give us. The familiar is too painful now.

We start home at 9 A.M. after breakfast. We have an uneventful trip and arrive in Marlborough by midafternoon. The waiting begins. Finally we receive a call from the movers. They have been delayed because of another pickup but will arrive later that day. When they do get to us it is very dark and too dangerous to try unloading, especially down the hill to our apartment where most of the things are going. They return early the next day. When they give us the bill we are astonished at how low it is. We expected it to be much more. We thank Mr. Cianetti for his kindness. People, strangers never know how much their thoughtful, generous gestures touch our hearts.

We quickly unpack and find places for Margie's belongings, now ours, in the bright new apartment. Seeing Margie's things here is both comforting and upsetting—just another reminder that her death is real. We won't have much time to get used to having them because we are leaving for Florida in two days.

CHAPTER 15

Seeking Solace
in the Sun

On the morning of Saturday, January 11th, Steve planned to help us take a sofa, two end tables, and some of Margie's clothes to Kathy. We were going to leave Delilah and Felicia, our cat, with her then. Kathy would watch them while we're in Florida. But she calls, "I don't want anything. Take Delilah and Felicia to the vet's. I don't ever want to talk to you again." I've cleaned up her language a little bit.

I'm stunned. We have no choice but to have Felicia put to sleep so I call the vet. We hate to do it since she isn't in any pain and we've had her for 21 years but she would get too lonely for two months in a cage at the vets and we can't take her with us. I know Kathy loves Felicia and she has taken her many times before so her refusal is intended to hurt us.

Kathy calls again. "I just called the Windsor Police and told them you stole my dog from me. You better get her back to me right now or you will be arrested." Then she starts on a long venomous tirade about all the evils I have committed as a mother—including giving away the horses and having other dogs put to sleep because they were old or sick. She ends by telling me Margie had never forgiven me either. She knows all the right buttons to push. We take Felicia to the vet and then deliver Delilah to Kathy. We follow her instructions: "Ring the apartment and I'll buzz open the door. Just leave her there. I don't want to see you."

We leave Delilah, seventy-five cans of dog food, and her dishes and toys. I'm a little nervous about leaving her that way but can't deal with Kathy's anger and hate. We go to the Windsor Police Station and tell them her dog has been returned. They aren't concerned about a family squabble. We get home and there is a message from Kathy: "Why did you leave the dog food and stuff and not Delilah? That is some sick thing to do." I won't call her so Larry does and he tells her that we saw her get Delilah. She is lying and probably under the influence of drugs and alcohol.

Not a great send-off but we leave on Sunday and stop in Venice, Virginia, at Larry's brother Riley and Esther's. We go into Washington to visit the Smithsonian both Monday and Tuesday. One evening we go to the Kennedy Center to see a play, Shear Madness. I didn't ask what it was about before we went. It is a murder mystery/comedy. An oxymoron? Isn't this a contradiction? Lines such as: "I blacked out or she made me do it," aren't funny when your daughter's murderer is also using them as a defense. I am not yet aware of the Parents of Murdered Children national campaign against murder as entertainment but I am uncomfortable with the play.

On Wednesday we drive south and play tourist in Charleston, South Carolina. We take a horse-drawn carriage through the historic district and learn that Charleston is on an active fault line, which explains why many of the buildings have small black screws that are used to straighten them after an earthquake. We enjoy the breathtaking walled gardens on the sides or in back of magnificent old homes lining the waterfront. We visit the warehouse that is all that is left of Larry's navy base and tour Fort Sumter. I feel a tinge of regret as I tell Larry, "Lucky I'm not teaching. They have wonderful books for fifth graders."

We spend Thursday in Savannah, Georgia. I am enchanted with the historic district which has been mostly restored. There are beautiful squares with trees, flowers, statues, and fountains every few blocks just the way James Oglethorpe designed it hundreds of years ago while still in England. The rich and vibrant past comes alive. A recent book, which I buy immediately, tells of a murder case that involved people living in the beautiful homes in the historic district. Midnight in the Garden of Good and Evil is by John Berendt. Reading it distracts me from my own loss. On a tour we see where the book's main character, Jim Williams, lived and have his friend "Mandy" pointed out to us.

While we are in Savannah we hear that Bill Cosby's son, Ennis, was murdered on a secluded section of road near a freeway in Los Angeles. My heart goes out to his family and my pain intertwines with theirs. Ennis, like Margie, had dedicated his life to helping others. I empathize with them and hope the killer will soon be caught. Years later I read an interview Oprah Winfrey does with Camille, Ennis's mother, about the experience. She seems to be a wise and caring woman who has worked to make her life meaningful since his murder. Her idea that you have to go through the pain, not around it, makes sense to me. I'd like to talk with her.

After spending a night in Baldwin, Florida, we arrive in Englewood on the afternoon of Saturday, January 18th. The modular home is bright and airy. We have a freshwater canal in our backyard with a nearby bird sanctuary. Our first visitors are a great blue heron and a great white egret. They boldly walk into the carport in search of food. We learn later the boy who had been living here fed them every day. I try feeding them bread, which they disdain. A disgusted neighbor, who doesn't want the birds encouraged, explains that the birds are looking for meat. I have none so I'm off to a shaky start with my feathered guests.

There is so little work here for us to do. However, there is no dishwasher or washer and dryer so we do spend about two hours a week taking care of these tasks. I'm not complaining but I do wonder why I'm not using the time to work harder on my book about Margaret. Kathy's behavior and my concern for her safety contribute to a feeling of being in limbo. I decide to let the weather and beautiful beaches work their magic, restore my sense of joy, and get me motivated to pick up the pen, so to speak, and begin putting my story of Margaret to paper in an orderly way. I have lots of handwritten notes to rely on for guidance.

We eat out often because it is almost as cheap as, and easier than, preparing food at the house. We find Tiffany's, a family restaurant, less than a mile away in the small strip mall at the edge of our development. Sometimes we walk there for a good old-fashioned breakfast and in the early evening we drive there for the specials. The food is good and we enjoy having the waitresses recognize us.

One night at a restaurant in Englewood, I sit facing a family of eight. One young woman looks like Margie. Of course, she isn't quite as pretty, but her mannerisms are so similar. She tilts her head, looks at someone she isn't quite sure whether to believe or not, scrunches up her nose, narrowing her eyes, and then she laughs. The sight and sound are delightful, except I will never see or hear Margie's again. I'm both sad and happy when the family finishes and leaves the restaurant. I've had enough reminders for one night but then a collage of memories of all the times we went out to eat with Margie takes over.

We have a message from Kathy when we check our answering machine in Windsor. She's sorry but we should understand that she isn't responsible for what she said and did. After all she was hearing voices. I refuse to talk to her. Larry writes her a letter telling her why I was so upset. We don't hear from her again until the morning of January 20th—my birthday. Her excuses for why she acted the way she did include being sleep-deprived and hearing voices, and she may be schizophrenic. She is going to a doctor. She understands if we don't want to talk to her.

The temperature remains mostly in the high seventies or the low eighties. There are several beaches nearby, so on January 20th I spend my first birthday ever—and the first one after Margie's death—on a beach. It is too cold for swimming, but just right for walking and collecting shells and sharks' teeth. On Wednesday, January 22nd, Kathy calls to wish me happy birthday. Right, Kathy! It was enjoyable but not because of you.

Later that day we drive to Miami to see the University of Connecticut Huskies men's basketball team play. It's fun to see them in person, instead of on TV, but we jinx them. They lose for the first time ever to Miami and by over twenty points. We're seated right behind the Miami bench so we take some rough teasing. I'm glad we went anyway.

We drive back to Englewood along "Alligator Alley" in the Everglades and are reminded of the time we brought the girls to Florida when Margie was only six. There are lots more alligators now than there were twenty-five years ago. Conservation and environmental protection must be working—for the alligators at least.

Exploring all the beaches and parks of Florida is a bittersweet experience because we are reminded that in the future Margie planned to ask for a transfer to the federal prison in Florida. We might have been doing our exploring with her. In Englewood one of our favorite quiet spots with a nice breeze is Indian Mounds Park. It has marked trails and a nice picnic area, and is right on the intercostal waterway. Across the water we can see Manasota Key, where all the beaches are. Lemon Bay Park is also in Englewood and on the waterway. It has several trails and the facilities are great with butterfly gardens and many planned activities.

Soon we develop a routine of being home to sit beside the canal at sunset with a cocktail and food for our visitors. One afternoon I cut up some old steak and take it out to feed the great blue heron who was visiting. He flies away, but soon I have an egret. I'm not paying much attention as the crowd grows so I'm startled when I finally realize that two wood storks are standing about three feet away. They're really big and ugly. I feed them and they come even closer—too close for my comfort. There are now two blue herons, two egrets, three moorhens, lots of gulls, and very little meat left. Am I going to be attacked? I remember the Hitchcock movie with the birds. Scary! I picture that movie with wood storks—real scary!

I make it inside safely. "Larry, come look out the bedroom window." The wood storks see us and come right up to the house. Of course, they appear much more friendly when their twelve-inch beaks are no immediate threat. They stay and chat until they're certain I'm not coming out again. Later, Larry cooks steaks on the grill but near the door. Better safe than sorry. However, we enjoy countless hours feeding and watching the birds fly to roost at the sanctuary each evening. Bud and Shirley and Steve and Abby enthusiastically participate when they visit.

One afternoon Larry and I drive around a development area called Rotunda. It is huge and impressive because much of it is covered with wild plants. There are a few homes and cleared lots, but basically it remains undeveloped—except for the roads and canals dug through it. It's strange—sort of like a Stephen King or Dean Koontz landscape. We don't know what happened here but imagining different scenarios distracts from our grief and pain.

While staying in Englewood we enjoy visiting open houses and reading ads for homes. We aren't sure if spending part of each year in Florida is still something we want to consider but we do like the area. If we decide to buy, it will be on the spur of the moment, or at least it will appear that way. I feel helpless and lost when I think of ever again being so far away from family for very long. The time we were separated from Margie now seems wasted. I dream of all the things we could have done together if we hadn't been separated geographically. Right now, I doubt I will ever again willingly make the decision to be separated for an extended time from my family.

Larry's brother Bud and his wife, Shirley, who live in Knobleton, north of Tampa, come for a few days. It feels good to be able to return their hospitality. We have stayed with them in Florida and in Jamestown so many times. We go to Fort Myers and visit the Edison and Ford estates, where we receive interesting history lessons while walking the lovely grounds and taking tours of their homes. I am particularly impressed with the huge Banyan trees whose roots and branches spread over large areas. I'm touched by Mrs. Edison's memory garden, which was built with a pool and statues as a loving tribute by her son. Back in Englewood we eat dinner at Mad Sam's, a seafood restaurant that catches our attention because of the huge colorful fish sculpture penetrating its roof. It is just before the drawbridge to Manasota key. Inside the decor is pleasant and the food tasty.

At the end of January, I begin putting my story of Margie onto the computer. I use my handwritten notes for guidance. I've done so much pre-writing and organizing mentally, it could be considered procrastinating! I feel all the pain of those first days roll over me as I type the story of that day and how we heard the news. It is painful but therapeutic. I work hard to balance my days with pleasant new activities that counter the older painful memories. I do well most of the time except when I go to bed. Then the floodgates open up. My mind just won't stop. Neither will the tears.

I am extremely upset when Ruth tells us a letter that Mitch wrote shortly after Christmas Eve just arrived. She reads it to me over the phone. He expresses his loneliness and sympathy for his family and ours trying to celebrate the holidays without Margaret, but writes nothing of remorse or a sense of being responsible. He even says he misses his wife. Does he really expect us to be concerned about his feelings? The guards must go over everything he sends out—guess he doesn't want to incriminate himself. I know they check any mail delivered to him so I don't even bother to tell him what I think. We send the assistant U.S. attorney a copy of his letter, which is all printed in capital letters. I wonder what a therapist would think of that. This is an unedited copy of that letter.

Dear Mr. and Mrs. Bostrom,

This past Tuesday, Christmas Eve, was an extremely emotional night for me. For many years we gathered together as a family over the holidays. This year I was gripped with an overwhelming emptiness, sick at the thought of celebrating Christmas without Margaret. I cannot even pretend to know the grief you, Ruth, Kathy, Abby and Jake feel. All I know is my own interminable suffering and sadness over my loss of my wife.

My parents are also devastated. I can hear it in their voices, see it in their eyes, their faces, and even though I cannot physically touch them, I can feel it as well. They to truly looked forward to getting together as one big family during this time of year.

Each night I pray for your family and for mine. You are in my thoughts and I cry uncontrollably when I think of the pain so many people are feeling. I know I am probably the last person you wanted to hear from, and if you have read this far I thank you. We are all hurting and grieving, I wanted you to know that I am too.
Sincerely,
Mitch

News follows that the trial has been delayed again because Mitch was going to be hypnotized at his attorney's request on February 6, but it had to be postponed because the psychiatrist, Dr. Sadoff, was at the John E. duPont trial. The weathy duPont in January 1996 shot Olympic wrestler David Schultz, who had been living with his family on the duPont estate. Mitch's hypnosis has been rescheduled for March 7th. He claims he can't remember what Margaret said to him that morning, or killing her. Hypnosis is supposed to help him find out. Jury selection is now set for April 2nd. I didn't need to bring my winter coat and boots to Florida after all—in case we had to fly or drive to Williamsport. We are just beginning to understand how slowly the wheels of justice work.

Larry has to go to a doctor in early February. He has this rash on his legs, but now his ankle has started to swell and hurt some. I was afraid he had that flesh-eating virus or a strong reaction to all the stress. The doctor says it is probably the second because he finds no infection or circulation problems and his blood pressure is fine. He gives Larry a cream to apply four times a day.

Joyce Wrabel, a fellow fifth-grade teacher, visits during school vacation week. Her parents live just a couple streets away from where we are renting. She says people back home at South School have Fifths Disease. The symptoms sound like what Larry has. Eventually it goes away.

We are very disappointed when Ruth tells us she and the kids may not get down this winter. Calie, the trial, Ruth's job, as well as Jakie's fear of the large people dressed up as Mickey and Goofy are all contributing factors. Abby is as disappointed as I am. She remembers the fun we had last year when she came to Florida with just Grandma and Grandpa. We laugh about Margie teasing us—saying she was jealous because Abby was getting such a special treat. Abby wants to share the beaches with Grandma and suggests, "I could fly down by myself. Kids do it."

I want to see Abby but we're apprehensive about her traveling alone even though she is almost eight. Ruth talks to Steve and he accepts our invitation to come for a week with Abby. We await their arrival with great anticipation. We go to the beach all five days she's here. Hardworking Abby drags the Florida snow shovel, which is a wire basket on the end of a long handle, through the shallow water. We collect unique shells and ancient sharks' teeth. Having Abby, the sunny beach, blue skies, turquoise water, and the gentle breeze is my description of heaven on earth. Only having Margie with us could make it better.

Boca Grande is a long strip of land connected to the mainland by a bridge and causeway. With its two old lighthouses, long empty beaches, blue skies, and breathtaking sunsets it quickly becomes one of our favorite spots. I christen Abby "Miss Boca Grande Bathing Beauty for February 1997."

We travel north to the Jungle Gardens in Sarasota. Abby poses with flamingos and riding a pony and holding a baby alligator. It is a warm day but we all enjoy the exotic animals and jungle plants. I take a picture of Abby with her daddy to give her as a souvenir and one of Abby with a carved statue of a fertility goddess to remind Steve that his little girl is growing up.

The Monday before Abby and Steve leave we go to Busch Gardens. I try to visualize Margie next to Abby and conjure up their conversation. I can almost hear their giggles. Abby is a real animal lover so we enjoy our eight-hour visit. Grandma gets lots more pictures. Abby hugging a gorilla, Abby sitting in a hippo's mouth or riding an elephant—all statues. Any excuse to take a photograph of my only granddaughter!

They fly home on Tuesday. I have trouble saying goodbye to Abby because the world is not a safe place for me or my family anymore. Who knows when a goodbye will be a last one? I try to stay positive and show how deeply I care but worried thoughts persist. It is hard to watch them go and very lonely without them.

Several years ago while sitting in a doctor's waiting room I read about an island paradise off the Florida shore—Cayo Costa State Park. It is the largest undeveloped barrier island in the country. We locate it and find that we can get there from Punta Gorda on Port Charlotte harbor. We make reservations with the King Fisher Fleet, take our cooler, buy our lunch at Fisherman's Village, and pack it before we board the early morning charter boat. The ride is long and relaxing. I'm reminded of times Margie and I sat watching the water foam and fall away behind us. I shed lots of nostalgic tears but no one else notices.

We have three hours to explore the island. After putting our things on the beach we investigate the small area that has about twelve compact cabins that can be rented. They are rustic and conditions are primitive—no electricity, no windows panes or stoves. The bunks are hard without mattresses and outhouses provide the only toilet facilities. It's fun to try to picture what it would be like at night. Maybe scary, especially if it was really dark, but wouldn't it be beautiful under a full moon?

We go back to the beach and discover hundreds of prickly dead sea urchins. I'm confused. They don't look anything like what I see in the tourist shops. A kind woman shows me how to gently remove the spines. Then we swim in the turquoise water, eat, and swim some more. I'm very glad we made the effort to see this paradise.

Another day we drive back to Sarasota, this time to visit John Ringling's home, art galleries, and circus museum. Beautiful gardens and statues surround the huge Italian-style palatial museum, which is full of fine art. He built a lovely home as a tribute to his wife, but we are stunned when we learn the Circus Museum was built after his death. He apparently wanted to leave a very different legacy. I wonder why.

We also visit an antebellum plantation in Ellenton, the site of the oldest building in Manatee County. It is a memorial to Judah P. Benjamin, a Confederate secretary of state, who was sheltered here while he waited to escape to England. Again I am struck by the uniqueness of the trees surrounding the mansion and the nearby Patten House, which has been preserved as an example of the pioneer Florida farmhouse. Larry and I both find history fascinating and our visit brings alive one of the most difficult periods in our history.

Television news informs us that the body of a woman has been found, bound and wrapped in a blanket, in a drainage ditch next to the highway near Fort Myers. They assume she is a prostitute and that drugs and alcohol are involved. When we return to Connecticut and the next Survivors of Homicide meeting we are stunned to meet her mother and sister. She was a loving daughter on her way to a new job and planned to visit her parents who were wintering in Florida. Her family believes it was a mob-related killing. Lisa, because of her job as a bookkeeper at a restaurant, was in the wrong place at the wrong time. Four years later, no arrests have been made.

We also hear of a murder in Tampa, committed by a man who had just been released from a prison because of overcrowding. Previously, he had raped a fifteen-year-old girl in California, cut off her hands and feet and left her for dead. She survived by shear willpower and determination. Now he has murdered the woman he was living with here in Florida. We can't get away from the constant reminders of man's inhumanity.

It has been an unusually warm, dry, and sunny winter. Just what I needed. It hasn't rained once in the two months we have been in Englewood but on March 15th, the day we leave, it does. We stop at Larry's brother's home in Knobleton for a three-day visit before driving home.

On our way back to Connecticut we'd love to stop and see my brother Dave and his friend Margaret in Kentucky, but the trial is scheduled for April 2nd. We know there is much to see in their area so we decide to postpone that visit until we can spend more time with them.

We drive to Beauford, South Carolina, where we spend a few hours looking at the lovely homes from the eighteenth and nineteenth centuries. I fall in love with Beauford and wish we could stay longer but Larry is ready to get home. The next morning I am able to get him to drive to the nearby Hunting Island State Park. We visit the lighthouse and walk along a deserted beach filled with driftwood.

The weather deteriorates as we drive north but we stop for lunch at a tourist trap called South of the Border, on the South Carolina–North Carolina border. It appears gaudy, honky-tonk, and carnival-like, but no one we see working there smiles or acts happy. It isn't the fun it was meant to be. Even with my problems I feel like I could cheer them up.

The weather driving from Virginia to Connecticut is damp, rainy, and grows increasingly colder. We arrive at our apartment at Ruth's Thursday evening. It's wonderful to see everyone and during the next week we have three beautiful days in the high sixties. We go hiking in a nearby state park with Ruth, Jacob, and Calie on Good Friday. I even show Jake how to skip flat rocks across the lake water. He throws rocks in the water just to hear the kerplunk when they hit. On Easter Ruth invites a family that is visiting from England—friends of her au pair—to dinner. On Tuesday Connecticut gets hit with a storm—about eight inches of snow, and in some parts up to twenty-four inches. It melts quickly but I enjoy my one snowstorm even if it is late in the season.

There is a lot of work to be done on the condo before we are ready to sell or rent it. After almost thirty-seven years of married life, we have collected a lot of things even if we moved five times. We also have a sentimental attachment to anything that was Margie's. We are excited about getting our apartment settled and living there full-time. It will be August before we sell the condo and officially change our address.

It is better with Kathy—at least her behavior toward us is. She is at Ruth's for Easter and tries to be friendly but gets sick. She is seeing a psychiatrist and he is giving her medicine. I worry that she is misusing it.

In April I'm tired and sick to my stomach much of the time. I don't know if it is physical or mental but I discuss it with my doctor when I go for a checkup. He decides it is time for me to try an antidepressant. I start taking Prozac and attempt to be patient with myself. Because Margie was away so much of the time and I didn't see her every day, it is easy for part of me not to really accept her murder—to think that someday I'll pick up the phone and it will be her. Truly accepting her murder and our loss is terrifying and painful.

Both Larry and I needed that time in Englewood. We wanted to be away from everyone and everything that reminded us of Margie. Our spirits were soothed, but I find that no matter where I am my thoughts return to Margie. I tell myself, Margie would have loved this, or this is like when we went…with Margie. My imagination becomes my best friend and my worst enemy. Our respite in Florida is only a prelude to the main events of 1997, in which the criminal justice system consumes our thoughts, time, and energy.

CHAPTER 16

The *Criminal* Justice System—1997 Style

Jury selection was scheduled for February, postponed to March and then postponed again because the defense wants to have a psychiatric evaluation done on Mitch. They plan to use a nationally known expert, Robert L. Sadoff, M.D.

Dr. Sadoff is the psychiatrist who examined duPont in a Philadelphia case in which duPont shot and killed his wrestling coach. It received much media attention. Dr. Sadoff found that duPont could not aid in his own defense. We are apprehensive. Will he do the same with Mitch?

Kenneth A. Kool, M.D., had done a psychiatric consultation at the Snyder County Correctional Facility on October 2nd, 1996. The defense requested his opinion prior to the bail review hearing. Dr. Sadoff's report, while more detailed, supports key findings in Dr. Kool's report.

The April jury selection date is then postponed because the government is performing its own evaluation of Mitch at the United States Penitentiary (USP) at Butner, North Carolina, during April and May. Sally C. Johnson, M.D., an associate warden of heath services, is in charge of the 60-day evaluation, including psychological tests. Even though she is a Bureau of Prisons employee, she submits a report that to me seems to support Dr. Sadoff's findings and Mitch's version of events. We receive both written reports in mid-June.

Later, Dr. Johnson will do a competency evaluation of Ted Kaczynski, the Unabomber, prior to his acceptance of a plea. She will help to get him a life sentence instead of the death penalty.

Dr. Sadoff's report is devoted to Mitch's history, his version of their relationship, Margaret's problems, and his recollection of the murder and events leading up to it.

I think Dr. Sadoff was hired and paid by the defense—so I expect his document to indulge their position. He states there is no insanity defense and Mitch knew what he was doing and that it was wrong. But he found Mitch had been adequately provoked, responded in the heat of passion, and had not premeditated the killing.

On March 7, 1997, the hypnotic interview was done at Dr. Sadoff's request by Dr. Louis Dublin. During the interview Mitch recalled going up to get his cat and finding the knife under the bed, taking it to Margaret, who was just getting out of the shower, and having her grab it angrily. Her fault, again? Isn't it convenient, if not convincing, that Mitch's supposed hypnosis produced only information that helps his case? He is Mister Nice Guy burdened with a bitch for a wife.

Dr. Johnson reports that while Mitch was under hypnosis with Dr. Dublin, he commented that his head hurt, he couldn't see straight, and felt he was falling over. Right after he remembered Margaret telling him to give her the knife, he coughs, gags, and breathes raggedly.

Poor Mitch. My question—was he thinking about what he had done or what might happen to him because of it? We're back to "she made me do it"! He doesn't remember the actual stabbing. Of course not. Why would he want to?

Certain details Mitch gives to the psychiatric examiners conflict with what we heard from Margie or what we ourselves know. Mitch mentions not being able to find work in Lewisburg. Margie complained that he didn't look for work. He says he returned in March or April. We know it was the middle of May.

Mitch reports to Dr. Sadoff he planned to stay in a dorm at Cornell, but he had rented an apartment. He claims to have saved enough while at his job in California to pay to go to Cornell, but it is reported that he took out an 11,000-dollar student loan.

From my knowledge of him, Mitch doesn't perceive financial issues to be a major strain on the relationship, but on numerous occasions Margie complained bitterly of his high-handed, unilateral decisions about what they could afford and how the money should be spent. Our family heard several of these heated exchanges.

He recalls that they broke up in 1989, which they did, but on his birthday Margaret called and asked him to return. Did she? She told us Mitch was doing poorly at his job and was going to lose it because he missed her so much. He followed her to California.

Mitch keeps referring to Margaret's drinking problem. The truth is Margie's autopsy showed only traces of alcohol in her body, she obtained a Ph.D., got licensed as a psychologist, maintained a good attendance record at work, and was just promoted. She had no arrests related to drunkenness. Mitch or his family never expressed any concern to us about Margaret's drinking—not even in the two phone calls we received from him the week he killed her. Why? Maybe it wasn't a real concern. But a glass or two of wine could have made her less amenable to his efforts to maintain control of her. She might have spoken her mind more freely.

Who invited Bill for dinner on the night of August 8th? We will never know. Mitch claims she did. She told us Mitch planned the evening so he could catch them together. He says Margie and Bill were drunk and she wanted to go out drinking some more when he came home from the basketball game. She maintained that he accused them of having an affair and said he became very aggressive. She was afraid and asked Bill to get her out of there. She admitted they had sex later that night—for the first time.

Mitch claims Margie told him she had forty or fifty affairs during their relationship. Again, when did she have the time? It is possible she told him this to try to make him so disgusted he would leave. My daughter was not perfect but she was not the vixen he describes either. The FBI could find no evidence of any affairs prior to her relationship with Bill.

The consensus of both Dr. Sadoff and Dr. Johnson is that Mitch cannot use an insanity defense, but he was provoked by Margaret and did not formulate a plan to harm her, and there was no premeditation. Dr. Sadoff concludes that Mitch experienced a dissociative disorder and amnesia concerning the event. Dr. Johnson terms it "adjustment disorder with mixed disturbances of emotions and conduct."

I feel Margaret is portrayed as a one-sided caricature. I don't think Dr. Johnson verified any of Mitch's accusations with other reliable sources, including the FBI. But isn't he just a little too good to be true?

I write a letter to Wayne Samuelson about Dr. Johnson's report. I send copies to Kathleen Hawk, director of the Bureau of Prisons and to Attorney General Janet Reno, expressing my dissatisfaction and concerns.

My fervent wish is to see what this woman psychiatrist, Sally Johnson, looks like. Not long after I had seen her report, I watch Tim McVeigh's sentencing on TV. There is a news clip showing Dr. Sally Johnson, who was consulted on that case too. I think she looks just as I pictured her; probably late forties or early fifties, straight brown hair pulled back and a plain face with glasses. She is wearing flat shoes and a nondescript raincoat. I feel she disliked Margie because of her apparent beauty and ability to attract men. Is that why she quotes Mitch when he calls Margie a "coke slut" in her report? I think of contacting her, but she would probably write me off as a crazy old woman who contributed to my daughter's wicked ways. This is part of a letter I would like to send her, but won't.

Dear Sally, (no undue respect here)

My search for a way to appropriately acknowledge your forensic evaluation of Mitchell F. Paster has come to an end. Enclosed is a book, *Women Who Love Men Who Kill* by Sheila Isenberg. It reflects the kind of thinking employed in your report.

It is apparent to me that you bought Mitch's line, believed the person who betrayed our daughter and our family. You dismissed, or didn't learn of the broken lock on the bedroom door which enabled Mitchell to steal Margaret's pets. If she had lived I'm sure her version of the argument and the bathroom scene would have been very different from his. Death keeps her from telling it and we are not asked, but shouldn't the professionals seek to determine the truth? One side is not enough.

Mitchell may be out of prison in his early fifties, able to have an intimate relationship and kill again when his partner isn't per-

fect or wants to end the union. I wouldn't want this to happen to
any woman—not even you or someone you love.
With great feeling,
Shirley Bostrom
An outraged mother

It is hard to read the same old accusations, fabrications, inaccuracies and distortions of the truth that we have been subjected to for
all the months since he killed her. I suffer some of my most debilitat-
ing grief. Getting out of bed takes too much effort. Besides, why
bother? My doctor starts me on Prozac, 20 milligrams, increases it to
40 milligrams, then 60 milligrams.

Janet Reno makes her decision. The prosecutor cannot seek the
death penalty because Mitch only killed one person. And even
though she was a federal employee she wasn't on duty at the time of
the murder. We don't want Mitch to die, mostly because of what it
would do to his parents, but Ms. Reno has taken away a tool that
could be used in plea bargaining.

Margie's worth continues to be devalued. She has no voice. As
Wayne Samuelson often says, "My star witness is dead." She cannot
tell her side of the story or defend her reputation, which is being
systematically destroyed.

Jury selection dates are never officially scheduled for June or July.
The new date is August 13th. Receiving a court date gives us hope
that finally we may see this case resolved. Tension builds, already-
made plans may have to be changed, everything is on hold, the wound
has been opened wide again. At the last minute this date is also
canceled.

In the middle of October we receive a voicemail message from
Wayne Samuelson informing us that jury selection has been moved
to November 4, 1997, with the trial following immediately after. I
have been told I will need to testify, mostly about the phone calls
from Mitch and Margie during the week she was murdered, but also
about their relationship. I wrote about the calls in my journal so I
have an accurate account of them. I send Wayne the following recollections:

Monday night, August 12

Our answering machine had this message on it when we returned around 8 P.M. from Rhode Island. We assumed Mitch made this call from his parents' home in New Jersey.

"Mr. and Mrs. Bostrom," (we knew something was wrong because he always called us Mom and Dad) "This is Mitch, I'm leaving Margaret. I just found out that she has been having an affair with her boss (Bill) for over a month. I really loved your daughter but unfortunately it wasn't enough." (This is almost an exact quote. He sounded upset and was breathing hard—spoke rapidly and had an angry inflection in his voice.)

I called Margaret at around 9 that night, Monday, August 12th. Margaret said, "So you got the call." She reported that Mitch had been back for about a week and had been being very nice to her. Over the weekend they went out to dinner with Bill and his wife, who kept questioning Margie about whether she and Bill were having an affair. When Bill and Mitch were not at the table Margie admitted the affair to her. Margie claimed Bill told her he loved her and was getting a divorce, but his wife responded that Bill had just told her that she was still important to him and he realized he wanted her and the kids back. Margie added, "Of course she could have been lying to me."

Later, Margie did admit the affair to Mitch—because she felt it was the one thing he wouldn't forgive her for. I told her how foolish it had been to tell him. She agreed. Mitch had called his father to come get him and some of his things. He asked her to leave before his dad got there. She tried but was just going when Mr. Paster arrived. He was cool but polite.

While we were talking Mitch called her on the phone. She had call waiting. She told me, "I don't know if I should call him back or not. What do you think I should do?"

I told her, "Margie, if you are serious about this divorce then you need to be firm—now."

Margie responded, "I feel so alone." I reminded her that there were hundreds of thousands of women who don't have men, but lead perfectly happy lives.

She said, "I know, I was so proud of myself too." She felt like she was getting everything together—she had passed the exam for her license as a psychologist in Pennsylvania, got a promotion to a pay level GS13 and lost the weight she had gained the previous year.

I encouraged her to believe in herself because she was doing fine. I also told her to keep in touch. She didn't call during the week but she was coming home on her way to the conference on Cape Cod. I wasn't as much help as I could have been. I was tired and losing patience with all of Mitch and Margie's nonsense.

Thursday evening, August 15

Between 10:15 and 10:30 P.M. I came home from a class. Larry told me the phone had rung but when he picked it up whoever was on the other end hung up, so when it rang again I answered. It was Mitch—no greeting. Just, "What do you know?" His voice was calm and deliberate, with good clear diction. Breathing was normal. I asked what he meant. He said, "About Margaret. She called me and asked me to forgive her and to please come back so we could talk about it. Now I'm here and I saw her car go by. When she saw my car in the driveway she sped up." (which was his mother's because his was being repaired)

I told him I hadn't talked to her since Monday night after he had called and left the message. I also told him, "Mitch, I hope this works out so you are both happy."

He said, "Un huh," and hung up.

When we got to Margaret's house Mitch's car was in the garage, so he must have moved it inside so Margie wouldn't know he was there and felt it was safe to come home. Her car was parked within two feet of the garage door. He couldn't get his out without moving hers.

This statement is basically what I told Dick Rodgers when he interviewed me on August 17th.

On October 24th, Wayne Samuelson calls us. He has received a letter from George Lepley, one of Mitch's defense attorneys. In his letter Mr. Lepley refers to several conversations he has had with Mr. Samuelson over the last few weeks. Mitch is willing to enter a guilty plea to the charge of voluntary manslaughter. Mr. Lepley also states that he anticipates what Wayne's response will be—a negative one.

Wayne does reject that plea but informs Mr. Lepley, "The government may consider accepting a plea to second-degree murder, with both the government and the defense being free to argue whatever adjustments they feel appropriate to either enhance or reduce the calculated guideline sentence. Should your client be willing to agree to such a disposition, please contact me so we can further discuss such a potential resolution."

We do not realize how important this language is until sentencing. The guidelines for second-degree murder fall between eleven and fourteen years, but attorneys get to argue upward and downward departure from the guidelines. Mitch could still receive life in prison, but it isn't likely, or he could receive less than the eleven years at the lower end of the guidelines. It is all very complicated.

Knowing I *might* be called as a witness and *actually receiving* the official "United States District Court Subpoena in a Criminal Case" are very different. I'm now convinced we are going to court. Wayne has received no response to his offer to consider a second-degree murder plea bargain.

Wayne, the FBI, and BOP staff feel strongly that legally it is not in the realm of the psychiatrists to determine whether Mitch's act was premeditated, so Wayne submits a brief to exclude the anticipated expert testimony of the psychiatrists on the "ultimate issue" regarding premeditation. These opinions are inadmissible and should be excluded by the court. The jurors, the triers of fact, should make the decision regarding "ultimate issues." He isn't sure what his chances are but feels it is worth the effort.

At noon on November 3, 1997, Larry, Ruth, and I leave Marlborough. Traffic is light and construction work slows us down in only two places near Scranton so we get to Williamsport before dark. It helps that Williamsport is in the western part of the eastern time zone. It would already be dark in Connecticut at 5 P.M.

Ruth and I unload the luggage onto a cart and take it to the elevator. Larry has registered and gone to move the car. Ruth looks at the woman behind the desk and says, "Didn't she say 'Bostrom'?"

I see a clerk talking on the phone and I think I heard "Bostrom" too, but she doesn't look at us as the elevator arrives. "It's okay, Ruth," I say. "The red light will be flashing on the phone in the room if it was for us."

It is. Wayne has called to make sure we got in safely and wants us to call him back. Larry makes the call. Wayne asks if we can come to his office the next morning at nine. He'll fill us in on developments and discuss the procedure for jury selection before it starts at 10 A.M. We agree.

When we are finished unpacking we go downstairs to the Shadow Lounge for happy hour. Then we walk five blocks down Pine Street to Charlie's Caboose for dinner. There is a light, misting rain and the cool air is refreshing. The restaurant is nearly empty on a Monday evening. As we are seated in the actual caboose, I tell Ruth and Larry, "I can't wait to tell Abby and Jacob about this. They'd love it."

Ruth and I have the catch of the day, which is attractively presented with carrots cut on the diagonal to form oval petals which are placed on the plate in the shape of a flower. The fish is covered with thin strips of carrots and leeks. When I taste the leeks I'm surprised. "I can't believe these are leeks. They are so mild. When I was a kid if we ate leeks they sent us home from school because the smell was so strong."

"Those were wild leeks, Shirley, and you ate them raw. These are cultivated and cooked. Maybe that's the difference," Larry reasons. Keeping our thoughts occupied with trivial details helps distract us from the reason we are in this restaurant in western Pennsylvania on a Monday evening in November. We walk back to the hotel, crossing West Third Street where the Federal Court Building is located two blocks to the west. We're in bed by 10 P.M. Tomorrow the people who will decide Mitch's fate—and ours—will be chosen.

In the morning, we are delayed on our way to Wayne's office by our encounter with long lines at the court house metal detector. Ruth has to leave her pager—it might cause an interruption in proceedings. In Wayne's office he and Harold Schmidle tell us how the proceedings will work.

We learn the trial will not take place immediately after jury selection as scheduled but has been postponed until November 19th. We start discussing the trial. Wayne plans to call only fourteen witnesses. He will not call Bill Corey. He wants the defense to have to introduce the infidelity issue—and therefore not be able to cross-examine government witnesses. He explains there is no need to muddy the waters. This is a murder trial—pure and simple.

At 9:50 A.M. we go to the courtroom that is full of potential jurors. At first we are directed to chairs along the side wall near to where Mitch will be sitting. Wayne comes and takes us to sit next to him and Harold at the prosecutor's table. Mitch's mother and father take the seats where we had been.

Judge Malcolm Muir, a slightly stooped distinguished man, well past seventy with white hair, prominent features, and glasses, follows Mitch into the courtroom. I've grown accustomed to his no-nonsense approach and I'm sure he's aware of our terrible loss.

The judge begins his instructions to the potential jurors, "Listen to all the questions. Don't daydream." He grins. "Once every five years someone does." Then he asks, "Would you have answered yes to any of my questions? If so, which ones?" He doesn't expect an answer. "You may be called on to answer them later."

The court clerk spins a wooden drum and twenty-eight names are selected from the larger group. They are instructed to enter the jury box, which is within inches of where we are now seated.

Wayne reads the Grand Jury indictment. The judge instructs the jury that the indictment by the Grand Jury is the accusation of the U.S. government—not an inference of guilt.

We listen as Wayne introduces himself and Harold. Then George Lepley does so for himself, Kyle Rude, and Mitchell Paster. It is another reminder that the victim and her family play no part in this action.

Now the judge wants the potential jurors to answer his questions. Do they know the counsel or defendant, or do they or any family member do business with any of them? There are no affirmative replies.

The judge states that the lists of probable witnesses can be changed if new evidence arises, but they are to be as accurate as possible. Wayne is required to read his. The defense exercises its right to refuse to divulge its list at this time. *Criminal* justice. "That is what it is—justice for the criminal." This is a favorite expression among Survivors of Homicide for this reason and many others.

Judge Muir asks if any potential jurors know the witnesses. One knows Graham Showalter. Another knows the 911 operator. Eventually they are not selected for duty.

The next question is about whether they have served as a juror or grand juror in either federal or state court. Two people had been on county court cases that were disposed of out of court, while a third person had been an alternate. One is eventually picked as a juror, one as an alternate, and the other is excused from duty.

The judge asks Wayne how long the trial will be. Wayne estimates two weeks at the most. George Lepley agrees. The judge then asks the jury pool if the length of the trial would cause undue hardship on anyone. A locksmith and a student indicate they would find it difficult. They are asked to approach the bench and a loud fan is turned on to keep the conversation private. The judge listens to them and they are excused.

The next question potential jurors are asked is about any ties to law enforcement personnel or agencies. Several people have friends or relatives in the business but feel it would have no effect on their ability to be fair. Other questions include: "Have you read or heard about this case? If you are selected are you unwilling or religiously unable to render a verdict based on law? Are there medical or other reasons you cannot sit on this case?"

Wayne has no questions for the jurors. Lepley asks, "Do you have a close relative involved with counseling? Are you involved in counseling? Is there anyone who is not willing to accept the findings of a psychiatrist?" He is told to approach the bench—the fan does its job but we presume he explains why he is asking these questions. He then continues with: "Is there anyone who believes the insanity plea should not be allowed? Would you give added credence to law enforcement officials?" He gets no response to any of his questions.

One woman was late and the judge excuses her from the case at the request of the defense. She hadn't heard the beginning of the instructions. Wayne does not object to her. He explains later that he wants the jury to see him as a nice guy—easy to get along with.

The twenty-eight potential jurors are farmers, an archeology student, teachers, clerks, an engineer, truck drivers, a realtor, emergency personnel, factory workers, professors, a bus driver, a machinist, an attorney, and a psychologist. They work at Woolrich, an animal clinic, a fitness rehabilitation facility, Penn Light, Penn State University, Bucknell University, Wise Foods, or local school districts. Some are homemakers or retired. There are no African-Americans or Hispanics among the seventeen men and eleven women.

The defense can make ten preemptive dismissals. The government has six. *Criminal* Justice! These are made in silence with the list of names being passed back and forth across the aisle between attorneys. It is an uncomfortable silence for everyone else in the courtroom.

When they are finished the court clerk reads the list of jurors: Stephen A..., Franklin R..., Harold F..., Robert R..., Norman P..., Theodore R..., James W..., Michael P..., Robert N..., Gary B..., Gerald B..., and Kenneth G....

Alternate jurors are selected in the same fashion. Nine men and three women whose names were randomly drawn from the drum are questioned. All but six are dismissed by the attorneys. The alternates are Ricky A..., Robert L..., Richard W..., Richard M..., Willard M..., and Charles P....There is a stunned silence in the courtroom. Ruth and one of the women not selected for the jury look at each other and whisper in disbelief, "They're all men!"

I've been watching the blue-suited, matronly court clerk call each name. The weight pressing down on my body got heavier with each additional masculine choice. What does it mean? Anything? There were so many more men in the pool. My God, is it possible Mitch's lawyer did it on purpose? Why? I feel tears of frustration and shock run down my cheeks. This is the hand we've been dealt. I've never heard of an all-male jury before. Will it really work in Mitch's favor or will men be less tolerant of what he did? Who knows? I hope they are fathers with daughters.

The judge instructs the jurors to call the clerk's office after 5:30 P.M. on November 18th to find out when the trial will begin. Court is adjourned. We gather our belongings and quickly slip out the side door and start down the narrow hallway to the stairs and the safety of Wayne's office. Just as we reach the corner, Jordan and Aileen come around it toward us. Jordan looks at me and winks. Did he really? Was it an unconscious, nervous reaction or a signal that he felt they had won this round? Either way, I wish he hadn't done it.

Wayne admits he hasn't seen an all-male panel before, but he is happy he got rid of the four people he didn't want. A female attorney, a woman psychologist, a male college professor, and a man who informed the judge, "I'm divorced and I don't know where she is!" are all gone. He tells us blue-collar people make the best jurors—they don't overanalyze everything.

Wayne looks at me and says, "I don't like schoolteachers on a jury."

"You know I'm a retired teacher, don't you?"

He smiles at me. "Yes, and you're an old softy too."

I don't agree, but figure it is useless to argue the point—with tears still filling my eyes.

Abby wants to be in court, but we are not sure she should be. Wayne tells us she can be, but doubts we want to expose her to the grim details. We'll wait to decide but know he is right.

We want to see the crime scene pictures but Wayne refuses, saying they are too gruesome. He also advises us to leave the courtroom when the photos are shown. I don't think I can walk away while others watch. He does agree to show us the coroner's charts, which are outlines of the female body standing—one of the front, one of the back, and one of only the skeleton. Even though each wound is shown, I have very little reaction to seeing these diagrams. They are too impersonal.

Then Wayne asks us how we feel about a second-degree murder plea bargain. *Is this what it is going to be?* We tell him we don't like it. He says he hears us but reminds us we have no part in making the decision. *Criminal* justice, again! He will keep us informed of any new developments.

We go back to the hotel and reschedule our meeting with attorney Andrew Lyons. We will meet him at his office in Lewisburg at six tonight instead of tomorrow to discuss a possible wrongful death civil lawsuit against Mitch and/or the federal government. When we meet, he is pleasant but doubtful about the outcome. He tells us we will have to file right after the criminal trial to meet the two-year deadline for filing wrongful death suits because the paperwork is extensive. With Mitch we have a case because of anticipated lost wages for Margaret and our pain and suffering, but realistically what are our chances of ever collecting on it? Mitch might write a book in prison, inherit a large sum of money, or we'll just be hassling him. We have to decide if it is financially and emotionally worth it.

Mr. Lyons advises us against suing the government. The BOP is a close-knit group and will stick together. Margaret was a part of their family while she worked there. You are not part of that family. We know that. We've had no official contact with staff at the penitentiary for months. Their attorneys have not been at court proceedings since Dave Lamer retired as warden.

Mr. Lyons tells us our issues with the Bureau of Prisons: a guard should have been stationed at a guardhouse at the entrance to the reservation, and the report that a woman heard screams and called security but they didn't respond don't necessarily prove neglect or make the BOP responsible for her death. He goes on to explain that even a case for sexual harassment against her supervisor has difficulties. We'd have to prove the authorities knew about it and did nothing. We know Margie would not have wanted us to pursue this matter. She did not feel Bill forced their relationship.

We are cautioned that the government will use all its resources against us and won't settle out of court. So much for all the free advice we got from others telling us we had a strong case. Larry is relieved when Ruth and I agree not to file a suit against the government. Ruth tells him, "We know, Daddy, you didn't want to do it."

I hope we are making the right decision. We will wait to make a determination about filing against Mitch. It is dark outside as we finish our discussion and say cordial goodbyes. I'm pleasantly surprised his bill is so reasonable.

The three of us go to Kings Restaurant in South Williamsport for dinner. The dining area is attractive with white tablecloths, mirrors, and flowers. When we were here before with Margie, Abby, and Jacob, the owner came to our table and gave Abby and Jacob each a balloon, told them how much he enjoyed his grandchildren, and that he loved having kids at his restaurant. A three-piece band was playing and there was a small dance floor at one end, separated by only a curtain Abby and Jake peeked around. When dinner was over we moved to little tables near the dance floor and soon Margie and Ruth were dancing with Abby and Jacob. I had so much fun watching them.

Tonight there is no band and the restaurant is not busy. The food is good, but we're all tired and haunted by everything that happened today. The plea bargain we are sure will happen and the memories of that happier evening bring our emotions to the surface. During dinner Ruth tells me, "Your friend Lillian told me I was angry because Margie took you away from me. It's true, Ma. You aren't the parents you used to be."

Lillian is the therapist I see and whom I convinced Ruth to see at least once. *Thanks a lot, Lillian.* I admit to Ruth, "You're both right. I'm not the parent I was, and I never will be again."

Back at the Sheraton in Williamsport I watch *NYPD Blue* and we make plans to go to the Woolrich Store. It is north of here, but we have the time. What better way to forget for a while than to go shopping? Margie loved taking us to Woolrich. Today we buy Christmas presents, coats and snow pants for Abby and Jacob. It is a successful detour on our way home to Connecticut.

On Wednesday, November 12th, the telephone rings, "Hello, Mrs. Bostrom, this is Wayne Samuelson." I know what he is going to say and dread it. Larry picks up the other phone. "George Lepley has called. Mitch will plea to second-degree murder without agreement as to the sentence.

"I'm meeting with my supervisors to discuss it this afternoon. I wanted you to know and see how you feel."

We're not sure. There will be no defaming her at a trial and there is no risk he will not be found guilty. Wayne has told us he is not sure he can prove premeditation. However, we wonder if Mitch will kill again if he gets out too soon? We are upset the system appears to be saying this is all her life was worth. A trial would have given us a chance to tell her story. Wayne tells us we will get a chance at the sentencing to give our impact statements. We're still not sure.

Wayne answers, "I hear you. I'm not either. That is why I'm talking to my supervisors. I'll call you after we talk and tell you our decision."

There is no call on Thursday but on Friday, Wayne calls us in Marlborough. Our fears are now a reality. Mitch signed the plea agreement. We are stunned. Why did he make us go through the jury selection? Then plead. Sounds sadistic to me.

The hearing will be Wednesday, November 19th, at 4 P.M. Wayne tells us it really is best. He will ask for more than the eleven to fourteen years. The psychiatrists' reports make it hard to get first-degree murder. He advises us to call Marty Carlson, the criminal chief in the U.S. Attorney's office, for more details. We do and are told, "It is the psychiatrists' reports that cause us to agree to the plea." This may be true, but I know homicide trials cost the government money and take time. Under 10 percent of them ever reach trial. Maybe they should be brought to trial and less violent crimes disposed of in other ways.

We discuss the plea agreement with Ruth at dinner. I think she is relieved and my doubts seem foolish to her. We argue and I tell her, "You lost a sister. I lost my baby. How would you feel if something happened to Abby or Jacob?" I go downstairs to our bathroom where I moan like a wounded animal—over and over again. It is the first real release I have had since the day Margie was murdered. Thankfully, Abby and Jacob are with Steve, but Larry, Kathy, and Calie are all worried about my well-being and feel helpless.

Ruth apologizes, "Ma, I don't know what I would do if I lost one of them. I can't even imagine how awful it would be."

On November 19th, at 4 P.M., Mitch goes before the judge. His rights and what he is giving up by entering into this plea bargain are explained over and over again. Each time he is asked if he understands. Has he been advised by his attorneys? Has any deal been agreed to outside of this court? Does he understand the United States may recommend the maximum sentence and his attorneys may ask for downward departure? Does he understand the victims will be able to comment on the crime and sentencing? The judge wants to ensure Mitch is in no way impaired or unable to make the best decision for himself. I look at his parents across the aisle and feel their dismay at all Mitch is giving up with his admission of guilt. They know we are devastated because he took Margie from us but he is their son. I write this poem on the ride home to Connecticut.

Two Lonely People

His parents sit outside the courtroom door
Isolated from the world by their pain and grief.
The father waves as Margie's family passes by.
An acknowledgment of defeat and despair.

All hopes and dreams for his only son are
Suddenly cruel fantasy and torment to his heart.

The mother stares straight ahead seeing only the future.
Wishing for what was and could have been,
But will never be when her beloved son admits,
In anger, he stabbed his wife to death.
The past holds all the precious memories they'll have
Of Mitch—precocious child, football star, and business whiz.

In the courtroom, brevity is mercilessly denied.
The judge needs to be sure Mitch understands
The gravity of a guilty plea to murder two.
The prosecutor tells of six wounds to the heart
Others to the lungs, liver, and abdominal aorta,
Her damp, nude body bathed in blood.

Their thoughts are for the people across the aisle,
Friends who have lost a precious daughter.
Do they have the same ugly nightmares?
Hear the helpless cries and ask why he didn't just leave?
Wonder if he knows what he is doing—giving up his rights?
Feel it's too late? We've all suffered for fifteen months.

Court adjourns. Her family reaches across the aisle.
Two grieving families embrace, share the pain,
Murmur words of comfort. So sorry.
Agree it never should have happened.
Tears and silent sobs release the tension.
Surely, the healing can now begin? No, but maybe soon.

There will be no more trips to Williamsport this year. Our Impact Statements and letters supporting an upward departure are due in probation officer Drew Thompson's office before February 9, 1998. The sentencing is scheduled for March 18th and 19th. Now, we'll have something to do during the Christmas holidays. Preparing our impact statements well is important because it is all we can do for Margie.

I take the Prozac from April 1997 until February 1998 when it becomes apparent the increased dosage is causing fatigue—the same problem I had before I began the medication. Writing the impact statement makes me face what is gone. I think of the adult Margie and her potential that will never be reached because of Mitch. I am grateful for those poignant remembrances.

CHAPTER 17

From Lynchburg to Lewisburg

Margie's dad often misspeaks, saying Lynchburg when he means Lewisburg. Perhaps this is a subconscious psychological attempt to return to the earlier, happier memories when Margie's young adult life was just beginning—pre-Mitch.

Margie, in her typically independent way, selected which colleges she wanted to apply to, sent for the applications, and filled them out on her own. She decided to go to Lynchburg College after we visited it during the April vacation of her senior year in high school. In April 1983 we drove south through Scranton, Pennsylvania, and were amazed when we encountered a major snowstorm. The road through the Appalachian Mountains was snow-covered and slippery but soon we were into Virginia where spring was in full swing.

The city of Lynchburg is located on the banks of the James River south of Charlottesville. Its brick streets, hills, and old mills reminded Larry and me of Jamestown, New York, where we grew up. We drove by Liberty College. Jerry Falwell founded it for conservative Protestants, which he claims are the *moral majority*. The extensive construction and numerous temporary buildings housing the students indicated that religion was thriving in the South. Randolph Macon, an all-girls school in 1983, was a typical, stately, well-established institution of higher learning located in town.

Lynchburg College, with its red brick structures and white pillars and trim, sits in a park-like setting atop a hill. When we met with a representative of the college she reported it had snowed in

Lynchburg the week before but assured us snow was unusual in April. A student from Brewster, New York, gave us a tour of the college. The grounds were well tended and attractive with large trees, flowering shrubs, and colorful flower beds— a college campus worthy of a movie set. We spent the night and had dinner at the Hilton Hotel, where Liberty College was holding a banquet, and we were surprised when our waitress made some negative comments about that institution. It reminded me of the bumper sticker that proclaims *The Moral Majority is neither.*

We liked southwestern Virginia, which is rich in American history, and looked forward to visiting many of the famous homes in the area, including the plantations of presidents Madison and Monroe. All of us were impressed with what Lynchburg College could offer academically and Margie would be able to work part-time to help with expenses. The warmer weather was certainly a factor in her choice of this small liberal arts college nestled in the mountains of Virginia.

We went back to West Suffield and completed plans to sell the farm and move into a condominium in Windsor. We were having it built in an area called Strawberry Hills, which was only four miles from where Larry and I worked in Windsor Locks. It would be quite a change. No more lawn or muddy drive to care for. The chores connected with caring for three horses were already part of the past because I had given them away to what I hoped were good homes. Selling the farm was a difficult decision for me because it felt like home, but it still required major repairs including a new roof and siding, extensive work on the foundation, and the remodeling of the upstairs rooms still needed to be finished.

Larry's demanding work as an electrical engineer and his natural tendency to procrastinate frustrated me. If we had spent the money necessary to completely renovate the farm we wouldn't have been able to keep our commitment to Margie. We had promised to pay for her education because she did well in school and knew, while still in high school, that she wanted to become a clinical psychologist. The farm sold quickly and by July we were in the new condo. Margie and Kathy shared a large, attractive room with two huge closets—very different from their bedrooms on the farm.

That September we packed up the car and took Margie to begin her college career. We went through the ritual all parents of college students experience twice yearly—loading and unloading the car and lugging everything into or out of a dorm room that is too small to hold the necessities of teenage roommates. Of course, Margie's room was on the top floor, but there was an elevator.

We met her roommate, a short bubbly blonde from New Jersey who was interested in the theater and acting. When it was time to leave, my heart was in turmoil. I was leaving my baby but she was embarking on an exciting new chapter in her life and I wished her well.

During the two years Margie was at college in Virginia we visited Jefferson's home, Monticello, and the University of Virginia, both of which are splendid examples of his architectural genius. On the tour of his home we were impressed by all the gadgets he invented to make his life more convenient. We admired his huge entryway clock with a pendulum that dropped through a hole in the floor. We followed the tunnel to the kitchens, walked the flower-filled grounds, viewed the small burial plot where Jefferson is buried, and the living quarters of his favorite slave. It was both a fun-filled and educational excursion we recorded on several rolls of film.

We also stopped at the University of Virginia so Larry could search for the famous, spartan, living quarters on the quadrangle where his brother Bud lived while he was a student during World War II. When we found them we were struck by their small size, austere decor, and lack of modern conveniences. Small nameplates indicated that several important figures in American history spent their formative years here. Although Margie was impressed, I was sure she preferred the comforts of her dorm at Lynchburg.

In Lynchburg we visited the home of a famous black woman poet, Ann Spencer, who was part of the 1920 Harlem Renaissance. Her cottage was on Pierce Street; Pierce also happens to be my maiden name. We met her son, who was a decorated World War II hero, but his mother was not home at the time. We planned to return but never did. Each time we visited Margie we enjoyed exploring historic sites, attending college events, and dining in good restaurants, but mostly we relished being with her.

During the winter of Margie's second year there, Kathy decided to visit her. They went to Florida for a break—without telling us they were going. Kathy has always felt we blamed her but I knew Margie had a choice and she wanted to go too. We, the parents, are not sure what happened, but believe that either before or after their trip some trouble occurred on campus and Kathy was told to leave and not return.

Later Margie evaluated what she wanted from college. She realized she had allowed herself to be distracted from her goals and decided she wanted a new start nearer home at the University of Connecticut.

She came home and we met with personnel at UCONN to determine if this was the right decision. She liked it there and they accepted her credits. We were thrilled to have her nearer home and it was less expensive, but we worried when she was assigned to "the Jungle" because it was known as the party dormitory. She adjusted quickly and successfully to the change. Her studying was done in the library and she came home if she needed to complete a paper or prepare for an exam. She continued to earn excellent grades and when she was selected for Phi Beta Kappa, I was delighted she had earned that honor. Her hard work paid off and she graduated magna cum laude.

After being at UCONN for less than a month she met Mitch, a bright business student, who came to the university on a partial football scholarship as a place kicker. However, he had dropped off the team, blaming the coach for capriciously choosing to use another player more. Margie and Mitch quickly became involved in a volatile relationship. They weren't happy apart but had frequent, heated arguments on the phone or when they were together. The quarreling was matched by equally intense loving. Their interaction troubled us, but we had no knowledge of the characteristics of an abusive relationship so we decided that interfering would only drive them closer together. We hoped Mitch would get tired of her and move on to someone else. Unfortunately that didn't happen. We also hoped, to no avail, that the physical separation—when he graduated and went to New Jersey to work and she was still at the university getting a master's degree in Marriage and Family Therapy—would end their involvement. It didn't.

Margie meets Mitch at the University of Connecticut and the volatile relationship begins.

We made Mitch welcome in our home because Margie wanted us to, and they spent many weekends in Windsor. Larry and I observed one incident I remember clearly: Mitch stormed down the stairs into the living room followed by an angry Margie. He headed toward the front door about the time I noticed a police cruiser pulling into our driveway. When the policeman knocked on the door Mitch opened it and told him, "She has my wallet and credit cards and won't give them back."

The policeman looked at Margie who didn't deny Mitch's accusation but countered, "He posted nude pictures of me in the dorm at UCONN. I want them back. Then he'll get his wallet."

The officer asked Mitch to step outside. They sat in the cruiser and talked for a long while. When they returned the policeman told us, "He says there are no photographs at UCONN. He was only teasing. I've told him this isn't a joke and he says he is sorry. I've warned him that such behavior is serious and he could be in trouble with the law. I think he understands, but in any case he should go back to New Jersey now." The policeman waited while Mitch packed and left. The neighbors must have gotten an eyeful.

Later, I received a long letter from Mitch trying to justify his behavior. In it he explained that it was not his fault. He had a cold, it was a bad day at work, traffic was horrible, and he was distressed because he had stopped to see his beloved grandfather who was terminally ill with cancer. He was tired and hungry and anticipated Margie being loving and supportive when he arrived. Instead he felt she had been angry and argumentative. Too late, I will learn that blaming others for their unacceptable behavior is a characteristic of most abusers.

Many times we tried to explain to Margie that although she was in love with Mitch, we saw him through eyes not clouded by that emotion. We accepted him because she wanted us to but our reservations grew.

Three sisters in 1987. Ruth is the bride with Kathy and Margie. (Photo by Richard Berozsky Studios, Enfield, CT)

On March 1, 1989, Margie was in New York City interviewing as a candidate for a doctoral program when her niece, Abigail, was born. That summer Ruth returned to work after her maternity leave and Margie, who had completed her master's program, delighted in being Abby's nanny. She loved Abby and surprised me with her competence in caring for the newborn. They formed a close bond that lasted until Margie's death.

In July, Larry and I went to San Diego with Margie to invest in a condominium where she would live while she pursued her degree. She had been accepted into the California School of Professional Psychology's Ph.D. program for clinical psychologists.

We had agreed to help pay her living expenses and buying a condo seemed like a good investment. We stayed at the Seven Seas Motel where Larry had stayed on business trips to the Miramar Naval Air Station. When we weren't house hunting we enjoyed the pool, cocktail hour hors d'oeuvres, and the nightly piano bar where customers with excellent voices sang their favorite songs.

After several disappointing visits to condos in the price range we were considering, we knew we had to go at least ten thousand dollars higher to get a suitable dwelling in a safe community. We all fell in love with a lovely, one-bedroom condo in a stucco building with red Spanish-tiled roof and a veranda. There was a swimming pool and a laundry building, and each resident was assigned a covered parking area. It was located in Mira Mesa, north of San Diego, close to the CSPP campus. Everything she would need could be found on nearby Mira Mesa Boulevard or further down on Miramar.

After all the paperwork for buying the condo was completed, we began our search for furniture. We bought a sofa with an abstract pastel print, light oak tables and lamps for the living room, a glass and wrought-iron table set with white plastic seats for the dining area, and a pine double bed with mattress and box springs. Everything was to be held at the store until Larry and Margie returned in late August.

Back in Connecticut the search for a carrier to take Larry's, soon to be Margie's, little red Hyundai across the country began. She packed what she would need and shipped it so it would arrive in August at the same time Larry and she did.

While Larry and Margie were in California they bought some plants and patio furniture to dress up the veranda, a dresser, a GS

Apple computer, a printer, and a desk. Dad came in handy for setting everything up. Secretly, I envied him his time alone with Margie but I was also pleased they had this chance to relate to each other. Besides I was working and teachers don't want to be away from their classrooms during those important formative days with a new class.

She was her daddy's little girl.

Margie spent many happy hours in the months that followed, shopping for just the right accessories for her new home. She soon began her love affair with the Target store, where she bought linens, tools, and household items such as: wastebaskets, pots and pans, throw rugs, and plastic storage containers.

When Margie had decided to go to California to get her Ph.D. in Clinical Psychology, she and Mitch argued and broke up. We hoped that this time it was a clean break and Mitch wouldn't know how to reach her. We were relieved when she dated briefly, but soon he visited her. It is possible that his claim that she called him on his birthday, October 22nd, is true. It is hard to believe she begged him to move to California, but she had given him her phone number. Margie told us he called her frequently, claiming he needed her and that he was doing poorly at his job because he couldn't concentrate without her. Classic examples of the honeymoon phase in the cycle of domestic violence, which none of us recognized.

The first winter Margie was in California, I went to visit her during my February vacation. It was before Mitch moved there and Larry was working. It was my time to be alone with her. She went to classes during the day and I sat at the pool where I met her neighbor Maggie. Maggie was older than I and adored Margie, who had wisely explained to me that Maggie went into the pool wearing a raincoat because she was allergic to the sun.

Margie and I enjoyed relaxing together, so when Larry called and asked who was doing the cooking, we looked at each other and giggled. We ate out every evening. One special night we returned to the piano bar at the Seven Seas Motel—a real women's night out. I felt having grown daughters to enjoy spending time with was my reward for the worry and sleepless nights that were required when my daughters were babies or teenagers.

Shortly after my visit, Mitch moved to California to live with Margie.

On June 25, 1991, Larry and I began a month-long vacation. We flew to Margie and Mitch's and began our tour by driving to Las Vegas. It was the only place we could get reservations for the Fourth of July weekend. Margie and Mitch went with us but drove in his car because they would return to San Diego the following Monday. We drove through Victorville and stopped in Calico—a ghost town on the side of a hill that was covered with greenish-colored soil. There were decaying wooden ruins and a reconstructed main street, but I was most impressed with how hot it was. The temperature was 128 degrees. When I took a can of soda from the ice-filled cooler, the can was too hot to hold before I could finish drinking it.

In Las Vegas the daytime temperature was 116, but I still posed for a picture next to a cardboard cutout of Elvis. We stayed at El Rancho, which is no longer there. That evening we walked along the street and I kept making 360-degree turns—I didn't want to miss any of the amazing visual stimulation. Bright neon signs were flashing everywhere.

Mitch didn't want to see the Rich Little show so we agreed to meet afterward. We returned to the hotel and Margie was upset because Mitch wasn't there. He arrived later and wanted to bowl at the alley in the hotel but she went to bed. Larry and I decided to play peacemakers so we stayed up and bowled with Mitch. We were surprised we had such a good time.

Larry and I went on to Utah to visit St. George, Snow Canyon, Zion, and Bryce before returning to California through Joshua Tree Monument. We saw some spectacular scenery, so we weren't prepared for the deterioration in mood caused by the abandoned shanties we saw as we approached Twenty-nine Palms. Further south that negative aura was reinforced when we found the Salton Sea, a deserted lake surrounded by ruined modular homes. No people, no boats, and no birds—it was a disturbing and desolate sight. The mystery increased when we discovered the AAA guidebook described the area as a thriving saltwater wildlife and recreational area that developed early in the twentieth century because of a mistake. A cut had been made in the Colorado River to irrigate the Imperial Valley and water accidentally flowed into an ancient sea bed. When was it abandoned? Why? We returned to San Diego on a narrow winding road over the Santa Rosa Mountains—with no guard rails.

A few days later, Larry, Margie, and I flew to San Francisco where we did what tourists do. We went on the harbor cruise under the Golden Gate Bridge. Seagulls patrolled the fog-shrouded metal spans and tall reddish supports that reach to the sky giving the bridge a delicate geometric beauty. Alcatraz, the haunted island, sat in the middle of the harbor—so close to the unreachable freedom symbolized by the San Francisco skyline. The prisoners' depression and despair could still be felt, yet it was a fascinating and thought-provoking sight. One building near the water seemed to have been repaired, while molting white stucco ruins still perched on top of the rock near the white tower that stands guard over the prison. As the cruise ended, the bright morning sun cast a silver glow over the Bay Bridge.

At Pier 39 we saw lots of tourists, the carousel, and one lonely sea lion. We learned this was the season they go away to mate and this one was too old. Margie and I bought unique earrings that spiraled through the pierced holes in our ears. (I now have both pairs.)

We rode a cable car to the top where we visited the Ansel Adams and John Paul Getty museums. Back at the bottom we went to the Natural History Museum where I made friends with a dinosaur—well, at least we talked to each other. I don't think Margie was embarrassed but Larry might have been.

We had dinner at the Cliff House with Larry's niece Janet. She and Margie seemed to hit it off and I hoped that perhaps these cousins would get acquainted. Janet, a Ph.D. working at Stanford University, did offer to help Margie make contacts that would be helpful when she started writing her dissertation. Unfortunately, there was a mixup and it never happened.

Larry, Margie, and I took Lounge Car Tours from San Francisco to Los Angeles. The bus seats had been replaced with huge padded swivel lounge chairs. There were only seven people so each of us had at least two seats so we could spread out. It was wonderful. Margie was the youngest member of the group and soon became a favorite of everyone.

Traveling south along the Big Sur was an awe-inspiring experience. From the narrow and winding road we had a spectacular view of the rocky cliffs being buffeted by the strong ocean waves. Scary!

The bus took the Seventeen Mile Drive past Clint Eastwood's former home. It was a foggy day filled with drizzle and everything was gray—the ocean, the rocks, the birds, the seals, the sky, the wooden home, and even the cypress trees surrounding it. We saw deer on the Pebble Beach Golf Course as we drove by before stopping. We bought Mitch a souvenir pad and pencil with the course name inscribed on it. He probably couldn't afford to play there, but now he could pretend he did.

We ate lunch in Carmel and later stopped to see the Lone Cypress, near Monterey. It was old and bandaged, held together with wires and cement, and supported by stone walls that reinforced a rocky cliff that jutted out into the water. Three deep-green tufts of needles atop the gnarled trunk were silhouetted against the sea and sky. I was distressed to learn the tree is owned by a Japanese company that claims it as their logo and have copyrighted it.

We continued on, looking back at bridges we had crossed. They spanned huge ravines where water descended to the ocean. There were a few sandy stretches along the shore but I wondered how anyone got down to them. We spent the night in Monterey and visited the shops at Cannery Row, which was made famous by John Steinbeck.

At San Simeone we stopped at the visitor center at the bottom of the hill and boarded a bus to tour Hearst Castle, which sits at the top. Beef cattle grazed on the golden hills surrounding it. The outdoor pool had Italian-style statues and columns and was lined with blue and white tiles forming intricate designs.

The large rectangular indoor pool with a small alcove was enclosed with huge arched windows. Statues and large floor lamps surrounded it. Each room in the castle was more lavish and ornate than the one before, but Margie and I were most intrigued by Randolph's relationship with his mother, his wife, and Marion Davies, his lover.

We drove over the mountains into Santa Barbara through forests that were destroyed by an arsonist's fire. For us, the main attraction was the mission with its two stone towers topped by pink domes and the triangular steeple with a cross at its peak that sat between them. Six pillars encompassed large front steps that led to the huge arched entrance. Its simplicity was stunning.

We looked for souvenirs at Solvang, a small Scandinavian settlement, because my girls are proud of their Swedish background. Margie found a small wooden horse painted red and decorated with the typical Swedish designs. She wanted it but it was expensive and I felt we had already spent enough on her. It is one of the few times I said no. Later, she and Mitch went back and she got her red horse. She was a determined woman. Now, I wish I, instead of Mitch, had gotten it for her.

In Los Angeles we went to Universal Studios where we saw the Bates house and motel, the set for *Miami Vice,* and rode the *E.T.* bikes. Then we took the train to Del Mar, where Mitch met us.

In April of 1993 Larry and I, Ruth and Steve, Abby, and Kathy were all invited to stay for a week with Margie and Mitch at their new home in Poway. Mitch was a gracious host and being together was very special. Abby loved the San Diego Zoo and Sea World, where we sat in the danger zone for getting wet when the killer whales splashed. Kathy wasn't happy when we got wet but Abby thought it was funny. Before the show started they projected pictures of people in the audience onto a huge screen. We were startled when four-year-old Abby's picture materialized inside of a star frame. She looked so cute but we almost missed her brief appearance.

One day the "girls" went to the beach while the "boys" played golf. We were amazed as we sat watching the rescue teams practice in the violent surf. Then Abby and Grandma made a sand castle and later we walked along the boardwalk, rode the merry-go-round, and steered little electronic boats mostly into each other or the sides of the canal. We ate lunch at a beachside café and watched kites perform complicated routines guided by skilled handlers. It was a day for creating happy family memories. All my girls together!

The next day we all went down to the harbor and took a cruise. Abby loved the sea lions that played or sunned on rocks and buoys. Larry described the different naval ships as we passed each one. Back on shore, we shopped at the stores along the harbor. Then we walked the boardwalk to find a place to eat.

Another day we drove to National City and crossed the border into Mexico. Tijuana shops lured the girls with their substantial discounts on expensive perfumes, jewelry, and leather goods. We all enjoyed the cafés that served margaritas, cerveza, and chips with guacamole. Steve finally became aggravated with the persistent street vendors and asked one little girl why she wasn't in school. It was time to return to Poway.

Abby relished the attention of six adoring adults. She sat on a float in Margie and Mitch's pool—just like a little princess. She wanted Sebastian, Margie's cat, along with her human subjects, to demonstrate complete devotion. At first, Sebastian had other ideas. He was shy and not used to small children but gradually Abby won his affection, or at least his curiosity, with toys and treats.

Leaving was sad. It was one of those special times you know instinctively can never happen again. Everyone had worked very hard at being considerate and cooperative. Fortunately, Grandma was faithfully videotaping our experience. I called it *Abby Does San Diego*. Before we left we gave Mitch some extra money to help pay for the additional expense caused by five houseguests. Shortly after we returned to Connecticut, Ruth told us she might be pregnant. The doctor confirmed it and the baby was due in early January. I could hardly wait.

On July 2, 1992, our anniversary, Larry and I were visiting Margie and Mitch and we took Margie to the famous Del Coronado Hotel. I felt only a little guilty that Mitch was unable to join us. As we drove toward the Coronado Bridge, which is long and curves at an angle with little visible support, we could see the red cone roof of the historic landmark. At the hotel we parked and strolled through the grounds to the large rectangular pool. A wooden deck, white furniture, and buildings with red roofs surrounded the pool. Beyond a wire fence was the beach.

Inside we found a luxurious cocktail lounge with a piano player. Next to this area was a huge, elegant restaurant that was a little intimidating at first. But the waiter put us at ease and we had a great meal. When Larry and I were back home in Windsor, Connecticut, my friend Barbara asked, "Did you get to the Del? Isn't it marvelous?" Yes, Barbara, it is.

Larry and I visited Margie and Mitch at least twice a year. We always went to Old Town with its historic village, gift shops, and authentic Mexican restaurants. We seldom left Old Town without making a purchase at Margie's favorite garden and pottery shop. Those pots now sit on my patio in Marlborough—reminders of the interest in gardening Margie and I shared.

A trip to San Diego usually meant a trip into Mexico. It was easy to take the trolley to the border and cross over and take a taxi to the center of Tijuana. Sometimes we drove to the border crossing and once we even walked from there to the markets and shops. On one occasion Mitch couldn't go and he suggested that Margie have her father drive. Of course, this made her determined to prove she could do it. She drove. I was proud of her determination and relieved she accomplished the drive without incident.

Early one morning Larry and I and Margie and Mitch drove to Oceanside and took the ferry to Catalina Island. Avalon is nestled at the foot of mountains that reach down to the protected bay. Houses climb up the hillside or sit on top, blending into the landscape. I watched two people parasailing and remembered that Mitch got Margie to do that when they went to Acapulco. That was one thing I really liked about him—he encouraged her to stretch her bound-

We are happy tourists on our way to Catalina Island.

aries. We took a tour bus to the top of the mountains and the guide told us about the Wrigley family, who own much of the island and have established reserves to protect the environment. He showed us where Zane Grey, a favorite author of mine, had lived. It is now a private home but there is a plaque identifying it. At the top of a mountain, there is an airport where the runway seems to disappear over the edge—an awesome sight. We saw herds of buffalo that have developed from the ones that were brought over for a movie and left behind when the picture was finished because it was too expensive to transport them back. They seemed happy enough with their new home.

There was always something to do in the San Diego area. We went to the Del Mar Fair, La Joya, the Scripts Aquarium, and the Balboa Park Art Museum, which is near the zoo. A nicely landscaped tree-lined parkway leads the visitor into the grounds full of beautiful flowers, plants, and trees. One afternoon we drove to the First Mission on el Camino Real. It was a white stucco building that had been recently restored. It was located on top of a hill overlooking much of old San Diego.

The guide explained to us that this was the Plymouth Rock of the West. Even though I understood what he meant I told him, "Don't sell the mission short." When he looked at me quizzically, I asked, "Have you ever been to Plymouth Rock?" He hadn't so I explained. "It is a small ordinary rock encased in a cement hole with a black, protective iron fence around it that does not keep out the trash." He didn't enjoy that history lesson any more than I did when I first visited the historic rock.

In April 1995, during my spring vacation from teaching fifth grade, Larry and I went to see Mitch and Margie in California. The weather that week was awful—which is unheard of in San Diego County. It rained four days straight, and the three of us decided to go to Death Valley. Secretly, I was happy Mitch couldn't go because he had just started a job. (He and Margie had been arguing about money and he wanted her to get a low-paying job as well as work at her post-doctoral clinical placement. Besides we always enjoyed getting her away alone.) She was so much fun without Mitch there to demand her attention. She got excited and enthusiastic about everything.

It was vacation week and the only reservations we could get were at the Furnace Creek Inn, which cost nearly three hundred dollars a night. Larry only blinked for a moment before deciding to splurge. We were soon on our way—in Margie's little Hyundai. I had the backseat all to myself and was surprisingly comfortable. I watched as we glided past cactus, Joshua trees, and surreal rock formations on the desert landscape. I was glad we were seeing this part of California now. If Margie and Mitch settled back East, our chance to explore California would end soon. But I wanted her nearby when I retired.

Death Valley was hot and dry and full of ghosts of old prospectors, the twenty-mule teams that transported the borax on *Death Valley Days* and Zane Grey characters I recalled from books I devoured while a teenager.

The desolate vistas were foreign to our eyes, which were accustomed to New England's lush green spring landscape, but the resort was truly an oasis. Later, under the afternoon sun, we approached the fancy lodge. The pale, peach-colored adobe building sits in front of barren hills. The magical scene was complete with balconies, red-tiled roofs, and an outdoor swimming pool surrounded by profuse flower gardens and walkways that would be lighted at night under a sky full of shining stars. Fancy dining rooms, a bedroom furnished with Victorian antiques, and the footed bathtub that was really a Jacuzzi all catered to our comfort.

We hiked along trails, delighted by the sight of the dainty wild-flowers covering the desert floor, and marveling at the surreal landscapes. Zamboni's Point, solid rock swept smooth by the wind, appeared to flow like sand. It was breathtaking at sunset. Salt crystals seeped up through the soil at Devil's Golf Course, forming ever-changing magical castles. Margie was enchanted by the experience and we enjoyed her enthusiasm so I was surprised when she refused to buy Mitch a gift. Instead she picked up some unique-looking stones, which we later realized was against the law, to give him as souvenirs. She explained, "I'll make Mitch happy. He is so worried about me spending money. He wouldn't want me to waste it on him."

Later, when she gave them to him he complained, "Is this all I get?" She had hit her mark.

From Death Valley we went to Joshua Tree Monument, where we had fun taking photographs of all the odd-shaped trees and rock formations. We also met a large, healthy-looking coyote on the road. He was as curious about us as we were about him and he posed for pictures before disappearing into the ocotillo cactus and scrub brush.

Back in Poway, we spent a few days at Margie and Mitch's home helping Mitch trim a palm tree and Margie get the ice plant that was taking over the sidewalk and patio under control. Margie and I walked on the desert trail behind her home. Spring is the perfect season for collecting wildflowers, which I took back to the house and pressed inside cardboard. We either cooked out or went to nice restaurants. At one in a nearby plaza, Mitch talked Larry and me into trying a drink with raw oysters instead of olives or lemon rind as a garnish. Margie laughed at us but we all had a great time.

On Saturday morning we followed Margie's ritual of going to the local farmers' market. Along with fresh strawberries, melons, arugula, green beans, and corn, we bought huge Hawaiian flowers that appeared to be from an alien world. I still have them, dried, in my living room.

Larry and I received a call from Margie shortly after we returned to Connecticut. She had changed her mind. She would spend the money to participate in the graduation ceremony, which was less than two months away. We happily agreed to return to San Diego in mid-June to watch her receive her Ph.D. in Clinical Psychology. Larry and I were so proud and happy for her—and Mitch certainly appeared to be too.

Dr. Margaret E. Bostrom and her proud parents celebrate.

After the ceremony we took "Dr. Bostrom" and her husband to Ensenada, Mexico, to a beachfront resort where we relaxed and had fun. Margie and I went horseback riding on the beach. A goal of mine was to ride a horse along the beach—hooves splashing the surf—like in the movies. I am so grateful Margie was there to help me fulfill that dream and I have pictures of us riding. Later we ate at the old St. Tomas Winery again.

The next day Margie was anxious to get back to Poway early so she and I could go pick up the golden retriever puppy we were giving her as a graduation present. She and Mitch argued about whether there was enough time before our plane left. I had to be back to school the next day. Margie and I drove quite a distance to the small ranch home where

Margie helps fulfill her mother's dream of riding on a beach.

the breeder lived. The puppy was a small bundle of golden fur that I got to hold on my lap all the way home because I don't do standard stick shifts—and that was what Margie's car had so she had to drive. I teased her that I was bonding with my granddog. She kept saying, "What should I call her? I was thinking of California Girl, Calie for short, or Golden Girl, Goldie for short." I thought she liked Calie better and so did I. Calie it was! When we got her home we took her for a walk in the desert but we soon ended up carrying her because

Calie and Margie are bonding.

her legs were so tiny. She had to take too many steps to keep up. That didn't last long. Within weeks she was a lanky, leggy, energetic adolescent.

In September 1995, Margie finished her post-doctoral work, which she did in a facility for victims of domestic violence in the San Diego area. After she was murdered we learned that her supervisor there had been told by her coworkers Mitch was abusing her, but apparently Margie was in denial. The one time she called the police she refused to press charges—the laws were different then. Now, the police can decide whether to arrest.

Margie learned there were openings in the Federal Bureau of Prisons for psychologists. She thought the experience would be beneficial and she could pay off some of her student loans. Each year she worked for the federal government would reduce the amount she owed. There was an opening in Lewisburg, Pennsylvania, so she came back East to interview. She and Mitch flew into Baltimore and drove up to central Pennsylvania. She was offered the job, which she would begin in November. Everything seemed perfect. They would drive cross-country, while the government shipped their furniture. Mitch came with her and we all had Thanksgiving with the Pasters in New Jersey, which is only three hours from Lewisburg. On Friday we went to help her unpack and settle into her new home. Mitch returned to California for three months and planned to come home at Christmas. But the three months dragged to six and during that time the relationship deteriorated further. Margie was finding that she was capable of managing her life on her own without his control and criticisms. She was successful at her job and was making friends without regard to his preferences. She was gaining back her self-esteem. We all missed the signs that she was still in a dangerous relationship.

CHAPTER 18

Elizabeth Helps
Solve a Mystery

Elizabeth! This name appears in strange ways in the days and weeks following the murder. Margie's friend Ed at the penitentiary puts a memorial piece in the prison newsletter. In it, Margie's name is given as Margaret Elizabeth. He's terribly upset. "Mrs. Bostrom, I knew her middle name was Eleanor. I'm so sorry. I don't know what I was thinking."

"It's the thought that counts. Don't worry about it. We appreciate all your attempts to keep her memory alive." I feel close to him. He is one of the few members of Margaret's "penitentiary family" who have kept in touch during the long months of waiting for justice following the crime.

I often ask myself, *What kind of family is that? They don't answer my letters. How can they forget so soon? Don't they understand what we are going through or how much a card or a call would mean?*

The October after Margie's murder Ed sends me a purple ribbon for Domestic Violence Awareness Month. I tie it on the inside mirror in my car and make a pledge to keep it there until Mitch is brought to justice.

A news article and Margaret's obituary appear in the Jamestown, New York, newspaper. Both Larry and I grew up in that area and all three of our daughters were born in Jamestown. Many relatives and friends still live in western New York State. One of my best friends, Agnes, died in 1977 from pneumonia and complications caused by blood clots. In 1964 we both were pregnant with due dates in early December. I had Margie early and Agnes went three weeks beyond her due date. I saw Agnes twice the year she died. Our visits were so natural and we quickly filled each other in on what was happening in our lives. She promised they would visit Connecticut again soon. My mother was very ill with emphysema and died in late September. Agnes was at her funeral. Two months later Agnes was dead. Her husband has now remarried so he and his new wife send us a sympathy card. Inside she writes, "We read in the *Post-Journal* about Elizabeth and we want to let you know how sorry we are. God bless you, Shirley!" There's that name again. Of course, they mean Margaret.

Another friend, Pat from my writing group, sends me a newspaper clipping about a woman's shelter called Elizabeth House. I ask my daughter Ruth, "What significance does the name Elizabeth have? I can't make the connection but I know there is one." She just shrugs her shoulders.

The phone rings one evening while I'm watching the news on television. It's Sam Rieger, president of Survivors of Homicide. "Shirley, I just talked to a woman whose daughter was murdered by a boyfriend. She lives in Colchester. She'd like to come to the Waterbury meeting on Wednesday. Would you and Larry be willing to bring her since Marlborough is so close to where she lives?"

"Sure." I'm glad to have the chance to help someone else just as we've been supported through our grief by other survivors. "Let me have her phone number."

Sam explains, "She said she would call you but you may want to give her a call—if you don't hear from her soon."

I agree. It meant so much when strangers reached out to us, especially people like Sam and Wanda who have shared a similar loss. "See you Wednesday."

"Yeah. By the way, her name is Elizabeth."

Elizabeth! There is that name again.

I wait before making the call. I want to give her the chance to reach out. She does and we make the necessary plans. We also talk about how hard it is to keep going when a child is dead. I give her directions to Ruth's home. We'll see each other the next afternoon at 6 P.M.

Elizabeth calls me the next afternoon at five. "I can't go."

"Why? Is there anything I can do to help?"

"No, I'm just not ready to hear everyone's sad stories. I'm having enough trouble dealing with my own grief. I can't handle any more."

"Elizabeth, that isn't how it works. In some strange way sharing each other's pain gives everyone more strength. The support is essential for healing to start and keep going."

"Oh, I'm sure, but I'm really not ready to meet so many new people. I'll pass this time."

"Why don't we get together soon? Just the two of us—for lunch or breakfast. That way you will know at least one person before the next meeting."

She agrees.

On a clear, sunny October morning I drive to Colchester. Elizabeth is standing in an open door when I arrive. Obviously, I'm not too early. Elizabeth is young, mid-forties, and the jeans and black sweatshirt accentuate her slender body. Her short, sable hair with a hint of red defines a delicate, round face with high cheekbones. Large, sad, brown eyes smile through the thin, dark-framed glasses that sit on the well-shaped nose. "Hi, I'm Elizabeth. You didn't have any trouble finding the house?"

I like her soft pleasant voice with its slightly Southern sound. "Hi, I'm Shirley. No, not at all. Your directions were complicated but very accurate."

Elizabeth reaches for a canvas bag. "I take this everywhere with me. Are you hungry? Let's go to Herman's Diner for breakfast."

We go the short distance in my car. Soon I relax. I like her. She's a good listener but also willing to share. I like her openness. She seems strong and independent.

When we enter the restaurant it is obvious everyone knows her. "Hey, Elizabeth, where's Ted today?"

"Don't you squeal on me—for being here without him." She turns to me and explains, "Ted is my friend who is a widower in his seventies. He isn't doing well without his wife."

I think, *So she's compassionate, too. Even with all her own problems.* My cheese and mushroom omelette and coffee are well-made and tasty. Elizabeth has her "usual," which includes eggs and home fries. We tell each other of our tragedies while sitting at the small wood-grained Formica-topped table in the corner. Three months ago Elizabeth's eighteen-year-old daughter was shot in the back of her head by an ex-boyfriend. She asks, "Will you come back to my house? I have to be there to meet my son's bus." She reaches for her bag again and promises to show me its contents when we get to her house.

On our way out of the restaurant, I notice the walls are covered with photographs of a young man and different race cars. Trophies won by the owner's son fill the shelves. I'm reminded that we all have our precious mementos of our children's lives. Mine are in the photo albums, degrees and awards hanging on the wall, and term papers or theses stored in a trunk—even her doctoral dissertation. Elizabeth's are in her canvas bag.

I sit at her dining room table with a glass of ice water and look at clippings from a Greenville, South Carolina, newspaper. Elizabeth points to a picture of an empty lifeguard's chair. "She was sitting there when he came up behind her and killed her. That is her blood you see on the cement. Front page news!"

I wonder when the media will understand the effect something like this has on the victim's family and friends. But I know the answer. Not until they are faced with tragedies of their own that equal ours. I remember my fury when a Hartford paper put Margie's murder on page 11 and called Mitch the alleged killer, but identified her as an adulteress—based on Mitch's statement. The killer has all the rights. The victim none.

I turn the album page, sickened. There looking back at me is a beautiful, wholesome, all-American face. The perfect features and large soft brown eyes form a smile in the halo of long light-colored hair.

"That's not her real smile. If you knew her you'd know she is scared to death. Her ex-boyfriend stalked her for weeks before and after she graduated. Her father found threatening notes he had given her. He killed himself too. At least I don't have a trial to go through."

My tragedy is horrible but I understand it could be worse. I ask, "Elizabeth, can you imagine not knowing whether your child is alive or dead? I couldn't have handled it if Mitch had killed Margie and disposed of her body. Not knowing what happened must be the worst of all." Elizabeth concurs.

We continue talking and Elizabeth's husband's unkind and aggressive behavior comes up several times. In my search to comprehend what happened to Margie, I read a book *The Batterer: A Psychological Profile* by Donald G. Dutton, Ph.D., that clearly portrays the threat such behaviors signal. Now I know enough to be worried about Elizabeth. "I'm worried about you. You are in a dangerous relationship."

She tells me, "I know but he isn't as bad as the last husband."

"Elizabeth, abuse progresses. Mitch wasn't always physically abusive. Most of the time his assaults were verbal. Consider your options. Make a plan to get out safely while you still can. I didn't know enough to protect my own daughter. All I can think of is I don't want the same thing to happen to you."

We hug and say goodbye. Elizabeth says, "Call me when you get home."

"Are you serious?"

"Yes."

It is fourteen months after Margie's death when I first meet Elizabeth. Driving home from Colchester after five hours of sharing, which is healing, I know I have to write about her. I'm not sure why yet but I know our meeting is significant.

I call and tell her, "I couldn't figure out why your name, Elizabeth, kept surfacing in connection with Margie's murderer. Until today. Now I understand. Meeting you will help me find a way to make Margie's life meaningful and give purpose to mine. I haven't figured out how but it will."

"Shirley, I heard what you said about being afraid for me and I will do something. I promise."

I hang up almost satisfied but truly exhausted. I've been thinking about volunteering at a women's shelter but I realize I'm not strong enough. The trauma and hopelessness that abused women face would be too much. Maybe in the future.

On Thursday, Elizabeth again cancels her plans to go with Larry and me to a Survivors of Homicide meeting in Wethersfield because she can't get a baby-sitter, but she tells me, "I saw a lawyer today. My brother sent airline tickets for my son and me to visit my parents in Texas. My mother is sick. It is a good excuse to go."

"When are you leaving?"

"Oh, not for a couple weeks. I have things to do. If my brother had his way I'd be on a plane tonight."

"Elizabeth, I like the way your brother thinks."

"Tomorrow morning he is going to talk to my attorney. I was so rattled I'm not sure I got everything straight."

Friday morning Elizabeth calls me. "Will you drive us to the airport? We have a three o'clock flight out."

"I'd be delighted and since I'm going to Windsor Locks to have dinner with my friends it isn't even out of the way."

Later that night, after a decadent, delicious Greek meal at Golden Irene's with three very supportive friends, Barbara, Shirley, and Marj, my brain works frantically to figure out what it is I'm supposed to do that will give my life and Margie's death some meaning. I know I'll never be the same person I was before she was murdered, but everything I read assures me that I will survive and be a stronger person because of my overwhelming loss. *How can I make that be true?*

My answer comes like a flash of lightning. Meeting Elizabeth is not a coincidence. It is the key that opens sesame. I'm a teacher. I love doing workshops for the Connecticut Writing Project and Windsor Locks students, parents, and teachers. Why not about domestic violence—warning of the danger signs that should not be ignored in a relationship? Prevention! Yes, that's it.

I work all day Saturday, outlining the contents of my presentation. I gather photographs, letters, documents, and items made by Mitch to keep winning Margie back. My words tumble out as I enlist my engineer husband's help. "I could talk to Bette from camera club. I'm sure she would help me make slides of the material or I could have color transparencies made and use an overhead projector. Or we could be real fancy and make a computer presentation to project onto a screen. But I don't know where to start. That's where you, dear husband, come in. We'd develop the presentation together and you'd take care of the visual display while I'm speaking. Wouldn't that be nice? We would both be doing something positive in Margie's memory."

He agrees and I think he wants to help. It isn't just his usual brush-off to get some peace and quiet.

On Sunday we go to a surprise retirement party for Sam, the president of Survivors of Homicide. He has left his position as a chemistry professor at Naugatuck Community College, where each spring they hold the Melanie Ilene Rieger Memorial Conference Against Violence. The conference is one way Sam and Wanda give meaning to their daughter's murder by her ex-boyfriend. National speakers come. Polly Klaas' murderer was already a two-time sexual offender who had been out on parole. Marc Klaas, her dad, comes to talk about limiting parole for child molesters. Megan Kanka's mom keeps fighting to have child molesters registered with the local police and parents informed of an offender's presence in a neighborhood. Thus we have Megan's Law. They hope to protect other families from the grief they endure. I want to follow their examples.

If I can help one woman escape an abusive relationship or one family become aware of the danger signals that should not be ignored in a relationship, Margie's death will have meaning. And my efforts will be worthwhile.

When Donna, the social worker who is organizing the conference, comes by our table and tells me she enjoyed what I said about Sam during the roast, I brazenly tell her of my plans for a workshop on domestic violence. "If you don't have all the speakers you need for the conference, I'd like you to consider me." I can't believe I really said it.

She doesn't have all the time slots filled and she is interested. She asks me to come to some of her classes to talk about it. "This will give you a chance to speak in a small setting and get feedback from young women." I agree.

Monday evening I present my ideas to my writing group. They are mesmerized by the subject and encourage me. I talk about Margie for twenty minutes without becoming emotionally overwrought because I have found a socially significant reason to focus on the tragedy. I will expose the myth that abuse doesn't happen in well-educated, middle-class families. I know it does.

I choose "Funny—He Doesn't Look Like a Murderer But Margie's Dead" for my workshop title because a batterer is often charming, seeking approval from those at work, his friends and family. We expect a person who does bad things to look the part, but many times he doesn't. Except when he is in a rage—usually in private.

I have found a way to honor Margie and give my life a purpose. Thanks, Elizabeth, for helping to solve that mystery. I now have a purpose I can focus on during the long *criminal* justice proceedings that lie ahead.

CHAPTER 19

The *Criminal* Justice System 1998 Style—Part A

The need to prepare an effectively written impact statement to send to Drew Thompson, the U.S. Probation Officer, before February 9, 1998, takes precedence over everything. After several drafts and the careful selection of pictures and poems to include, I finally send the following statement on February 1st:

> There are no words capable of expressing my loss or the pain caused by Mitchell Paster's cruel act. I have not looked at the crime scene photos of Margie's murder. Mr. Samuelson and Mr. Schmidle feel they are too gruesome for a mother's eyes. Let me assure you, Judge Muir, the images I create in my mind are also too hideous to bear.
>
> Mitchell planned his attack for when she would be most vulnerable. He waited for her to step out of the shower just as he had once before. Only this time he had a butcher knife instead of a camera. She was completely unaware of the danger she faced or she wouldn't have gotten into the shower. I hear her cries and screams, see her startled expression. Wonder if she calls to me for help? When does she realizes she is going to die? Obviously, from the wounds, she didn't die quickly. I see their bodies tangled together. I watch him raise his arms and stab her again and again—16 times.
>
> I picture that all white bathroom with her damp, nude, bloody, body lying there exposed for everyone to see. I watch as the pool of blood grows larger. Wonder if she is lying on her back or stom-

Once before Mitch waited outside the shower with a camera.

ach. Are her hands by her sides, flung over her head, or clutching her wounds? I envision each possibility over and over again. I hear her golden retriever, Calie's, traumatized barks and wish she was a pit bull.

I feel my painful inadequacy—a parent who could not protect her child! Her premature birth wasn't an easy one, but the joy, love, and pride she brought to me transcend any words I could use to describe their depth. My pain caused by her untimely brutal death has not diminished and I know it will continue to be my constant companion. I struggle to survive because of the rest of my family and because I know that is what she would want me to do.

Margie and Mitch's relationship was rocky from the start. We were not sure how long it would last, but we accepted him into our home and our hearts because she wanted us to. We enjoyed many visits with them in California with trips to Mexico, Catalina, and Las Vegas. Mitch shared my passion for the University of Connecticut basketball teams and during halftime in close games we would call across the country to give each other support.

Our family planned and paid for a large Jewish wedding. We accepted her decision to convert to his religion because it would make her life easier, but Christmas was a special holiday for Margie and us. She always came home then. In 1995 she came from Pennsylvania. Mitch wasn't coming from California, but Margie's niece, Abby, cried so hard because she wanted Mitch to be with us that they decided he would come. We have wonderful family pictures of those happy times. Because of what he did Margie hasn't been home for the last two Christmases and never will be again.

Mitch, Margie and I are celebrating Christmas 1993.

Aunt Kathy and Margie are delighted with Jacob.

Margie and Mitch were with us in June 1996 for my retirement party. Margie looked so beautiful and smiled most of the time. Mitch took video of the event asking my friends to say something about me. He charmed everyone. I was so proud of my family and they were proud of me. None of us suspected the devastation that was less than two months away.

The last time we saw Margie alive was in Rhode Island at our trailer. Mitch and she had been in New Jersey along with Ruth, and her children for the July fireworks that Abby and Jacob call, "Jordan's." Abby loved all the attention the Pasters gave her. Later Margie and Mitch, and Ruth drove to Ruth's house in Connecticut before going to our trailer in Rhode Island. Soon Margie and Mitch were arguing about when he should jog—before we went to dinner or after. Ruth shook her head and whispered to me, "They've been going at it like this since they got to New Jersey. Last night in Marlborough he got on her case because she was having another glass of wine. She got mad and went to bed. Then he poured himself a glass of Scotch. Make sense to you? It hasn't been much fun for me."

I got Margie alone, "Margie, It doesn't make that much difference. We're only talking twenty minutes."

She told me, "Ma, you don't get it. He's got this new guru whose book tells him how to make his life perfect. He wants me to jog with him after I've worked all day and he's sat around the house. Some days I just can't do it. You should see all the lists. He has them posted all over. Little reminders to keep him on track. He tells me, 'When I get my MBA you won't be good enough to be my wife.'"

Things calmed down and Mitch told us he was treating Larry and me to dinner because our anniversary was July 2nd. We interpreted this as a positive sign that Mitch was maturing. But Margie said, "He spent a lot on dinner for his parents' anniversary last week so order what you really want. He has to do it."

Mitch told her, "Margie, that's not called for. I want to do it for your parents."

Margie answered, "Oh, I know. I'm just teasing." I knew she wasn't. She perceived financial issues to be a major strain on their relationship.

Abby rode on Mitch's lap in the back seat of our car. Dinner was pleasant. Margie's nephew, Jacob, entertained us with his two-and-a-half-year-old antics. Abby sat happily at the head of the table between her aunt and uncle.

Our trailer sleeps four people comfortably. There were five adults and two kids. Mitch told us he didn't mind sleeping on the queen sized air mattress. Abby asked, "Can I sleep with Uncle Mitch?"

Mitch agreed and that's what happened. Abby slept in the same bed with the man who killed her aunt. I can't comprehend how we let that happen.

Mitch had to visit his uncle on Long Island and go out in the boat Sunday. Margie told him it was too much and they should do it another weekend. But they were gone when I woke up Sunday morning. They didn't want to disturb me. Tears flood down my cheeks each time I remember I didn't even get to say goodbye!

Many of the cards of sympathy advised us to let our precious memories of her help us heal. But the awfulness of Mitch's betrayal tarnishes the last eleven years of wonderful memories of Margie. How is it possible to treasure the times we spent with them while knowing he is responsible for our loss?

Memories that include Mitch hinder the healing process. Because of him I will have no new memories of her. I will never see the woman she would have been at thirty-five or forty. I'll never hold her child.

I am thankful she lived long enough to reach several important goals. She had her Ph.D. in Clinical Psychology, had a good job and had been told she was getting a promotion. She had passed her licensing exam with flying colors, and found out she had the highest academic score possible at her Bureau of Prisons training in Glynco, Georgia. She even had the car of her dreams—even though we had to loan her the $2,000 for the down payment. Mitch wouldn't let her spend their money for it.

Certain memories will forever haunt me: seeing her dog, Calie, or learning that her cat, Sebastian, streaked past the emergency squad and disappeared when they opened the door. Shaking the hands of her fellow workers, seeing their tear filled eyes full of sympathy—questioning how we are able to function under our burden. Writing the obituary in a motel room far from home.

Learning that the prison chaplain called Mr. Paster before us and told him of Margie's death, believing he was her father. Knowing Mitch called his mother and a lawyer while Margie lie dying or dead and he only called 911 after he was told to do so. Hearing that he never asked the FBI agents about his wife. Having to make the arrangements for the funeral. Being told that we couldn't use the dress we selected even though we brought one of Ruth's scarves to cover the chest wounds that might show above the neckline. The short sleeves wouldn't hide her defensive wounds. Seeing her in the casket, eyes closed, slender hands crossed, and all her fingernails cut short. Knowing some had broken in the attack and that the others were probably cut off and scraped for evidence. Knowing her body suffered further wounds from what was surely an intrusive autopsy. Feeling the paper stuffed in the sleeves of her dress and above her abdomen. Touching her hair one last time. Hearing Abby ask, "How could Mitch kill Margie? He said he loved her." Jacob's four-year-old questions make me cry every time. "Is Margie dead? Where is she? When will she come back? When can I go see her? Is Mitch a bad man? Will the FBI give us back the knife?" I know he doesn't remember her love or playful giggle.

Margie told me she was lonely in Lewisburg. She sat in bed studying for her Pennsylvania licensing exam in psychology with only Calie and Sebastian for company. Yet he stayed in California because on March 1st he was to receive a bonus at work. We all wondered why he stayed in California for two and a half months after that. Margie questioned if he was involved with another woman.

But during the six and-a-half months Margie spent alone in Lewisburg she gradually began to see herself as capable, competent, and successful at work. She began to make friends without regard to whether Mitch would like them. She managed her home and became much more independent. He insisted that a large part of her paycheck be sent to him, but he couldn't control how she spent the rest. She wasn't constantly being told to stand up straight, lose weight, do this, do that. Yet, she wanted him to come. Was hurt because he wasn't in any hurry. When I went through their house I found letter after letter that she had written him asking him to come. Telling him how much she missed him.

So many things Mitch did destroyed her self-esteem. He told her she wasn't as bright as he was. She had just completed six years of work getting her Ph.D. in Clinical Psychology, but he taunted her for not having life goals. She was tired after a day of work at the penitentiary, but he wanted her to open a private practice as a therapist in the evenings. He did not work from March 1st through August 16, 1996. He planned to leave her and go to Cornell to get his MBA. Margie supported his plan, but questioned why he couldn't stay with her in Lewisburg and go to Bucknell. Especially since he wanted her to get pregnant. The emotional and physical support she needed from him during a pregnancy and in the early months after a child's birth would not be there. Is this the behavior of a man passionately in love with his wife? No! He just wanted to control her. He murdered her because he lost control of her. It wasn't passion or frustrated love, but his driving need to control her. Seeing Mitch alive in court knowing she is dead because of him keeps our wounds wide open.

We have been betrayed by Mitch, but also by the federal government and the criminal justice system. First by Janet Reno's refusal to allow Mr. Samuelson to seek the death penalty. Margaret wasn't a policeman, but was a federal employee on federal property. Not that we wanted Mitch to die, but it would have given Wayne more options when plea bargaining and been a validation of her life.

The psychiatric evaluation done in Butner, NC obviously weakened the prosecution's case. Dr. Johnson is not legally qualified to make her statement that the murder was not premeditated.

November 19, 1997 was the hardest day for our family since the August 16, 1996 murder of our daughter. We are not happy that Mitch was given the chance to plead to murder two. Wayne, the Assistant US attorney, has listened to us and taken our wishes into consideration. However, we feel Mitch's heinous act would have convinced a jury that a murder one verdict and life in prison without parole were justified. Not wanting to show us the crime scene photos is a strong indication of how awful her death was. Please don't betray Margaret and us again by giving him anything less.

We live with the guilt that we didn't recognize the warning signals that were escalating in both intensity and frequency. When

Mitch broke the bedroom door to get to her dog and cat so he could take them away from her because he said she loved them more than him, when she sued for divorce, even when he called me the night before he killed her, we had no warning of the imminent danger. That night he was calm and collected. Gone was the emotional turmoil I heard in his voice three days before when he told me he was leaving her. I think he knew then he would kill her when she returned home. The timing was intentional. She was planning to come to see us that day.

When the defense expressed the belief that Mitch should be freed on bail so he could pursue his MBA at Cornell we understood just how insignificantly Mitch perceived his taking of her life. He told us later in a letter from prison that he knew how hard it was for us to go through the holidays without her. He knew and yet he killed her! He told us he missed his wife. I couldn't believe it. He didn't say he was sorry he killed her. Having him referred to as a widower in a psychiatric report grates on our nerves and seems a preposterous choice of words considering…

Margaret was our youngest daughter and we are very proud of what she accomplished in thirty-one years of life. We supported and appreciated the focus needed to reach her goal. However, it required that she be away from her family for twelve years. All of us willingly tolerated the separation and looked to the future. Would we have done the same if we had known how short a time she would be with us? She only had ten months to use her Ph.D. in Clinical Psychology after all her years of effort and sacrifice. In anger Mitch took her life and destroyed our dreams. His betrayal overwhelms us. For 17 months our life has been hell. Mitch could have made it much easier for everyone if he had taken responsibility for killing her and pled guilty to begin with. Instead he degraded her and made her out to be an awful person who deserved what he did.

Losing a child is never easy and it has changed Larry's and my retirement dreams. We are so proud of her and she was to be a comfort in our old age. Ruth and Kathy no longer have their sister to share life's joys and sadnesses. Abby has lost one of her greatest supporters and Jacob will never know this aunt who loved him so. It hurts to acknowledge Ruth's statement, "When Margie died she took the parents I knew and need from me." She's right, we aren't the same people. As great as our loss is, we understand that society too has lost. She was a care giver—wanting to help others.

We all made mistakes. Margie paid for hers with her life. We are paying for ours every day. Mitch should pay for his mistake by spending the rest of his life in prison. He made the choice to destroy both their lives—and so many more. We acknowledge that Jordan and Aileen Paster have suffered greatly and certainly did not wish Margaret harm, but they can still see and talk to their son. We can't see, talk to or hug Margie. Mitch took that right from us.

I remind the court that many people have written telling of their surprise and dismay at Mitch's murder of Margaret, vouching for his good character, giving their assurances that he would present no danger to anyone else. 15 months later he admitted to that crime. Should the court take a chance with another woman's life and cause another family the grief and loss we have suffered? No! Forgiveness can only come with justice.

I also help Abby write her statement. We share our grief and remember all the things we love most about Margie. It is an incredibly touching time. Margie would have enjoyed being part of the discussion and we wish she could be. This is eight-and-a-half-year old Abby's statement, typed by me:

> I want to tell you how sad I am about Margie's death. I don't understand why Mitch had to kill her. I think what he did is wrong and he is a jerk. He should be in jail for his whole life. I miss Margie. She was very pretty. I'm going to miss visiting her and seeing her cat, Sebastian. I liked having her come to see me. She was there for my seventh birthday and she helped my mommy have a party for me. Then the three of us went out to dinner and listened to jazz music. She wasn't at my eighth birthday party and she will not be at any more.
>
> I miss having her as part of my family on the holidays. The last Christmas she was at our house she knocked over the Christmas tree—twice. I miss how she let me open her presents for her on Christmas Eve. When it is her birthday I miss blowing out the candles on her cake.

I loved her and when I was younger she helped me reach things like my food. I was so lucky because she baby-sat for me when I was a little baby and my mommy had to go back to work.

When I visited her in California she had a big sign that said, "Welcome, Abby." She took me to Sea World, the San Diego Zoo, the beach, and I saw the Pacific Ocean for the first time. I swam in her pool.

Margie won't be here when I graduate and go on to college. I will honor her by trying to go to the University of Connecticut. I'll miss her at my wedding and when I have a baby I will name her Margaret. I miss her all the time.

I would like to ask Mitch how he could kill Margie when he said he loved her and knew how much I loved her.

(Abby's drawing) Calie is very angry at Mitch for killing Margie.

Larry and I discuss our statements several times during their writing and decided to cover different ways we have suffered from our loss. This is Larry's letter:

Each member of Margaret's immediate family is suffering her loss in their own way; therefore, we must explain how we are affected separately rather than jointly. I have, however, included the effects on others when I felt it was appropriate.

I was the one who received the call from Lewisburg Penitentiary with the terrible news that my daughter Margaret had been killed. The trauma of the call made me feel numb, almost like being in a trance. I wish I could have broken down into a weeping, raving, non-functioning person completely overcome with grief at that time. My love for Margie demanded that I should but I couldn't. I still carry the guilt that I did not grieve for her with enough intensity. In those moments following the call, however, it was fortunate that I remained functional. I was home alone and the remainder of the family had to be informed immediately. I don't believe this is an indication of character or courage; I think it's the way our minds insulate us from a tragedy and help us get through those first terrible days; however, I still feel insulated from the horror of her death. (a year-and-a-half later)

I still subconsciously believe Margie is alive and I will see her again when the next holiday arrives. Since she had been away from home for so long not seeing her every day, week or month is normal. So subconsciously believing she is still alive is logical even though I consciously know she is dead. I now know denial of a loved one's death can be an early phase of the grieving process, I wonder if I must endure the other phases of the grieving process; disorganization, depression and helplessness before returning to the so called normal life. I know my future will be effected by her murder in ways that are unknown to me now.

Probably the greatest sense of accomplishment and pride a father can feel is when his child achieves goals that are almost beyond her God given abilities. Margaret was this source of pride and accomplishment for me. Margie did not possess the ultrahigh intelligence that produced dazzling scores on standardized tests or A's in college courses while only expending a minimal amount of effort. Her achievements were the result of hard work and perseverance. At the time of her murder she had fulfilled all the requirements for her position in the Bureau of Prisons. She had a Ph.D. in Clinical Psychology. She was a licensed psychologist in the State of Pennsylvania; the license was obtained by working the required time in post-doctoral intern positions and passing the licensing examination. She had successfully completed the

Bureau of Prisons training program in Georgia; I understand that her academic scores were the highest ever obtained by a trainee in that program. I can now only wonder what her future achievements would have been. Obviously her death was a devastating loss to her family and friends, but it is also a loss to society because she was a care giver. How many suicides would have she prevented? How many murders would have she prevented? How many criminals would have she converted to law abiding citizens? How many marriages would have she saved? How many troubled people would she have helped? Would her counseling have prevented other women from becoming involved with controlling, abusive, violent men like her husband? I will never know! The world will never know!

The psychological impact of her death is so immense that I, and also my wife, have sought help through individual and group counseling, joined a support group and we attend conferences and workshops dealing with either grief or violence. Never before in my life have I felt the need for external help with my emotional problems. Fortunately Margaret's murder has drawn my wife and me closer together rather than driving us apart, but it has changed our lives socially. A great deal of our time is now spent at activities associated with the support group Survivors of Homicide. Being with people who have experienced the death of a loved one through a homicide is very comforting and helpful. They will always listen to my story and I will always listen to theirs; others tire of hearing the story that has become the focus of my life. I now attend trials and hearings related to other group member's homicide cases to offer them support.

Not only are my wife and I closer, the whole immediate family is closer. We now live with my eldest daughter Ruth and her two children Abigail and Jacob. Our other daughter Kathy spends at least 70 percent of her time at Ruth's house even though she still maintains an apartment in Hartford. Our move was a direct result of Margaret's murder; my wife and Ruth feeling the need for the mutual support that can be gained by living in the same house. We recently sold our condominium making us non-property owners for the first time in over thirty-two years. Our grandchildren are ages eight and four; I don't think I have to elaborate further to show that my day-to-day life has changed drastically.

The Christmas season is very difficult for me and the other members of the family. Margie always came home for Christmas. Being closer together as a family makes it easier to cope, but it magnifies her absence. Little things like buying stocking stuffers; I must think to buy two not three.

In the June preceding Margaret's death my wife, Shirley, joined me in retirement after teaching twenty-eight years in the Windsor Locks, Connecticut public schools. Our retirement plans included many visits to Margie in Lewisburg. Her murder has required many trips to Lewisburg. Every one brings back memories of things we did with her there and things we planned to do in those never to be future visits. We had also talked about relocating to Florida for part of the year: Margie said she would transfer to a prison there if we moved. These retirement plans can never be fulfilled.

I have no physical health problems that are unquestionably caused by my daughter's murder. Naturally I have had insomnia; a condition that occurs even when a loved one dies from natural causes. Fortunately it was not so severe that I required a physician to prescribe medication. This is not true for my wife who has required drugs for both insomnia and depression.

I am enclosing a copy of the itemized funeral bill which includes related services. We were not reimbursed for these expenses by either the States of Connecticut or Pennsylvania. Her estate does not contain enough funds to cover this expense. This, however, has not been a financial burden to us.

As you undoubtedly know by this time I, and the other members of my family, consider life imprisonment as the only acceptable punishment for Mitchell Frederick Paster. I cannot deny that this belief is partially a retaliation for Margaret's murder. It is difficult to think of him being free to enjoy his family and friends when we will never see Margie again. This feeling is intensified when I realize that this could be possible in less than fifteen years.

My granddaughter, Abigail Grover, said shortly after learning that Mitch had murdered her aunt, "How could he kill somebody he said he loved?"

I say, "How do we know he will not kill somebody else he says he loves?"

Margaret was involved with Mitchell Paster for approximately ten years. As their relationship progressed I became familiar with

Mitchell's personality and observed his behavior in various situations. He could be very polite and the complete gentleman. I, and the rest of the family, had many good times with Mitch. Overshadowing this was his desire to have complete control over Margaret. He also was very egotistical about his intelligence, looking down upon Margaret even though her academic achievements far surpassed his. I observed verbal abuse several times and suspected physical abuse. Following bitter arguments they would breakup; immediately after Mitch would ply her with lavish gifts and apologies to gain her back. Once back together the cycle would start over again. Now with a limited knowledge of domestic violence I recognize this as the pattern of a typical "batterer." In your position you are most likely very knowledgeable about domestic violence. I urge you to investigate the events in Margaret and Mitchell's lives during the six or seven weeks before her murder and make your own conclusion about Mr. Paster. I believe Mr. Wayne Samuelson has this information.

The only way to positively prevent Mitchell Paster from murdering another women is to incarcerate him for the rest of his life.

Thank you for listening to the victim's survivors and considering their feelings.

During November and December of 1997 and continuing into this January, I have asked relatives, neighbors, my counselor, my doctor, my lawyer, and all my friends to write letters telling of how they have witnessed the impact on our family. Some send me copies of their letters when they send them to Mr. Thompson, and Mr. Samuelson gives us copies of all the letters. Those who wrote are articulate in expressing their outrage that Margaret and our family have been the victims of Mitch's selfish actions. They tell of the pain her death has caused and encourage the judge to give the maximum sentence. Wayne tells us such letters do affect judges' decisions. I am including excerpts from several letters and wish I could include them all.

The most heart-wrenching is one from my seventy-six year old aunt Margaret:

...So I encourage you to sentence him to life without parole for the brutal slaying of Margaret Bostrom Paster who not only was my niece but my namesake as well. His vicious killing has taken a great part of my life from me.

Many letters express the wish that Mitch be sentenced to life in prison without parole so he could have no new victims. The following are examples of other sentiments:

We know the anguish of our brother and sister-in-law, as well as the entire family. They have suffered since this crime was committed and will never find their lives returned to normal....We were so proud of Margie and all her accomplishments. *Uncle Bud and Aunt Shirley*

I met Mitchell a number of times, and stayed with him and Margaret on a visit to San Diego. I found him a charming young man and very likable. But behind that surface charm I sensed that he always had to be in control and dominate his relationship with Margaret. When I played golf with Mitchell I found him a poor loser. *Uncle Riley (Roland)*

I am a friend of the victim's mother....Consequently, I have some idea of the devastating effect this horrific crime has had on the Bostrom family. They will spend the rest of their lives dealing with the images that they have in their minds of the suffering Margaret must have endured. *Barbara C., friend and social worker*

My son, Andy was a student in Shirley Bostrom's class. Andy is now 18. He is a special kid. He has cerebral palsy....She was not only his teacher but also his friend. She treated him with such compassion....I had only met Margaret Bostrom a few times, but I knew that she was the light in Shirley's life. *Joe M., friend and fellow teacher*

...Mr. Paster committed a terrible crime against humanity, against women in particular. It was one of terrible enormity having used his superior physical strength to exert control over this wonderful person, using such an overpowering force to end her young life. It is a tragedy that is hard to bear. *June H-A., Superintendent of Schools*

It is easy to be taken in by Mitch....I read a copy of the report from the court-appointed psychiatrist and I could see where he fooled her. He will attempt to give people what he feels they want to hear and see in order to control them. *Marjorie B., longtime friend and school psychologist*

I did not know Margie personally, but I was plunged into a spiritual crisis of my own in which I felt that evil was winning in our supposedly civilized society....Paster need not have tried to smear the name of his victim because, *in fact, she did not make him murder her.* I believe he acted out of his own free will and now needs to take responsibility for his actions. *Pat K., CWP friend*

The act was deliberate, vicious, grotesque and entirely fatal in its intent. However, a lesser sentence will allow this person to be free, in all probability, for a majority of his remaining life. Such punishment belittles the value and worth of the victim's life and life itself. *Joe F., attorney and parent of one of Shirley's students*

Dr. Bostrom will not have the opportunity to fulfill her dream to be able to help people with emotional difficulties. How ironic that her life was taken from her by such a person—her husband....The most outstanding fact of this crime is the number of times Mr. Paster stabbed Margie—16 times, 9 of which were life threatening. This man did not intend to hurt his wife—he wanted to kill her...*Barbara M., longtime friend*

Margie's murder was a horrendous deed committed by a man who swore to love and care for her....He has refused to accept total responsibility for his crime, choosing instead to blame Margaret for what he did, and wrapping himself in the cloak of depression as an excuse. *Judy and Leo S., longtime friends*

Mitch had a choice and he made a bad one. Now you have a choice. I urge you to make the right one. (Margaret didn't have a choice) *Kathy B., friend and parent of one of Shirley's students*

After many hearings and presentations, many of them degrading and humiliating the murder victim who was unable to defend or protest, the judicial system has one sidedly elected to reduce the first degree sentence to second degree. Because this was his first offense does not in any way alleviate or minimize his despicable act. *Larry and Elaine (Dot) C., longtime friends*

He killed her in a most terrible way, so I feel that he should be put away for life so that he never gets another chance to hurt anybody again. *Shirley K., longtime friend*

Ruth's mother, Shirley, calls me her "fourth daughter." I do not know Mitchell Paster. I *do* know that *anyone* who could be so cruel and heinous to such a gentle person, who could "snap" and fatally wound Margaret needs to be locked away and *never* be given freedom. *Mary Ellen B., longtime friend of Ruth and the Bostrom family*

When a family suffers the ultimate tragedy of losing a child to homicide, it is the worst event that can ever happen. Then to have to deal with the justice system as it is currently constituted, is almost as tragic. *Sam R., President of Survivors of Homicide*

What surprises me is that some people choose not to become involved even in this manner. Why? Do they think Margie deserved to die or that Mitch somehow deserves leniency? Do they feel it won't do any good so why waste their time? Maybe their lives are just too busy or they can't be bothered. Some people tell us they sent letters that were not given to us. When I ask Mr. Thompson if he has more letters he tells me no. I feel betrayed by these people I trusted and have shared my grief with. But I am overwhelmed by the love and understanding displayed in the letters that were sent. They are now treasured mementos of our friends and their compassion and love.

Margie's sister Kathy tells me she is too distraught to write an impact statement. I am terribly angry. She is so preoccupied with herself that she can't or won't write a letter. My needs and what might help keep Mitch in jail longer don't seem to count with her.

She tells me she holds everything in until she explodes. *Yeah, well so do I. I dread that day. I fear that I'll pop like a balloon.*

Ruth sends in a statement but doesn't tell me that she has until I ask. I couldn't believe that she wouldn't, but I needed to know for sure. I wish she had mentioned it without being prompted.

Wayne calls us on February 9, 1998, to tell us they held the closed-door hearing on the sentencing. He feels Drew Thompson's report is a good one, but we feel left out because we were never contacted by Mr. Thompson. Mitch's attorneys don't like it because they claim Mitch took responsibility. Yeah, fifteen months later. It now appears that Mitch will receive seventeen years and with good time will be out in twelve-and-a-half years. Wayne will present a brief supporting upward departure from the sentencing guidelines and the defense will write one supporting downward departure. Then new briefs in opposition to these briefs will be submitted by each side before the sentencing occurs.

Even with all the emotional turmoil regarding what the sentence will be, February provides new and unique experiences for me. I am off the Prozac and able to wrap myself inside Margie. She is a cloak of comfort and love, keeping me warm and safe—shutting out the cold and pain. At times I feel incredible peace. My body relaxes and I'm happy to be alive in this glorious world—but only for a moment because that feeling itself triggers the pain I feel because of my loss. I remember why this experience is so remarkable now and sadness overwhelms me, but recapturing my sense of joy at being alive makes it a valuable gift—or is it a prize I have earned by working so hard at grieving? I know that any brief moments of future happiness will be outweighed by sadness but I'm going to enjoy each benevolent opening.

On February 13, 1998, the government files its twenty-five page *Government Brief in Support of Motion for Upward Departure from Sentencing Guideline Range.* In it the government agrees with the probation officer's suggestion that two separate factors may warrant an upward departure. Extreme conduct and premeditation take the offense outside of the "heartland" of second-degree murder cases. "The Government not only agrees that each of these individual factors warrants an upward departure under the circumstances of this case, but also recommends an additional upward departure based on…use of a weapon or dangerous instrumentality."

The brief cites a court opinion in another case regarding guidelines, "However, since it is difficult to prescribe a single set of guidelines that encompasses the vast range of human conduct, a court may depart from the range if it finds an aggravating or mitigating circumstance of a kind or to a degree not adequately considered in formulating the guidelines."

We, Margie's family, are pleased to know the judge is permitted to depart upward and feel secure that he will not depart downward.

The brief uses quotes from the *United States Sentencing Guidelines (5K2.8)*. "If the defendant's conduct was unusually heinous, cruel, brutal or degrading to the victim, the court may increase the sentence above guideline range to reflect the nature of the conduct. Examples of extreme conduct include torture of a victim, gratuitous infliction of injury, or prolonging of pain or humiliation.…The probation officer concluded that the 'cumulative damage caused by these numerous injuries went significantly beyond the threshold necessary to kill the victim.'"

We agree!

Mitch says he and Margie had argued the morning of August 16, 1996. The brief goes on to state, "The evidence in the instant case reveals that minutes before the murder, the defendant was encountered outside by a neighbor at the back of his residence. They engaged in a conversation during which the neighbor described the defendant as, 'very calm, pleasant, and very soft-spoken.' Thereafter, the defendant entered his residence, and heard his wife getting out of the shower upstairs. He took a knife from the butcher-block in the kitchen and started upstairs with it—traveling the approximate 49 steps to the bathroom where he murdered his wife by stabbing her 16 times. During that journey he had abundant time to consider and reflect on what he was going to do.…The murder of Margaret Bostrom was premeditated."

The government brief states that his use of a knife warrants upward departure and the extent of the increase "should depend on the dangerousness of the weapon, the manner in which it was used, and the extent to which its use endangered others."

We are impressed with Wayne's arguments and thoroughness. Surely the judge will be too.

On February 17, 1998, the *Defendant Brief in Support of Downward Adjustment and Departure from the Sentencing Guideline Range* is submitted. They object to the two-point enhancement for obstruction of justice, in the Pre-Sentence Report, because no specific findings of "willful" obstruction were made. They argue that even though the judge made the following statement at the November 22, 1996, suppression hearing, "…we [the court] are of the view that Paster's claim that he did not understand the effect of signing the form is not credible," the judge did not find that the defendant willfully impeded or attempted to obstruct the administration of justice.

They argue that "Mitch is entitled to an additional point reduction because he pleaded guilty in a timely manner, permitting the government and the court to conserve scarce judicial resources."

Fifteen months after the crime!

They further argue that, "Because the defendant's actions were the result of extreme emotional distress suffered as a result of the victim's incessant emotional cruelty, this Honorable Court should depart downward for aberrant behavior and victim conduct." Dr. Sadoff and Dr. Johnson are quoted explaining that he was adequately provoked and suffered from dissociative amnesia. Mitch was pushed beyond his limits.

Here we go again—she made me do it. Why doesn't he just take responsibility?

On February 24, 1998, both the government and the defendant file briefs in opposition to the other side's request for downward or upward departure. We are shocked to learn that after rejecting the defense's October 24, 1997, offer (which the government didn't received until five days later) to plead to voluntary manslaughter, the government wrote on October 31 that it "may consider accepting a plea to second degree murder, with both the government and the defense free to argue (departures)." We had no idea this was taking place until we were in Williamsport for the jury selection on November 4, 1997.

The government refutes defense claims that the victim's conduct caused Mitch to murder her by citing the U.S.S.G. Victim's Conduct Policy Statement. Factors to be considered include:

(a) size and strength of the victim compared to the defendant;

(b) persistence of the victim's conduct and any efforts by the defendant to prevent confrontation;

(c) the danger reasonably perceived by the defendant, including the victim's reputation for violence;

(d) the danger actually presented to the defendant by the victim; and

(e) any other dangerous conduct by the victim.

The government explains that Mitch was larger and stronger than Margaret. He didn't avoid confrontation but waited in her home all night and started the argument. She presented no danger as she was taking a shower. His actions can be viewed as his response to the divorce complaint that was due on August 15th. The defendant did have a choice. He could have left. It was evident his wife did not want to see him.

The thirty-three page government brief cites several other court cases for the judge to consider in making his decision, but mostly it continues to restate the government's position and review the evidence.

The defendant's opposition brief claims that extreme conduct doesn't apply here because Mitch's actions were not unusually heinous or torturous "in light of the mental state of the Defendant during the stabbing."

They quote the probation officer as concluding "...the cumulative damage caused by these numerous injuries went significantly beyond the threshold necessary to kill the victim."

I'd agree.

But the defense claims Mr. Thompson did not review the psychiatrists' reports. If he had he would understand the murder was committed in the heat of passion with adequate provocation by Margaret. They further argue that the murder was not premeditated and refer again to the psychiatric reports.

The defense brief states, "An upward departure for use of a weapon or dangerous instrumentality should not be approved by this Honorable Court because use of weapons does not fall outside of the 'heartland' of cases for second degree murder." They present several cases in an attempt to prove their point. And conclude with the request "that the Honorable Court not depart upward from the sentencing guidelines."

After reading the briefs we eagerly await the sentencing hearing, unaware that the same arguments will continue to plague us and the courts for years. Wayne has written that the hearing may take place between March 18ᵗʰ and 20ᵗʰ or around April 20ᵗʰ. When Larry and I receive Subpoenas in a Criminal Case in the U.S. District Court in the case of *United States of America V. Mitchell Frederick Paster* on March 18, 1998 at ten A.M., I believe we are finally going to be heard and that our tiring, frustrating, and degrading journey is nearing an end. I know we will never stop missing Margie, but I am naive in my hope that we will soon be free of Mitch and done with the criminal justice system.

On St. Patrick's Day, 1998, Ruth, Larry, and I drive the 319 miles to Williamsport and meet Larry's brother and friend Esther, who will become his wife in December, at the Sheraton. We relax and talk in the lounge. Having people who care share this terrifying experience with us bolsters our spirits.

We meet briefly with Wayne before the Sentencing Hearing begins promptly at 10 A.M. on March 18ᵗʰ. He tells us he hopes to have all three of us give our impact statements. Silently, I add, *So do we.* In the courtroom there is a coolness between the Pasters and us. I'm sure they were surprised by the sentencing guidelines suggested in the report, which were much longer than the eleven to fourteen years they expected. Although we understand he will not get life in prison without parole, as we hoped, we will not be satisfied with the length of any sentence given. They are fighting for their son's life, but we have lost our daughter forever.

The judge proposes a procedure that includes both counsels making opening statements regarding "outstanding objections to the Pre-Sentence Report and two motions for departure from the guideline range...." Then he will ask members of the immediate family of the victim whether they wish to make a statement or present any evidence that is directed toward the imposition of sentence. Closing statements will follow that. His reason for this is to allow us to hear the other evidence before we take the stand so we can respond to what is presented today. Both Wayne Samuelson and Kyle Rude agree to the proposed procedure. Mr. Rude informs the court that he feels the opening arguments will be short since the judge has six briefs before him.

Judge Muir responds, "I not only have six briefs, I've got probably hundreds of letters. And it's a very complex problem legally and factually as far as I'm concerned as to what is the proper sentence in this case." He then asks who should go first.

Wayne suggests that the defense has the burden of proof regarding their objections. Kyle Rude agrees and says the defense is ready. He quickly reviews the contents of his briefs, which we have all read and heard several times before.

Then, Wayne puts the defense's objections into two categories—factual and legal determinations or conclusions made by the probation officer. The first factual objection is to what Mitch said at the beginning of the 911 tape. Whether he said, "Hi, I just stabbed my wife" or "I just stabbed my wife." Wayne suggests that the judge listen to the tape and decide whether it is even relevant.

Regarding the other factual objection, Wayne will present evidence to show what Mitch told the investigators about the knife when he was first questioned. He believes the Pre-Sentence Report contains the information the court needs to make a decision on the legal issues. The report also thoroughly covers the government's claims of premeditation and use of a weapon for upward departure. However, the government plans to present further evidence to support upward departure for extreme conduct. The pathologist's testimony regarding the nature of the wounds and photographs of the victim—and the defendant at the crime scene will help the court make a determination about upward departure for extreme conduct. Wayne finishes and thanks the judge. Mr. Rude also asks that the judge listen to the 911 tape to resolve the issues of what was said.

The defense calls its first witness—Jordan Paster. He is sworn in, gives the court his name, spells it, and tells where he lives and his relationship to Mitch. Mr. Rude asks about his educational and employment background.

Jordan responds that he was at the City College of New York for about two-and-a-half years—in marketing and sales. He works in sales.

Mr. Rude asks the name of his employer. Jordan answers, "Right now I'm self-employed." I'm stunned. The last we knew he worked for a metal company—for thirty years. Was he fired or was the stress of the murder, the charges, and knowing Mitch was in jail too much? I know how hard he worked and how proud he was of his success. He doesn't deserve all this any more than we do.

On the stand, Jordan is the proud father describing all of Mitch's academic and athletic triumphs. He explains that Mitch was fifth in his high school graduating class of 250 to 300 students and on varsity teams in track, baseball, and football. He was in Key Club, worked for the local Kiwanis Club, and helped kids learn sports. Mitch officiated at basketball games while he was in high school. When he graduated from college he took it up again. He even went to school to be trained—then he was paid for it.

Jordan's answers to the questions about Mitch and Margaret's early relationship are accurate. Then he tells of the breakup in 1989, when she went to California, and their reuniting several months later when Mitch joined her there. When asked to describe their relationship up until their marriage he describes it as "very loving."

I look at Larry and mouth *sometimes.* Jordan makes no mention of Mitch's extended periods of unemployment or of Margie's paying jobs at hospitals and treatment centers while she was working for her degree. He claims that Mitch remained in California to earn a bonus and to sell the house they (his word not mine) bought. He recalls that Mitch came to Lewisburg in March or April, when in fact he returned on May 15th. He gives his version of Mitch's taking the pets, the divorce papers, the alleged affair, Margaret coming for the pets, their reconciliation, and trips to a seminar at Fort Dix that Margaret was attending, which I later learned was about domestic violence. He describes their visit to Cornell on their wedding anniversary as a second honeymoon.

Then on August 12th, Jordan received a call at work from Mitch telling him the affair was still going on. Jordan went to Lewisburg to help Mitch pack Jordan's truck and the car that belonged to Mitch's mother, which Mitch was using, and they drove to New Jersey. On Thursday, August 15th, Mitch left his parents' home and returned to Lewisburg. His family didn't know where he was going or if it was Margaret's or Mitch's idea.

The following testimony has caused a deeper breach between our family and Jordan than the murder itself did. Mr. Lepley, one of Mitch's attorneys, asks if there were other concerns or conflicts between Margaret and Mitchell. Jordan answers, "I don't know how you mean that. Margaret had filed papers for divorce, and she did that angrily after Mitchell took the pets. And then at some point she called the lawyers and said, you know she got the pets back so just stop the action or...."

Wayne objects on the grounds that it is hearsay.

Mr. Lepley agrees. "I believe it was. It was not what I was anticipating as an answer." A few questions later he asks, "Was there any concern expressed to you by Mitchell with regards to drinking patterns or habits by Margaret?" I wonder if this is what they call leading the witness.

Jordan answers, "Yes, there was."

Wayne objects to it as hearsay and the defense explains that even if it is hearsay it goes to Mitch's state of mind. The judge wants to know which it is—hearsay or the exception to the rule? After checking in the legal text they decide it qualifies as the exception.

Wayne objects further on relevancy. Mitch has already pled guilty to a murder that "requires an intent-to-kill state of mind at the relevant time frame. So, his state of mind days before is really not relevant to any issue in these proceedings."

The judge sustains the objection and Mr. Lepley changes his line of questioning to Jordan's first-hand knowledge of Margaret's drinking problem. Jordan explains that Margaret and Mitch always argued "...but we found that they would get a little more serious when Margaret drank a little more wine." I listen, thoroughly disgusted, as he tells the court they advised Mitch to go to Al-Anon.

As I've asked so many times—why didn't Jordan or Mitch mention their concerns to us? My answer is always the same—because it was never a concern. His first-hand knowledge of her drinking too much was at a wedding, with a cocktail hour, where Margaret stayed in the bride's room for most of the evening because she had a terrible cold and was heavily medicated. He tells how loving and supportive Mitch was of her.

I shrug and wonder if he has convinced himself that what he is saying is true or if it is a father's desperate attempt to help his son—the murderer of my daughter.

Defense questioning continues. Jordan is asked about the day of the murder and Mitch's personality and reputation. Then he is asked if he has anything further to add that he thinks the court needs to know to help it make a decision. Jordan responds, "Yeah…I do not think my son is a murderer. This to me is a crime of passion. He—this is total aberration—he needs medical help, we all know that. And we're just hoping that he gets that."

He tells the court Mitch has a reputation as peaceful and non-violent, a well-liked kid, honest and truthful, and handled his stresses very well.

I want to ask why Mitch had seen a counselor in California and been on medication to help him manage his stress.

Jordan continues, "…He was driven due to certain circumstances to God knows what that morning. But it certainly—what the prosecution described is not my son. I know my son as a parent. I'm an expert on that. And I know what his character—and I know what his background—I know what he's capable of doing. And he's certainly not capable of murder. So, he—snapped—something snapped, something overcame him."

I listen and think, *My daughter is dead. He killed her in his rage. He should pay the price.*

Mr. Lepley ends with, "Thank you, I have no further questions."

Wayne begins by reminding Jordan of the crime scene photo shown to him at the bail reduction hearing. "But you don't believe that?"

Jordan tells him, "It is an aberration. It happened but it wasn't Mitch."

Wayne elicits the fact that Margie did indeed work in California and reviews Jordan's recall of the events of June, July, and August 1996, establishing that Jordan perceived that Mitch moved out of the house on August 12th and was going to Cornell the next week.

On redirect, Mr. Lepley asserts that Mitch did not take furniture but only what he would need at Cornell. Jordan agrees.

Aileen Paster, Mitch's mom, takes the stand and identifies herself. She has a master's degree in education from City College and taught elementary school for seven years. She has been a paralegal for nineteen years at the same firm—which does not practice criminal law.

When she is asked to describe Mitch's behavior during the week before Margaret's death she says he was very upset and depressed. "He was—he went out and bought a computer and he was studying."

She has just confirmed that the computer was purchased and he had it. This explains the charges to Margie's credit card that were placed on it a week before she died. We are never reimbursed for that charge.

Aileen attests to Margie and Mitch's talking daily and believes both of them originated calls. Next she is asked to recall the morning Margaret was stabbed and died and the procedure when Mitch's call came into the office where she works. She heard the receptionist paging her from the other side of the office where she picked up. She talked to Mitch for only a short time.

Mr. Lepley asks, "And what did you do after he told you what he told you?"

"I was hysterical. One of my coworkers came over to me and said to me, 'What is the matter?' And I said, 'Please, just put my boss on the phone. I can't talk.'"

Mr. Lepley asks her to describe her son's tone of voice.

"He was crying. He said, 'Something terrible happened. I stabbed Margaret.' And I just—lost it." That is when her boss took the call. She did not talk to her son again until that evening.

When asked if there was anything she would like to add she says, "And I just—I love him. Yes, I would like him to get help. I think that he does need help. And I would just like to have him back in my life. My deepest apologies to the Bostroms. I don't know what else to say."

We understand her feelings and appreciate her thoughts for us. Her pain is real. But she can see Mitch and we can't see Margie. The prosecution wisely does not question this mother.

Jory Schlenger, who has known Mitch since he was four, is called next as a character witness. He confirms and expands on Jordan's description of Mitch as the all-American boy. Wayne has no questions and a short recess is called.

Mitchell Paster is the next witness. When Mr. Rude asks, "As you sit here today, Mr. Paster, do you have any doubt in your mind that you stabbed and killed your wife?"

"No."

Mitch now admits that finances were a problem but only when he was laid off and he had to control the spending. There had been lots of fights but they never turned violent. In the psychiatric evaluations he had denied that Margaret and he argued over money. He classifies their relationship as loving and says it was excellent just before they married and right after.

Mitch claims, under oath, he came to Lewisburg at the end of March, admits he didn't seek employment but did earn some extra money refereeing basketball games. He tells of his concerns about Margaret's drinking, his version of the Thursday night dinner, of Margie and Bill being drunk when they left the house, and of conversations he had with Bill's wife about the affair. He acknowledges that he took the pets because he realized it would upset Margaret. Later, he felt really bad about it and told Margaret she could come get them. While he was in New Jersey he received divorce papers, but Margaret and he decided to go to Ithaca together at the end of July and see how it went. Mitch describes it as an up time in their relationship.

Mitch says that on August 11, 1996, while at dinner with the Coreys, Margaret confirmed the affair for Bill's wife, who later called Mitch to tell him. That night Bill came to Mitch and Margaret's home to get the pager because "Margaret was too drunk to answer it." Mitch was civil and told Bill he wasn't going to hit him and to just leave. Mitch called his father the next morning. His father came and they packed and left for New Jersey.

Mitch reports that Margaret and he talked at least once a day from August 12th to August 15th and agreed to meet. That is why he went to Lewisburg. Here he tells Mr. Rude and the court he knew she was leaving for a conference and he was going to Cornell the next Monday. When he arrived Margaret was not at home. He says she did not come home that night but did drive by the house twice with Bill, another friend, and Calie. He is sure she saw him standing in the driveway. He claims it was raining and he put his car in the garage when he arrived.

Mitch says he spent the night waiting and spoke with Bill's wife several times. Margaret returned home at about 7:45 A.M. Mr. Rude asks him to explain what happened when she came home.

"Well, as soon as she walked in the house, I gave her a hug and asked where she had been. And she went—kind of said something about this motel because she was drinking. And I asked her if she was with Bill, and she said she wasn't." Mitch says the phone rang then and it was Bill's wife telling him that Bill was now home and had admitted he was with Margaret the night before. When he confronted Margaret she became angry because he refused to tell the acting warden that he didn't mean the complaint he had made on Monday. He says Margaret threatened him with her friends and what they could do to him. She was furious and began telling Mitch about prior relationships.

Wayne Samuelson objects.

Judge Muir is troubled by the line of questioning.

Mr. Rude explains, "Your Honor, this is not offered for the truth of the statements. This is offered to show how the defendant acted as a result of the statements. This is not hearsay."

Wayne objects and reminds the court that Mitch has already admitted to intentionally killing Margaret.

But the court overrules the objection.

Mitch continues. "She started telling me about other things that were going on pretty much throughout the whole length of our relationship. Her infidelities, affairs with people, a lot of things, doing drugs, doing other things."

I'm outraged that he can make up anything and tell it, and no one can refute it because he killed the other participant—Margaret.

Mitch says he was overwhelmed by what she told him. "It was almost as if I was in a fog, in a daze."

At noon the lunch recess is taken. When we return Wayne asks to take a witness out of order. The defense agrees and so does the judge. Dr. Samuel Land is sworn in. He is a graduate of the University of Virginia and received an M.D. from the Medical College of Virginia in Richmond, where he also did a five-year residency in anatomic and clinical pathology. He had a one-year fellowship at the office of the chief medical examiner for Virginia.

Dr. Land, a forensic pathologist, has performed over fifteen hundred autopsies and has testified as an expert witness at least one hundred times. He is currently employed by Forensic Pathology Associates, Inc., in Allentown. Wayne asks us if we would be willing to leave the courtroom while this testimony takes place.

"No! If others are going to hear it I want to hear it for myself."

Blow-ups of clinical drawings of the female body, with Margaret's wounds marked and labeled, are displayed as Dr. Land methodically explains what Mitch did to her.

Most of it is in medical terms and very clinical and doesn't have a strong effect on me at the time. In the last chapter of this book, I write about seeing the actual report and discuss its contents.

What I do remember is that all the wounds to the chest and one to the back are immediately life-threatening, including eight or nine in the area of the heart. Several incised wounds, caused by a sharp object dragging across the skin, indicate she tried to defend herself.

Mr. Samuelson asks, "So, would your conclusion be that the victim put up a struggle in this case?"

"Absolutely." Dr. Land reports that there were fresh abrasions to the left shoulder and right wrist and "multiple bruises to the buttocks and lower extremities of varying ages."

I wonder if this means that Mitch was beating her all along.

Wayne asks, "Doctor, of the homicides you've seen and performed autopsies on, how does this rate in terms of violence?"

Dr. Land's answer is recorded in the court transcript as, "This was a very violent attack." He goes on to explain why and finishes his answer with, "This was a very violent death. Those [intimate murders] are usually the most violent deaths because it's such a personal crime. This was one of the more severe cases I've seen."

"Based on the number of injuries that were suffered by the victim in this case, assuming she were in the—in an operating room in the best hospital in the country as the last wound was being inflicted, would she have been able to be—would she have survived?"

"I don't think so."

Do we need any more proof of how awful it was?

Mr. Lepley begins questioning for the defense by asking how long it would have taken Margaret to die from the wounds to the heart. The doctor tells him it would have happened in minutes, but he wants a more specific answer, which the doctor says he can't give because there are no controlled studies of how long it takes and there is the complication of wounds to several vital organs besides the heart.

"Would you be able to render an opinion as to whether she was deceased as of the time of the last stab wound?"

"With the amount of blood at the scene, I think she probably survived for a few minutes after the last stab wound, but I can't be sure."

After several attempts to clarify the testimony Mr. Lepley asks, "So, isn't it true then that it's equally likely that she was deceased as of the time of the last stab wound?"

"I actually considered that. The problem is that all the wounds have hemorrhage along the wound pathways and you need to have some blood pressure to have hemorrhage...."

When the pathologist is excused, Mr. Rude claims Mitch is trying to compose himself and asks for a five minute recess. The court grants it. I haven't noticed any remarkable reaction by Mitch to the testimony.

When Mitch retakes the stand, he reports he was confused on the morning of the murder and it is difficult to express what happened that day. He says he met with the government psychiatrist for over two months trying to sort it out. He implies that part of his trouble is because he hasn't seen a counselor since last June. He is taking an antidepressant medication and tries not to think about the murder—it is too painful. He denies any recollection of what happened between the time he went upstairs and finding himself on the phone with his mother.

Mitch underwent hypnosis under the direction of Dr. Sadoff but didn't learn what he had said until Dr. Johnson, the federal psychiatrist, informed him that on the tape he remembered going upstairs to look for the pets and he had found the knife under the bed. He then confronted Margaret with it. This is his second version of the story.

Mr. Rude asks why he called his mother and Mitch says, "We've always been a close family and when things happen—I didn't even realize I was on the phone until I heard her voice." He confirms it was his mother's boss who told him to call 911.

Mr. Rude asks what his purpose was in calling 911 and Mitch answers, "To get help for my wife."

"But you've testified here today that you don't recall anything from the time she went upstairs to the time you were on the telephone. How do you know you stabbed your wife?"

"I just—I don't know....There is no doubt."

Mr. Rude then asks several questions about the suppression hearing testimony hoping to establish that Mitch was not trying to obstruct justice. This line of questioning is followed by questions about the plea bargain.

Mitch explains, "The decision about going to trial was something that we [his family] talked about a lot with the doctor [Sadoff] and Butner [the government psychiatric facility]. The—as depressed as I was, given all the circumstances, it was just—I was told that i[t] would be compounded by going to trial, nor did I want to subject my wife's family, my family to the—to more of the traumas of a trial."

When asked if there was anything else he wanted to say he responds, "Hum, well, Your Honor, I'm not a criminal. However, I am responsible for my wife's death. And I regret that no amount of grief, no amount of prayer can change that terrible, terrible fact. And I'm not trying to justify what happened. I'm trying to understand what happened. I feel tremendous remorse. I offer my apologies to my wife's family, to my family, and to everyone that has been impacted by this."

He never looks at us and his words are cold and impersonal but they are all we'll get. A real tearful expression of emotion would be more like—*I'm so sorry I killed Margaret. I know everyone is suffering because of what I did. I wish I could bring her back.*

Cross-examination focuses on the discrepancies in Mitch's various statements. He told the 911 operator he stabbed his wife but didn't say that to the FBI agents. Mitch admits it could have been May when he moved to Lewisburg and that he was laid off for as long as two years while in California, but is adamant he did not tell the agents he took the knife from the kitchen and started up the stairs.

Wayne methodically attacks his testimony about finances, his choice of Cornell over Bucknell, the divorce papers, and money he removed from their joint account, and elicits the information Bill is a much larger man than Mitch. My suspicion that Mitch had put the car in the garage so Margaret wouldn't see it is confirmed. Apparently Bill's wife suggested it. Wayne asks Mitch why he didn't leave that night when he saw Margaret and Bill in the car together and they saw him but she didn't come home. Mitch says he doesn't know.

Mitch admits he was upset but relieved that she was okay when she came home. As for the hug, Wayne asks, "She had been out all night, you had seen her with Corey that previous night in the car, and yet you gave her a hug, is that right, when she came in?" Wayne's tone implies that this is a very unusual reaction.

Mitch is now saying that the first thing he remembers after their fight was being on the phone with his mother, but Wayne asks him if he didn't tell the agents that the first thing he remembered was being on the phone with 911. Mitch doesn't recall.

Mitch denies that he cleaned up, changed clothes, or washed his hands after killing Margaret. (But when they permitted Margie's family to go into the house, I found a bloodstained towel in the sink in the guest bathroom.) He doesn't recall putting the knife in the kitchen sink but believes he told the 911 operator he did. He doesn't recall if he asked the agents how his wife was that day. In short, Mitch doesn't recall anything that would hurt his case further and presents himself as a loving husband who knows he stabbed his wife but doesn't remember it.

I feel that Wayne establishes doubt about Mitch's credibility.

The court takes a five-minute recess; then the defense rests.

Wayne begins the government's case with his first witness: Special Agent Richard L. Rodgers, who retired from the FBI in 1997. He was a supervisor and helped investigate Margaret Bostrom's murder along with Agent Schmidle.

Wayne asks, "Did he specifically say that he went into the kitchen and got the knife from the butcher block?"

"Very definitely."

"Did he say he then started upstairs with the knife?"

"Yes, he did." Agent Rodgers says Mitch described the knife as silver with a black handle.

"Now, you say you have no doubt whatsoever that he said that. Why is that?"

"I have a daughter the same age as Margaret. And when he said he was—started up the stairs, I thought at that point in time how little time she would have had left to live."

I'm grateful to Dick Rodgers for pointing out that Margaret is the victim—not Mitch. The real victims can get lost in the judicial process. Wayne begins taking the agent through the crime scene photos. Mr. Rude offers to stipulate that the photos are authentic so the court can accept them. Wayne feels an explanation of what the photographs depict is in order.

Judge Muir agrees, "Yes, I'm not eager to look at these, but it's my duty and I'll do it...."

Crime scene photos numbered 3 through 7 are of Margaret's body in the bathroom, 8 through 10 are pictures of the kitchen sink and the knife. Number 9 is a close-up of the knife and a ruler that shows the knife was about 12½ inches long. Photographs 11 through 21 are of Mitch, his bloodstained cheek, clothes, hands, and fingernails. Photo exhibits 3, 6, and 7 are sealed at the government's request. The defense asks that number 4 also be sealed.

After a brief cross-examination, Wayne plays the 911 tape then calls Ruth Grover, Margaret's sister, as a witness. After establishing facts about her employment, our family, and the sisters, Wayne asks about Ruth's relationship with Margie.

"We were very close from childhood. There was more of a bond between, you know Margie and myself than probably between Kathy and me. And it was that way through adulthood. Obviously, I named my daughter after her."

Later Wayne asks if Margaret confided in Ruth and if Ruth knew about her relationship with Bill. Ruth simply answers, "Yes" to both questions.

When asked if Margaret ever confided in her about other relationships, Ruth's answer is, "No, just about a relationship with Mitch."

"Could you relate to the court the impact her murder has had upon you?" Wayne's question unleashes an emotional response from Ruth and a tirade from Judge Muir follows her description of the questions Abby and Jacob ask her. My heart goes out to Ruth, who seems completely confused on the witness stand.

The judge allows Wayne to ask her questions but she is not allowed "to read a lot of melodramatic data....But I tell you people this: There is a statement in the Pre-Sentence Report from the mother saying, 'Judge, don't betray us.' I consider that grossly inappropriate and I'm not going to tolerate that kind of statement or inquiry in this courtroom. I'm just going to shut it off. So, you better counsel the mother when she gets on the stand that she's not to say anything out of line."

The judge has to hear another case at 4 P.M., so our case is adjourned after Judge Muir tells Wayne that he will be able to ask Ruth questions tomorrow but that he wants an oral response, she can't read what she has prepared before. "I also want to know whether she wishes to be designated as a person who under the statute, a family member, to make a statement....I'm perfectly willing to consider designating one or two others on behalf of the family."

Judge Muir appears a little calmer, but we are still very confused about whether both Larry and I will be able to speak along with Ruth. That evening is very hard for us. We are angry and confused. The judge doesn't want us to talk about feeling betrayed but how else can we feel? I feel bad that my honest thoughts have caused trouble for Ruth, Larry, and Wayne.

We go back to the hotel and discuss our concerns and dismay over cocktails before we go to dinner. We end up at a local microbrewery with Riley and Esther. It is long and narrow and crowded but the shiny vats and polished wood make an attractive setting. Back at the hotel I make some quick handwritten notes—in case I do make it to the stand.

The next morning the judge speaks before Wayne gets a chance to say anything. We are pleased when he has no objection to Ruth making a statement to the court relating to the sentence to be imposed, but he wants it separate from testimony.

Wayne apologizes to the court and takes responsibility for calling a witness out of order yesterday. He explains that he has three family members who will be giving brief testimony and would also like to give impact statements. The judge is in agreement with all of us speaking. After a short discussion it is decided that each of us will give our statement immediately after our testimony—eliminating the need for us to be recalled.

When Wayne is through asking Ruth questions, there is no cross-examination so he calls Rebecca Smeltz, Graham Showalter's legal assistant who dealt with Margaret's divorce case. Margaret was at their office on August 13th and confirmed that Mitch had signed the return receipt for the certified mail. She also stated she wanted to go ahead with the divorce.

Larry is the next witness. Wayne guides him through all the financial help we gave Margaret and Mitch while they were in California. We bought the condominium in Mira Mesa and a car, helped with living expenses, and made house payments when Mitch was out of work. We paid the down payment on her Volvo and bought Calie for her.

Wayne asks about Margaret's drinking and Larry responds that she was a social drinker. We spent time with her in California and Lewisburg and never saw her intoxicated. Then Wayne asks what the impact of her murder has been on him.

Larry begins by telling of seeking help from Survivors of Homicide and becoming active in that group—actually we are co-vice-presidents. He also declares that the federal court and the prosecutor have been cooperative.

Judge Muir demonstrates his sense of humor when he asks Larry to repeat his last statement because he didn't hear it. Sure! He just wants to have the praise repeated to offset my "betrayal remark." Larry expands on his tribute and gives an abbreviated version of his written impact statement. He states, "I think what hurts so much is that we'll never see Margaret again. But they can visit Mitchell. We know they hurt. We know they feel bad that—Mitchell's parents— that Margaret was killed. But still in the future, he may come back and conduct a fairly normal life....This is very hard to take....You know, we just—holidays are hard. We remember little things she did. Like she used to touch me—pat me on the back and say, 'Oh, Daddy,' when I said something that was a little bit too hard, like fathers do....I'll go to the grave with this, I'm sure."

Then I'm called as a witness. Wayne asks how many children I have. I say, "How do I answer that question? I had three. I sort of still feel like I have three." I'm asked about the phone calls on August 12th and if I knew about the affair, her filing for divorce, and Mitch's phone call the night before he killed her. I answer questions about my advice to her and my dismay at not being contacted by anyone from either psychiatrist's office when Mitch was being evaluated.

I begin my impact statement with, "I guess our whole family dynamic has been so drastically changed. We didn't lose only Margaret, but we lost Mitch. And we lost the friendship of the Pasters....He called us Mom and Dad. We called him son. My granddaughter always called him Uncle Mitch...." While describing how Mitch and I used to cheer for the UCONN basketball teams I begin to sob.

The judge tells me I can ask for a recess if I need it, but I continue telling of our plans with Margie. I explain that we have our faithful old friends and new dear friends. But we have lost some friends who can't handle our tragedy. I explain that my workshops about violence against women are a way to keep Margie's memory alive and help keep others from the same experience.

I'm a part-time writer and since Margaret's murder I've been writing about my feelings and memories of her being alive. "My other daughters think we don't care as much about them anymore because we're so involved with Margaret. And that's not true. But when you lose something, that's something that you sort of concentrate on. You can't help yourself.

"The other thing is no matter how many times I've tried, I cannot accept the fact in my heart that it wasn't premeditated. I just cannot understand waiting for someone to get out of a shower and that not being premeditation. Having the knife itself, no matter where he got it, to me that's premeditation. And I think Mitch knows that as well as I do."

Wayne then shows me an eight-by-ten photograph. He asks if this is my daughter, Margaret, Larry, and me. Yes, it was taken when she received her Ph.D. I thank Judge Muir, both FBI agents, and Mr. Samuelson for their support and understanding. Before I step down I remember to tell the judge about Margie changing the beneficiary on her insurance policy two weeks before Mitch killed her.

When I am finished Ruth is called to the stand again. She is hurt Mitch hasn't said he was sorry and that no one from his family has asked about the funeral or where Margie is. "So, it's almost as though not knowing is going to make this not be there, but it is there. And just so everyone knows, she was cremated and sits in my family room every day, so I can see her there."

Ruth talks about the things that are in her house that were Margie's. Then she says, "It's [a house] filled with a lot of grief and sorrow…it's difficult to deal with people grieving." She tells the judge she has to be the strong one; her sister, Kathy, will not accept that Margie is dead. "Kathy expects Margie to come walking in—sometime." Ruth tells the court about being on a plane with two elderly sisters who were visiting one of their daughters who was having a child. "I'll never have that. My whole life, I will never share with my sister…that kind of bond that those two women then shared as they went through life. I lost a friend, a companion…a whole piece of my life."

Ruth says that as a Christian she is trying to forgive Mitch but sees that as separate from these proceedings. It is hard when Mitch has made so many vile statements about Margaret and her character. He claims she drank too much. But Ruth wonders—is that a reason to kill her? She had an affair—is that a reason to kill her? Ruth wants Margie remembered for what she accomplished, not for what happened that day.

The government has no more evidence and the defense has no rebuttal evidence. The court will hear closing arguments. It is agreed that the defense should argue first. At 11:04 A.M., after a short recess, Mr. Rude will begin a twenty-five minute presentation. When the prosecution finishes its remarks the defense will be given five additional minutes for rebuttal.

Mr. Rude tells the judge he has completed his findings of facts and conclusions of law report and has his computer disk for changes that may be necessary after he meets with Wayne Samuelson later this afternoon. The judge will have both the defense and the government's reports today. Judge Muir is happy he will have them while everything is still fresh in his mind.

Mr. Rude begins his statement, "May it please the court, opposing counsel, Your Honor, in my short career I've made this statement on four different occasions for three other people who have been accused of murder. What makes this one different from the other ones, I believe, is the great losses that are suffered on both sides of the aisle. I believe Mrs. Bostrom has stated it that the Pasters have lost a daughter; the Bostroms have lost a daughter and a son-in-law.

"By no means through the facts that we presented did we attempt to disparage or to minimize the life of Margaret Bostrom. We presented these facts in an effort to try to explain why this occurred from the defense view." He goes on to argue there isn't a preponderance of evidence that Mitch willfully obstructed justice or purposely gave testimony that is not credible at the FBI suppression hearing. Mr. Rude says Mitch's attempt at a defense by seeking psychiatric evaluations was taking responsibility because he did not recall what happened. He goes on to challenge the government's case for upward departure based on premeditation, use of a weapon, and extreme conduct.

Mr. Rude admits, "…Yes, it [the murder] was brutal, but it wasn't unusually heinous or it wasn't unusually brutal." He then asks for a downward departure for a single act of aberrational conduct. Mitch never acted violent in the past. He recognizes he needs help and his family want him to get that help. "Mr. Paster knows he will be punished for this crime but he also wants to know why this happened…what we are asking here is for him to receive the help, not the lengthy time the government is seeking, and to be able to get on with his life, to take the next step to—once he does realize what happened, to become another productive member of society and hopefully someone who is better for this."

Inside my mind is screaming, *Oh, if only Margie had a second chance. Mitch took that away from her. Why should he have one?*

Mr. Samuelson begins the government's closing statement by saying he does not find Mitch's testimony credible. He reminds the court that in the FBI interview Mitch had a very good memory of the two months leading up to the murder. Wayne continues, "If you look at the 911 tape and listen to the transcript of that, that is probably the most revealing portion of the defendant's statement because it's really pretty much before he had any time to think about what he is going to say."

Wayne suggests Mitch was doing plenty of thinking when he carried the knife back downstairs and placed it in the sink, not the butcher-block holder, because it was covered with blood. He also washed his hands and called his mother, who works at a law firm. He didn't call his father because he didn't work for an attorney and might have been out of his office at the time. "Amazingly, though, four hours later, when it is time to sit down with investigators and he's in trouble at this point, after having been advised of his rights…he conveniently does not remember what happened upstairs."

Wayne presents the evidence of premeditation. Before the actual killing, Mitch hid the car in the garage after talking to Bill's wife, so Margaret wouldn't know he was there when she came home. At the time of the killing he took the largest of the butcher knives and waited patiently for her to finish her shower. She was trapped in the bathroom. The attack was quick, shampoo bottles and conditioner on the top ledge of the shower were not disturbed, even though she tried to defend herself.

Next Wayne explains why the government considers Mitch's attack extreme conduct by reviewing Dr. Land's report and testimony. Then he explains that Mitch obstructed justice by trying to suppress his statement to the FBI and continued to do so on the stand in this hearing by contradicting the agents' testimony and reports.

The government does not believe the defendant has taken responsibility for his actions. "Simply standing here saying, 'I'm very remorseful for this,' doesn't mean he is remorseful. Does his demeanor show remorse? Did he turn to the parents in the courtroom and say, 'I'm really sorry for what I did? I can't believe I did this. I accept responsibility for my actions. I will take my punishment.'? No....There's only been an attempt to minimize his involvement, highlighted yesterday by his testimony on the stand—I am not a criminal."

Wayne concludes his statement by taking issue with the victim's conduct causing the attack. Mitch had choices; he could have left several times but he chose to stay and intentionally stabbed her to death.

Mr. Rude responds that Mitch has never denied he stabbed his wife. What he has been trying to do is determine why it happened.

The judge asks who said Mitch found the knife under the bed.

Mr. Rude explains that this information was obtained while Mitch was under hypnosis. Then, the defense claims Mitch took responsibility for his actions by calling 911. Mr. Rude asks, "Why didn't he just leave after this occurred?...Why did he do everything the operator told him to do?...He didn't even seek to run. This was a single act of aberrant behavior."

Court is adjourned at 12:10 P.M.

On Having No Voice

My life is shrouded, with clouds of injustice,
by a system concerned, not that
my child is dead, but for the rights of the criminal.
A grieving mother's voice is as hard to hear
as a needle falling in a haystack.

A dangerous cliff called despair, full of anger and
depression, hides in the lonely mist.
I lick my wounds and yearn for life as it was
before his vicious act of murder
and my introduction to this unjust system.

We drive back to Connecticut and when we listen to the messages on our answering machine we learn that my uncle Rance has died from a massive heart attack. The message was left on March 17th. The funeral was today, March 19th. I call to express our sympathy and I talk to each of his three sons. None of us has pleasant news to share, but I cannot truly accept that death is the end. I know Margie's spirit is with me now and that I'll see her and all my loved ones again in a more perfect place when I die.

CHAPTER 20

More Messages
From Margie

What happens when we die? Did I really live before? Did I share those lives with people who are part of this life? Do events in past lives influence who I am now? Can we communicate with the dead? These are all questions I have asked for a very long time. In fact, Margie helped me in my search by giving me Brian Weiss's book *Many Lives, Many Masters*. Since her death my search has gained purpose as I focus on Margie. A bibliography at the end of this book includes resources I found helpful in answering my questions.

I have already mentioned Margie's visit to her niece shortly after the murder, her comforting touch when I was feeling desperately overwhelmed in the Lewisburg motel, and her sending Colleen to be with me during my breast surgery. Margie has continued to make her presence felt and let us know she is aware of what we are experiencing here on earth.

The night of October 16th, two months after Margie's death, I'm in bed unable to sleep and mourning my loss when a small white light appears at the corner of my right eye. It's Margie's spirit moving across the room encouraging me to relax and enjoy my dead friends and family members she has brought to visit me. Soon her spirit is joined by other frolicking shapes.

Night Visitors

Margie visited last night.
She brought dozens of playful friends
To entertain and illuminate
Her lonely mother's spirit.

Tentative, at first, not wishing to scare,
They hid just out of sight.
Then, gradually they came into view.
Their intense light filling the room.

White, blue, red, and yellow, too.
Colorful moving shapes dancing
And playing for me.
Then, fading from view.

A filmy gray shape floating
Through the room.
Deep black shadows changing forms.
Moving closer, then away.

At first, they frighten me.
But Margie is there I know.
Ma, open your eyes and spirit to our dance.
I do. It's heavenly.

I suspect that Mom and Dad, Grandma Bo,
Jack, Ted, Dolly, Agnes, and Sue,
Even baby Maxine, the sister I never met,
Have made the visit with Margie.

Come again, my night visitors.
Come to comfort or play,
Or to share your wisdom.
Your reality sustains me.

Teach me, guide me along

The healing path filled with
Pure love and endless joy.
Perhaps, I will dance with you.

Margie continues to visit. Sometimes she comes alone as a single bright dot of white light. Other times she brings additional spirits. Sometimes she appears as one of a thousand little, light blue butterflies that fill my field of vision. Their tiny wings make a soft fluttering noise that fills me with peace.

While Larry and I are vacationing at Mexico's Copper Canyon her spirit floats across the deep chasms to let me know she is happy that I have this chance to fulfill my dream of visiting this geological wonder. Her spirit visits always leave me refreshed and wanting more.

I tell people I came out of my mother's womb a New York Yankee baseball fan. It is a genetic trait. My dad was knowledgeable and enthusiastic about their legacy. DiMaggio, Berra, Rizzuto, and Mantle were my heroes. During September and October of 1996, I jokingly tell Margie, "If you have any pull up there do something to help the Yankees." It is a great time to be a Yankee fan because they get in the race and surprise everyone by their magnificent comeback in the post season. I give her credit for their becoming world champions in 1996. I know Joe Torre thinks his brother is responsible for their triumph and many fervent Atlanta Braves fans have sought their deceased loved ones' efforts to help their team win. However, I'm sure Margie's interest in events on earth that I care about prevailed. It is another way to feel close to her. In 1997 the Yankees win their division and in 1998 they have arguably the best baseball team ever— winning 114 games in the regular season and taking the World Series in four games from San Diego. They also win the World Series in 1999 and 2000. Even if Margie isn't responsible I'm sure she is celebrating with me.

In October 1996 I visit a psychic in East Hartford. It isn't completely successful. She receives information from the spirit world, but it is vague and not quite accurate. She tells me she keeps seeing two, then three, then two again. She asks if I have two children or three. That is a question I am unsure how to answer since the murder, so her confusion makes sense to me.

"I keep seeing a man with curly, dark hair. One of your children must be a son."

Oh, no, she is seeing Mitch. Am I thinking so much about him that his presence is stronger than Margie's? "No, that is my son-in-law."

I purposely work at not giving her any clues that might help her identify the source of my grief and reason for my visit. Later, I wish I hadn't done that. It certainly did not make her task easier and I might have lost the chance to receive helpful information.

At the end I tell her about the murder. She tells me Margie is happy and safe. That justice will be done. Mitch will pay for his actions. I ask how soon and she assures me in three or four months. Wrong! It takes 22 months for him to be sentenced. Even though I'm disappointed with the limited information, I know I'll try again.

Margie communicates with us through Calie, the golden retriever, who has become an immediate source of comfort and a constant reminder of Margie. Calie loves Abby and Jacob but chooses to spend most of her time with Larry and me. She shares our grief and sometimes cries in her sleep. She was there when Margie was murdered and hates it when anyone raises a voice in anger or fights. The first few times I put on one of Margie's sweatshirts, she picks up Margie's scent and excitedly chews and tugs on the sleeve—a behavior Margie permitted. Having so much of Margie's furniture here helps ease the transition for Calie. She claims the same spot on the same sofa she had with Margie. My poem "In Her Image" describes how Calie's deep brown eyes, playfulness, and loving behavior remind us of Margie.

We all get comfort from Calie and Jacob.

In Her Image

The huge brown eyes
looking into mine with
such love and devotion
are Margie.

The tilt of the head,
the ears alert and waiting
for my welcoming words
are Margie.

The sleek and slender body,
the long, lean legs
bringing her toward me
are Margie.

The curly windswept hair,
the limbs eagerly embracing
me with affection
are Margie.

The slightly raised lips
in the smiling face
caught at play
are Margie.

The pleading head placed
next to mine, the awareness
that she'll get what she wants
are Margie.

The golden retriever called
California Girl, Calie for short,
and the spirit within
are Margie.

In July of 1998 Larry and I visit our family in Jamestown, which is in western New York State. Nearby is Lily Dale, a renowned spiritualist colony. I was curious about it during the many years I lived in the area, but never dared to break the taboo placed on it by the larger community. Thirty-three years later my pressing personal need to gain information about Margie gives me the courage to schedule a reading. I tell my husband and aunts about my plans and Peggy, the widow of Uncle Rance, tells me, "I went there once with Dottie Carnahan against your uncle's orders. While I was there the toilet tank in our upstairs bathroom broke and flooded the kitchen light fixture—ruining it and several ceiling tiles. He said it happened because I broke two rules. The first was thou shalt not disobey thy husband. The second was thou shalt not tamper with things that God alone should know."

I laugh. "Sounds like something Rance would have said. I'm proud of you for going anyway."

The next afternoon Larry and I go to Lily Dale. Sherry Lee Caulkins, the psychic I have my reading scheduled with, is at a public demonstration held at the historic "Stump." Several psychics are there displaying their abilities but I'm satisfied with my random selection from among the over fifty individual psychics who are at Lily

Dale in the summer. Sherry has a pretty, round face with striking blue eyes and a blonde, bouffant hairdo. Her manner is quiet and friendly, yet professional.

At her house I feel comfortable entering the small, bright, cluttered room. I sit in a soft chair across a table from her. After a brief prayer she explains she has a spirit with her who is going to help her draw a picture with information for me. She picks up a piece of blue chalk and quickly draws five blue lines all starting at a common point toward the top left hand side of the paper. They fan out an inch or two while extending in a large circular path downward. "Ah, angel wings. No, one angel wing. I see someone with five children. You may only know about four. Do you know who this is?"

Relieved that she is right so far, I answer, "My mother had five children, but my sister died five years before I was born."

Next she takes gray chalk and draws a long slender shape that curves slightly and comes to a point at the edge of the paper. "Oh, my God! It's a knife. Where did that come from? Yes, it is a knife. I don't understand. Do you?"

I nod. Relieved, she continues, "It's also a slide. This gentleman with me tells me he went down a playground slide when he died. It was a very pleasant feeling. He took over as your guardian angel in March."

The irony of the very uncle who forbid his wife's visit to Lily Dale being my guardian angel strikes me as fitting. As I mentioned earlier, Rance died March 17, 1998. He always did have a unique sense of humor. I'm a little upset Margie gave him the job, but later I'm told she has some very important things to accomplish where she is now. I'm relieved that everything she learned here is not going to waste.

Sherry uses yellow to divide the paper into two sections. Then she asks, "Who do you know on the other side who has the initial R?"

"My mother is Ruth and my uncle, the guardian angel, is Rance." What are the odds that she would pick that initial if she was just guessing? Then she holds up the picture and shows me two clear Rs—previously drawn. I'm speechless.

Sherry tells me the pink and turquoise in the drawing show that I am a psychologist, meaning I help individuals with their problems and I'm a teacher who works well with groups. I am also a communicator who is beginning to speak to very large groups of people. This information feels right to me.

"This past February a big change took place in you. What happened?"

"I suddenly felt more energetic. I began enjoying myself and life, if only for brief moments, for the first time since Margie's death. Getting out of bed wasn't a chore. The only reason I can think of is I went off Prozac after ten months." She has given me enough information to make me believe she is real—so I relax.

"You and your husband are friends now?" I nod. "You will be even better ones later on. Do you have children—besides Margie?"

"Two daughters—Ruth and Kathy."

"You and Ruth are very tight. I mean close. Tell her not to give up on her sister. Kathy will achieve success by September of 2000." I'm stunned that she knows about Ruth's concern for Kathy. (However, that date passes without a significant change in Kathy's status.)

Sherry asks, "Do you have any questions for me?"

"Yes. Does Margie approve of what I'm doing?"

"She is sad you are still so stuck in your grieving. She has forgiven Mitch. Oh, that doesn't mean she doesn't think he should be severely punished, but she doesn't want to spend time thinking about that."

"That's not what I mean. I'm doing workshops about violence against women and I use her story to help inform other women. Am I invading her privacy?"

"Honey, who do you think planned the workshop? Your mother and Margie! You are only their earthly tool. Remember the white spaces on the angel wing? They are there because God can get his message across through you."

Sherry continues, "Margie knew, in her subconscious, in March of 1996 that she was going to die and she prepared for it." I wonder if this might explain why she named me beneficiary of her life insurance.

We have gone five minutes over our half hour session. We hug. I pay. She gives me the picture. When I get in the car Larry can see my tear-stained face and red eyes. I tell him, "It was scary how right she was, but there are a few things I can't connect. She told me my aura is white which means that God wants to communicate through me. It has been that color since I had a near-death experience while riding in a car with a dark-haired woman. When I told her I couldn't remember anything like that, she explained I might not have even known. It happened a long time ago."

My years in college spent at Bob Jones University, a Christian school in South Carolina, and my later questioning of so narrow a definition of God rise to the surface. I tell Larry, "God and I working together? I'm not sure. I'm still angry at him for Margie's murder and confused about how a loving God let it happen." Perhaps this is God's attempt to expose himself to me in a way I can accept.

Later, I tell Peggy about Rance, saying that dying was like going down a slide on a playground and really quite pleasant. She says, "Yes, that could be because he sat on a stool in the bathroom after taking his shower and when he had the heart attack he slid off onto the floor."

I feel better because of my visit with Sherry Lee Caulkins. She confirms for me that we can receive messages from departed loved ones if we are open to them. Many of my questions remain unanswered but my search continues.

In March of 1999 Larry and I fulfill my dream of visiting Machu Picchu in Peru and the Galapagos Islands off the coast of Ecuador. We travel with a Special Expeditions tour that is very expensive but promises to be educational. We use some of the life insurance money Margie left us to pay for the trip. As always, I try to determine whether Margie approves of this expenditure. She answers me, clearly affirmative, making the trip an unqualified success.

Unlike Hiram Bingham, who in 1911 trudged up Machu Picchu from the Urubamba River Valley with the help of Indian guides on July 24th to discover this remarkable site, we take a bus up a winding dirt road with sixteen switchbacks. When Hiram arrived he found two Indian families living in the northeast corner of the ruins. One young man volunteered to show Dr. Bingham the sacred ruins, which were completely covered by subtropical growth. Larry and I have Julio, a native anthropologist, to tell us about the Incas. Listening to what he has to say about these remarkable people is fascinating and informative; however, the visual stimuli of rocks so carefully and skillfully placed together to form aqueducts, terraces, temples, and residences sitting among the green mountains, some with their peaks in the clouds, is inspirational by itself. I try to picture buildings covered with stucco, and visualize gold and silver temples and palaces for the high priest and the king.

I can't really feel Margie's presence but I sense that this perfect sunny day is a gift from her. In the afternoon we are free to explore on our own. Larry and I go to the only large tree on the site, a flame tree, and sit for a while watching the shadows move slowly across the terraces and the Hitching Post of the Sun. We move to the section where the eight hundred women chosen to honor the Inca gods lived. There on the ground is a stylized stone carving of a condor. Later we see two round stones hollowed out in the center. For grinding corn, perhaps? No, at night filled with water they reflect the stars, eliminating the need to look up—much easier on the neck.

At dinner we sit with the two Peruvian guides, Julio and Julia, making plans for our return to Machu Picchu in the morning for the sunrise. We awaken early to mist and a thick cloud cover, but decide to go anyway. The winding road is slick and rutted by the rain and the tracks of other buses. Larry and I decide to climb to the watchtower or guardhouse on our own, taking our time, even though we are not sure we will see anything but clouds. Which is exactly what we see during the long climb up the damp steps. But when we reach the top the clouds clear—completely for about two minutes. I can see the ruins and the young mountain, Huayna Picchu, behind them clearly. Perfect for pictures. Today I feel the mystery surrounding the ruins, but more rewarding is the sense of Margie's presence. Who else would have guided me safely over the wet, slippery rocks and made the clouds disappear just as I made it to the top? I seek a quiet spot alone near the terraces, spread a plastic bag, and sit to watch the mist move across the ruins and mountains, one moment obscuring them and the next revealing surreal forms. I also feel the presence of the Inca spirits.

A movement in the grass nearby catches my attention. A small bird, probably a finch, with black and brown stripes from the front of its head down its back, hops around, comes over, looks at me, but leaves before I think to take a picture. Margie? Yesterday, I was sure she was a large lone flower sitting on a terrace high above me, her long red petals reaching toward the sun. I searched for a path or steps up to her, but I couldn't reach Margie—which I can't—but today Margie comes to me.

We fly from Peru to Ecuador and on to the Galapagos Islands. My first impression as we approach the islands from the air—not on the ocean as Charles Darwin did so many years ago—is of flat land covered with small scrubby brush and hot temperatures. On April 1, 1999, I feel Margie's presence again. We are on a beautiful protected beach surrounded by ancient lava flows. We are actually in a volcanic crater that crumbled into the water on one side allowing the ocean to form a huge bay—Darwin Bay.

On the "short walk" we see all kinds of birds—frigates with the male sitting on low bushes displaying his bright red balloon-like neck pouch and calling raucously to attract females who are flying overhead trying to make a wise decision in choosing a partner for one season. What makes a good mate for a frigate? Is it looks and charm— a romantic tongue full of endearments?

The swallowtail doves are nesting on the rocky sand. What beautiful intelligent faces—black heads with red rings around the eyes and a white ring across the beak. Red-footed boobies with unique webbed feet capable of gripping the branches for support nest in trees. Several nests hold big fluffy feathered babies about seven weeks old. They are adorable.

On my way back to the beach for a much anticipated swim, I meet three sea lions resting in the sand and rocks. Another photo opportunity! Soon I'm in the water. It is wonderfully refreshing. I snorkel among the rocks and encounter lots of sea urchins and two small fish. Two young sea lions are playing in the water, moving slowly closer to me, curious about this creature. I am enthralled by the lack of fear any of the animals show when we appear. I wait patiently to see if they will come to play, but I'm interrupted by Larry's summons. The panga, a motorized rubber dingy, is ready to head back to the ship. I obey but resent leaving this paradise at 10:30

instead of 11:15 A.M. as scheduled. I'm feeling so sorry for myself when Margie steps in. They can't get the panga off the beach. After several tries they tell four of us to get out—temporarily. As I step out I hear Margie, "Ma, I've done all I can. It's up to you now," I sense her impatience with me. Delighted, I grab my bag from the floor of the panga and head back to the beach and thirty more minutes of swimming. How thoughtful of her to intercede for me. This is the only time a panga has gotten stuck on a beach.

While in the water, I see a clear plastic tube floating toward me and decide to retrieve it to protect any birds or sea creatures who might be tempted to taste it. It is a roll of film. Later I learn it belongs to a woman named Margie who was in our Peru group and is also here. Margie—the significance of the name strikes me. Not a coincidence, I'm sure.

The next day an optional 6:45 pre-breakfast walk to the top of Bartoleme Island's highest peak is scheduled. Rumor has it that the view from the top is fantastic. The island's lack of rainfall makes it barren except for two types of plants that were able to colonize. One of them is a cactus with short multiple tubes. The other a silver gray bush that grows close to the ground and has small dainty leaves. There are also a few mangroves near the beach. I can't resist seeing the strange formations of lava in all their surreal beauty. So off we go. There are wooden steps—only 372!

After a dry landing on the panga, we begin a gradual climb up the lava, which is in fine gravel form. A large lava cinder is blocked from my view by other hikers. I find it and trip. I'm not hurt and this is the only mishap clumsy me suffers on the whole trip. Margie?

When we get to the wooden steps they are very steep. As usual my lungs complain about a lack of oxygen. About three-fourths of the way to the top, I decide this is it. I can't go on. Then I hear, "You're no quitter." Ashamed and with new resolve, I start again. Surprise—my lungs don't hurt and my legs are strong. Margie helps me to the top. I feel energized as I gaze at the spectacular view. Thanks for the trip of a lifetime, Margie. The only thing that would have made it better is if I had been able to give you a hug.

At times Margie's intervention saves lives. I make plans for Larry and me to spend his sixty-seventh birthday, October 27, 1999, in the Litchfield Hills of Connecticut. It is a little late in the year for the famous fall foliage of New England, but we will wander through the tiny shops, check out the used bookstore, and eat lunch at the West Street Grill. I'll show him a park that is hidden at the end of a tree-lined lane on a hilltop. We'll visit the small winery I found then lost and found again earlier this month. We'll sample and buy the wines we enjoy the most.

I want to share with him the place where I feel such peace while at the writing retreat. I'll show him the back roads lined with ancient maples that lead to Wisdom House, the large red brick building, the farmhouse, the labyrinth, and the huge pine tree that inspired my friend Kathy's poem.

However, our relaxing plans are changed on I-84 West. Larry becomes distracted and the car drifts toward the concrete Jersey barrier on his side. I watch with horror, having envisioned this happening a million times. All I can do is draw in my breath but it is enough because at the last second he realizes what is happening and swerves to the right. All but the rear tire escapes contact. The tire blows out but we safely cross several lanes—all traffic-free—to the right shoulder. Anyone who is familiar with this stretch of I-84 near Flatbush Avenue will realize this is a true miracle. I know Margie is with us—perhaps because it is her dad's birthday—and saves us from being seriously injured or killed. She even encourages AAA to respond quickly to our call.

Visiting Litchfield will have to wait for another day.

Other times her interventions are lighthearted and playful. They serve to let me know that she's aware of what's happening. One morning, while driving to my writing class with the Middlesex Adult Learning Center, the light rain becomes a downpour. I plead, "Margie, please make it stop before I get there. My papers and prompts to inspire their writing will get soaked if you don't." The heavy rain keeps up until I am in the parking lot ready to get out of the car—then it stops completely. I arrive at the class dry and amazed. We begin to write and the rain starts again. I tell the class my story. We laugh and they advise me to ask Margie to intervene again when we are ready to leave. I do. She does.

I'm still dry when I reach my car, but it rains heavily until I reach home. I tell Margie, "Thanks. I know asking you to keep me dry is frivolous so you don't have to stop the rain this time." But she does anyway.

It is comforting to know that Margie's spirit is alive, actively interested in her loved ones here on earth and growing wiser and more beautiful every day.

Most recently she sends me a two-part message. Larry and I are in Mesa Verde with an Elderhostel group, climbing steep ladders and large steps carved into the rocks when I twist my right knee, slightly—I think. I rest it and it seems better but three weeks later, when I finish speaking to ninety people in New Hampshire at the Intimate Partner Fatality Review Team Workshop, I unexpectedly fall to the floor. When I try to put weight on the leg the pain is excruciating. Two months later I have arthroscopic surgery for a torn cartilage followed by physical therapy. At first, the knee appears to be healing but the pain continues.

When I speak at Becker College, Kevin Woods, a policeman and professor at the college, asks me if I think this is Margie telling me to slow down. He may have a point. If so, I appreciate Margie waiting to get her message firmly across to me until I was safely standing on a carpeted floor and not hanging from the sandstone rocks near Balcony House ruins in Mesa Verde.

Margie gives me comfort and communicates her wishes but she also encourages me to be patient with people who have not experienced the murder of a loved one. She reminds me that our reaction to survivors before our tragedy would not have always been caring and helpful.

CHAPTER 21

We Are Not Contagious
But Healing Requires Effort

Ironically, what survivors need most is a smile, "I'm so sorry," and a hug. However, our culture doesn't teach people how to approach someone who has suffered the devastating trauma caused by a homicide. We fear death and the mortality of our children is unfathomable. When a child is a victim of homicide, everyone feels inadequate. One natural tendency is to avoid dealing with the grieving family either out of fear of doing something wrong or being inadequate for the task.

The reality of what happened to us may pose a threat to your own family. If it can happen to us it can happen to you, so it is safer to cling to the myth that murder only happens to strangers. Murder is happening more and more to people like us, but it is not contagious. You can't catch murder from comforting the survivors.

The effects of being ignored or the thoughtless remarks intended to comfort are devastating for an aching survivor. However, a thoughtful choice of words will soothe our spirits. Many times an awkward or senseless remark, intended to give comfort, can be altered slightly, so that it doesn't provoke more grief, guilt, or anger in the survivor. People tell me: "*I think about you all the time.*" I want to tell them: Don't think about me. Call me. Write to me. Ask me to spend some time with you. Even if I refuse, you have told me you care. Don't tell me to call you. I'm much too tired to do that. Please call me. Don't tell me you will call, write, or keep in touch if you can't do so. I expect you to keep your promise and feel betrayed when it doesn't happen.

"*I don't know what to say.*" You don't have to say anything. Just being here is enough. Listening to me is even better.

"*You're so strong.*" No, I'm not! I have shed more tears than I knew I had. I weep mostly in private, in my car, in the shower, in my bed at 2 A.M., with caring friends, and while writing. Watching me cry may make you feel uncomfortable and inadequate. Remind yourself that I need this release if I am to heal. Expect me to be irrational. I'm not thinking clearly. I feel guilty when told I'm strong. I wonder if you are really telling me that I'm doing better than you could. Why? Do you think I didn't really love her? Did I? Of course I did. I could agree with the slightly different comment, "*It must take all your strength to keep going.*"

"*I don't know how you do it.*" Of course you don't. Neither do I. I do it because I have no real choice. Life is still precious. I have people I love and things I want to do. Your thoughtfulness and prayers give me the strength I need.

"*You look so good.*" What? And I shouldn't? I feel guilty. My daughter's dead—I should look awful. Maybe, if you said, "*I'm glad to see you are taking care of yourself. Margie would want you to.*" I'd feel validated.

"*Having other children must make it easier to bear.*" You'd think so, but this doesn't feel easier. Siblings are often reluctant to discuss their pain and loss, but certainly, having other children to love and who love me is a comfort.

"*Time heals all wounds.*" People really do say this! I'm not going to heal—at least, not without lots of scar tissue. Should I wear a bracelet with the inscription, "I get keloids when I'm opened up. See my appendix scar for confirmation"?

The most insensitive remark I've had to deal with was, "*It has been three months. You must be over it by now.*" It is my daughter who is dead, not a friendly chipmunk who lived in my yard. I'll never be over it.

The worst example of insensitivity I have heard is the spiritual leader who actually tried to console the father of a murdered teenager by telling him, "*At least now you won't have to worry about his behavior problems."* Dealing with teenage behaviors is a natural part of life. Burying a child isn't.

"Maybe this will give you closure." In a murder case the wounds keep being reopened. There is no chance to heal or move on. A state of limbo exists. Lawyers, courts, judges, and a live criminal blessed with civil rights control my life. Survivors say, "Closure will come when they close the casket on me."

"At least the murderer is in jail." Yes, but do you understand how tenuous a situation that is? Come to court with me and write letters to the judge when we ask. Judges tell us this support makes a difference. But please don't promise to write and not carry through. Above all don't tell me you wrote if you didn't. I will see the letters. If an expected letter is not there I feel betrayed—again.

"You must be strong. Your husband, daughters, and grandchildren need you now." I'm aware of their needs, but I'm also struggling to keep from drowning in this cesspool of pain. *"You need to support each other now,"* would be more helpful.

"You need to take care of yourself." Why do you think I eat, try to sleep, take showers, brush my teeth, and get my hair cut? I have to. I know that even healthy and with all my strength I'm not going to deal well with my loss.

"How are you doing?" How do you think I'm doing? The best I can. My daughter was murdered by a man she loved enough to marry. She spent eleven years of her life with him and he brutally killed her. Would you like to see how crazy a grieving mother can be? Or hear my primal scream?

"How is your husband doing?" I don't know. Probably shitty. (He keeps his feelings to himself.) I know I am.

"What can I do?" Be specific. If you are too general I will tell you I need nothing or ask for what I really want—bring her back.

"Did you know the killer was capable of murder?" No. I feel terribly guilty and inadequate as a mother. I should have known and done something to keep her alive. I hate being a failure.

"I can't think of anything more horrible than losing a child." Well, I can. What if he had killed her and we couldn't prove it because she just disappeared? If there were no body or its various parts the uncertainty would gnaw at me. What if I lost more than one family member to brutality—my husband, other daughters, or my grandchildren?

Or what if I were responsible for a terrible accident that took the lives of those I love? How could I deal with the kidnaping or disappearance of a grandchild—not knowing if they were tortured and raped? It is a very violent world we live in. I know.

Margie's death was horrendous, but I have learned not to ask how it could be any worse. I know it could be and ghastly things can still happen to those I love. Margie's murder has not given us immunity from more such tragedies. Rather, it has forced me to acknowledge my world isn't safe anymore. When I see newspapers and TV reports of other people's tragedies, I comprehend their loss and pain and experience the first sharp thrusts of mine again. I know it can happen to my family, so I don't ask why me, but why not me. And I wait.

Don't avoid me. Being ignored hurts deeply. I know being around me is uncomfortable, but I'm doing the best I can. I need all the support you can give me. If you don't feel strong enough to help, please tell me. I'll accept that. I know what it is to feel weak.

Holidays are difficult. Pray for me. Make plans to get together. Let me know you remember her birthday and the day she died—that she existed. I need to celebrate her life and acknowledge her death. Your call, card, or visit help me and my family through these tough times.

You can help me work to heal. I can't escape the pain but must acknowledge it and make the decision to live the rest of my life with purpose and meaning. Caring friends make that a possibility. Keep trying. Sincere effort counts the most. And don't forget the hugs.

After Margie's murder my family and friends support me through the awful nightmare that follows, but I soon realize this pain is mine and I must find my own way through it. In the first weeks and months after Margie's death, I search frantically for every book written on grief and loss—especially of a child. I find solace in reading what others have felt. Their pain, so similar to mine, reassures me that what I am feeling is normal under the circumstances.

I am including a bibliography at the end of the book, but I want to share with you some passages that have been especially meaningful to me.

Antoinette Bosco, Toni to her friends at Survivors of Homicide, is an author of several inspirational books. In *Finding Peace Through Pain*, formerly titled *The Pummeled Heart*, she tells of her journey through the pain of one son's suicide and the murder of another son and his wife. Her book is subtitled *The True Story of a Journey Into Joy*. Toni and her book remind me that I do not have control of everything in my life but I do have choices.

> To grow from pain requires that you make the choice early to hold on to your power. That's extremely difficult because when you've been pummeled, you also get at least temporarily blocked due to the anger you feel at the injustice of the blow. You suddenly learn that life has its own agenda. You are not in control of it. You get overwhelmed by the reality of your powerlessness when it comes to what can happen to you against your will.

Giving up the myth of my control over my universe is extremely difficult, but the fact that I have the power to choose what I will do in the face of Margie's murder gives me a purpose in life. Having a friend like Toni, who understands my pain, inspires me to serve others in Margie's memory.

Other books validate what I am feeling. Nicholas Wolterstorff's *Lament for a Son*—Eric, who was killed in a mountain-climbing accident—captures many of the same feelings I experience. Sometimes I think insanity or senility would be a blessing. I could refuse to acknowledge her death, pretend that she was away and would be home soon.

> It's the *neverness* that is so painful. *Never again* to be here with us—never to sit with us at table, never to travel with us, never to laugh with us, never to cry with us....All the rest of our lives we must live without him. Only our death can stop the pain of his loss.

I, like Mr. Wolterstorff, have been wounded and know my tears make others uncomfortable, but is it too much to expect tolerance for my expression of pain?

> And why is it so important to act strong? I have been graced with the strength to endure. But I have been assaulted, and in the assault wounded, grievously wounded. Am I to pretend otherwise? Wounds are ugly, I know. They repel. But must they always be swathed?

When I read these passages from *Lament for a Son*, I'm struck by how my life is divided into the Before Margie's Murder (BMM) and the After Margie's Murder (AMM) phases. Each experience I have is diminished because I can't share it with her—in person. Knowing that Margie can see the brilliant fall leaves isn't the same as viewing them together.

> Nothing fills the void of his absence. He's not replaceable. We can't go out and get another just like him.
> Something is *over*. In the deepest levels of my existence something is finished, done. My life is divided into the before and after....All I can do is *remember* him. I can't *experience* him.

Eric's father's feelings are comparable to mine. I feel I have changed for the better, just as all the self-help books promise. However, as I reflect in the last chapter of this book, I'd gladly exchange my growth for Margie's return.

> I have changed, yes. For the better, I do not doubt. But without a moment's hesitation I would exchange those changes for Eric back.

Both Nicholas Wolterstorff's and my writing reflect an ongoing search for God.

> How is faith to endure, O God...You have allowed bonds of love beyond number to be painfully snapped. If you have not abandoned us, explain yourself.

We strain to hear. But instead of hearing an answer we catch sight of God himself scraped and torn. Through our tears we see the tears of God.

Gerald Sittser's mother, wife, and daughter were killed by a drunk driver while riding in the van Gerald was driving. In *A Grace Disguised* he writes about "how hard it is to face the loss and how long it takes to grow from it."

Recovery is a misleading and empty expectation. We recover from broken limbs, not amputations. Catastrophic loss by definition precludes recovery. It will transform us or destroy us, but it will never leave us the same....Whatever that future is, it will, and must, include the pain of the past with it.

There is a bitter irony here that cannot be avoided, however much we grow through loss. The people whose death enabled me to change for the better are the very people with whom I would most like to share these changes.

I know that Margie is proud of her father's and my attempt to warn others about the dangers of domestic violence but it isn't the same as seeing her smile of approval, feeling her pat on my back, or hearing, "Wow, Ma, you really did that?"

In *Give Sorrow Words* by Tom Crider (copyright 1996 by the author, and reprinted by permission of Algonquin Books of Chapel Hill, a division of Workman Publishing), a father describes his journey through grief. His daughter, Gretchen, died in a fire in her room at college. His thoughts are similar to what I thought as I stood where Margie was murdered and when I took my last look at her in the casket.

Can my daughter, my only child, have been what is called a corpse? Can her precious body have been so cold and still? Did people around her whisper or make jokes—the hospital workers who wheeled her body to the morgue, the coroner who examined her, the man or woman who slid her small body into the furnace....Oh how I wish I had been there to hold Gretchen, to stroke her, to kiss her, as she died.

I experience the fear that my memories of Margie will fade and drift away, leaving me in a joyless void, just as Mr. Crider feared would happen to his recollections of Gretchen.

> But I know the fog is moving in, making memories less clear. Her face, her eyes, her smile were once as precious and familiar as anything I've ever known. Can't love hold them fast?...Not knowing whether it is true or not, we play with the notion of immortality, and it makes us feel a bit better.

Rosalie Deer Heart's fourteen-year-old son, Mike, was electrocuted when he touched a downed power line. She writes of her pain and growth in *Healing Grief: A Mother's Story*. I identify with her emotions and her questions about Mike's privacy. I have so many questions about reading what Margie has written, writing about her, and sharing her story. Apparently, both Rosalie and I feel it helps to keep our children alive—in our memories, at least. Rosalie describes how normal his room looks. She wasn't prepared to see his handwriting. She wondered if she had the right to read what he had written and if it contained awful things about her. She read it anyway. I read Margie's writing too. We keep our children alive a while longer this way.

After C. S. Lewis' wife died of cancer he wrote *A Grief Observed*. After some time had passed he found the earlier grief returned. He described emerging from a phase that subsequently returned. He wondered if he was going in circles or if on a spiral—which direction, up or down? He decided sorrow is not a state but a process.

My grief does not follow a straight path either.

When George Lardner's daughter was murdered by a jealous jilted boyfriend, he set out to learn the truth about the crime. In *The Stalking of Kristin* he wrote about his daughter, her killer, the law that did not protect her, and his efforts to keep other women from the same fate as his daughter. He is someone I can identify with and respect. My attempts to help prevent future intimate partner homicides by educating women of the dangers are validated by his experience.

Brett Lott was one of the authors we met at the authors conference in Maine, shortly after Margie's murder. I am surprised when I learn he wrote a novel about parents whose young son is killed by a car. *Reed's Beach* reminds me that being a parent is full of risks and none of us can be sure that our child is safe. The father expresses many thoughts I have experienced. He likes the feel and sound of his son's name, Michael. I say my daughter's name over and over, using different inflections and tones: "Margaret, Margie, Margie, Margie." He made everything become something to do with Michael. Nothing was what it seemed, but contained a part of his son. Every important new thing in my life must somehow be connected to Margie if it is to have meaning, just as with Michael's father.

A friend, Karen Carney, who is a counselor at a grief center, recommends a small paperback book *Water Bugs and Dragonflies* by Doris Stickney for explaining death to young children. In its wonderful fable I find a new hope and understanding. A dragonfly, who has been transformed from his previous state, tries to keep his promise to let the water bugs know he is okay but he can't go back in the water. However, he knows that even if he could go back, the water bugs wouldn't know him in his new body. He decides that only when they become dragonflies will they understand what happened to him and where he went.

Like the water bugs, I must wait until I cross from this life-form to the next before I can comprehend what dying really is. Today, my own death does not hold the fear it did before Margie's untimely parting. She is waiting for me.

My own poems, which I have dated, reflect my healing process. In April of 1997, eight months after her death, my pain is still raw but spring does reach my spirit even if God can't—directly. At the Connecticut Writing Project retreat at Wisdom House, I write about knowing that I must enjoy life for both Margie and myself and not expect others to provide all the support I need.

Spring Writing Retreat

I'm not going to write about you this weekend.
I'll dwell in my childhood—innocent and happy
Near my dad and ma, the hemlocks, and river.
Unaware of the pain I feel today and every day.
Hopefully—a brief respite from present reality.

Other writers talk of their youngest children.

Agree these offsprings exhibit unique personalities.
I'm silent—it is the kind thing to do.
No need to warn them to celebrate their bounty
My presence is reminder enough.

The sign says, "This cemetery closes at 5 P.M."
I drive in seeking solace and a private place to grieve.
Soon, I'm followed and told, "We're closing now."
If this groundskeeper knew of my loss would he care?
I glance at my watch and leave—it isn't even 4 P.M.

I visit a shrine, sit in front of Jesus.
He says, "Come unto me."
I can't. His retribution for my sins is too cruel.
Recapturing the peace I felt in his care isn't possible.
A loving God could not be so merciless.

I walk among the yellow daffodils.
Soak up the new green growth of spring.
Breath in the bright blue sky.
Pain, my constant companion, loses control.
I enjoy this moment for two—Margie and me.

At the November 1997 writing retreat, the tone of a new poem still reflects my painful loss but with a clearer sense of acceptance, strength, and purpose. I am clearly making choices.

Ladybug on the Ceiling

Snow, sleet, freezing rain
Should I? Shouldn't I?
Am I being selfish? I know Larry'll worry.
He doesn't want me to go.
But tells me the choice is mine.
He means it, too. A sign of his growth.

I'll start early, turn around if it gets too bad,
Call when I get there.
Daylight, above freezing temperatures, and

facile, careful traffic bring me safely to
Wisdom House and the writing retreat.
I hear the friendly greeting. *You're the first to arrive.*

I explore the farmhouse and choose a
large airy bedroom with four windows.
Time passes, Penny arrives.
We've both brought sandwiches.
No West Street Grill tonight.
We chat and two more "retreaters" arrive.

Back in my room I see a ladybug
on the ceiling. No, not one, but two.
A good sign—my time here will be productive.
I'll write, feel my pain and loss,
deal with all-male juries, and desperate,
last minute pleas of, *I did it. I'm guilty.*

We're told he's beginning to understand
what he did was awful,
how it hurt his family and ours.
Unanswered questions plague me.
How would Margie feel?
Is he truly repentant? Or is this another ploy?

It doesn't matter. We have no say.
Oh, they listen to us—politely
and do what they want anyway.
He will be free to marry and murder again.
I wish Solomon, not our justice system, were in charge.
But little ladybugs, snow-white hills and writing help.
So do snowmen and angels in the snow.

In June 2000, almost four years after Margie's murder, I attend a
poetry workshop conducted by Steve Strait for the Connecticut
Writing Project. In the following poem I'm able to recognize not
only that God may not have planned the murder, but may be distraught because of this kind of senseless behavior.

God's Psychiatrist Was Tired

God's psychiatrist was tired of
his client's irrational guilt.
The therapy of Dr. Albert Ellis
wasn't working as it should.
But, Jehovah, You did the best you could.
You created us in your image—gave us free will.
You aren't responsible for our choices.

But I'm omnipotent, God replied,
I should have realized, programmed
you differently or limited your options.

God's psychiatrist was tired so
he used Carl Jung's method of reflecting
on what God had said,
I hear Your fear of losing control.

God insisted, *No, I'm just sorry—*
for all the needless pain—I thought
mankind would always prefer what is good.

God's psychiatrist was tired.
As a last resort, he tried Fritz Perls' technique.
The sound of God's primal scream shook the universe.

I'm not letting God off the hook, quite yet, for the birth of handicapped children or making mothers in Ethiopia watch helplessly as their children starve to death in their arms. Eventually, I may even recognize that God's ways are mysterious and I need not understand everything to accept that a caring God exists. I'd like that.

At the same workshop I have fun writing the next poem. When I read it weeks later I realize I've given up the idea that I control my destiny. I accept responsibility for my choices, ask for help, and look for answers but know the irony is that my search must continue.

Driving to Paradise

One Sunday morning
I was driving to Paradise.
Along the way I made
A wrong turn.

Ended up in Trouble instead.
The traffic was horrendous.
I asked for directions but was told
Sorry, I don't live here.

Finally, I referred to my map.
It was complicated and out of date.
I searched for Paradise and found
You couldn't get there from here.

I suggest to other survivors of a tragic untimely death that you acknowledge your grief, accept that your life has changed forever, and decide how to give meaning to your existence. Only you can determine that the killer doesn't have the power to destroy you too. One victim is enough. Choosing to be a survivor and not a victim is hard work, but it is the only constructive choice you have. You cannot escape your sorrow but you can find a reason for living.

CHAPTER 22

The *Criminal* Justice System 1998 Style—Part B

On April 21st the prosecutor calls to tell us the judge's decision on the sentencing range. The judge will pronounce the actual sentence on May 4th at four P.M. The twenty-five-page decision is being faxed to Ruth; we will learn the details tonight.

In his written opinion and order, Judge Muir gives an introduction, which is a brief review of court proceedings. Then he gives the court's finding of fact. Among the fifty facts listed are: The government had attempted to obtain permission to seek the death penalty. Paster's testimony during the November 22, 1996, suppression hearing was inaccurate. Paster was extremely upset during his call to his mother when he told her, "Something terrible has happened, I stabbed Margaret." Paster cooperated fully with the 911 operator and was extremely upset. Paster was cooperative with Bureau of Prisons personnel and was detained for approximately four hours. At times he was very upset, crying and shaking, and was often despondent.

As I read about Mitch being "extremely upset" I grow apprehensive. I'm unsure of what this means in the judge's mind. Does he think Mitch is showing remorse? For what? Killing her or for what he has done to himself and his life?

The judge finds that although Paster didn't remember many of the details of the murder, he did tell the FBI he had taken the knife from the butcher block and started upstairs. His testimony at the sentencing hearing that he did not tell this to the agents is not credible. Paster did change his story about what happened upstairs from not remembering to he didn't want to talk about it. He did tell the operator he stabbed his wife and the knife was in the sink downstairs. But up to a few minutes prior to the stabbing, Paster had no plan to kill his wife.

The judge reviews the facts regarding Dr. Land's qualifications and experience as a forensic pathologist. He discusses the number and severity of the wounds as described by Dr. Land. The pathologist found that excessive force was used and that "Margaret Bostrom suffered an extremely violent death…the most severely violent death he had ever seen." Furthermore, Dr. Land characterized the stabbing as including "considerable struggle" by the decedent. The judge repeats Dr. Land's conclusion that "it is highly unlikely that Margaret Bostrom would have survived if she had been on the operating room table in the best hospital in the country as the last wound was inflicted." He accepts Dr. Land's statement that Margaret was alive throughout the attack.

Judge Muir completes his findings of fact with information about Mitch. He has no prior history of violence. Initially, Paster did not act violently but left the residence. He was not violent toward Mr. Corey. Dr. Sadoff's opinion is that "Paster lost control during a heat of passion with adequate provocation by his wife" and that "outward explosion of violence is atypical and foreign for Mitchell Paster."

There isn't really anything new here. It is all the same old stuff. At least we now know what the judge believes are the important facts in this case. I wonder, as I read it, how many more times will I be subjected to all the details?

Judge Muir follows with a discussion of the departure issues. These include the government asking for upward departure based on Paster's extreme conduct. The judge determines this is warranted based on Paster's unusually heinous, cruel, and brutal conduct. After studying the guidelines and case law he writes, "We consider that a nine level upward departure for Paster's extremely brutal conduct is warranted."

The government is also requesting upward departure for premeditation. A discussion of the difference between first-degree and second-degree murder follows, in which the judge states, "Premeditation is the only distinguishing factor between the two crimes." He determines that since this "was taken into consideration by the Sentencing Commission in formulating the guidelines for first and second degree murder, it is not a valid ground for departure." The judge denies this request.

The judge responds to the upward departure requested by the government for the use of a weapon. "The relevant guideline for second degree murder is silent with respect to consideration of whether a weapon is used....We took Paster's use of a knife to stab his victim sixteen times into account as the predominant factor when we decided to depart upward for extreme conduct and we decline to depart upwards again for the use of a weapon."

Next, the judge considers Paster's request for downward departure for aberrant behavior. "Aberrant behavior justifying a downward departure must involve a lack of planning: it must be a single act that is spontaneous and thoughtless, and no consideration is given to whether the defendant is a first time offender. Here, there are indications that the murder was spontaneous. Dr. Robert Sadoff, a psychiatrist retained by Paster, stated that an 'outward explosion of violence is atypical and foreign for Mr. Paster.'

"There is insufficient evidence to show that Paster had planned the killing of his wife." The judge does not accept the government's claims that hiding the car in the garage or taking the knife upstairs demonstrates planning. "However, the murder was not committed in a thoughtless manner....Paster had ample time in the minutes preceding the stabbing to think about whether to murder his wife. Further, the number of times Paster stabbed his wife indicates that he thought about the act as it was being done." The judge denies the request for downward departure based on aberrant behavior.

The defense has requested downward departure due to victim's conduct. The judge quotes U.S. Sentencing Guidelines K52.10, which the court should consider in making this decision:

1. The size and strength of the victim in comparison to the defendant;

2. The persistence of the victim's conduct and any efforts by the defendant to prevent confrontation;

3. The danger reasonably perceived by the defendant, including the victim's reputation for violence;

4. The danger actually presented to the defendant by the victim; and

5. Any other relevant conduct by the victim that substantially contributed to the present danger.

Because Mitch's claim of Margaret's threats and his allegations of her affairs could not be substantiated, the judge denies the downward departure.

In a mother's mind, the fact that she was completely helpless getting out of a shower, and faced with his superior strength and possession of a weapon as he waited for her, certainly fall under these guidelines.

The next section of the judge's decision deals with adjustment issues. The judge responds to Paster's objection to the two-level upward adjustment applied by the probation office for obstruction of justice by reviewing the court's order of December 6, 1996, in which Mitch is described as confused and upset. The judge writes, "That confusion was reflected in his testimony at the suppression hearing which although not credible was not made with a willful intent to provide false testimony." This upward adjustment is denied.

I think, Oh, Judge Muir, of course it was. Mitch had time to think. Even if only for a few hours. He's bright and has narcissistic tendencies so I'm sure he began to regret his actions which incriminated him. This is evident in his changing stories. Many people would have asked themselves, "Why didn't I calmly dispose of her body and go quietly to Cornell. Later I could tell everyone that Margie was fine when I left but has since disappeared. I could have mounted a frantic search for her and played the grieving widower." Mitch took the lawyer's advice and look where it got him. After all, he should have been allowed to pursue his MBA even after the murder. Instead he has been behind bars.

Guidelines for reductions in the offense level for acceptance of responsibility tie it to whether the defendant obstructed justice. Drew Thompson adjusted upward the offense level for obstruction of justice, and he did not recommend a reduction in levels of accepting responsibility. However, the judge finds that Mitch admitted stabbing his wife, told the 911 operator where the knife was, did not flee the scene, and pled to second-degree murder. "Paster has accepted responsibility for the murder of his wife and is entitled to a two-level decrease in the offense level." However, "Paster did not timely notify the authorities of his intention to plead guilty, which would have permitted the government to avoid preparing for trial. Paster is not entitled to an additional one level decrease in the offense level for acceptance of responsibility...."

Judge Muir did not find that any of the factual disputes were relevant and states they will not be taken into account in deciding Paster's sentence.

Section IV. Recapitulation follows:

Total Offense level as determined by the Probation Officer	35
Upward departure for extreme conduct	9
Downward Adjustment of acceptance of responsibility	-(2)
Downward Adjustment for obstruction of justice (reflects denied upward departure of 2 recommended by Drew Thompson)	<u>-(2)</u>
Total offense level	40

The Criminal History is 1. On page 22 of Judge Muir's written opinion, item 11 under V. Conclusions of Law, he states, "The guideline imprisonment range is 292 months to 365 months, or 24 years 4 months to 30 years 5 months."

We, Margaret's family, have no real understanding of what all the numbers and levels mean. While it isn't a life sentence, it is more than we expected and we hope he gets the thirty years and five months, even though we suspect that won't happen.

On Monday, May 4th, we return to Williamsport Federal Courthouse with what we later realize was a falsely optimistic hope of never having to return. This time, both Ruth and Kathy are with us. We arrive at the Sheraton in Williamsport to find that four friends from Survivors of Homicide are already there. Sam and Wanda Rieger, Marie Pelligrini, and Joan Charette traveled together from Waterbury and have been shopping at a local grocery store.

We drive the few blocks to the courthouse because it is hard for Marie to walk. When we arrive at the metered parking lot across the street from the courthouse the Pasters are there. We avoid direct contact, but Marie asks, "Is that his mother? My God she looks awful." I glance Aileen's way and feel real empathy for her. She does look haggard and defeated. "Who is that big man?" She is looking at Mitch's uncle Julius, Jordan's sister Fran's husband who is a coin dealer. Michelle, Mitch's sister, is not here. We manage to reach our seats in the courthouse without having to acknowledge the Paster family; however, we are aware of their curious glances across the aisle at the strangers who are with us. They can't place the people who are with us. We are surprised and pleased when Kathy Yeager, a wellness counselor who was involved with Survivors of Homicide, enters. She has driven alone from New York City to give us support. Ed Soboleski is the only one I recognize from Lewisburg Federal Penitentiary and I'm sure he is here on his own, not as a representative of the Bureau of Prisons. So much for that tightly knit family they described at the time of the murder.

The judge calls the attorneys and the defendant forward. Wayne states, for the record, which case this is. Mitch is sworn in and asked if he has seen the report and reviewed it with his counsel. He has. After several questions regarding the order of the court, Judge Muir asks Mr. Lepley what he wants to say on behalf of his client.

Mr. Lepley responds, "What we would like the court to do, though, is to indicate, if the court has this opinion, that the place of incarceration not be Lewisburg penitentiary due to the fact that that's where the victim worked up until the time of her death. So we would ask, if the court feels it appropriate, to include a recommendation that he not be incarcerated there....We would also ask, if the court feels it appropriate, that any recommendation be—that there be a recommendation that he be incarcerated at some place that might be susceptible to be traveled to by his parents for visitation."

Only a lawyer could word a simple request in such a manner.

Judge Muir answers. "Our recommendations as to places of imprisonment of defendants have been rejected with such frequency by the Bureau of Prisons that I'm not going to give them any further opportunity to reject our recommendations. This occurs almost universally, and for that reason I decline to make a recommendation."

I silently applaud both the judge's refusal to be a pawn for Mitch, and the Bureau of Prisons' rejection of defendant wishes when choosing a place of incarceration. We have no such privileges and visitation isn't an option for us.

Mr. Lepley then asks the court to impose a sentence toward the low end of the range that was determined after the pre-sentence hearings. "We think that all of the positive things that have been brought to the court's attention, while certainly I'm assuming the court took them into consideration in fashioning the order, I think that those items impact more, and I'm talking about his character and his lack of record, impact more in determining where in the range the sentence should fall as opposed to whether the court would grant the government's motion which resulted in the guideline range of twenty-four years plus to thirty years plus."

Judge Muir listens, then asks, "Mr. Paster what do you wish to say in your own behalf over and above what your counsel has said for you?"

"No, Your Honor. No, Your Honor."

"Well, I asked you what you wanted to say. If you want to say, 'I have nothing further to say,' that's all right. Is that what you mean?"

"Yeah."

For a moment I can sense how difficult this is for Mitch. In his worst nightmares he never could have pictured himself being sentenced for murder. He must be terrified. Quickly, I remind myself of what Margie suffered to pull my thoughts away from Mitch's plight.

The judge asks if the victim's family has anything more they would like to say. We confer and decide that nothing would be gained by further comment. Wayne then asks that the court impose a sentence at the top of the range and reminds the court that Mitch is to make restitution to Margaret's family of sightly more than four thousand dollars.

Wayne continues. "…Despite all the information that was presented, we unfortunately can't hear from one person herself today, and that is Margaret Bostrom, the victim in the case, whose life was tragically and violently ended at age thirty-one by this defendant. Her life was ended at a time when it was actually just beginning. She had just finished years of schooling and training and was basically just starting her career with the Bureau of Prisons as a psychologist.

"As a result of the choices we make in life, we must all suffer the consequences of these choices. The defendant chose to commit a deliberate, vicious, brutal, and gruesome crime, and he must live with the consequences of those actions."

I can't help think—Margie paid the ultimate price for her choices. If she had not decided to leave Mitch she might still be alive.

Wayne reviews the reports of both Dr. Sadoff and Dr. Johnson. "In layman's terms, Your Honor, at the time he murdered Margaret, the defendant knew exactly what he was doing and he knew that it was wrong.

"Each crime, no matter how specifically directed at an individual—single individual person, leaves many victims and leaves many deep scars...."

The moment we have been both anxiously awaiting and dreading has arrived. The sentence of the court is going to be announced. Judge Muir states, "This is a particularly reprehensible crime. The reasons for the sentence to be imposed in this case are to provide just punishment for the offense, to deter Mr. Paster and others similarly situated, and to protect the public....It is the judgment of the court that the defendant, Mitchell Frederic Paster, be committed to the custody of the Bureau of Prisons to be imprisoned for a term of 365 months or 30 years and five months."

There are relieved sighs on our side of the aisle but we hear the anguished gasp that is torn from Aileen Paster. The judge further orders that Mitch will pay restitution, be placed on supervised release for the five years following his release from prison, must report to a probation officer, submit to drug testing, not be involved in a crime, and must participate in mental health treatment as directed by the probation officer. No fine is imposed because the court considered Mitch's lack of financial resources.

Even before the sentence has had time to really sink in, we hear the judge continue. "We advise you of your right to appeal your sentence to the U.S. Court of Appeals for this circuit. If you are unable to pay the costs of an appeal you may apply for leave to appeal in *forma pauperis* and if approved, counsel will be appointed for you and you will not be required to pay any costs."

Court is adjourned at 4:17 P.M.

Wayne leads us through a side door to the grand jury chambers. He invites our friends from Survivors of Homicide to join us. Thus we avoid an encounter with the Pasters. Our being in this room for the first time—where Mitch was indicted on August 28, 1996—seems serendipitous but we know it isn't over. Mitch has ten days to file a notice of appeal and we are sure he will. Wayne explains what will happen next and that the appeal will be considered in Philadelphia. The U.S. Court of Appeals for the third Circuit Court will set a schedule for briefs from both the defendant and government. Wayne promises he will remain on the case and keep us informed of all developments. He considers any questions we have and takes time to answer them. He listens to the other survivors' stories and expresses his sympathy. We are proud of Wayne and of our friends who care enough to be here.

Larry and I show our appreciation by offering to take everyone to dinner at an elegant Victorian-style restaurant in Williamsport. Wayne declines our offer and Kathy Yaeger decides she can't stay, but the eight of us enjoy a splendid meal and exploring the house's nooks and crannies. Ruth falls in love with a large Goya-like painting of a nude woman that is placed in a focal point above the stair landing. We tease her about where she would put it in her house. Most of all we relish being with our daughters and friends. We hope they know how much their being with us helps.

Back in Connecticut we write the letter we had discussed with Agent Schmidle to Wayne Samuelson's boss.

Dear Sir:

We are the parents of Margaret E. Bostrom, Ph.D. who was murdered on Lewisburg Federal Penitentiary grounds on August 16, 1996. We want you to know how much we appreciate Wayne P. Samuelson's efforts to assure that Mitchell F. Paster, Margaret's husband and murderer, pay for his crime. Wayne made this difficult time in our lives and our introduction to the criminal justice system less foreign and threatening.

Wayne listened to our thoughts and feelings. He carefully explained the legal issues and the options available within the laws. He met with us before and after every court proceeding to keep us informed and answer our questions. As soon as a court date was scheduled he called us to let us know. When we had other commitments he obliged us by trying to schedule dates around our appointments. He made us feel we were part of the process even though we know legally we have few rights. The extra things he did showed respect for us and concern for our needs. We were particularly impressed and pleased that he bought and read the book, *The Batterer* by Donald Dutton, that we had recommended to him.

The length of Mitchell's sentence reflects Wayne's efforts to secure justice. He is a skilled and knowledgeable attorney with a forceful court personality and presentation. When we heard him confront Mitchell we were happy to have him on our side. His briefs were thorough, carefully prepared, and well organized. He obviously takes his work seriously.

The U.S. Department of Justice and the Middle District of Pennsylvania are fortunate to have Wayne. He provides a truly positive image of United States Attorneys. We know the process is not over and are extremely grateful that Wayne will remain on the case.

Thank you for your attention.

Sincerely,
Lawrence and Shirley Bostrom

On May 12, 1998, Wayne sends a copy of the U.S. District Court's judgment in a criminal case against Mitchell F. Paster. It is exactly what Judge Muir indicated we could expect. So is the copy of Mitch's notice of appeal. Ten days later we receive a copy of the transcript of the sentencing hearing.

At the end of May we take our fourteen-day cruise, which was delayed because of possible court dates, with Bud and Shirley to the Mediterranean. Starting in Greece we travel west through the Strait of Gibraltar, up the Atlantic coast to Dover, England, and from there to the Netherlands to fly home. We visit the Acropolis, tour Athens and the Greek Islands, visit Capri, Rome, Monte Carlo, Lisbon, and take a side trip to the mountain town of Sintra, Portugal. We fall in love with the small picturesque French town of Honfleur and on a rainy day in Dover we see Jo, one of Ruth's former au pairs. We always have a good time with Larry's brother and Shirley but the distraction of places we always dreamed of seeing is a welcome change for us. It is good to be away from reminders of the ordeal we still face.

In June we receive a letter from U.S. Attorney Barasch thanking us for our kind remarks about Wayne, expressing his sympathies on our loss, and assuring us he will forward our kind remarks, along with his, to Wayne. We appreciate his thoughtfulness.

As residents of Connecticut and through our work with Survivors of Homicide, we know that the victim's family is entitled to notification on the status of the inmate convicted in their case. We want this information from the Bureau of Prisons so I begin my written search on July 2nd, our wedding anniversary. After several delays, on September 30, 1998, I receive a letter from the warden at Florence Federal Correctional Institution in Colorado. With it is a one-page form completed by the acting unit manager. The information is limited and some of it is inaccurate. For example, they assume that Mitch will return to live in the Middle District of Pennsylvania. I cannot imagine that this is so. He has no family or other ties to that area.

A release date of February 15, 2023, is given because of anticipated good time he will earn. They promise to keep us informed but we do not receive any new information in the next three-and-a-half years, even though we know he may be transferred to a new facility and the release date has been changed significantly. In this matter, the federal system needs to catch up with Connecticut, where the Department of Correction keeps the survivors informed about who visits their perpetrators and how often. My friends know if there has been disciplinary action, the inmate is taking courses or has a job. Not every victim's family wants this information but it should be available to those who do. The federal form indicates we will be informed if the inmate dies, escapes and is recaptured, or is released but not if he is transferred. Nothing more.

On August 27, 1998, the defense files its brief with the Court of Appeals. On September 22nd, we receive our copy along with the government's forty-nine page counter-brief and a letter from Wayne. We are not surprised to see that Lepley and Rude have been replaced by the firm of Walder, Sondak & Brogan from Roseland, New Jersey. The issues presented for review are regarding the "unreasonable" upward departures and rejection of downward departures made by Judge Muir in his ruling, especially because the victim substantially provoked the crime.

The Procedural History of the case is reduced to less than seven double-spaced pages. There is nothing new here.

In their Summary of Argument, the defense claims the district court's upward departure based on the defendant's unusually heinous, cruel, and brutal conduct was erroneous for four reasons, which include (1) not applying clear and convincing standards of proof, (2) the factors relied upon were already considered when the sentencing guidelines were drawn up, (3) Paster's conduct wasn't unusually heinous, cruel, or brutal, and (4) the degree of departure was unreasonable.

Furthermore, the district court erred when it denied downward departure for aberrant behavior because downward departure is warranted by reason of Mitch's behavior being spontaneous and unplanned. The district court's conclusion that the victim's wrongful conduct did not substantially provoke Paster's violent reaction, as well as its denial of one more level of downward departure on account of Mitch taking responsibility for the crime by confessing, are argued.

The defense makes legal arguments regarding five points in its next twenty-eight pages. The most disturbing for us is the section on victim conduct. "Paster's crime was provoked by his wife's revelation of 40-50 affairs. Paster overreacted, with tragic consequences. Whether she had the affairs or not is irrelevant. She told him she had, and in direct response to that shocking and degrading revelation, he stabbed her....It is undisputed that Dr. Bostrom's adulterous revelations were the direct, immediate and *only* cause of Paster's violent response."

Who is there to dispute what was said that morning? He killed the only person who could have told the other side of that story. We only know what he claims—what helps him. We were not surprised when the FBI, after an extensive search into her background and questioning her friends, family, and acquaintances, found no evidence of other affairs.

The government's fifty-page brief refutes each claim by the defense and makes counter-statements of facts regarding the last months of their relationship including her seeking a divorce, her attorney's statement that Margaret never withdrew the divorce complaint, and a neighbor's statement that she saw a friendly and pleasant Mitch outside minutes after the supposed argument and before he killed Margaret. He did not appear upset.

Wayne's brief reports an incident that occurred on July 19, 1996, which I had either forgotten or didn't know about. It is upsetting because I now know that if it had been taken more seriously Margaret might still be alive. Margaret was returning from a BOP party when she noticed Mitch's car in the driveway. She thought this was strange since he had moved to his parents' home a few days earlier. "She advised Bureau of Prisons officials that Paster had just returned to her home, and she was afraid to return home alone. As a consequence, two bureau of prisons officials, an attorney, and a captain accompanied her to her residence." They waited outside while she went in to talk to Mitch. After a short while Margaret told the officials they could leave. They drove away, going about two blocks before deciding to return to check on her. She was all right, but upset and afraid because Mitch had recently taken twelve thousand dollars from their account. She now had her dog and cat back, both of which he had taken to New Jersey the week before.

The brief restates, from the government's view, all the details of the murder, the autopsy report, Dr. Land's testimony, the evidence collected, and the interview with Mitch and his conflicting stories of what happened. It argues that in the district court's view, Mitch did not make a timely notification to authorities of his intention to enter a guilty plea. It reviews Mitch's attempts, even in interviews with the probation officer for the Pre-Sentence Report, to minimize his role in the offense and to place the blame on the victim and her actions.

The other arguments for upward departure due to the heinous and brutal nature of the crime, against downward departure for aberrant behavior and victim conduct are the same ones presented over and over during the past three years. Several other court cases are referred to in support of the government's position. The brief states that "...a sentencing judge is in a unique position to evaluate a defendant's acceptance of responsibility, and that the determination of the sentencing judge is entitled to great deference on review."

We hope so.

We receive the twenty-page Reply Brief of Appellant Mitchell Frederick Paster on October 13, 1998. It focuses on the same five arguments and objects to the government's "new" claim that Mitch's actions immediately after the murder denied Margaret medical attention.

On October 8, 1998, we receive a letter from Wayne telling us the case is tentatively scheduled for the week of November 16th or 30th. We reschedule everything else. On October 15th, we receive another letter with the news that oral arguments are scheduled for either the week of December 7th or 14th. We will be advised when he knows the actual dates. We reschedule again—painfully aware that Jacob's birthday and Christmas can't be rescheduled. On November 9th, we learn that the case will be heard on Tuesday, December 15th, or another day during that week.

On December 2nd, the U.S. Court of Appeals sends the following letter to Wayne, which he forwards to us:

Dear Counsel:

The Court has directed me to advise you that counsel in the above-entitled case is scheduled on the merits on Tuesday, December 15, 1998, will be allotted *15 minutes* oral argument time for each side, pursuant....Court will convene at 9:30 A.M. and argument in this matter is scheduled in *Albert Branson Maris Courtroom,*...Counsel who will present oral argument should register with the Court Crier *in the courtroom* at least 30 minutes prior to the time when court is scheduled to convene....You are hereby advised that your appeal will be argued before the following panel: SLOVITER, COWEN, Circuit Judges and OBERDORFER, District Judge.

It is signed by the Calendaring Clerk.

On the late afternoon of December 14th, Larry and I meet Ruth and Frank Blackford, the counselor/advocate for Survivors of Homicide, at the Hartford Civic Center in time to drive to New Haven. We eat at a Subway and meet Wanda and Sam Rieger before boarding the 7:30 train to Philadelphia. We arrive at the 30th Street Station at 11:10 P.M. It seems that all of Philadelphia is in a festive mood. Trees, skyscrapers, and streets are decorated with bright Christmas lights signaling good cheer. We regret that our circumstances preclude such festive thoughts. We take a taxi to the Holiday Inn on Independence Mall.

In the morning we are pleasantly surprised when we see Wayne in the hotel restaurant where we are having omelets for breakfast. Later, we walk past the Liberty Bell, which is encased in a glass building, to the courthouse. I find it ironic that the first time I see this symbol of liberty and justice we are involved with a system that seems unconcerned with our rights. The U.S. Constitution guarantees numerous rights for the accused but none for victims. Survivors of Homicide, Inc., is working to get a national amendment to the Constitution similar to what we now have in Connecticut.

We enter the courtroom and sit quietly in the last row while other cases are being heard. We know that Mitch will not be present but are surprised his family is not here yet. Soon, I realize they are not coming—probably on the advice of their new attorneys. Seated to our right in the row ahead of us are three young people, two men and a woman, who watch us with apparent interest. We guess correctly that they are from the firm now representing Mitch. When our case is called, we move forward. The round room has an alcove and the seal of the United States above and behind the three judges whose seats are raised with a long table in front of them. Judge Cowen, to our left, is a white-haired man. The woman in the middle is Judge Sloviter, and the white-haired man to our right is District Judge Oberdorfer. They are flanked on each side by several flags. The courtroom walls have portraits of seven somber, robed judges. The ceiling is peppered with round recessed lights that barely illuminate the few spectators on the long benches at the back of the room. We are the only six people seated in the purple leather chairs at the front.

Both attorneys are given longer than fifteen minutes to present their cases and the judges each ask questions and make remarks. However, they never once glance our way or acknowledge our presence. We are gratified when the woman judge jumps out of her seat when the defense attorney states, "This was not a heinous crime."

She reminds him. "He stabbed her sixteen times when she was getting out of the shower—that sounds pretty brutal to me."

However, we listen in shock as Judge Cowen states it wasn't heinous. Mitch didn't drag the killing out over several days or torture the victim. We hope the district judge will understand Judge Muir's position and be the deciding factor in getting this appeal turned down.

When we leave the courthouse we have no idea how the judges will decide or when we will get their decision. We stop to take a closer look at the Liberty Bell before we walk to the famous Bookbinder's Restaurant. After a delicious and filling lunch we buy cans of their famous soup and Beanie Babies to take to Abby and Jake.

The train ride home is delay-ridden and we are emotionally drained by our experience. We face Jacob's birthday, our third Christmas holidays, and a new year without Margie, filled with fear Mitch's sentence will be reduced.

Criminal Justice

August 1996
The Crime

Murder One, no doubt.
The prosecution might ask for the death penalty.
How do we, her family, feel about that?

June 3, 1997
Attorney General's Decision

Murder One, no doubt. Death penalty?
Sorry, Janet Reno says it's not allowed.
That's okay. We want life without parole.

June 27, 1997
We See the Psychiatric Reports

Murder One, no doubt—well maybe not.
Not premeditated say the psychiatrists.
But he got a knife—waited while she showered.

November 4, 1997
Jury Selection

Murder One. The all-male jury hears the charge.
Only men will listen to the evidence.
See her damp, nude, bloody, body and decide.

November 19, 1997
Plea Bargain

Murder One? No. He pleads Murder Two.
He'll get eleven to fourteen years, maybe more.
That's justice? Not for Margaret!

March 19, 1998
Sentencing Hearing

At last, we get to speak—tell her story.
Please hear our pain and Margie's too.
Assert the value of her life. Demand payment.

May 4, 1998
Sentencing

We do not breathe—awaiting the judge's words.
Judge Muir says thirty years and five months.
Yes! It is not enough but more than we expected.

September 1998
Mitch appeals

The confessed murderer's appeal is heard.
He took responsibility—the sentence is too cruel.
But so was Margie's painful tragic death.

December 15, 1998
Appellate Court Hearing

We go to Philadelphia—the City of Brotherly Love.
Supported by 'Survivor' friends to hear Mitch's claims.
Only legal issues count. Not Margie. Not our devastation.

We know that it is unwise to tie our healing processes to what happens in the justice system so I continue, with Larry's support, the work of educating others about the dangers of domestic violence. It helps.

CHAPTER 23

Janet Reno Is a Real Person—Margie's Gift

When the Melanie Ilene Rieger Memorial Conference Against Violence is held in April 1998, Peggy Panagrossi, the Executive Director of the Women's Emergency Shelter of Waterbury, and I are co-presenters at a breakout session. She is a sensitive caring professional with a wealth of knowledge and understanding about domestic violence. The registration for our session is so large that we are on the main stage of the auditorium.

I wear the green and navy blue, two-piece dress I bought to wear when I testified at Mitch's trial, which didn't happen. But I did wear it when I gave my victim's impact statement at his sentencing hearing. The top has vertical stripes, which I heard make you look thinner. Before the lights dim I see the audience that nearly fills the hall.

I tell them, "I chose "Funny—He Doesn't Look Like a Murderer But Margie Is Dead" for my workshop title because a batterer is often charming and seeks approval from those at work, his friends and family. We expect people who do bad things to look the part, but they don't look violent except when in a rage—usually in private. They don't wear an M on their foreheads for murderer or A for abuser or V for violent. It would be helpful if vicious people looked the part."

I want to expose the myth that abuse doesn't happen in well-educated, middle-class families. I know it does. I show slides of Margie as a child, teenager, college graduate, professional, and an integral part of our family so they will recognize that abuse can happen to women just like those in the audience. I suggest that if a woman wonders if she is in an abusive relationship, she probably is.

I describe Margie and Mitch's volatile relationship—the fights, the distancing from family and friends, his need to control her, their breaking up and making up. I emphasize the phases in abuse patterns as I show text slides of my research to explain why a woman stays. In the *Build Up* phase there is tension. He makes demands and puts his partner down because he feels inadequate. When the *Eruption*, which he says she always causes, occurs, he may be both verbally and physically abusive. The eruption is followed by a period of *Repentance and Forgiveness*. The abuser tells his partner he can't live without her. He gives thoughtful gifts that convince the woman she has his love. Many men give expensive presents but Mitch gave Margie token gifts. He wrote a newsletter telling how talented, sexy, attractive, and bright she was. He also surrounded a picture of her with adjectives that he cut out of magazines—wonderful, super, fantastic. He also placed a picture of them on a heart shape, which he cut in two along a jagged line. She was supposed to put it back together again.

A batterer claims he'll lose his job or flunk out of college if he doesn't have her because he can't concentrate. She becomes responsible for the relationship and only at this time, enjoys a sense of power. This cycle is repeated over and over again. The frequency, duration, and severity of the eruptions usually increase over time while the honeymoon phase is shorter and happens less often.

A batterer needs to control his partner. He owns the woman, picks out her clothes, makes decisions for her, wants to improve her, and finds fault with her posture and weight. He controls the money. His attitude toward women in general is one of superiority so any problems are her fault. He blames the victim or an outside force, maybe drugs or alcohol, when he loses his temper and beats and berates her.

I want everyone to know that a successful woman with good self-esteem and satisfying personal alliances can get trapped in an abusive situation. Being in a relationship with a batterer is enough to destroy a woman's self-respect unless she gets out soon enough. Intimate abuse isn't just hitting and punching. It is psychologically and physically controlling a victim's time and space to isolate. Verbal abuse destroys a woman's self-esteem and is very dangerous because it can lead to physical abuse—without much warning. It needs to be taken seriously.

Annihilating a woman's sense of self-worth makes her manage-able. To combat this, a woman should stay physically and mentally fit and have outside activities to preserve her confidence. It is im-portant to develop and maintain a support system and to get to know herself, her friends, and family.

The most dangerous times for a woman are when she tries to leave an abusive partner or if she is pregnant. He sees his control slipping away and this brings up feelings of worthlessness and panic. Mitch killed Margie when he realized he couldn't have her. He made sure no one else would.

I advise women to have a plan that assures their safety. I warn them to be careful of restraining orders. Often they don't work but give her a false sense of security. Seek help. Women get killed when they think they have it all under control. Margie did!

If a loved one or friend is in an abusive relationship, be aware of behaviors that indicate the violence is escalating. Offer support. Tell the woman what you can realistically do for her. She knows what she should do better than an outsider does. Help her develop a plan for leaving when she is ready. Have her get help from one of the professional resources available to battered women.

Our loss of Margie, the loss of any child, especially to violence, is devastating. The survivors of a victim of intimate violence experi-ence guilt and anxiety. We should have known and prevented it. We feel grief, loss, and betrayal—our world isn't safe anymore. Many years, more than a thousand cases of intimate abuse end in murder, leaving the surviving family to grieve and deal with the criminal justice system. It becomes their job to seek justice. The victim isn't here to contradict the killer and there is no law against libeling the dead.

I end my presentation with, "My loss is no less now than it was when Margie was murdered, but by speaking about our tragedy and warning others of the dangers in domestic abuse I have found a way to make it meaningful."

Then Peggy reinforces what I have said and provides the partici-pants with information on the resources available to women who are in abusive relationships. We end the session by answering questions from the audience. I am amazed when a woman tells us she feels women are partly responsible when they are abused. Both Peggy and I repeat previous statements that identify the abuser as the one with the problem. I wonder if she heard anything we said.

Since that day I have been speaking to groups of young women, caregivers, correction officers, educators, church fellowships, and civic groups, emphasizing the danger of intimate violence for women at all social, economic, and educational levels. I have appeared on local television and my message has made the front page of the *Waterbury Republican–American* newspaper and numerous smaller publications. When I finish writing *Funny—He Doesn't Look Like a Murderer: But Margie Is Dead*, it will be available as a valuable resource to workshop participants.

I am honored when Dr. Mario Gaboury from the University of New Haven asks me to give my presentation at the 1998 Connecticut Statewide Crime Victim Conference. Other speakers include: John Armstrong, Commissioner for the Connecticut Department of Correction; Maureen Whelan from the Connecticut Coalition Against Domestic Violence; Joseph LaMotta from the Connecticut Office of Victims Services; and Michael Lawlor, a state representative and co-chair of the judiciary committee. There are speakers from the Connecticut Board of Parole, the Office of the Chief State's Attorney, the U.S. Attorney's Office, MADD, and the Connecticut Sexual Assault Crisis Services.

Most of the comments on the forms evaluating my workshop are positive. "Powerful presentation. Great strength, great legacy. I won't forget Margaret!" or "Excellent workshop...very real and emotional. Thoroughly impressed by the courage of Shirley and her husband— to commit to helping others through their own pain." However, I very humanly focus on the one negative response. At least, I think it is negative. "Congratulations for letting a highly charged, sentimental, emotional woman give a workshop to balance the slick professional ones." I read sarcasm into "congratulations" and think "sentimental" and "slick" are put-downs of the conference in general and my talk in particular. Nevertheless, many of my future engagements are the result of someone hearing me at this conference.

Kristine Hazzard, the chief operating officer of Communities Against Violence In the Home (CAVITH), was at the state conference and asks me to be the keynote speaker at their fifth anniversary breakfast celebration honoring three attorneys who generously donate their time to help victims of domestic abuse. CAVITH is a consortium of sixty-five agencies in the greater Bridgeport area that are working together against domestic violence and sexual assault. As I stand at the podium facing the 250 people seated around the white tablecloths, I'm relieved they can't see my knees shaking.

Later, Maureen Regula, the director of CAVITH, tells me, "I admire your dedication to this cause and respect your courage in sharing your daughter's tragic story in hopes of educating young women in abusive relationships. Your presentation also served to remind the professionals in attendance about the impact of domestic violence on the surviving family members."

I am impressed and heartened that so many people who have not personally experienced domestic violence care so much and are working hard to heighten the community's response to abuse.

In addition to the slide presentation I speak at vigils and rallies. I address a vigil in April 1998, sponsored by Survivors of Homicide in Waterbury at the First Congregational Church. Wanda Rieger has worked hard to organize it and the intimate chapel is full. A videotape showing several victims of homicide is playing. The lights are low and there is soft music in the background. Each of us receives a small white candle in a holder, which we will light later.

The service begins when Sam Rieger introduces the local dignitaries who speak briefly. Then the survivors begin. By the time I speak I have already shed many tears. I share who Margie was, what she meant to us, the joys we shared, and how awful it is not having her here with us. I end with part of Ruth's eulogy and two of my poems.

Then Stuart Brush conducts a very moving service. He and his wife, Laura, lost one son to murder and then their second son committed suicide because he didn't want to live without his brother. We light our candles and when it is my turn I say, "This candle is for Margie."

Later that month I speak at a rally at the state capitol in Hartford. I tell them:

I'm Shirley Bostrom. I'm a survivor of Homicide. By the luck of the draw, my husband got the call every parent dreads—but believes they will never get—Margaret, our thirty-one-year-old daughter had been murdered. We didn't believe such a horrible act could happen to us. We are law-abiding, hardworking, taxpaying, college educated citizens. Such violence didn't happen to people like us.

We learned that having a Ph.D. in clinical psychology doesn't protect you. My daughter knew all the facts and statistics about intimate abuse—but she didn't think it could happen to her. Neither did we—but it did. Her husband stabbed her 16 times when she was getting out of the shower. She wanted a divorce and he wasn't going to let her go.

Many of us here found out the hard way that violence in today's world does affect anyone and everyone. Including entertainers, religious leaders, lawyers, judges, policemen, and politicians. This knowledge makes us unwelcome among those not yet affected. We serve as too real reminders that it can happen to anyone. We are shunned as lepers were because others may catch our disease. We are told to get on with our lives. But our lives are changed forever. We know no one is safe. It is impossible to return to the complacency we felt before our loss.

I recall listening to news reports of violent deaths and reading of other families' losses. For a moment I was touched and asked, "How do they survive?" But I pushed aside any lingering thoughts and went on with my busy life.

When that violence strikes your family you can never push it aside again. Those of us who are Survivors of Homicide must deal with our own loss—and some of us take on a crusade to inform, comfort, and support those who suffer such a loss in the future. We work to bring changes to a criminal justice system and laws that favor the criminal and forget the victim. Not for ourselves, but for the next victim. Yet, our appeals often fall on deaf ears. All but a few legislators are too busy to listen when we speak before a judicial committee. Some don't show up. Others talk and eat while we make our pleas. How large do our numbers need to grow before we will be listened to with the respect we deserve? Survivors of Homicide is a club that wants no new members and no one willingly joins. But just while I've been talking our membership has increased.

We hold rallies like this one—to wake up society. Everyone needs to view violence seriously and take up the cry—NO more Violence. Prevention is the only solution. That begins with taking a close look at our values and priorities and then working to make the necessary changes in society. YOU ARE NOT TOO BUSY! Do something before you, or your daughter, or son, or mother, or father, or grandchild, or grandparent, or friend becomes a victim. If there is one way I can give meaning to the brutal murder of my lovely daughter, Margaret, it is by helping others avoid the life changing pain that the violent death of a loved one brings.

At yet another candlelight vigil I tell the audience about a verbal game Larry and I play called "What If?" What we never ask—at least when we play the game together—is, "What if we had never met, fallen in love, and married?" After thirty-nine years that is beyond my imagination and hopefully his.

This is the way our game goes: What if we had stayed in Jamestown, New York, instead of moving here?

What if Larry had taken an engineering job at Westinghouse, near Baltimore, instead of Hamilton Standard (now Hamilton Sundstrand), a division of United Technologies Corporation?

What if we had stayed in Bloomfield in the duplex we first rented? That's easy. I'd have gone crazy. Too many people too close. I'm a country girl.

What if we had never bought the horses or the farm in Suffield? That's easy too. We'd be rich.

For the last two-and-a-half years, the follow-up to all our what ifs has been: Would Margie ever have met Mitch? Would she still be alive?

Then we ask: What if Margie had stayed at Lynchburg College in Virginia and not transferred to the University of Connecticut her junior year?

What if Mitch hadn't followed her to San Diego when she went there to get her Ph.D.?

What if we had refused to accept him as a part of our family because we knew their relationship was a troubled one? Would we have lost her sooner? Or would our disapproval have kept her alive?

What if Mitch had come to Pennsylvania with her when she took the job at the federal penitentiary at Lewisburg instead of remaining in California for six months?

What if we had gone to Lewisburg when he broke the lock on the bedroom door and took her dog and cat to New Jersey—because she loved them more than him?

What if he had left for Cornell and his MBA a week earlier than planned? He was to leave two days after he murdered her.

What if she had never met her boss—or if he had been a fifty-year-old grandfather?

What if she hadn't asked for the divorce first, had let Mitch have the control? He had told her she wouldn't be fit to be his wife when he got his MBA.

What if she were still alive? Would she have stayed with the Federal Bureau of Prisons? Maybe become a warden? Or even its chief?

Would she have taken a position with the BOP in Florida—as we talked about—so Larry and I could live near her six months and near Ruth, Abby, Jacob, and Kathy in Connecticut for the rest of the year?

Would she have found the right man? What kind of mother would she have been? She called from across the country to find out how to stuff a Thanksgiving turkey. Would she have called me every time the baby sneezed? I'd have loved that. Would these grandchildren be as cute as she was, with the curly hair and devilish smile?

Would she have written the book she talked about writing— How to Live with a Neurotic Cat? Or have been an expert guest on the Oprah show counseling people with problems?

Would she have talked us into taking one of Calie's pups instead of leaving her golden retriever for us?

How many lives would be different if she had not been murdered by a man who swore his undying love? Her family and friends and those she would have helped professionally?

She was a beautiful, caring, young woman. I'll never know what she would have been like at forty or fifty. I've thought of having one of those aging things done to one of her photographs. But I decided to let her be forever young....

At Middlesex Hospital I speak to a group of interns who plan to be general practitioners or family doctors. There are signals that might warn a doctor a patient is the victim of domestic violence. These include a patient reporting a change in sleep patterns, overeating, loss of appetite, stomach problems, fatigue, allergies, back pain, depression, or any other extreme change in behaviors or body functions. In the month before her murder, Margaret went to a doctor with many of these symptoms. The female doctor put her on Prozac and gave her pills to sleep and medicine to treat her allergies, which always acted up when she was under stress.

Most women will not volunteer the information they are being verbally or physically abused, so the doctor must take the time to ask the right questions and listen carefully to the answers. To do this, the doctor must be aware of the patterns and symptoms of domestic violence. Signs of physical abuse such as suspicious bruises, broken bones, discomfort when touched, ducking, or flinching. Does the patient show signs of mental or emotional stress? Does she cry easily or have a flat affect? Doctors must establish themselves as compassionate listeners and take the time to ask the right questions. HMOs and managed health care make this difficult.

I challenge the doctors with, "If you are to make a difference your role is not simple or easy. It can be time consuming and disheartening, but if you take the time you may help save the life of a woman like Margaret who didn't know the danger she was in and had her whole life ahead of her as a helping professional. That is why I'm here. If the doctor Margie went to had been aware of the signs of abuse she might still be alive today."

The young doctors, mostly women, are attentive. When I finish, one of them who has a striking resemblance to Margaret seeks me out. "Thanks for coming. Now I'll be aware of the signs." It hits me then. I don't know how many women I may be helping. It is a heady feeling.

At the next Melanie Ilene Rieger Memorial Conference Against Violence, I do a presentation called, The Homicide Story Part 2 with Toni Bosco, another survivor who lost a son and daughter-in-law to a brutal double murder. They were sleeping when the attack occurred; no motive has been established but the killer is in jail serving a long sentence. The focus of our presentation is getting beyond our grief.

After a brief review of the murder, I tell of keeping busy to avoid dealing with my feelings. I still feel, at times, like an actor playing a part. When reality hits, I feel the urge to shut down. I'm never sure what will bring back the tears. It is important to understand that survivors react differently. Feelings of anger, despair, guilt, denial, and depression occur but not in neat stages. Larry and I are fortunate that our ways of grieving are compatible. However, many marriages deteriorate or end in divorce because of different methods of dealing with the pain. One of the hardest things for me to deal with is the fact that my world isn't safe anymore. Eventually every survivor has a choice to make. I know I want to live, and beyond that, I want to be as happy and productive as I can. Writing about my experience helps me deal with my emotions and evaluate my progress. Survivors of Homicide helps me focus my pain. Reaching out to others aids my healing, and going to therapy helps me understand that what I'm feeling is normal.

I believe we begin to heal by keeping active, reaching out to others with similar losses, and doing what we can to keep others from experiencing what we have. The why, when, and how of each survivor's decision to work for change may vary, but the emphasis needs to shift from *poor me* to *I can make a difference*. If it doesn't we get stuck in our despair. Speaking out to prevent domestic violence has given my life a positive focus.

I end the session with an activity I hope will involve the audience. I use the chapter of this book, called "We Are Not Contagious But Healing Requires Effort," to make them aware of how survivors feel and what can be done to comfort them more effectively. I share some of the insensitive remarks people make to survivors. Then, I ask how to change them so they are more helpful. I even give some examples. I find out that people don't have any idea of what to do or say to someone who has had a loved one murdered. I'm frustrated with how this exercise is going but don't know how to make it work before we run out of time.

When the conference is over, a touching tree-planting ceremony is held in a little garden that was established in Melanie's memory. Margie's name is mentioned and she will be remembered here along with Polly Klaas, Megan Kanka, Frankie Merrill, John and Nancy Bosco, and other loved ones of conference presenters.

Larry and I join the planning committee for the 2000 conference where I will be leading a panel of survivors. When that time comes, Frank Blackford, the counselor/advocate for Survivors of Homicide, shares how we have been making a difference by seeking new, victim-friendly legislation, going to schools to speak against violence, giving victim impact statements at prisons, and working against domestic violence. Wanda Rieger talks about starting the conference in her daughter's memory. John Cluny tells of his legislative advocacy. Anne Stone describes writing part of her son Ralph's Ph.D. dissertation about women in underdeveloped countries. She also did the oral presentation. Ralph and Anne earned his Ph.D. These are all wonderful tributes to loved ones who were murdered.

During this time, I receive a call from Maureen Whelan, training coordinator for the Connecticut Coalition Against Domestic Violence (CCADV). She asks me to speak at a noon memorial service for victims of domestic violence that is being held at the Hartford Public Library. The group that started the Silent Witness display and the wooden figures—each representing a victim—will be there. So will Connecticut's attorney general, Richard Blumenthal. I accept and the brief service is touching.

Dr. Gaboury also asks me to participate in Department of Correction staff training sessions at the Maloney Center for Training in Cheshire where I tell the social workers, guards, and supervisors that I want the criminals to understand they are responsible for their own actions. Nobody made them do it. There are consequences for their behavior. They had choices—they could have walked away. I want to make the innocent victims real.

My first chance to speak to offenders comes when I'm invited to Gates Correctional Facility. As usual, we are early when we arrive at the institution so we drive along the country road past farms and small homes on one side of the road. On the other side, high chain-link fences topped with razor wire surround the prison buildings and present a startling contrast. I recall hearing that living near a prison is the safest place to live because an escaped convict isn't going to stay in the area. Still I wonder how it feels to live so close. I suppose you get used to it—until something happens.

At 9:45 A.M. we turn into the prison grounds and park in the visitors parking area. We are met at the entrance to the facility by Carol, who is one of the facilitators for the group of offenders we will be sharing our story with this morning. These men are due to be released in the near future and the Department of Correction has developed an Offender Education Program, VOICES, to prepare them for that day. The impact that crime has on its victims is part of this course. When we are buzzed in through locked doors that close behind us, I am acutely uncomfortable with being locked in—*and* I know I'll be leaving in an hour.

It is early December but the weather is more like late October. Offenders are out and strolling around the level two facility. In Connecticut there are five levels of incarceration that reflect the severity of the crime and whether the perpetrator needs a highly structured confinement or not. This area, with low level offenders, feels safe and nonthreatening.

We enter a dormitory and walk through to the chapel where the group is in session. They are discussing Tracey Thurman, who was almost killed by her husband, and the lack of concern demonstrated by the response of the local police. Her case led to the strengthening of domestic violence laws in Connecticut. An offender states, "I'm human. If someone pushes me too far, gets me too angry, I'm going to act."

Another man tells the facilitator, "I bet if you got angry enough, if you caught your husband molesting your daughter, you'd blow him away."

She agrees that she would have violent thoughts, "But the difference is I wouldn't act on them." They laugh at her with knowing disbelief.

I listen to the topic and their statements and wonder what I have gotten myself into as I look at the note I wrote myself this morning. *My goals: to have them take responsibility for their actions and understand there are consequences for their choices. She didn't make me do it.*

I look at each young, nice-looking, attentive black or white man as I begin to speak. It is an auspicious moment. I explain how many victims there are to a violent crime. Several men are obviously touched by what we have experienced. Only one older white male has his eyes shut and doesn't look at the slides or me. My message is that Mitch took Margie's life, ruined his, ours, his parents' and robbed society of a productive member. He could have walked away and none of this would have happened. There were terrible consequences for his choice and behavior. When I am finished they have only one question, "How do you feel about being here?"

"I'm happy that I am here. I've wanted to do this. I hope what I've said has made a difference. It would help me if I knew what effect our story has had on you."

"I'm speechless. I have three children and I can't imagine the pain you feel." This offender seems to speak for the group.

When we are preparing to leave several men individually express their sympathy and thank us for being here. One tall, good-looking, reddish blonde offender sobs during much of my presentation and he is still sobbing as he approaches me. He tells me he was raised with golden retrievers, rode horses, and his father taught him that anyone who will mistreat a dog will do the same to a person. I am touched by the depth of his pain. I ask Carol if help is available to him and she tells me, "Elaine and I will help him deal with the feelings that surfaced during your presentation." I'm relieved.

Carol explains, "This is a very vocal group. They enjoy verbal sparring and banter back and forth. But they were deeply touched by your story—they were speechless. They will open up in the next session. Too bad you can't hear them. I'll call to let you know how it goes." I appreciate her thoughtfulness.

The last door closes behind me—setting me free and physically separating me from the men inside, but our encounter has been a powerful one. I'm drained emotionally and tears begin to flow down my cheeks unchecked.

On the way home I reflect on the experience and feel close to Margie. Margie worked with federal prisoners and would no doubt have conducted classes for those ready to be released. I tell Larry, "If Margie was the group leader, she would tell me about each person— verifying or disputing my reactions." She and I had talked about introducing writing as a therapeutic tool for the offenders she worked with at Lewisburg. She planned to investigate the possibility of my teaching writing groups. I know she was with us today and approves of my efforts.

In December, Sam Rieger, Larry and I meet with Mark Staiger, a counselor at the Danbury federal facility to discuss Survivors of Homicide participating on victim impact panels for small groups of inmates that he is counseling. Mark attended a week-long session of Victim Impact Training for Trainers at the FCI in Schuylkill, Pennsylvania, and decided to implement it at Danbury.

Mark heard about us through a coworker who attended the 1998 Connecticut Statewide Crime Victim Conference. Making inmates aware of how their violence changes lives and having them take responsibility for their actions are important parts of the Survivors of Homicide mission. We want to keep others from facing a tragedy similar to ours so we're excited about the possibilities.

At the end of our discussion I show Mark my notebook which contains copies of my slide presentation against domestic violence. He looks and listens courteously but I don't think he's very interested. However, less than a week passes before I receive his e-mail telling me that he shared our story and information about my presentation with a female counselor. She wonders if I will speak to the large drug rehabilitation group. There are two points she wants me to stress: one—women are sometimes the abuser, and two—a same sex partner can be abusive. I know I'll have to research these situations but I agree—unsure of what I'm getting myself into but determined to do it anyway.

So on January 19, 2000, the day before my sixty-sixth birthday, Larry and I go to the federal correctional institution for women in Danbury, Connecticut, where I will speak to the ninety-five female inmates in the drug rehabilitation program. My topic is domestic violence and its impact on the victims and society.

The morning is sunny and cold as we approach the entrance to the correctional institution. The area around the sign is well land-scaped with evergreens and shrubs that are probably azaleas or rhododendrons, in front of a decorative stone wall near the drive-way that winds up the gradual incline. Even in winter the facility is not visible from the street below. I feel a strong connection to Margie as I recall the paperwork she had completed, but had not yet turned in, requesting a transfer to this facility. For a moment I'm over-whelmed with what ifs. How different it would be if we were here at her request, but I know Margie's spirit is here with us.

Mark is waiting for us in the lobby. We do the paperwork and he asks for my driver's license. I don't have it. When I returned from a writing retreat on Cape Cod I left it in my parka pocket. For a while it appears that I will not be allowed to go in but Mark contacts the female warden who gives permission for me to enter. I tell Larry, "I thought you would be giving the speech while I waited here."

We are guided through an ultrasensitive metal detector, ultra-violet light sensitive stamps are placed on our left hands and we are led down a narrow hall to a locked gate. The small room on the other side is larger and much less scary than the one at Lewisburg. We place our hands in front of the light to verify that we have been approved for entry and the door on the other end of the room opens. The counselor takes us to her cramped office that is occupied by three visiting coworkers. We are introduced to two social workers and a secretary before we are taken for a tour of that building. The inmates' chambers are small—probably no more than six by ten with bunk beds. I can't imagine sharing such a small space with a stranger. Several of the doors are decorated with inspirational sayings. These quarters surround a long narrow room that is used for their group treatment sessions. From there we go to the department supervisor's office, but Dr. Lindgren is at lunch. However, she finds us later. *Maybe Margie would have that job—if she were alive.*

Mark has gone ahead to the auditorium to set up the projector and we follow shortly. We exit the first building and find ourselves in a large outdoor area which is completely surrounded by buildings. While we are being escorted along the sidewalk we meet two women who are introduced as psychologists. I tell them, "My daughter was a psychologist for the Bureau of Prisons. She was at Lewisburg before she was murdered but wanted to transfer to Danbury."

One woman quickly answers, "I know all about it. I was offered that job before she took it. I turned it down because Bill Corey freaked me out. Please tell me he lost his license over this."

I tell her, "No, but he was demoted and is at a facility in the South." She looks disgusted and walks away. I think, *He didn't kill her. Mitch did.* This brief encounter leaves me angry. She is invalidating my version of Margie's murder. I quickly put it behind me—for the time being—when I enter the auditorium. Larry gets the slides in focus, but the room is so light it is hard to see them from seats near the window. Mark is able to climb up and release one blind that was tied open and lower another. Not perfect but it will have to do. Soon women come in and start choosing seats from among the rows of folding chairs. Watching them, I remind myself there is no way I can predict what their reactions will be. If anyone becomes confrontational or obnoxious, I can remain calm and let the professionals deal with the situation. When I begin to speak it is quickly apparent that this is an attentive, supportive audience. I have eye contact and there is an interested silence.

At the end I take questions. Many women thank me for coming and express their sympathy for what we have suffered. They ask if I plan to talk at men's prisons, how my daughters are dealing with the murder, and about Mitch's family. Others tell me of being shot by a husband, a daughter murdered by her partner, or ask where they can get help to leave an abusive relationship. As we prepare to leave, women who would not talk in front of the group approach me privately. One attractive, petite blonde tells me her story, "I kept my husband from abusing me—he was abusive with his first three wives—by refusing to let him swear at me or put me down. By stopping it there, he never started physically hurting me." She goes on to tell me, "I'm HIV positive and my husband died from AIDS." I think about the potentially useful lives and silently curse the drugs and environments that have helped destroy them. I hope she will beat the odds.

On the way out I observe, "In Connecticut, Danbury has the reputation of being a country club. It doesn't look like one to me."

One of the social workers says she is from Connecticut and she heard the same thing while she was growing up.

Mark tells us that the facilities are old but remodeling has been done and there are tennis courts at the back of the grounds, but laughs at the idea of it being a desirable place to be. Being locked inside the walls of a prison has never been a pleasing thought for me either. Again, I'm relieved as we walk away—aware that the doors are locking us out.

I think I did a good job and the women were receptive, so I'm pleased when Larry tells me, "I thought it went really well." As we drive away I think, *Margie was here and she is proud of us*. Today we have shared her gift in a special and unique way.

On Tuesday, August 1, 2000, I speak at the National Organization for Victim's Assistance (NOVA) conference in Miami Beach. We fly to Fort Lauderdale and arrive at the Fontainebleau Hilton Resort and Towers on July 29th, the day the conference begins. We are impressed with the public areas which are ornate and spacious but our room is small and ordinary. We try to register for the conference and are dismayed when we're told we aren't on the list. We aren't happy as we get in the "new registration line," which is long and slow moving. However, seeing our friend Marsha Kight, whose daughter, Frankie Merrill, was a victim of the Oklahoma City bombing, improves our outlook. We first met Marsha in Connecticut when she spoke at the Melanie Ilene Rieger Memorial Conference Against Violence. She now works for NOVA in Washington, DC.

The first night we're bused to Señor Frogs where we meet a group from Arkansas. Angela, a young, attractive Heather Locklear look-a-like, introduces us to her supervisor who tells a comical story about her dog and President Clinton's old dog. Apparently, they are grandparents to the same litter of puppies. After that evening there isn't much free time. We don't swim in either the pool or the ocean, but we do take a brief stroll along the boardwalk. We're reminded that summer in south Florida is hot and humid with frequent showers when an unexpected downpour, just as our food is delivered, interrupts our plans to eat at the outdoor café. We are forced inside for sushi. Darn!

The conference runs smoothly, after apparent confusion about which kind of projector I need is clarified, and Christopher Greenslade, the conference coordinator, assures me I have a slide projector.

The majority of participants are professionals in law enforcement, criminal justice, or victims' rights and services, so we, as survivors of homicide, are treated with respect. Our thoughts and feelings are sought, acknowledged, and validated. This is quite different from the disinterest, discomfort, and disbelief some survivors faced with a few state agencies and some public servants in Connecticut, before they understood that many survivors of homicide wanted to work with the system and could offer the unique perspective of a survivor of a vicious crime.

We attend as many workshops as possible. At dinner we share a table with B. J., a Mothers Against Drunk Driving (MADD) worker from Austin, Texas. We learn that she will be in Arizona for the Parents of Murdered Children (POMC) conference later in the month, so we exchange business cards and promise to look for each other in Scottsdale.

I also deliver an information packet about my presentation to Marylouise Kelley from the Department of Justice (DOJ), who is considering me as a speaker for a forum on intimate partner homicide in September.

My NOVA presentation has a very desirable slot in the Burgundy Room on Tuesday morning. Larry and I attend the workshop which precedes ours. I am afraid that I might identify too closely with the presenters, whose daughter was murdered by a boyfriend. I don't want to be emotionally distraught before I begin my talk. Their discourse is touching and informative but I'm calm and focused as my time approaches.

The room's seating capacity is listed at one hundred-fifty and I was told to bring handouts for seventy-five participants. I brought one hundred—just in case, but I anticipate about forty. I joke that it is going to be lonely in this huge room with only five people. The room begins to gradually fill during the break. When I begin speaking I have a sense that the room is nearly full but no idea that they're bringing in additional chairs. Later, the volunteer assigned to my presentation tells me that I had two hundred people. I'm amazed.

Margie's and our story is powerful and the focus is on what I'm saying not on how well I'm doing. This helps keep me from being too nervous or critical about my delivery. The written evaluations and comments are positive—except for one person who doesn't like all the poetry, another who thinks I should move around more and one who suggests that I advance the slides myself—which I decide to do. I'm pleased with my reception but feel bad that there aren't handouts for everyone, so I offer to send copies to anyone who gives me their address. Several people wait to tell me they appreciate my openness, honesty, and courage. One is Brad Mitchell from the DOJ, Office for Victims of Crime (OVC). He asks me to speak at the forum in Washington. I thank him and explain that I think I will be there.

We fly home on Friday, August 4th to interview candidates for the new position of program director and grant writer for Survivors of Homicide. We also see a play in Rhode Island—*Joseph and the Amazing Technicolor Dreamcoat*.

Less than a week later, on Thursday, August 10th we speak at the national convention of Parents of Murdered Children (POMC) in Scottsdale, Arizona, where we stay at the Doubletree Paradise Valley Resort Hotel. It is a great facility and the first evening we go in the pool—for the only time. We finally meet Dan Levey, the member of the Valley of the Sun Chapter of POMC who arranged for me to speak. We are impressed by the chapter volunteers and leaders. Becky Miller and Sherry Kiyler, conference co-chairs, are friendly and open. Becky is the president of the Phoenix chapter of POMC and Sherry is an officer with the Phoenix Police Department where she has become involved with the local chapter of POMC.

We are not unique at this conference—almost everyone is a survivor of homicide. Many attendees come to share their stories and get answers to questions. The choice of workshops is varied. I attend 1) *Poetry Writing for Healing*, 2) Darcy Sims, *Wallowing: How to Have a "Good" Bad Day* and 3) *Impacting the Offender thru Awareness of the Victim Experience,* which are all excellent.

I also go to one on mother's grief because I feel that although I'm reaching out and helping others I may be neglecting my own grief and healing.

This time my workshop is early Saturday morning and about thirty people attend. It is a very moving experience. I quickly learn that several of the participants have experienced intimate abuse themselves or are very concerned about a loved one who is in such a situation. One young woman, a caregiver, reports that she has asked for a divorce and feels she is being stalked. We agree with her since she has received roses at the conference—she didn't think her husband knew how to contact her. He is proving he can find her anywhere.

We continue our discussion at dinner. Everyone at our table encourages her to take his behavior seriously. She is in real danger. After the meal several awards are given out to recognize the work of people who are supporting victims and survivors. It is an idea I will take home for the Melanie Conference.

Each day we eat lunch and dinner with B. J., the MADD worker from Austin. She promises to send me a book she thinks I'll like. *Hello from Heaven* is by Bill and Judy Guggenheim and gives firsthand accounts of after-death communications that use the different senses and include various forms such as butterflies and rainbows.

Sunday we have a delicious brunch with Darcy Sims as the keynote speaker and a touching closing ceremony. Later there is an ice cream social, which I enjoy while Larry goes to the airport to get our rent-a-car.

Larry and I have made plans to treat ourselves to a few days of sightseeing after presenting and participating in two very draining but fulfilling national conferences. We begin by visiting Frank Lloyd Wright's home, Taliesin West. I've been a longtime fan of his architecture, which blends in with the natural setting, but never thought I'd get to visit his desert home. We eat dinner at a local tourist attraction, Rawhide, a replica of a small frontier town complete with saloons, mines, general stores, and restaurants. My grandson would love it. We get him a sheriff's badge with "Jacob" on it before we return to the hotel.

Monday morning we take our sightseeing to Payson, Arizona, the site of the Zane Grey Museum. I learn that his cabin in the mountains, which I wanted to visit, burned down in the early nineties. The museum is small but well organized. I'm amazed at all the early movies that were based on his books. I also find three books I still need for my collection of his novels.

From there we go to Tonto Natural Bridge State Park. The pine forests and mountains are so different from the desert terrain near Scottsdale. The temperature is also more bearable, especially when the breeze brushes across our bodies. Then we drive northeast from Payson to Holbrook, located on the old Route 66, and spend the night before going on to the Petrified Forest and the Painted Desert. We enjoy the drive around the loop through Blue Mesa. The deep silence and the view of the multicolored formations in the muted pastel landscape below us creates a surreal scene. Later, on our way north to Chinle we stop at the old Hubbell Trading Post, which is still in business.

At 4 P.M. on Tuesday, August 15, 2000, the day before the fourth anniversary of Margie's murder, Larry and I arrive in Chinle, Arizona—a small town on the Navajo Reservation. We stop at the visitor's center for Canyon de Chelly (Canyon dSHAY) where a friendly ranger tells us, "The canyon will be spectacular tonight because of the full moon." He suggests that we watch it from the White House Ruins Overlook. Before we return to the motel we purchase tickets for the next morning's jeep tour into the canyon.

After dinner we drive along the southern rim of the canyon. It is almost dark. There are only a few other tourists and the Navajos selling their wares. I buy a small stone with pictographs painted on it from a young man who tells me, "My friend just moved to Norwich, Connecticut." Small world, since that is thirty minutes from our home. The darkness and silence are eerie as we watch a phenomenal storm approach. No canyon by moonlight tonight.

The next morning on our way to the canyon I photograph cows grazing along the main street of Chinle. At 9 A.M. we are waiting to board the jeep for the ride into the canyon. A woman asks me where we are from and we learn that they are from Connecticut, but recently relocated to a retirement community in Arizona. She asks, "Why were you in Scottsdale?"

I answer, "We were presenting at a conference." Hoping she will stop there.

"What kind of conference was it?"

"Parents of Murdered Children."

"Are you one of *them*?" It is apparent from her expression that she wishes she hadn't asked.

I react to that by telling her, "Yes, my daughter was murdered by her husband four years ago today. Actually just about this time if you allow for the time differences between Navajo and eastern daylight savings time."

"Oh."

She makes sure she doesn't sit next to us on the jeep and when, days later, we eat in the same restaurant at Monument Valley she acts as if she doesn't see us.

Being on the bottom of the canyon gives an entirely different perspective than you get from the rim—both are breathtaking. We ride along beside the small stream and green foliage thinking of all those who have lived and died in this canyon and all the children for whom this was a huge playground. Seeing the cliff dweller ruins is distracting but cannot change what happened to our family four years ago.

The canyon has two branches and I find it significant that the guide chooses to take us to the Canyon del Muerto (canyon of the dead) first so we are there at the time Margie died—four years earlier. I cry my own private tears hoping that no one notices. If they do they don't show it. I'm thankful for that. I feel that Margie's spirit is with us and the canyon promotes a feeling of continuity that I appreciate. The human spirit does survive.

In the afternoon we drive north to Kayenta and Monument Valley. I wish for the hundredth time that I were Zane Grey—maybe then I could find the words to describe the breathtaking vistas. On August 17th, we take a jeep ride with Fred's Adventure Tours into the valley, but this time it is only us and the guide. The silence brings peace. However, somewhere along the bumpy road exiting the park, I lose a small instant camera. I have tried since Margie's death not to let the little things get to me, but I'm distraught over the loss of these once-in-a-lifetime photos. It takes serious talking with myself before I can let go and enjoy our lunch at Gouldings Trading Post Restaurant. After all, I didn't lose all three cameras.

We decide to eat dinner at the motel restaurant and while we are there a huge storm develops. There's a strong wind, loud thunder, bright flashes of lightning across the dark sky, and the rain begins as we cross the parking lot to our room. I turn around to enjoy nature's demonstration of power and I see the most magnificent rainbow I have ever seen. It's complete from horizon to horizon. Each color is distinct and brilliant. Above the first rainbow is a second less-clearly defined one. I know it's a sign from Margie. For whatever reason she waited a day to let us know she is with us and is giving us a thumbs up. The rainbow lasts for thirty minutes before beginning to fade. Many grieving people report seeing rainbows at significant times. This is the first rainbow sign for me but only one of the many messages I have received from Margie.

The next day we complete our loop around northeastern Arizona, driving by Flagstaff back to Phoenix. We stop for lunch at a small diner in Camp Verde called Babe's Round-Up. It is a little bit of the "Old West" and I consider it a fitting end to our tour.

Back in Connecticut, we attend the annual picnic given for survivors of homicide by the State Department of Correction at York, their facility in Niantic. It is great to see everyone. Artie and Marie are here. He is making progress in his recovery from a devastating stroke but it is a long process. David Kaczynski, the unabomber's brother, is here and agrees to write the introduction to this book when I have it completed. He has already read the first eight chapters and has the next eight. I appreciate his time and effort.

The next week, we learn that the woman who was going to be program coordinator and grant writer for SOH quit without giving us a reason. So we interview and hire Lorraine Egan. I'm impressed with her understanding of our issues, hope she is self-directed and will get us structured, organized, and focused. I hope she can get us grants that will allow us to add to the services we provide but also remove the need for us to be fund-raisers. I hate selling things! Unfortunately these things will take time.

Larry and I see *Damn Yankees* at Theatre-by-the-Sea in Rhode Island before flying to the Baltimore/Washington airport for the Intimate Partner Homicide Forum sponsored by the Office for Victims of Crime. We plan to take the forty-five minute ride to the Renaissance DC Hotel on the Super Shuttle, but we get conned into going with another van. We're assured it will be quicker and cheaper. With that we are lured to the parking garage full of cars but few people. We begin to feel isolated as we wait in the strange dark surroundings. What have we gotten ourselves into? Even the rosary hanging from the rearview mirror contributes to the sinister plot I develop for murder and intrigue. We relax when another couple finally joins us and our ride is safe and uneventful.

We settle into our room and go to find the Department of Justice building where the forum will be held because I am the first speaker in the morning and we want to avoid any last-minute problems. As we are returning to the hotel I think I hear, "Mrs. Bostrom." *No, it can't be. Not in DC.* I continue on. "Shirley." When I turn around I'm pleased to see Brad Mitchell approaching. He greets me enthusiastically. Larry has kept on walking but comes back to hear Brad suggest that we may want to go down to the "mall" and view the monuments in the moonlight. Later, we hire a taxi for our tour. It is a pleasant, safe way to view the sights in Washington by night—besides, I want to save my energy for tomorrow.

The building at 810 Seventh Street has been beautifully restored with brass and glass doors into the entry hall, which has marble columns and floors that reflect in the large mirrored walls. We go through security and take the elevator to the third floor where we will spend the next two days in a state of the art conference room with about forty-five of the most prestigious researchers in intimate partner homicide, practitioners in the field, and Department of Justice employees.

I have thirty minutes to tell Margie's and our story. The focus is on our personal experience with intimate partner homicide. We are here to add reality and remind the researchers that their work is about real people—not just statistics. I feel Margie's presence in the room. She was an employee of the Bureau of Prisons which is a division of the DOJ. It would be better if she could be here herself but I know she is happy that our message is being heard—at this top policymaking agency. I learn a new term and a new concept—we are Margie's proxy. We speak for her.

Again, our reception is supportive, caring, and warmly sympathetic. We are deeply touched at the genuine emotions expressed by the participants. Knowing we have been heard is healing. While on a visit to the ladies' room a fellow participant tells me how important our message is and that Margie is very proud of us. I admit that at times I've wondered how Margie feels about our telling her story. She was a very private person. This woman puts her arm on my shoulder and tells me, "I counsel battered women. One question we always ask them is, 'If you are killed do you want us to tell your story or not?' They all answer, 'Yes, of course.'"

I start to joke, "If Margaret wanted to keep her privacy she shouldn't have gotten killed." The woman turns to leave, as if she doesn't want to hear this. It is then that I notice that her name tag identifies her as Margaret. Too strange to be mere coincidence!

Charlotte Clark, who is arranging for me to present at a symposium that the DOJ is holding in January of 2001, is at the forum. I contacted her after Mike Tafelski, the attorney from the BOP who was so helpful when Margie was murdered, suggested it. This chain of events was put into motion when Wayne Samuelson, the Assistant U.S. Attorney, had told me Mike had been promoted and might have the information I was seeking. I originally heard about the symposium from an employee of the BOP and followed up with Mark Staiger at the Danbury Federal Corrections Facility.

Earlier I had purchased a book, *Understanding Domestic Homicide* by Neil Websdale, because both Charlotte and Debbie Stanley recommended it. Debbie, a faculty member in criminal justice at Central Connecticut State University, is co-chair for the next Melanie conference and she is proofreading part of my manuscript. Neil is at this forum and graciously signs my copy of his book, "Dear Lawrence and Shirley, In memory of a life. And a life lost. Love Neil."

On the second day of the forum we follow a group process that develops recommendations regarding intimate partner homicide prevention, which the attorney general has requested and will be coming to hear this afternoon. I am amazed when several DOJ employees speak of Janet Reno with awe and respect. I have ambiguous feelings about her because of her denying the death penalty option for Mitch, but I do realize she has a very difficult job.

At 2:30 P.M. Janet Reno enters and is quickly seated. As I listen to her speak, I am impressed with her grasp of the subject and perceptive questions. It is obvious she is extremely intelligent and has spent time gaining knowledge and understanding of the depth of this problem. She is very different from the images of her on TV. I find her charming, warm, and personable. Robin Hassler-Thompson, a facilitator, kneels by my chair and asks if Larry and I would like our pictures taken with the attorney general. Of course we would. She tells me that when we see Ms. Reno start to leave we should go to the front, near the door. We do but she is quickly whisked out through the door by three secret service men. Robin is undaunted and pursues the attorney general into the hall. Ms. Reno stops and gives me direct eye contact as she expresses her sympathy for our loss and admiration for our courage. We are positioned with her in the center with her arms on our backs. After the picture is taken, she leans over to Larry and tells him, "I'm not patting your back—it's the Parkinson's." Then she is gone. I'm deeply touched and the tears come. *Janet Reno is a real person!*

Later, Larry reflects, "Margie could have worked for the DOJ for thirty-five years and probably never met the attorney general." I like to think she would have.

We hurry back to Connecticut where we are speaking the next day to new court-based victims service providers (advocates) as part of their training. We are very pleased the Office of Victims Services has asked us to present.

Robin Hassler-Thompson has invited me to present at a workshop about conducting intimate partner fatality reviews that will be held in New Hampshire in November. I readily agreed because I see this as an attempt to identify strategies that work and those that don't to prevent murder in intimate relationships. When we arrive we are pleased to see Neil and Caroline Nicholl from the DC Metropolitan Police Department—we met Caroline at the forum too. Maureen Whelan is there representing the Connecticut Coalition Against Domestic Violence (CCADV). I finish speaking to about ninety people and Larry and I begin answering questions. I turn to the right and unexpectedly fall to the floor. I am in too much pain to be embarrassed as I'm put in a wheelchair. After a fitful night's sleep we return to Connecticut, where I am diagnosed as having torn the cartilage in my knee—probably as a result of climbing at Mesa Verde in October while at an Elderhostel program. (Later I learn it is not torn cartilage, but arthritis.)

Since we feel the way we were told of Margie's death was flawed, Larry has now decided to talk about death notification during our speaking engagements. What he shares is very personal and touching. I'm proud of him and revise my brochure to include him as a presenter. We find speaking at colleges, high schools, and prisons—especially in Connecticut—rewarding. The positive feedback we get is encouraging and keeps us going. One young woman writes, "I asked God to give me a sign. He sent me you. You saved my life." Each time we speak, women come up and thank us. Their stories are different but similar to Margie's. They find that what we share helps them understand their relationships. We make their difficult decision to leave an abuser and seek protection easier.

Margie's gift has been the strength to survive her death and use it to warn others of the dangers inherent in intimate abuse. Focusing on this productive activity keeps us from sinking permanently into a deep depression. We know our daughter, the caregiver, would like that.

Promises Not Broken
Are Margie's Gift

She always told us,
I'm your baby.
The only baby
You'll ever need.

For thirty-one years,
She kept her word.
She was lovely and bright.
How we loved to spoil her.

She was growing stronger.
Ready to blossom fully
Into the woman
We knew she would be.

We had only a glimpse.
Then she was gone.
Her love gives us strength
To face our terrible loss.

She guides us as we search
For meaning in her senseless death.
She brings us other
Survivors who help us bear our loss.

Margie led us to helping others see
The dangers of domestic violence.
She left us Calie for comfort and
Her spirit is with us everywhere.

We fear death less, treasure life more.
Margie's gift—no broken promises.

CHAPTER 24

Life and *Criminal Justice* 1999–2000 Style

On May 6, 1999, Wayne Samuelson sends us a copy of the Third Circuit Court's April 19th ruling on Mitch's appeal. It requires that he be resentenced and that Judge Muir reduce the offense level by "one point" because Mitch did accept responsibility. The judge must also state his reasons for the nine level upward departure for extreme conduct, and address concerns about the proportionality of the minimum sentence for first-degree murder and the sentence Mitch received. Judge Muir has asked for briefs from both sides regarding these issues.

At the end of May we receive the prosecution's brief, which cites cases that support the nine point upward departure and applies those decisions to our case. In one instance, a husband strangled his wife on a cruise ship during the last night of their honeymoon, then threw her body overboard. Even though that perpetrator, like Mitch, had no previous record, the judge made a ten point upward departure. What Mitch did to Margie seems at least equally "extreme" to me. The brief also restates all the gruesome details of Margie's death.

Wayne argues that the proportionality concerns are nonexistent. There are only two sentence choices under federal statutes for first-degree murder—death or life without parole. The maximum penalty for second-degree murder under federal statutes is life without parole. Although federal guidelines may cause confusion, it is clear Mitch did not receive the maximum sentence for the crime to which he pled.

On June 11th, the defense submits their brief, which argues, "The court's conclusion was based upon erroneous interpretations of testimony by Dr. Samuel Land, the government's expert pathologist." They cite the court identifying the sternum as "one of the hardest bones in the body." Although the transcript records Dr. Land as testifying that it is, "a very difficult bone to penetrate—it's very thick and hard," the defense sees a discrepancy between Judge Muir's "an extremely violent death...the most severely violent death he [Dr. Land] has seen" and the transcript's record of Dr. Land reporting it as "a very violent death...this was one of the most severe cases I've seen."

The defense cites cases where the upward departure was not upheld and insists there was not sufficient evidence Mitch's crime falls outside the heartland (eleven to fourteen years in the sentencing guidelines).

They quote from their expert pathologist, Dr. Elliot Gross, who is prepared to testify Mitch may have stabbed her less than sixteen times because one stabbing could have penetrated more than one organ. He also gives a list of circumstances present in other stabbing cases but not in this case. These include "mutilation, torture, disfigurement, binding restraints, and most significantly, in excess of thirteen wounds to the torso." Dr. Gross would *not* characterize this case as, "unusually heinous, cruel, and brutal" or as "one of the more severe cases seen."

I'm incensed at these incredible statements but understand this report serves the defense's purpose. So does the argument that the convergence of the defendant's sentence with the guideline range for first-degree murder distorts proportionality.

The system is confusing and beyond my comprehension. Larry and I can't understand why the guidelines developed by Congress are so different from the statutes. Larry gets the address of the U.S. Sentencing Commission and has our friends join his letter-writing campaign asking for a change in these guidelines. No change yet.

At the same time the defense submits a brief in support of a motion to supplement the record by adding Dr. Gross's written review of the following items: photocopies of color prints, the relevant autopsy and toxicology reports, and the transcript pages 97 to 123 (Dr. Land's testimony).

At the end of June we receive the government's reply brief regarding the nine level upward departure and their brief in opposition to supplementing of the record. In this brief the government argues that the defense is trying to relitigate an issue already decided by the district court and the Third Circuit Court.

In July Judge Muir rejects the defense's motion to supplement the record. He found no evidence in the court of appeals' opinion that authorized him to hear additional evidence.

August 16, 1999, is a bright sunny day much like the one three years ago when our world fell apart. A dark and dreary day would feel more appropriate and match my sadness. This year we decide to go to Jamestown, New York, to visit relatives the week before the anniversary of Margie's death. We visit with Aunt Peg, Aunt Margaret, and my cousins Jim and Mark and their wives. We spend a pleasant afternoon with my nephew Dan and his wife, Jennifer, and her son, Alex. My nephew John and my niece Mary and her family and their Aunt Barbara stop by. We spend a pleasant afternoon talking about kids, dogs, and Alex's college plans. I tell them I stopped at Dad and Ma's graves in Bemus Point Cemetery but couldn't find my brother Jack's marker. He died the June before Margie and was cremated. His ashes were put in the same plot as my mother. Danny explains there has been a problem getting Jack's military plaque installed. I can't seem to get away from death or bureaucracy.

Eventually the conversation gets around to Mitch and what is happening in his case. Everyone is amazed at the appellate court's decision. How could they possibly believe he deserved a reduced sentence?

We hear the same incredulity every time we explain the situation. Why should logical, caring people understand how a system we have been taught will protect us really victimizes us over and over in its attempt to preserve the criminal's rights? We can't explain what we don't understand ourselves.

Being away from home, with people to see and places to visit, is helpful. Chub, my dad's ninety-six-year-old brother, is in a nursing home in Salamanca, and we combine a visit to see him with locating the cemetery on Bunker Hill Road in Steamburg where most of my Native American relatives are buried. My Grandmother Pierce's grave was moved here from Old Town when the Kinzua Dam was built and flooded much of the reservation, including my childhood home—a loss for which I still grieve. The location is pleasant and peaceful but Margie is never far from my thoughts. I wonder if she has met Grandma or Cousin Dolly, who was Uncle Chub's daughter and my close friend. Dolly was in her thirties and had two children when she was killed. Her car was hit by a milk truck. I contemplate her telling Margie about the trouble we got into together. Dolly met Margie, a toddler, once, at my father's funeral.

We drive Aunt Margaret to her home in Conesus on August 15th and stay overnight. Being with her seems an appropriate way to remember Margie. Aunt Margaret is seventy-eight and told us that until she was seventy-six she felt good and could do most everything. Now she talks of dying and concern about what will happen to her Yorkshire terrier, Daisy. When I assure her that we will take Daisy, she is grateful and relieved. It was hard leaving her and Peg because both are aging and Peg is in poor health. I wonder as we leave—will I see them again or are these our last goodbyes? I never had a chance to ask that question the last time I saw Margie—but I wouldn't have known to ask it anyway. (We do see them again at Margaret's eightieth birthday party.)

Larry is driving east on Route 17 across New York State as the time of

Ruth, Abby and Jacob go on without a favorite sister and aunt.

335

the murder comes and goes. My thoughts return to that day and how unaware we were of the tragedy we faced until the call came when Larry was all alone. Later, at home with Ruth, Abby, and Jacob, we have veal Marsala, look at pictures of Margie, and face another year without her. These rituals we now accept as helping to keep Margie alive in our hearts and minds.

On August 17th we are pleased when Wayne tells us that on August 6th Judge Muir denied the defense motion to supplement the record with Dr. Gross's report. Wayne was not there. Neither was Mitch and because of a mixup, neither were we. This is the only time we weren't notified of a court proceeding.

I request a copy of Dr. Land's autopsy report. Now that I've seen Dr. Gross's report I need to see exactly what Dr. Land wrote. Wayne agrees to send it to me. Then I say, "Please choose the three crime scene photos that are the least gruesome, put them in a sealed envelope, label it, and send them to me. I will not look at them until I'm ready, but I need to know I have the option if I ever choose to see them." He will send them to me but warns me to think hard before I look at them. I have not yet chosen to view them, but knowing I have that option is empowering.

On August 25th we learn the judge's decision. He has reviewed his findings of April 21, 1998, and the case law submitted in the briefs. He states, "There is a paucity of relevant cases with respect to the extent of the upward departure for extreme conduct." He points out that if Mitch had pled guilty to first-degree murder, his mandatory sentence would have been the statutorily required minimum sentence of life in prison. After stating all this, the judge rules that with the upward and downward departures, Mitch's offense level is now 37 or 210 to 262 months—much less than given in the original sentence. He ends his narrative with, "The sentence previously imposed of 365 months in our view satisfied proportionality requirements [between first- and second-degree murder]. If it did not, the sentence to be imposed in accordance with this opinion after only a seven level upward departure for this extremely heinous, cruel and brutal crime certainly satisfies those requirements."

Mitch will serve somewhere between seventeen years six months and twenty-one years ten months. The judge's reasons for this sentence include, "Just punishment for this brutal and outrageous offense." The sentencing date is set for September 22, 1999.

On September 21, 1999, we go with a group of Survivors of Homicide to a city council meeting to support John, a fellow member. He is asking for the interest on his property taxes to be reduced or eliminated because of the loss of his wife's income when both she and their son were brutally shot to death by their fourteen-year-old, next-door neighbor. He broke into John's house and a locked gun cabinet. Then he shot the dog and lay in wait for the family members to return home. John has succeeded in getting legislation changed in Connecticut so that juvenile perpetrators of violent crime can be tried as adults. He also lobbied, with less success until the 2000 Connecticut Legislature passed it, to get low interest-loans approved for innocent victims of violent crimes who are suffering financial hardships because of loss of income. The government supports such loans for disaster areas and losses due to hurricanes, earthquakes, floods, or drought. People whose oceanfront mansions were knowingly built in harm's way qualify for assistance when damage occurs. John asks, "Why not an innocent victim of homicide?"

John makes an impassioned plea that I fear falls on deaf ears. Seldom have I seen public officials, even local, show less interest or compassion. They appear rude, impressed with their own importance, and in a hurry to be rid of us. Marie, one of our members, gets fed up and finally tells one official, "I hope you never have to go through anything like this. You keep looking at your watch. If you don't have time for the meetings, you shouldn't sign up for the committees." Later John tells her the man is the city manager. We decide she didn't help John's case. On the way out we see a sign on the hall bulletin board informing us that the tax collector accepts Visa and MasterCard. We laugh cynically. John has filed bankruptcy so this is not an option for him.

We have dinner at the Old Tyme Café and I enjoy the laughter and companionship that keeps my mind off tomorrow—for a little while. I spent most of today preparing autopsy diagrams of Margie's wounds to be made into slides that I will now use in my presentation "Funny—He Doesn't Look Like a Murderer But Margie Is Dead" to show how heinous Mitch's attack was. The awful graphic reminders of

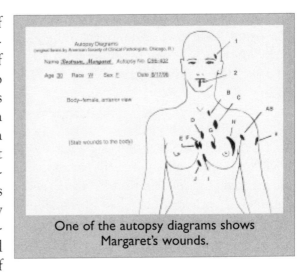

One of the autopsy diagrams shows Margaret's wounds.

her death made me unbearably conscious of the injustice that will occur tomorrow.

In the morning, Ruth, Larry, and I leave at 8 A.M. to meet six Survivors of Homicide who are going to Williamsport to give us support. Sam and Wanda, Marie and Artie, and Joan and Don have put aside other responsibilities to be with us. We feel guilty but also grateful. It is unlikely we would have met in our previous lives, and if we had our different backgrounds would have kept us apart. Homicide as a unifying force—I'll have to think about that more.

During the drive to Williamsport I sit in the backseat of our car and write what I would like to say in court today if given the chance.

My problem is not with the individual representatives of the criminal justice system—Judge Muir, Wayne Samuelson, or Harold Schmidle—but with the system itself that can tell a mother that the murder of her daughter by a man who claimed to love her is not in itself a cruel and heinous act. How can the taking of her life, her potential, and the love we shared be considered anything less than barbaric? How can anything less than life in prison be just?

I've read the autopsy report. Perhaps if the defense attorneys and the appellate judges had to read about their daughters' penetrating stab wounds, labeled A to N and described in detail, they would feel the outrage I feel. How can civilized people decide the perpetrator shouldn't serve the maximum time in prison?

There was damage to the ribs and sternum, and each section of the heart was pierced. All the lobes of the lungs were punctured and one wound that infiltrated her lungs went through her slender body. Margie's spleen, pericardium, aorta, and liver all suffered severe damage. Four wounds penetrated the diaphragm and parts of her stomach protruded through these holes.

The many wounds to her hands and arms prove she fought to live and didn't die easily or quickly. The pathologist indicated that she was alive throughout the attack—through the last stab wound.

I would remind the defense attorneys that there is still the death penalty and life in prison for those who commit the barbaric crimes your "expert pathologist" describes in his report. However, I wouldn't put too much stock in his opinion. Maybe if all of you had to read your daughters' autopsy report, wake up every morning to gnawing agony, go to bed with the despair I feel, and know it would be with you for the rest of your lives, you'd develop some compassion and a conscience.

To Michelle and Aileen—I know you are suffering and I empathize with your pain, but we are separated by a chasm too wide and deep for me to cross—now. To Mr. Paster and Mitch, I suggest you read the autopsy report but substitute Michelle or Aileen or Fran's name for Margaret's. If one of them had been killed by a jealous partner would you not agree that what was done to her was savage and deserved to be severely punished? Would you want to hear her falsely labeled on the stand? Margaret was not a whore or a drunk or an addict. You both know that.

You claim Mitch is not a criminal, but he did commit a crime. Mitch, you should take responsibility for your actions. It is deplorable that you blame her for her death. She didn't make you do it. You could have walked away.

I never heard any concern about Margie's drinking while she was alive, Mitch. Not even when you called me the night before you killed her. If either you or your dad, who claimed to love her, had real concerns why didn't you tell us? Weren't we all part of one big happy family? The truth is it is just another failed attempt to excuse Mitch's behavior. Margaret's autopsy showed only traces of alcohol and no drugs.

Mitch, I don't believe you ever loved Margie. How could you—then kill her—then try to destroy who she was? I don't care what she told you in anger. You knew her better than that. I hope the short time you spend in prison will help you take responsibility for your actions—otherwise you will return to society and the next woman who wants to end a relationship with you will be in danger of being murdered—just as Margaret was.

I miss her and everyday is a fight to keep going, but I won't let her death be excused. Neither will I let her be forgotten.

We arrive at the federal courthouse and meet briefly with Wayne Samuelson, who tells us, "The defense submitted copies of previous letters and some new certificates presenting Mitch as a model prisoner. There was even one with a smiling picture of him as employee of the month at the U.S. Penitentiary at Florence, Colorado."

"Oh, what a good boy," is my sarcastic response. We all laugh as we picture a young child coming home with a note saying he plays well with others in a structured setting.

Wayne promises me I will have a chance to say something, but it is obvious he is uncomfortable with what he fears I might say. He thinks the judge will go with the high end of the sentencing guidelines and he doesn't want anything to jeopardize that. I assure him, "I don't intend to criticize the judge."

Wanda wants reassurance. "You can ask that Shirley be allowed to speak? It is important to her." Wayne tells her he can.

This time we are in a different courtroom. It is much smaller and the judge sits at an angle in the left front corner of the room. I'm uncomfortable with the more intimate surroundings. There is a railing a few feet in front of us and the prosecutor's table is right in front of that. Someone asks Wayne if we are allowed to wear our Survivors of Homicide buttons. He says we can. Ruth arranges the seating so she is sitting on the end of the front row nearest to where the Pasters will sit—only three feet away. When they come in I glance their way but don't really look at them. Seeing them earlier, in the parking lot, was difficult enough. I can't handle trying to deal with their pain too.

Mitch enters the courtroom between two marshals who are dressed in slacks and sports jackets. I'm surprised to see Mitch in orange prison garb. Later Wayne tells us Judge Muir remarked that no one has ever appeared in his court dressed this way. I think he was offended by it but I thought it was appropriate.

It is disturbing that Mitch is now only fifteen feet away instead of thirty as in courtroom one. The change in his appearance since the original sentencing is remarkable. He has slimmed back down. He isn't bloated and his affect is natural—showing no signs of over-medication. Wanda leans over to tell me she can't keep from looking at his hands, which he holds behind his back, without remembering what he did with them. It helps to know she understands.

A defense attorney makes a few remarks in favor of the shortest sentence possible, pointing out how Mitch is being a good, productive citizen even in prison. The judge asks Mitch if he has anything to add. He doesn't. *Couldn't he at least pretend to be sorry?*

Wayne refutes defense remarks by reminding the court that while Mitch is getting "Worker of the Month" certificates, Margaret Bostrom cannot. We will never know what Margaret might have accomplished. Wayne is brief but effective. When the judge asks him if he has anything further his answer is no. I'm stunned. My dismay and disappointment at not being allowed to speak are eclipsed when I hear the judge decree—the sentence is twenty years and ten months. It is the most Mitch can get under the newly established guidelines. *Thank you for that, Judge Muir.* In three years we have gone from the death penalty or life in prison to thirty years and five months to this. Are we to feel this is justice? I'm relieved it isn't less but feel cheated out of the chance to say what I needed to say. Mitch is given the right to be heard. Why not me? He has ten days to appeal this decision and we will begin all over again. We cannot appeal.

We walk out, eyes straight ahead, past Aileen and Jordan. Neither family is a winner. We want more and they want less. We go to Wayne's office, where he explains that appeals in the case can go on for years. Neither he nor I mention his broken promise.

Criminal Justice **Continued**

May 6, 1999
Appellate Decision

Three appellate judges have decreed—too severe.
Judge Muir must shorten Mitch's sentence.
Margie's sentence and ours are still for life.

September 22, 1999
Mitch's Resentencing

Almost nine years are deducted from his prison term.
Healing and resolution must come from within us.
Justice is a callous fantasy we were lured into believing.

Later, I'll have to write part 3.

We drive to Scranton, hoping to never have to come to Williamsport again. We have dinner with our friends at a restaurant called Coopers. Wayne Samuelson suggested it, but I think Margie chose it because its unique decor will provide a welcome change from the sterile atmosphere of the courtroom. Outside, a huge wooden statue of a bear greets us, while pirates and a huge octopus on the roof perform to piped out music. Inside there is a model railroad near the ceiling with a train that makes a trip around our dining room— on an eight-minute schedule. Display cases hold original Barbie and Ken dolls and old magazine covers with Mickey Mantle, John Wayne, and Marilyn Monroe hang near historic photographs of the area.

When we finish eating it is near 8 P.M. Larry, Ruth, and I are tired and emotionally exhausted so we decide to drive to an area motel for the night. I look out the car window and see the harvest moon.

The Beholder

There is an almost full moon
but the gleam is gone.
Its allure diminished.

Or is it only the dirty window
of crime and injustice

342

I am seeing it through?

I miss its mystical magic,
the dreamlike thoughts
its light used to inspire.

I must wash the window,
rid it of my tainted view,
to savor life's enchanting moments.

We return to Connecticut and wait for the news we are sure will come—Mitch's attorneys have filed notification he is again appealing the sentence. That news arrives on October 4, 1999.

On November 5, 1999, the day before Margie's thirty-fifth birthday, Larry and I are driving back from the court in New London, Connecticut, where we supported another victim's family. It is a long and complicated case! I tell Larry, "I wonder what we would be doing on this bright, brisk windy November afternoon if Margie hadn't been murdered." Then I know my answer, "We'd probably be driving to Lewisburg, or wherever she'd be working, to celebrate her birthday with her." He agrees and I can almost pretend that is what we are doing. Almost.

Our family has decided to celebrate Margie's birthday on Sunday, November 7th instead of November 6th because Abby and Jake will be with their father on her birthday. On Saturday, after a very busy week speaking and supporting survivors in court, I sleep late and relax before going to the cleaners for the prom dress a friend allowed Abby to wear as a wedding dress for Halloween. Then, I go to the florist to get four red roses, in remembrance of the four birthdays without Margie, to put next to her urn. I reread the chapter I wrote earlier about her birth, which helps me relive those very precious memories.

Marie and Artie send us an electronic card; Stuart Brush, the registrar for Survivors of Homicide, calls; and Kathy Yaeger's card arrives with the mail. Bill Corey sends an e-mail to let us know he is thinking of us. Even with this show of support I feel my depression deepening, my blood sugar dropping, and all I want to do is stay in bed—sleeping if I can.

Toward evening the phone rings. It is Colleen Mahoney, Margie's best friend from fourth grade through high school. Ruth saw her last night at a restaurant in Hartford and told me, "Colleen says she is going to call you."

I laughed and told Ruth, "She's been going to call me for over three years and I haven't heard from her yet."

Hearing Colleen's voice lifts the depression and I enjoy reminiscing about the good old days. We talk for about an hour. She promises we will get together when she gets back from a vacation to Aruba. Maybe we will. Friday night I had asked Margie's spirit to get in touch with me. She does—through Colleen just as before when I was in the hospital and Colleen appeared.

On Sunday Kathy joins us and Larry prepares the veal Marsala and pecan pie. It is a quiet evening. We discuss plans for going to Lewisburg Federal Penitentiary to see the two memorials to Margaret. Warden Romaine has invited us to visit the tree that has been planted near the training center and the plaque, which I wanted hung in the psychology department where it would be a daily reminder of what violence costs all of us. Conflicting schedules dictate that the trip to see the memorials will have to wait until spring.

On January 3, 2000, the first day the mail is delivered in the new millennium, we receive copies of the defense and prosecution briefs for the new appeal. Mitch's new lawyers claim a new judge should be appointed to replace Judge Muir because he didn't follow the circuit court's mandate. He didn't provide objective standards for his seven level upward departure and ignored case law where fewer levels of upward departure were applied. They also argue that Dr. Elliot Gross's proposed testimony is relevant and the defense should have been allowed to cross-examine Dr. Land on the areas of dispute between the two pathologists.

The defense—foolishly, I think—cites Judge Muir for the appearance of partiality. "The court appears to be bending over backwards to achieve a particular preconceived result. *i.e* as large a sentence as possible." They also object to the "sudden and unexplained ruling," Mitch's uncorroborated testimony about the conversation Margie and Mitch had the morning of the murder was not believable.

Wayne's brief refutes these claims. He points out that Judge Muir reduced the upward departure by two levels and quotes the judge's earlier remarks discrediting Mitch's statements at the suppression hearing. We realize we must wait, helplessly, for the judges' decision so we keep busy, but the nagging concern is always there. When we return from Ireland on March 28th, we have a message from Wayne Samuelson. The three judges from the appellate court, Mansmann, Greenberg, and Alarcon, have turned down the appeal. We feel no elation but some satisfaction.

On April 17, 2000, Ruth, Jacob, the current au pair Lydia, Larry, and I go to Lewisburg. We stay at the Country Cupboard Inn and Tuesday morning we drive the short distance to the penitentiary to view the two memorials to Margaret. We are met by Warden Romaine and an assistant. Brian Patton, who planned the memorials, is on vacation. It is not possible to be unaware of her house, across the street just to the left, as we stand in the slight drizzle near the entrance to the prison grounds.

We view the new sign for the U.S. Penitentiary and the beautiful red maple trees directly behind it. The warden explains that the piece of marble the bronze plaque is placed on is from the original steps at the penitentiary. It seems fitting to us since Larry was born the same year, 1932, as it was built. At night there is a light on the site. They have brought the plaque from the psychology department to show us because Jacob cannot go inside the prison. It is the same as the one near the entrance but is mounted on dark wood. I had hoped the memorials would warn about the dangers of domestic violence as we were promised, but they don't. We don't know either man and they didn't know Margaret. There isn't much to say so our visit is brief. We appreciate their effort but miss any personal connection with them.

I'm reminded of the tree I had planted for her at Windsor Locks High School where I hope her death will cause young people to think about intimate abuse and avoid its consequences. That plaque reads:

> In memory of
> Margaret Bostrom, Ph.D.
> 11/6/64—8/16/96
> Victim of Domestic Violence
> Daughter of WL Teacher Shirley Bostrom

The defense has asked the whole appellate court to hear the case, but on May 19, 2000, we receive word that the Third Circuit Court of Appeal has declined to hear Mitch's appeal of Judge Muir's resentencing. Now Mitch has the option of taking his appeal regarding the length of sentence to the U.S. Supreme Court. However, Wayne doesn't feel Mitch would be successful in that attempt either. No doubt, habeas corpus appeals will follow. Mitch can claim he had incompetent defense when he was advised to plead.

We learn he has been moved to a less-secure facility—not a penitentiary but a federal medium-security prison still located in Florence, Colorado. We fear that because of his sentence reduction, he will be moved to a penal institution nearer his home—making it easier for his family to visit. Fortunately for us that hasn't happened yet.

I know healing doesn't happen magically or automatically, and I'll always bear my scars but with effort the periods of intense pain will not occur as often or last as long. Focusing on all the wonderful things people have done for us because of our loss helps me to live the rest of my life as fully as possible. There will always be bad days, but I can work to make more days better. I've accepted that I must reach out and ask for what I require from others. It is foolish to sit back and wait for them to guess.

This book, the workshops about violence prevention, and the attempts to establish intimate partner fatality reviews in Connecticut are steps I'm taking toward healing. Working together and being involved with other survivors of homicide helps both Larry and me accept our tragedy and draws us closer together. These people have suffered similar losses, been asked the same questions, and know we all received a life sentence the day our children were murdered. They understand and share the emotions we feel: grief, guilt, anger, frustration, sorrow, and depression. We mourn our loved ones but share hope and comfort. We learn to laugh again and find pleasure in our lives. We are survivors—not victims—an important distinction. Survivors work to make the world a safer, more just place and give solace to new survivors. Victims stay mired in self-pity.

Driving to the fall of 2000 Connecticut Writing Project retreat at Wisdom House in the hills of Litchfield, Connecticut, I relax and watch the season change. I remind myself that my life since Margie's murder hasn't been all bad—in fact, some of it has been good. No, not just good, but rewarding and enjoyable. Do Margie's murder and the torment of Kathy's disease help me appreciate the difference and distinguish between mere existence and fulfillment? Is it an exchange? Insight for pain? Pain for insight?

Then I wonder, do the people who have not paid with aching grief for the pleasures of life have a lesser understanding or appreciation for the joys of life—because they have not been assaulted by its tragedies? Sort of like, you don't fully delight in a sunny day until it has rained for a week. If this is the way it is I would gladly surrender my increased perception in evaluating and treasuring life for an incomplete grasp of its extremes.

Much of the literature on loss and grief assures readers that while they will never be the same person they were before the tragedy, they most likely will be better and stronger people. Am I—because of my experience? I don't think so. Wiser—certainly, happier—no, just more aware of life's gifts. I'm a teacher and an Aquarian so it is my nature to care about other people. Now, I'm more aware of when I'm not nurturing someone who is in need and I work harder to reach out to them. But I liked who I was before I faced my demons. I miss the security of feeling strong and having control. Accepting my weakness and domination by events is a humbling experience.

I never wanted to be who I am today. This journey is too difficult and hazardous to choose. I am reminded of what I wrote while at a writing retreat at Norcroft in Minnesota: This path of grief is mine to walk along 'til I die—so I'll go forward striving to help others.

In spite of my loss, the continued court proceedings, and the changes I've been required to make in my life, I can still say, "I was lucky to have Margie for thirty-one years, ten months, and ten days. I wouldn't trade my memories of her even to escape the terrible events of August 16, 1996, what has followed, and all the days that are still to come."

I'll leave you with an epitaph I found on a Vermont gravestone: "To live in the hearts of those left behind is not to die." Margie lives.

"It Ain't Over Till It's Over"

We speak at the Department of Justice Symposium in Washington in January 2001. Joe Pryor, the BOP chaplain who was at Lewisburg, has been promoted and he attends this meeting briefly but we miss each other. Larry and I are at the DC police department talking with Caroline Nicholl about helping homicide detectives work more effectively with the survivors of a homicide victim. Joe leaves his card for me and we e-mail each other.

Larry and I take a trip to Aruba with Ruth, Abby, and Jacob. Jake and Larry are sick the whole time but us girls go horseback riding and shopping, and enjoy the food and nightly shows. In February Larry and I meet his brother Bud and his wife, Shirley, at Jekyll Island for an Elderhostel about the ecology and history of that Island.

In March Robin Hassler Thompson has Larry and me speak at a fatality review meeting in Santa Fe, New Mexico. This time we visit Chaco Canyon, another ancient site of the Anasazi. When we return to Connecticut, we approach Lisa Holden at the Connecticut Coalition Against Domestic Violence about starting a review team in Connecticut. She is very enthusiastic about the idea. Establishing one would help us identify what services were used by the victim, what worked, and what didn't so we could work more successfully to prevent more intimate partner homicides. It will be a great tribute to Margie's memory.

In early April Kathy is a passenger in her car when it hits a pole. Her left leg is badly crushed. She has several operations and is placed in a nursing home to recuperate. Eight months later she moves into her new apartment but may always be in a wheelchair. We hope for the best for her.

Larry and I continue to find speaking at colleges, high schools, and prisons in Connecticut rewarding. We hope we help prevent more violence. The June 2001 Melanie conference is a chance to meet old friends and make new ones. Debbie Parnham and Loretta Winn from Life Sentence, Frances Driscoll, Bill Jenkins, Leslie Charles, and Judith Meisel become valued acquaintances. It is great to see Marc Klaas and David Kaczynski again. I give a writing workshop *Pain, Pen, Pad.* It demonstrates how writing can be used to deal with grief.

My aunt Margaret turns eighty in July and I invite all her relatives to a party in Falconer, New York. Ruth, Abby, and Jacob meet many cousins for the first time. I'm sure Margie is there too.

August 16, 2001, is the fifth anniversary of Margie's murder. It doesn't seem possible! The pain is still raw and I now know it will never completely disappear. We recognize the day with the usual dinner of her favorite veal Marsala and pecan pie.

On August 19, 2001, Larry and I return to the NOVA conference, which is in Edmonton, Alberta, Canada. We see Linda Corraro, the federal victim advocate for Connecticut who has been such a support for both of us and B. J., our friend from MADD, along with Elaine and Gordon Rondeau and Amy Dawson who are with Fight Crime: Invest in Kids. We are Connecticut representatives for that group. Bill Jenkins, Loretta Winn, and Debbie Parnham are also there. Again our session is filled to capacity—this time the room holds 250 participants. Later, Larry and I receive an invitation from Marlene Young to present at the 2002 NOVA conference in Nashville, Tennessee. We are thrilled to accept.

After the Edmonton conference we take a self-guided tour from Jasper to Lake Louise and Banff. We stay in luxury hotels and have marvelous food. We walk on a glacier and bathe in hot springs. One night the handsome waiter gives me his business card. I'm impressed.

We are home for a short while before September 11, 2001. Every survivor I know feels retraumatized by the events and the devastation each family of a victim faces in the months ahead. It is as if August 16, 1996, the day my daughter was murdered, is happening over and over again.

September 11, 2001

God sends out the call,
everyone is to report to
the light at the entrance.
We are about to receive
thousands of souls.

Stunned, we look at each other.
What?
All at once?
How can that be?
Earthquake?
Flood?
Hurricane?

God shakes his head sadly.
Evil acts have occurred.
Four airliners filled with passengers
and fuel have crashed.
Two from Boston exploded in flames
as they hit the World Trade Center.
Both towers have collapsed.
The third plane hit the Pentagon and still
another crashed in a Pennsylvania field
before it could hit another target.
Brave souls on board gave their lives
to save the lives of strangers.

Be gentle, sincere and reassuring
as you welcome them.
You see they didn't plan
to make this journey today
so they have left much

unsaid and undone:
Saying I love you. I'm sorry.
Paying the bills. Making a will.
Giving that one last hug.
They feel guilty leaving others to grieve.

Many of you gathered here today
will be greeting friends or family
who are unprepared for this journey.
Martin, John, Diana, Margaret and all those
who joined us because of unexpected violence,
you understand their shock and disbelief. Guide us.

The Yankees only make it to the series this year. I guess Margie thinks it's time to let another team win the World Championship, but I think it would have been special for New York to win this year. Next year, Margie?

On October 18, 2001, Larry and I return home from speaking at Gates Correctional Facility and I listen to the phone messages. I hear, "Hello, Mr. and Mrs. Bostrom. This is Wayne Samuelson."

"Oh, shit!" I know he isn't just making a social call. We call him back and learn that Mitch's latest attorney, Shalom D. Stone, plans to file a habeas appeal based on ineffective counsel because his trial attorneys failed to perform certain necessary tasks, provide the defendant with vital information, and give defendant accurate legal advice. He also wants to file the motion under seal until he has a chance to take dispositions from the trial attorneys—to get their unadorned recollections. The hearing is placed on the November calendar.

When we receive copies of the motions and briefs, we see all the old accusations about Margaret's character but new more disgusting claims are added. Mitch still isn't taking responsibility for killing her. His father is making statements he hopes will get Mitch less time—whether they are true or not. I no longer consider forgiveness or reconciliation; I now know they will not happen.

Wayne tells us that if Mitch gets this appeal granted, the government will take him to trial for murder one. Six years after the murder, I no longer want to go through that painful process. If the appeal is denied by Judge Muir, Mitch will appeal the decision to the Federal Appeals Court in Philadelphia. In late November Wayne calls. The hearing is now scheduled for January 2002. Will it never end?

So much has now happened that Margie is not a part of: Abby is nearly a teenager, Jacob is eight, we have a new car, and we are building a new house with Ruth. I know Margie will be watching over me when I have a cataract removed and a knee replacement in 2002.

We get word the hearing is now scheduled for February. Then it is delayed until March. No, April— The Habeas hearing happens during ten days scattered from May 1st to May 28th. We are surprised when our wait for Judge Muir's decision ends after 13 calendar days. Mitch's appeal has been denied. We know he has at least one more appeal he can make to an appellate court and perhaps the Supreme Court. As Yogi Berra said, "It ain't over 'til it's over."

ACKNOWLEDGMENTS

I was able to complete this book because of the many people who have nurtured and believed in me throughout my life—beginning with my parents who loved me and taught me that I was strong and capable.

Many teachers and friends have inspired and encouraged me to write. Special thanks to Vince Rogers, Mary Mackley and the Connecticut Writing Project Summer Institute, which is held at the University of Connecticut, and Pat Schneider, the Director of the Amherst Writers and Artists. My ongoing writers group—Mary Mackley, Sheila Murphy, Kay Saur, Jenny Shaff, Kathy Uschmann, and Pat Korol—along with all the writers who attend the semi-annual retreats sponsored by the Connecticut Writing Project, have given me empathetic support as I work through my pain. They encouraged me to write this book and get it published. In 1999, I was granted a residency at Norcroft, A Writing Retreat for Women, located in Lutsen, Minnesota. It provided a quiet, yet stimulating environment in which to pursue my writing.

Special thanks to the many people who read and commented on parts of my various drafts. Especially to Antoinette Bosco, Neil Websdale, Bill Jenkins, Karen Carney, Debra Stanley, and Leslie Charles, all published authors, for encouraging me throughout the writing of this book.

In particular, I thank David Kaczynski, who read my drafts with the eyes of a former English teacher and an open heart. You understood what I wanted to say. Thanks, David, for the touching and insightful introduction to this book. I especially value your friendship.

I appreciate the consideration shown our family by the Federal Bureau of Prisons personnel at Lewisburg who helped us through the days that followed the murder. A special thanks to Wayne Samuelson,

Assistant United States Attorney, FBI special agents Dick Rodgers and Harold Schmidle, and Judge Muir. Their skills, intellect, and compassion still guide us through the maze that is our criminal justice system. I am grateful to Attorney Graham Showalter and his assistant Donna Joy who took care of the painful legal details that surrounded the settling of Margie's estate, relieving us of that burden.

I'm grateful to Sam and Wanda Rieger and the other members of the Survivors of Homicide (SOH)—too numerous to name without forgetting someone—for their support. They understand our pain because they have experienced the devastating effects the murder of a loved one brings. Each month I meet new survivors that I hope to help along their path because that helps me on my journey. Frank Blackford, the counselor advocate for SOH, deserves a special award for the patience, understanding, and gentleness with which he treats survivors. Frank, consider it given! Pat Wright, thanks for trying.

My sincerest gratitude to the care givers, educators, justice department workers, legislators, law enforcement, correction officials, and the Connecticut Coalition Against Domestic Violence who have listened and encouraged us to speak about our tragedy in hopes of helping others avoid violence. Your dedication often goes unnoticed. You know who you are and believe me, you are appreciated.

I want to acknowledge longtime friends who helped me through the darkest days and are still close. They include: Dot and Larry Costello, Terry and Harry Fitzgerald, Sophie and Ed Basile, Liz Kay and Alan Rocklin, and Bill and Viola Orsinger. I am fortunate to have Judy and Leo Smith's friendship. She has enriched my life and provided comfort for over thirty years when I needed it. Our Literary Society; Shirley King, Barbara Masera, Marjorie Bruns, Carol Janssen, Judy Smith, and Brenda Ives lifts my spirits. It helps to know that Sue Black is in heaven with Margie—scolding her for what she has done to me. Also a special thanks to everyone in the Windsor Locks School System, especially Barbara Carman and everyone at South School—students, staff, and parents.

Family members give me strength. Thanks go to Bud and Shirley Bostrom, Riley and Esther Pank Bostrom, David Pierce, Abel Wilcox, Peggy Wilcox, Chub Pierce and all my nieces, nephews and cousins.

ACKNOWLEDGMENTS

My husband, Larry, does anything that needs doing from house-work to cooking to technical advice. He now speaks at our slide presentations and he performed most of the official responsibilities when we served as co-vice presidents of Survivors of Homicide, Inc. Most importantly, he shares my pain and understands when I need to cry. His love and support have kept me going. Ruth and Kathy miss their sister, Margie, and wish they could lessen my pain. They do. My grandchildren, Abby and Jacob, inspire me with their enthu-siasm for life. Their unconditional love and that of my aunt Margaret sustain me. And I cannot forget to mention the comfort that Margie's dog, Calie, and Kathy's dog, Delilah, provide.

I want to thank everyone at About Books, Inc. for guiding me through the process of publishing this book. Marilyn and Tom Ross, Deb Ellis, Kate Deubert, and Cathy Bowman have given me good advice and held my hand while making my book the best it can be. Sue Collier, my editor, displayed compassion and strengthened my book. Dick Hanna at Group Five Creative, LLC did a great job bring-ing my vision of the logo to realization.

This book is my gift to Margie and to all the friends and strangers who have shed a tear with me. We both know who you are. It is small payment for what you have given me.

Loss of a Child

Key:

A child dies*

A child is murdered**

Appropriate for children***

Bosco, Antoinette (1994). *Finding Peace Through Pain*. New York: Ballantine Books.**

Bramblett, John (1991). *When Good-bye Is Forever*. New York: Ballantine Books.*

Crider, Tom (1996). *Give Sorrow Words: A Father's Passage Through Grief*. Chapel Hill, NC: Algonquin Books.*

Heart, Rosalie Deer (1996). *Healing Grief: A Mother's Story*. San Cristobal, NM: Heart Link Publications.*

Jenkins, Bill (1999). *What to Do When the Police Leave*. Richmond, VA: WBJ Press.** (Written by a parent of a murdered child but is a guidebook for others who have to deal with a homicide of a loved one.)

Lardner, George Jr. (1995). *The Stalking of Kristin*. New York: Onyx, Penguin Books USA.**

Lott, Bret (1993). *Reed's Beach*. New York: Pocket Books.* (fiction)

Sanders, Catherine M. (1992). *How to Survive the Loss of a Child*. Rocklin, CA: Prima Publishing.*

Sittser, Gerald L. (1996). *A Grace Disguised: How the Soul Grows Through Loss*. Grand Rapids, MI: Zondervan Publishing House.* (It is an account of the accidental death of three generations of his family.)

Spungen, Deborah (1996). *And I Don't Want to Live This Life*. New York: Ballantine Books.**

Wiitala, Geri Colozzi (1996). *Heather's Return*. Virginia Beach, VA: A.R.E. Press.*

Wolterstorff, Nicholas (1987). *Lament for a Son*. Grand Rapids, MI: William B. Eerdmans Publishing Company.*

Loss of a Loved One

Kight, Marsha, compiled by (1998). *Forever Changed: Remembering Oklahoma City, April 19, 1995*. Amherst, NY: Prometheus Books. (Marsha is Oklahoma City bombing victim Frankie Merrill's mom.)

Noel, Christopher (1996). *In the Unlikely Event of a Water Landing: A Geography of Grief*. New York: Times Books, a division of Random House.

Lewis, C. S. (1961). *A Grief Observed*. New York: HarperCollins Publishers.

Stickney, Doris (1982).*Water Bugs and Dragonflies*. Cleveland: The Pilgrim Press.***

Dealing With Loss and Grief

Carney, Karen, RN, MSW, LCSW (1995). *The Barklay and Eve Series*. Wethersfield, CT: D'Esopo Funeral Chapels.***

Childs-Gowell, Elaine, A.R.N.P., Ph.D. (1992). *Good Grief Rituals*. Barrytown, NY: Station Hill Press.

Colgrove, Melba, Harold H. Bloomfield, Ph.D., M.D., and Peter McWilliams (1991). *How to Survive the Loss of a Love*. Los Angeles: Prelude Press.

Deits, Bob (1988). *Life After Loss*. Tucson: Fisher Books.

Ericsson, Stephanie (1988). *Companion Through the Darkness*. New York: HarperPerennial.

James, John W. and Frank Cherry (1989). *The Grief Recovery Handbook, A Step-by-Step Program for Moving Beyond Loss*. New York: HarperPerennial.

Jones, Mary (1995). *Love After Death: Counselling in Bereavement*. London and Bristol, PA: Jessica Kingsley Publishers.

Klass, Dennis (1988). *Parental Grief: Solace and Resolution*. New York: Springer Publishing Company.

Staudacher, Carol (1987). *Beyond Grief: A Guide for Recovering from the Death of a Loved One*. New York: Barnes and Noble Books.

Violent Controlling Partners

Brown, Lou, Francois Dubau, and Merritt McJeon (1997). *Stop Domestic Violence*. New York: St. Martin's Griffin.

Dutton, Donald G., Ph.D., with Susan K. Golant (1995). *The Batterer: A Psychological Profile*. New York: Basic Books.

Jones, Ann and Susan Schechter (1992). *When Love Goes Wrong*. New York: HarperPerennial.

Martin, Del (1983). *Battered Wives*. New York: Pocket Books.

Walker, Lenore (1979). *The Battered Woman*. New York: HarperPerennial.

Websdale, Neil (1999). *Understanding Domestic Homicide*. Boston: Northeastern University Press.

Weitzman, Susan (2000). *Not to People Like Us*. New York: Basic Books.

Life After Death

Altea, Rosemary (1997). *Proud Spirit*. New York: William Morrow and Company.

Altea, Rosemary (1995). *The Eagle and the Rose*. New York: Warner Books.

Guggenheim, Bill, and Judy Guggenheim (1999). *Hello from Heaven*. New York: Bantam Books.

BIBLIOGRAPHY

Moody, Raymond, A., Jr., M.D. (1988). *The Light Beyond*. New York: Bantam Books.

Moody, Raymond, A., Jr., M.D. (1990). *Coming Back: A Psychiatrist Explores Past-Life Journeys*. New York: Bantam Books.

Steiger, Brad and Francie Steiger (1987). *Discover Your Past Lives*. Atglen, PA: Whitford Press.

Van Praagh, James (1997). *Talking to Heaven*. New York: Dutton Books.

Weiss, Barry, M.D. (1988). *Many Lives, Many Masters*. New York: Simon and Schuster.

Give the Gift of

FUNNY—HE DOESN'T LOOK LIKE A MURDERER

to Your Friends and Colleagues

CHECK YOUR LEADING BOOKSTORE OR ORDER HERE

❑ **YES,** I want _____ copies of *Funny—He Doesn't Look Like a Murderer* at $19.95 each, plus $4.95 shipping per book (Connecticut residents please add $1.20 sales tax per book). Canadian orders must be accompanied by a postal money order in U.S. funds.

❑ **YES,** I am interested in having Shirley Pierce Bostrom speak to my organization. Larry and Shirley Bostrom give slide presentations at national conferences, schools, colleges, for prison staff and offenders. For more information contact the Bostroms directly by phone at 860-295-1217 or email SPBostrom@aol.com—or through the Office of Victims of Crime Training and Technical Assistance Center (TTAC) at 1-800-627-6872 or ttac@ovcttac.org.

My check or money order for $_____ is enclosed.

Please charge my: ❑ VISA   ❑ MasterCard

All mail orders must be prepaid in full by check or credit card, or accompanied by a valid purchase order authorization. Inquire about the bulk rate when purchasing more than ten copies. Please allow 3-4 weeks for shipping.

Name _____

Organization _____

Address _____

City/State/Zip _____

Phone_____ E-mail _____

Credit card number _____

Exp. date_____ Signature _____

Please make your check payable and return to:
Calie Books
24 Pond View Lane • Marlborough, CT 06447

Call your credit card order to: 860-295-1217 or 1-800-587-9339
E-mail: SPBostrom@aol.com   www.IntimatePartnerMurder.com